THE MEN
WHO RULED INDIA

By the same author

THE MEN
WHO RULED INDIA

PHILIP MASON

DELHI BOMBAY CALCUTTA MADRAS
in association with
JONATHAN CAPE LONDON

To the Peoples of India and Pakistan
whose tranquillity was our care
whose division is our failure
and whose continuance
in the family of nations to which we belong
is our Memorial

First published in two volumes as
The Founders (1953) and *The Guardians* (1954)
This abridged edition published 1985
Copyright © 1985 by Philip Mason

Dass Media Private Limited, 207 Bhandari House,
91 Nehru Place, New Delhi-110019, India,
in association with Jonathan Cape Ltd,
30 Bedford Square, London WC1B 3EL, England

ISBN 0 224 02277 6

Printed in Great Britain by Ebenezer Baylis and Son Ltd,
The Trinity Press, Worcester and London

CONTENTS

Part V The Demission of Power 1909–1947

COLOUR PLATES

AUTHOR'S NOTE

The first version of *The Men Who Ruled India*, finished in 1952, was about 400,000 words. It would have made three volumes. At the request of Jonathan Cape, I reduced it considerably and it was published in two volumes, *The Founders* in 1953 and *The Guardians* in 1954. In one form or another, the two volumes have been in print ever since. In 1983, the house of Cape suggested that I should reduce the book to one volume, which they would publish with illustrations. The question arose of whether this should be essentially the same book, terser and with omissions, or whether it should be entirely rewritten in the light of later events and changed opinions. With full agreement of my publisher, I decided that it should be the same book, shortened. It had been in no sense a 'definitive' book, but a personal view, written in the light of personal memories that were still fresh as I wrote; it had also benefited by the freshness of recent discovery, because I had only a very sketchy knowledge of Indian history when I started work. In abridging, I have tried to keep those elements of freshness. If any reader should think a comment too dogmatic, I hope he will refer to the longer version, where he may well find it qualified. The dedication reads strangely today – but in 1953 and 1954 it seemed an essential part of the book.

P.M.

INTRODUCTION

There comes a time in a man's life when he may well stand back and consider what he has built, planted, written or begotten and whether it was worth doing. If in such a mood the English – and by that I mean all those who speak English: Chaucer and Drake, Milton and Marlborough, Clive and Hastings, belong to us all – if the English look back on their varied history, the long connection with India will be an achievement that cannot be ignored.

It is too soon to say if it will last. But though the political structure may change to something unrecognizable, it is hard to believe that the impress of English ways of thinking will vanish altogether. And the achievement itself, whatever the future holds, is surely a matter for pride.

There are many ways of looking at it. The heart of one man will beat faster – though perhaps against his will – to remember how a handful of his countrymen mastered and ruled so many millions by the sword, by diplomacy, above all by a stubborn tenacity of purpose. To another, the main matter for pride will be that so few among so many had so slight a need for force, that so often the district officer really was at heart what the villagers called him in their petitions, the father and mother of his people. To another again it will seem that the years of renunciation with which the story ends are the finest in the long record.

For more than three centuries the effort was sustained. It was an effort in which two parts combined, as brain and muscle join in the sweep of a scythe. There was the will of the people of England expressed imperfectly by the Crown, by Parliament, by the Court of Directors of the East India Company; at the other end, there were men in India who fought, won, governed, trained and handed over what they had made, sometimes in conscious disagreement with the will of England but in obedience to it at the last.

In the years between 1914 and 1940, India was a problem not yet solved that lay on England's conscience; now that it is India's problem not ours, we can begin to look back with detachment. And there are things which should be set down before they are forgotten, the smell of dust thirstily drinking the first rain, the spicy peppery smell of a grain-dealer's shop, the reek of mangoes, marigolds and lush vegetation when the sun breaks through the clouds in August and the earth steams, things too that fade more quickly such as the sound of men's voices in petition, the look on a man's face when he is found guilty, a peasant's emotion when a wrong has been put right.

This book is an account of the men who ruled India, whether they began as soldiers or civilians, written in the light of such memories as these. The scene is a mass of land the size of Europe; the period is three centuries and a half. There were something over four hundred districts in British India and a district officer in each. To write a full-scale history of the Indian Civil Service would be the work of a lifetime. This is no such book. It is a rapid survey, while memory lives, of the surface only of a great mass of material. If the episode is considered as a whole, it lasts from 1600 to 1947. Within that stretch of time there are five periods to be distinguished. There is the beginning, when the servants of the Company were suppliants to the Mogul; then comes a time of transition, the brief startling score of years that left them masters of India; then the long stretch of a century and a half in which they administered the continent. This again may be divided into two: at first, the sovereignty of Parliament was exercised through a corporation known as the Company; from 1858 onwards the Crown ruled direct. The fifth act is the thirty years during which power was deliberately transferred.

I have tried to be concrete, to take one scene that illustrates a point and to dwell on that, passing mercilessly, though with regret, over many years and places before the next; it is a method less unfair to the reader than abstract comment though still unfair because it selects. It is a book about men, not about trends or tendencies or systems.

It is a play in five acts. In the second act, these men gain the mastery of India. With startling rapidity, they were transformed from corrupt Nabobs into a body of men who boasted that 'no public service in the whole world can evince more integrity'. Then came the survey and settlement of the greater part of the continent, over-rapid attempts to transform a semi-feudal system, and the reactionary outbreak of 1857, events of which each could easily have made a volume. The result has no claim to be a work of original scholarship; it is still less a work of reference, nor is it meant only for those who know India. It is meant for anyone who would like to know what sort of men carried out this one English achievement.

They were men who by the middle of the nineteenth century had brought peace to the country instead of anarchy, had mapped the fields and made lists of every man's rights and had made a beginning of the task of building roads, bridges and railways, of harnessing the rivers to irrigation. More important, they had associated Indians with them in their work and the greater part of the administration was carried out by Indians. But perhaps nothing the Company's servants did was of greater value in the end than their release in India of some gusts of that dry and searing wind, that bracing scepticism, which swept through Europe after the French Revolution and which in the milder climate of England had come to be associated with the name of Jeremy Bentham. It was a spirit which inquired sceptically whether an institution was defensible by human reason, whether it contributed to human happiness, and whether it was consistent with a respect for the value of human beings as individuals. It was a spirit which found much to question in India at a time when her own civilization had ceased to grow, when pity for human suffering seemed to be used up and finished. This alien breath provoked new life and indignant reaction; India began to grow again and her mind took on new vigour. Indians did not, as the English of the 1820s and 1830s had expected, accept the full doctrine of Christianity together with Western education but this side-wind from the main current of Christendom stirred their minds deeply and changed their conception of their own religion.

Here they are then, the civil servants of the Honourable East India Company, learning among their bolts of gingham and taffety that they must be diplomats, administrators and soldiers; thrown suddenly into positions where the opportunities for wealth and power were such as have been open to no men since the Roman Emperors asserted their control over the pro-consuls; abusing their power and then transforming themselves into a body of men 'minutely just, inflexibly upright', who used power not for selfish ends but as they thought was right, men who 'after ruling millions of subjects, after commanding victorious armies, after dictating terms of peace at the gates of hostile capitals ... return to their native land with no more than a decent competence'.

'Whenever we are obliged to resign our sovereignty,' wrote Munro, 'we should leave the natives so far improved from their connection with us, as to be capable of maintaining a free, or at least a regular, government among themselves', while Elphinstone, with still clearer insight, thought 'the most desirable death for us to die should be the improvement of the natives reaching such a pitch as would render it impossible for a foreign nation to retain the government ... '

It was in that belief that the best of them lived and worked. But the rulers of India were not cast in a mould; they were men, quick with fleshly desire, lust for power, and all the miraculous diversity of man; humorous, solemn and unpredictable; adventurous, soaked in routine, timid and bold. Yet they have something in common. Nearly all of them − after the transformation − believe that the performance of duty is something good in itself; hardly one questions the value of his work. But he will do his work his own way. He is critical and sometimes contemptuous of authority. I have stressed again and again the independence of these men, their detachment, their questioning spirit. But there is a contradictory tendency as well. Already in the 1840s and early 1850s, long before the Mutiny, there is a hardening of the arteries, a readiness to take the whole business of British rule for granted. This was to be expected, an inevitable result of the growth of system.

The system began when the college at Haileybury was founded in the first decade of the nineteenth century; it was still growing and hardening when the process was interrupted by the Mutiny. All through the nineteenth century, three Governors out of ten, an occasional Member of the Viceroy's Council, sometimes a Commander-in-Chief, a few judges – altogether between a dozen and a score of men in the highest posts – came to their appointments direct from England; but the majority of the government at the centre, almost the whole of the provincial governments, the officers at the head of each district, all belonged to a specially selected official class, never much more than twelve hundred strong, who were responsible not to the people they governed but to Parliament in Westminster, seven thousand miles away, and who in fact governed in the light of what they themselves believed to be right.

There is an ideal model for the Indian system, not consciously adopted and exactly followed, for that is not the way English minds work, but a model with which every English statesman in the nineteenth century was familiar. Plato pictured a state ruled by guardians, men specially chosen by their seniors in the service, trained in the use of their bodies and in the study of history, believing that they were a separate race from those they ruled, aloof, superior to the ties of marriage or fatherhood and to the attraction of gold, governing by the light of what they knew to be beautiful and good.

The names of England and Athens are linked in men's minds with the idea of freedom, because both liked to choose and control those who governed them. But the Athenians would not give the islands and colonies the freedom for which they had themselves fought at Salamis and Marathon; the English learnt only slowly the lessons of Yorktown and Saratoga. They did, however, learn in the end. They were moving all through the nineteenth century towards a society in which each individual had a right and means to express his views and make them felt; cautiously, year by year, in the Reform Bills, in the Repeal of the Combination Act, they pared away restrictions based on privilege and extended the circle within which men were free.

India too would one day be free; Macaulay said so, Queen Victoria said so, Gladstone said so. Munro, Elphinstone and Metcalfe felt in their bones that it must be so and it was the conscious will of England. But for the present it was guardianship India needed. And in fact it was to peace and unity rather than to freedom, that the effort in India was directed, to equal justice for all, roads, railways, canals, bridges. That was the mixture, very good for the child, to be given firmly and taken without fuss. And to give it, the means found to be best was a corps of men specially selected, brought up in a rigour of bodily hardship to which no other modern people have subjected their ruling class, trained by cold baths, cricket, and the history of Greece and Rome, a separate race from those they ruled, aloof, superior to bribery, discouraged from marriage until they were middle-aged, and then subjected to long separations. The merchants of the East India Company were there to hand; some memory of Akbar's civil service survived; every decision was made by men who had been brought up on Plato. That was the triple parentage of the service.

Plato taught that the guardians of the state should not know their parents; the English did not go as far as that, but when they were eight years old the children from whom rulers were to be chosen were taken away from home for three-quarters of every year, taught not to mention their mothers or their own Christian names, brought up in the traditions of the Sparta which Plato had admired. And the children grew up to be true guardians; no other people in history can equal their record of disinterested guardianship. But guardians seldom encourage change; it is not surprising that in the end their wards outgrew their tutelage. What is surprising is that so often there was real warmth and affection between the district officer and the peasant, that the system was always much looser than it looked, that so much freedom was always left to the individual.

To one invincible prejudice which runs through the book I will confess in advance. It is a belief in the Christian doctrine that a man must be judged not by his worst so much as by his best, and in the end not even by his best but by what he aimed at. And so English rule in India is to be judged by the conscious will of England expressed in Parliament and by the aims of a good district officer, not by the nasty little atavistic impulses that came wriggling up from the subconscious when an official at the Treasury scored a departmental triumph over the India Office, when a merchant fixed something over an opulent lunch. 'Not what thou art, nor what thou hast been, does God consider, but what thou wouldst be.'

P.M.

HET HUIS VAN · DEN

OOST INDISCHE COMPACNIE IN

LON DEN

The front of the old East India House in Leadenhall, London. It was from here that policy about India was decided before it came directly under the Crown.

PART I
Under the Moguls 1600–1751

THE FIRST ENGLISHMEN IN INDIA

1 The First Englishmen

Elizabeth by the Grace of God Queen of England, France and Ireland, Defender of the Faith, to all our Officers, Ministers and Subjects ... Greeting.

Pride rings in the formal words; you can hear the trumpets peal along the narrow city lanes. This is more than the charter of a company of merchants; it is a move in the war with Spain. Trade is the object, but Spain and Portugal claim a monopoly of the West Indies and the East and there will be no trade without fighting.

That much they must have known when they met on September 24, 1599, to petition the Queen for their charter. But just how much they were founding, not one of them can have guessed.

It was 'for the honour of this our realm of England', for navigation, trade, merchandise – and because it was what they liked to do. That was why the bold eyes of the Queen's captains and merchants roved East as well as West. They sought gold, fame and danger in every corner of the world they opened and devoured with such zest. They had been East already in ones and twos; they had found the Portuguese before them in India, the Dutch in the Spice Islands. Both treated the English as poachers. The Portuguese had the Pope's blessing; the Dutch had no blessing but the plain advantage of being first in the field.

The English were third in the field; they petitioned the Queen for the same backing as their rivals. But in 1599 there were hopes of peace with Spain; the Queen would not imperil the negotiations by licensing trespass in the East; she kept her hand on the jesses. Next year, 1600, the hope of peace died, and on the last day of the sixteenth century the Queen gave the Company their charter.

The words of the charter were peaceful enough, and no doubt the merchants of London would have liked nothing better than peaceful trade

3

that brought home gold. But in practice, the profits from the first two voyages were less from trade than from privateering.

Spices were the main object of the first voyagers but India was not yet thought of as a market where spices could be bought or English goods sold and there is no place here for the first two voyages. It is not till the Third Voyage that India is mentioned in the instructions from the Governor and Company to their servants. But even then India was not the first object of the venture.

The ships of the Third Voyage were the *Red Dragon*, of seven hundred tons, the *Hector*, of five hundred, and a pinnace, the *Consent*, of a hundred and fifteen. The General of this fleet of cockle-shells was William Keeling and William Hawkins was the Lieutenant. They sailed from England in March 1607, and reached the island of Socotra in April 1608, thirteen months from home. Here they were held up by contrary winds and in the end Keeling went on with the *Red Dragon* to Bantam while Hawkins in the *Hector* made for Surat. On August 24, 1608, sixteen months from home, the *Hector* dropped anchor at the entrance to the river Tapti, the first ship to fly the English flag off the coast of India.

Hawkins met, right from the start, the supreme indifference of the Mogul officials to trade. They simply were not interested in promoting commerce; not one exception appears. But each had a lively interest in avoiding the wrath of his superior and in supplying the Emperor with what the Elizabethan merchant called toys – presents that were novelties at the Court. The presents Hawkins had brought for Jehangir were confiscated; Mukarrab Khan would prefer to lay them before the Emperor himself.

Meanwhile Hawkins could get no answer when he sought permission to build a factory. By this he meant a warehouse for storing trade goods; prices went up when a ship came in and if you wanted to buy pepper or indigo the only way to get it at a reasonable price was to keep a man on the spot who could buy at harvest time, when prices were low, and store it till a ship came. The first of the Company's servants in India had to be diplomat before he could be trader and a factory was the first object of his diplomacy. In the end, Hawkins was told that only the Emperor could give permission; he must go to Agra himself.

He had many adventures. The Portuguese repeatedly tried to murder him and it was only when he engaged a troop of fifty Pathans, 'valiant horsemen', to protect him on the way, that he was able to start. This was on February 1, 1609.

Hawkins was a practical man, and too occupied with his own safety to have thoughts to spare for the country through which he passed. But the road he saw on his journey is a road still to be found in every district of India. It is a road of earth, very broad, so that there is room to go round a bad patch in the rains. It is striped in the early morning light by long shadows where the wheels have worn deep ruts in the pearly dust; it is

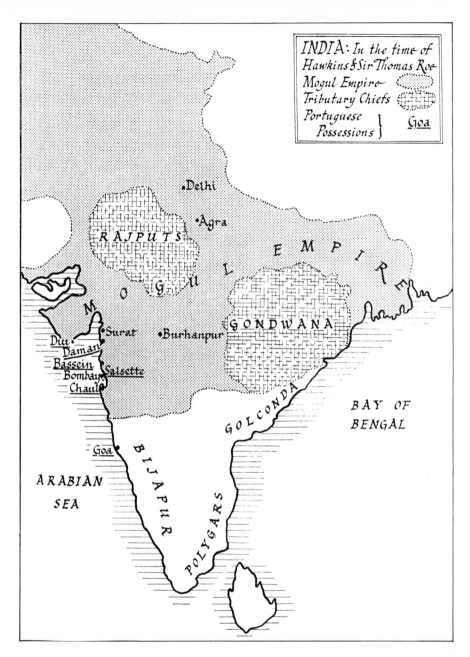

INDIA: In the time of Hawkins & Sir Thomas Roe
Mogul Empire
Tributary Chiefs
Portuguese Possessions } Goa

Delhi
Agra
RAJPUTS
MOGUL EMPIRE
GONDWANA
Surat
Burhanpur
Diu
Daman
Bassein
Bombay
Salsette
Chaul
Goa
GOLCONDA
BIJAPUR
POLYGARS
ARABIAN SEA
BAY OF BENGAL

flanked on either side by an intermittent hedge of cactus and tall plumes of elephant grass. In the first minutes of the day the dust is still too moist with dew to rise high above the ground; all is still clear and sweet. There are lines of camels pulling tall carts like gipsy caravans, droves of patient little grey-white cattle and black sullen buffaloes going to graze, a peasant carrying his shoes on the end of his bamboo pole to save leather, a potter

5

with his donkeys, traffic that will not change much in three hundred years.

Nor will the fields on either side of the road be very different then and now. In Hawkins's day as now there will be black partridges calling in the wheat and barley; the crops will be fresh and green, as high as the calf of a man's leg, heavy with dew. There will be grey partridges running in the tall pulse called *arhar* and among the little chick-pea known as *gram*. There will be blackbuck wandering between the plots of cotton and pepper; men will be beginning to cut into the squares of sugar-cane. Only there will be more opium and poppy in Hawkins's day and near Agra there will be indigo. Since it is February they will be working the wells and, not long after the sun is up, Hawkins will hear an inconsequent little song, rising and falling in a recitative more like a lark's than a man's; it is the song of the man who catches the great leather bag the bullocks have dragged up from the depths of the well, catches and swings it glistening over the watercourse to spill its cool glittering burden on the fields.

Hawkins reached Agra on April 16. Mukarrab Khan had taken all his presents, which was a bad start. But Hawkins recovered ground when Jehangir, the Emperor, learnt that he spoke Turkish – the family language of the Mogul Emperors. He was shown great favours – but not for long. The Portuguese were already in Agra and were plotting against him and every Mogul official had an interest in keeping out of favour a newcomer who had nothing to bribe them with. Altogether, it was a long tale of ups and downs. Everything depended on Jehangir's whim and his whim changed from day to day. Akbar, his father, had been a great man, but Jehangir was a drunkard and debauched by power as well as by wine and opium. Nor can it be said that Hawkins was always the pattern of what a diplomat should be.

It was Portuguese hostility, as much as Mogul apathy or his own mishandling, that caused Hawkins's failure. The Portuguese, like the English, had come to India for trade but – like the English later – had found themselves inevitably drawn into politics. They had built forts to protect themselves – but at first they had been very chary of continental commitments. A hundred years before the English company was founded, Almeida, the first Portuguese viceroy of the Indies, had written to Lisbon: 'the greater the number of fortresses you hold, the weaker will be your power; let all your forces be on the sea ... '

But by 1512, his successor Albuquerque had found that diplomacy was not a sufficient defence for his trade; he must have fortresses and he must go one step further and administer the territory surrounding them.

The Portuguese were for long thought invincible at sea. It was from the English that the first shock to their supremacy was received, when in 1612 a Portuguese fleet attacked the English *Red Dragon* with the pinnace *Ozeander*, where they lay before Surat. They had a great advantage in numbers, but were driven off – and now for the Moguls the thought was born that here at last was someone who could be played off against the Portuguese. By 1614, Mukarrab Khan was at war with the Portuguese and asking the English for help.

This changed attitude was undoubtedly a help to Sir Thomas Roe, King James's ambassador to the court of Jehangir. He was a man very different from Hawkins, a gentleman, a courtier, a former Esquire of the Body to the Queen, a friend of Prince Henry and his sister Elizabeth of Bohemia – 'Th' eclipse and glory of her kind'. He was 'of a pregnant understanding, well spoken, learned, industrious and of a comely personage'. He was the first Ambassador, Hawkins having been a mere trader bearing letters.

From the day he arrived in September 1615, Sir Thomas insisted that he must be treated as an Ambassador, and that he wanted a Treaty. But these were ideas quite foreign to the Mogul court. The Emperor could not be brought to sign a treaty; it did not seem fitting that he should bind himself, as though dealing with an equal, to any man, and certainly not to

Sir Thomas Roe, the first Ambassador from the King of England to the Great Mogul. He was in India 1615–18. A courtier, a realist, 'a man of pregnant understanding ...'

the king of an obscure and distant island of fishermen and wool merchants. A firman, an order to his officers, was quite sufficient. But Sir Thomas knew that a firman could be upset next day. He wanted a treaty – but he never got it.

He was in India until February 17, 1618, altogether nearly three and a half years. He did not much like India but he made some far-sighted remarks, arguing that 'our only dependence is upon the same ground that we began and by which we subsist, fear'. And almost in the words of Almeida, he wrote: 'Let this be received as a rule that if you will profit seek it at sea and in quiet trade.' And of the Moguls, he insisted: 'They have no written law. The King by his own word ruleth.'

This was true; in spite of the learning of Muslim lawyers, in the Emperor's dominions the Emperor's whim was law; it might change from minute to minute and no one would gainsay him. Muslim law ran only when the Emperor wished. And Roe saw too the next great difference between Europe and Asia, for the King, he wrote: 'is every man's heir'. 'The great men about him' he went on 'are not born noble but favourites raised'. He had seen that the nobles did not own land; it was assigned them by the King and 'as they die . . . so it returneth to the King, like rivers to the sea'.

Hawkins and Roe were there in Agra, groping, against the blaze of jewels and brocaded stuff, the swaying of elephants loaded with gold, the strange rituals, the prayers, the salutations, the savage executions, groping for a truth they could understand and convey to Englishmen. Roe

A Mogul palace and city when the English first came to India. 'The blaze of jewels . . . the swaying of elephants . . .' but 'the King by his own word ruleth'.

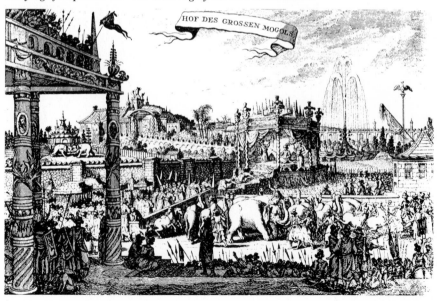

saw more truly than his successors, nearly two hundred years later, who turned those same 'raised favourites' into English landlords, but there was much he could not see. He and Hawkins could see the Emperor at his beads about the break of day, and again, when his prayer was ended, showing himself to the people. They could see him a third time at noon, when he came forth from his women and till three o'clock 'sat watching pastimes and sports made by men and the fighting of beasts'. Then at three they would see him 'sitting in his seat royal', the shadows of the awnings sharp on the red sandstone of the pavement, 'with every man before him in his degree, ready to do justice, and beyond and in front the master hangman, with forty hangmen, with a hatchet on their shoulders and others with all sorts of whips'; all this they could see — but they could not see how the land was ruled nor how the tiller of the soil had his living.

But we, who know that the men of his blood who follow Hawkins are to rule this Empire, who want to understand the tasks they will have to perform, we can rise high in the air till we see something of the greatness of Akbar, who built so much that the English were to strengthen and use as a foundation.

2 The Great Mogul

Akbar had died in 1605. He was a great man — great in his bodily vigour and his passions, in the spiritual restlessness that led him all his life to seek truth, in his occasional cruelties, in his startling and far more frequent humanity, in his wide tolerance.

He tried to give India the unity she had nearly attained once under Asoka, and once again under the Gupta dynasty; his was the third attempt and the fourth was to be the British. He was not the man to be satisfied by the tip-and-run raids of his ancestors — foreigners who never settled in India; he meant to establish a lasting empire.

And he saw what was needed if his Empire was to be stable. A fair rent must be fixed for the peasant; there must be a steady revenue for the Treasury; the land must be ruled by men who were responsible to himself; and the Muslim must live at peace with the Hindu. He went some way towards succeeding in each of those essentials; the English went further with all but the last. They failed in the end to make peace between Hindu and Muslim.

Akbar throughout the whole of his reign was experimenting with systems that would give his rule these foundations. His grasp of detail never slackened; he suggested new schemes, he directed and controlled them; his revenue minister was a servant who carried out the Emperor's policy, not an adviser to initiate. It was on his building that the English were later to build.

Taxes, social stability — everything depended on the tenure of land. In

Mogul India, no one could sell, mortgage, or bequeath land. All anyone had was a right to till the soil or a right to collect the sovereign's rent. What was most usual was the village community, who held the land of the village in common. Of the arable land, each shareholder held the right to cultivate a holding, but, if he died without heir, his holding reverted to the community and would be divided. All the shareholders had common rights of grazing and woodcutting, but they could not bring a piece of grazing-land into cultivation without the permission both of the other shareholders and of the King or his representative.

This is not ownership. The brotherhood hold the land in trust for their descendants and certain manorial rights are reserved to the sovereign, to whom they must pay a share of the produce.

Rent to the sovereign, the King's share, was paid traditionally by the simple method of sharing the produce. At harvest, each man's grain was piled in heaps on the threshing floor of dried and polished mud, a pile for the King, a pile for the village servants, a pile to keep for seed and food.

But from the point of view of the Treasury this was a poor system. The Treasurer did not know till long after the harvest how much grain there would be and there must have been heavy expenses on carting and loss by damp and mildew. With the paying crops, sugar, cotton, indigo and poppy, collection must have been still more unsatisfactory.

Akbar was constantly at work trying to find a better system. He tried having the crop estimated before it was cut – but this was obviously open to corruption. He tried to work out the average yield that an acre might be expected to produce for each kind of crop; of this a third would be due to the Emperor. But this was hard on a man with poor land – and at what price should the grain be turned into cash? Cash was what the Treasury wanted – but prices varied widely. In the end, he and his officials worked out a system of average yields and average prices applicable to a particular area.

It was the beginning of a fair assessment, but fell a long way short of what the British eventually achieved. This was to fix a yearly rent for each field based on the quality of the soil and on average prices in that district for the last thirty years.

Akbar had still to collect his share. There were two main kinds of territory owing him allegiance. Of one, the best example is Rajputana, where chiefs or petty kings, who had ruled before the Muslims came, acknowledged the suzerainty of the Emperor and paid him tribute. They were responsible in their own area for collecting the King's share of the grain, for keeping order and administering justice. It seems to have been Akbar's intention that the chiefs should take the equivalent in cash of one-third of the probable crop.

In his own territory, the country directly administered, Akbar's usual way of getting in the rent was to put so many villages in the hands of an assignee, a member of the imperial service. It seemed to the Moguls a waste of administrative effort to collect money from the peasant and then pay it out again to officials. Far better, it seemed to them, to let an official collect for himself in an area that would yield the amount of his salary.

The members of the imperial service, whatever their actual duties, were graded according to the number of imaginary horsemen they commanded. A commander of four hundred horse was supposed to be paid about £3,000 a year. The salary of a commander of one thousand would have bought as much in Akbar's day as thirty thousand rupees a month in 1914, three times the pay of the Governor of the largest English province; a commander of five thousand received five times the pay of an English Viceroy.

There were no rules for entrance or promotion, no division of function. A man might go from the Treasury to command an army in the field, from control of the library to the imperial stables. Great prizes there were, but no security; at any moment an official might be degraded, banished, tortured or executed, and at the last, the Emperor was every man's heir.

Though it sounded convenient, the system of assignments had grave disadvantages. The Mogul official probably had to spend at least as much of his time on getting his pay as he did on his duties. The assessment was too high and there was not much inducement to cultivate at all; press the peasant too hard and he would run away. He could always find land to cultivate somewhere else.

Akbar, like a wise bee-master, realized that it was impolitic to take all the honey, and limited the amount to one-third. He tried to build up a body of civil servants who would make just collections. But his successors did not concern themselves with justice and tried to take from the peasant everything beyond the barest needs of his existence. They eventually raised the King's share to one-half and abandoned all attempts to protect the peasant. In its final developments the system of assignment became one of merciless extortion.

Akbar saw that the system of assignments to officials who collected for themselves was inefficient. He made one attempt at complete reform, appointing Collectors who were paid directly by the Treasury. But Todar Mal, Akbar's great revenue minister – a Hindu incidentally – went off to fight a war. When he came back victorious, his bitterest rival had wrecked the scheme. It had, for the time, to be abandoned.

Akbar's India was the North. His rule did not reach to the Deccan or the far South; here the peasant seems generally to have been worse off. In the place of official assignees there were usually farmers of taxes, men not even supposed to be governed by any motive but rapacity; in Golconda, the farms of taxes were annually put to auction, a system probably the most extortionate yet devised by man.

This, then, was the India in which the first Englishmen found themselves. A brilliant court, profuse in display, for there was no point in saving for the Emperor; long processions of elephants with trappings of gold and silver, silks, jewels, servants, fans of peacock feathers, glowing carpets, horses from Persia and Arabia; it was not surprising that stories went to Europe of the wealth of India. And it was true that Akbar's revenue was many times that of Queen Elizabeth. But there was little commerce or industry; it was a country of peasants. The peasant was taxed twice as heavily as in 1914 and he was worse off in real goods. He had fewer cooking pots, his wife had fewer ornaments; his credit was even worse and his reserves less. It has been calculated that as a rule he needed about half the proceeds of the holding for expenses, to replace bullocks and carts, for seed, to pay village officials and the like; if the King's share was one-third he was left with one-sixth to eat – in a good year.

But many years were not good and famine was endemic; there were few years when there was not a shortage of food. And a shortage very quickly became a famine. In a country depending on animals for transport, it is impossible to do much to alleviate a widespread famine. The animals bringing the grain have to carry their own fodder, and if the journey is more than a very few days' march there is no room for anything else.

There are many descriptions of famine; two sentences must do. They come from Peter Mundy's account of a journey to Agra during the famine of 1631, one of the worst of the century: 'From Surat to this place, all the highway was strowed with dead people, our noses never free from the stink of them ... Women were seen to roast their children ... a man or woman no sooner dead but they were cut in pieces to be eaten.'

A people, then, who throughout India lived near to starvation; a people whose only refuge against oppression and extortion was flight; these were the people over whom the Moguls ruled.

It is not easy for honesty or pity to flourish at the court of absolutism anywhere, least of all where there is no permanence and 'the King is every man's heir'. No one need be surprised that such growths are hard to find among Mogul courtiers and officials. But somehow, among the peasants, in the stony soil of fear, hunger and poverty, these virtues did survive; they were still to be found in the villages, if you went to look for them, three hundred years later, together with a warm hospitality and the dignity of people poor in material possessions but conscious of long ancestry. It is hard to understand how these things survived but they did.

To this India the English came soon after Akbar died, when his fabric still stood, proud and strong to the eye, but already beginning to rot. Here they began to trade; here, by the exercise of diplomacy and no little courage and tenacity, they began to spread. By 1623, four years after Roe's going, they had factories subordinate to the main establishment of Surat at Broach, Ahmedabad, Agra, Masulipatam and Bramport – their name for Burhanpur. It was a tiny beginning.

2
SMALL BEGINNINGS

1 Pomp at Surat

During the century that followed that first small beginning in India, the English in the island settled whether King or Parliament should be ruler and found themselves confronted on the continent by Louis instead of Philip, by France instead of Spain, a new representative of the principle of personal domination which they had shown so effectively that they disliked. That power too they confined within bounds.

But it is depressing for a Western mind to turn in the same period from Europe to India, not only because the degree of cruelty and human misery is on the whole greater, but because there is no sign of growth in any desirable or even definite direction. There is none of that steady development of a principle or an institution by the yearly addition of small practical changes which in England gradually transformed society and government. Instead there is a melancholy record of insurrection, treachery and murder. The sons of each Emperor are rivals for the throne; before he is dead they are in arms against each other and against him. The most able and unscrupulous imprisons, blinds or kills the rest, as a queen bee stabs each young queen struggling out of her cell. If there was any principle of government at all among the Moguls who followed Akbar it was: 'a concentration on a barren struggle to divide, rather than a concerted effort to increase, the annual produce of the country'.

Outwardly, the Mogul Empire appeared firm enough – indeed, Aurangzebe increased his dominions considerably – but inwardly the structure grew steadily weaker because Akbar's objects were neglected. Year by year the peasantry were more grievously oppressed; year by year the civil service became more corrupt; while from the accession of Aurangzebe onwards any chance of Muslim and Hindu becoming one people disappeared in a wave of intolerance. The poll-tax was reimposed on unbelievers, temples were destroyed and idols were smashed. But it

13

was not till the death of Aurangzebe in 1707 that the decay appeared on the surface.

In this India the English wished to trade. They had first to contend with the Portuguese and the Dutch. But they had also to make their way with the Indian powers, and the servants of the Company had to learn something of India. They had learnt as soon as they came that they must be diplomats before they could be traders; they learnt more than that as, like the Portuguese before them, they began to administer and rule small numbers of Indians.

Peter Mundy, for example, made a journey in 1632 from Agra to Surat with 268 camels and 109 carts loaded with indigo and saltpetre. On the first day, he stepped into a small moving world of tents, men, bullocks and camels that in some degree every district officer was to know.

The danger from robbers was serious; Mundy was instructed to attach his caravan, with the hundred and seventy peons or footsoldiers he had for protection, to the troops of one Bakir Khan who was on his way to his new post as Governor of Gujerat. Many other merchants and travellers sought the same protection and it was a long straggling convoy.

> I am thrust out alone with little language, having nobody that I can trust or cares to take any pains to ease me to look after the company's goods, to help to compound the unreasonable demands of carters and camelers, to decide their quarrels and differences.

There was a small riot between his Baluch camel men – Muslim – and the Hindu cartmen. Then he was faced with exorbitant demands for protection money. He had to settle these affairs by the light of his own good sense.

To collect the revenue was the first duty of the Mogul official; to keep order and distribute justice were secondary functions. Merchants were expected to employ retainers and protect themselves. Anyone who has set up house in India knows that even in the twentieth century he becomes at once the arbiter between gardener's wife and washerman's, between table-servant and cook. When there was no regular police system, anyone who employed servants or labour was still more certain to find himself an administrator in embryo.

So gradually the English established themselves. In Surat, they were soon living a life of some formality. The President was treated almost like a Governor. There was a chaplain and a doctor; prayers were read twice a day and three times on Sunday. Life was more temperate than it was later to become; water or tea were the usual drinks. Yet when Peter Mundy returned to Surat on May 25, 1633, from his journey with Bakir Khan, he found only seven Englishmen alive out of twenty-one whom he had left there six months before, and of those seven, three more died before he finished writing up the last stage of his diary.

Life does not seem to have settled down into so formal a routine as at

An English factory at Surat in the seventeenth century. Here goods were purchased and stored until a ship came to take them away and leave British goods in exchange.

Surat in the English house at Agra, where the English lived to a much greater degree in the style of the country – 'sitting on the ground at our meat or discourse', wearing white linen coats and turbans.

Business increased at the Surat factory and more settlements are started. By 1647 the English have twenty-three factories and settlements in India. Sir George Oxenden successfully defended the Surat factory against 'that grand rebel Sivaji', first and greatest of the Maratha freebooters, who seized and looted Surat in 1664. Sivaji came again in 1670 in Gerald Aungier's first year of office, and again the factory alone held out. But there was no great change in the factors' way of life.

Formality grows. When the President is in Surat, there is a guard of English soldiers, consisting of a double file led by a Sergeant. 'The President besides these has a noise of trumpets and is carried himself in a palankeen, a horse of state led before him, a fan of ostriches' feathers to keep off the sun . . . '

Prayers at six; a morning of business; dinner, a little folding of the hands in sleep; in the afternoon, more business if a ship is in, but if not it is the custom to ride or drive abroad or stroll in the English garden. It sounds a tranquil picture enough, but for the President and Council crisis succeeded crisis with fair regularity, and no sooner was Sivaji's second raid over than Bombay became an anxiety.

2 Rebellion at Bombay

The island of Bombay, as everyone knows, was part of the dowry of Charles II's Portuguese queen in 1660. It was thus Crown property, not Company's. But Charles II did not like finding money for its maintenance; in 1668 he made it over to the Company.

Trade soon came to Bombay instead of Surat, merchants of all races being anxious to settle in an island where they felt secure against confiscation of their goods, and many also hoping for refuge from the religious intolerance either of Aurangzebe or of the Portuguese.

Sir George Oxenden had successfully defended the English factory at Surat against Sivaji and with dignified yet conciliatory firmness had composed a minor war with the Moguls; he was succeeded in 1669 as President of Surat and Governor of Bombay by Gerald Aungier, a man even more energetic, far-sighted and able than himself. Aungier saw the advantage of an island; on the mainland, he was at the mercy of Mogul and Maratha alike. He urged the Court of Directors to fortify Bombay and transfer the headquarters there. By 1674, when Dr Fryer wrote his description, a good deal of progress had been made:

> The Government here now is English; the soldiers have martial law. The freemen, common; the chief arbitrator whereof is the President with his Council at Surat; under him is a justiciary and Court of Pleas with a committee for regulation of affairs and presenting all complaints.
>
> The President has a Council here also and a guard when he walks or rides abroad ... He has his chaplains, physician, surgeon and domesticks; his linguist and mintmaster. At meals he has his trumpets usher in his courses and soft music at the table.

The justiciary was perhaps more versatile than learned in the law. Captain Nicholls, the first judge, was a retired sea captain; he was removed from office for refusing to pay his debts. He reappeared as captain of infantry, only to be again in trouble for an offence which 'we know not well how to put into such decent terms as may become us to your Honours'. His successor: 'condemned a man to be hanged on a Tuesday and the Man suffered according to sentence; but on the Friday after, the poor dead Fellow was ordered to be called before the court but would not comply with the summons.'

Bombay in those early days was built on tolerance – but it was dependent on the mainland for food. The mainland was held by the Marathas, who were perpetually at war with the Moguls. The English

1 An English traveller in India, early seventeenth century, when the English were still suppliants to the Mogul. Thomas Coryate, an independent traveller, reached Agra in 1620 and preached Christianity from a minaret of the Great Mosque. No one harmed him: they thought he was mad.

2 *Akbar crossing the Ganges, about 1600 A.D. Akbar, a contemporary of Queen Elizabeth I, was a far-seeing statesman who tried to give India unity.*

Sir Josiah Child, Bt., a director of the East India Company in London from 1677 till his death in 1699 and twice its Governor. 'Tempestuous and overbearing, he was a man who did nothing by halves ...'

wished to be neutral, but it was impossible to break with the Moguls, to whom Surat and the other factories were hostages; it was impossible to deny the harbour of Bombay to the Mogul admiral, who used it for constant raids on the mainland. And it was obvious that sooner or later the Marathas would retaliate.

In London, this was the beginning of the reign of Sir Josiah Child, who for twenty years directed the affairs of the Company as an autocrat, getting what he wanted by bribery, intrigue and sheer force of character. He was a man who did nothing by halves; he would use the language of Lear defying the storm in a letter about ordnance stores. Money had to be saved; he ordered that the defences should be left unfinished and the militia disbanded. To defend the island was a 'vain pompous insignificant course'. These orders were received when the Marathas had made up their minds to put an end to Bombay as a refuge for the Mogul fleet.

This is not the place for the whole story of those exciting years. There are battles, forays, sieges and ambushes, now and for two hundred years more, that would need not a book but a library to tell of them. But something must be said of the rebellion which Sir Josiah's behaviour produced.

The garrison of Bombay, confronted by hordes of indignant and war-like Marathas on the mainland, were filled with sullen anger at the tempestuous cheeseparing of Sir Josiah. They resolved at last to have no more of the imperious Josiah or the Company. They declared that the island had reverted to His Majesty Charles II, and in the King's name proclaimed as Governor Captain Keigwin, the commander of the Militia. Throughout the whole episode Keigwin insisted that he was the King's Governor. He surrendered a year later, as bloodlessly as he had rebelled, at the express command of Charles II. In the course of the year, Keigwin had told the Mogul admiral to keep out of the harbour, finished the fortifications, paid everyone his dues, and handed over the Treasury with as much in it as when he had taken it over. He had made the English a power; secure in their island, they could now ride out a storm on the mainland. The great Josiah is a changed man now:

> It is our ambition for the honour of our King and Country and the good of Posterity, as well as this company, to make the English nation as formidable as the Dutch, or any other Europe nation . . . in India; but that cannot be done only in the form and with the method of merchants, without the political skill of making all fortified places repay their full charges and expenses.

This was in 1685, a year after the Rebellion; two years later he was writing of 'the foundation of a large, well-grounded, secure English dominion in India for all time to come'.

3 Madras

On the West coast, the English won an uneasy independence as soon as they had an island to defend. But Bombay was not the first piece of territory to be administered. In 1639, Mr Francis Day obtained from a descendant of the old Rajas of Vijayanagar the grant of a strip of land on the coast of Coromandel, about six miles long by one broad. Within this husk was a kernel, only about four hundred yards by a hundred but defensible. The English built a wall and within it a college for the factors and merchants, a house for the Governor. This was the White Town; outside the walls but within the six-mile strip, sprang up the Black Town. This became Madras.

At Madras from the beginning there was a leisurely self-sufficiency, and in the seventeenth century there was also a way of being ahead of the other Presidencies. In the first place, the English claimed to hold this narrow strip in full sovereignty. They maintained soldiers to defend the place and they punished criminals. The Council met at eight in the morning every Monday and Thursday; the pettiest matters were discussed and recorded and a copy of the diary sent to England every year with a letter of review. The salary of the Agent or Governor was three hundred pounds a year; his three Members of Council drew one hundred pounds, seventy and fifty respectively. Factors received something between forty and twenty, Writers ten pounds and Apprentices five.

In the White Town, the Agent himself was commander of the garrison, and was the supreme authority for law and order. In the case of an offence committed by a European, the Agent and his Council were the judges and a jury was empanelled. Justice in the Black Town was more summary, the

Customer, or Fourth in Council, acting as Magistrate and condemning, flogging, fining or imprisoning at discretion, while the duty of keeping order and presenting offenders to the Magistrate fell to an Indian known as the Pedda Naik.

The Restoration brought a charter permitting the Company to build fortifications, raise troops and make war on powers not Christian. With the increase in authority came a succession of Governors who seem to have been usually men of a fierce vigour. Sir Edward Winter in 1665, indignant at being superseded, arrested his successor for high treason. Winter prolonged his tenure of office by three years and like Keigwin only surrendered to force sent from England to subdue him. Langhorn, Master, Yale, Pitt – all were men of character.

There was a period when the Governor and Council were allowed to hang Europeans only for piracy – but they ruled that piracy meant crossing a piece of water while in possession of property for which no strict account could be given. Governor Elihu Yale, whose name survives in the university, is said to have hanged his English groom, one Cross, for piracy, he having taken a ride on his master's horse without permission, stayed away two nights, and forded the river Koum, thus qualifying as a pirate.

It is the more surprising to find that as early as 1680 the Governor of Madras forbade the burning of a Hindu widow. And the slave trade was forbidden on September 18, 1683, and frequently thereafter.

By 1685, the doctrine of sovereignty was stated explicitly by Sir Josiah. He is directing the President how to deal with an appeal by the King of Golconda for help against the Mogul Emperor:

> You may ... tell him in plain terms that we own him for our good friend, ally and confederate, and sovereign and lord paramount of all that country, excepting the small territory belonging to Madras of which we claim the sovereignty and will maintain and defend against all persons and govern by our own laws, paying unto him, the King of Golconda, our agreed tribute of 1,200 pagodas per annum.

For a sovereign territory, it was by no means enough to provide men skilled only in measuring cloth and casting up accounts. Here is Sir Josiah defending the accelerated promotion of Mr Higginson because he is: 'a man of learning and competently well read in ancient histories of the Greeks and Latins, which, with a good stock of natural parts, only can render a man fit for Government and Political science, martial prudence, and other requisites for ruling over a great city . . . and for treaties of peace or war.'

Sir Josiah was undoubtedly a great man; he suggested a beginning of local self-government and added: 'Your people would more willingly and liberally disburse five shillings towards the public good, being taxed by themselves, than sixpence imposed by our despotical power.'

This is the voice of a statesman. As early as 1683, the Court of Directors had justified taxation for the defence of the town on the ground that the inhabitants 'do live easier under our Government than under any Government in Asia'. A house-tax was proposed, 'of three fanams a year for a small house, six for a middle size house and nine for a great house'. Nine fanams would be rather less than two shillings. The inhabitants stopped all work and presented a petition to the Council, protesting against the tax.

The Council however were resolute and insisted that they must pay the tax or leave, and at last they submitted.

4 Job Charnock

Madras had till 1688 no more formidable neighbour than the King of Golconda; but Bombay was menaced by the Marathas, while Calcutta was in the heart of the richest province of the Mogul Empire.

The Portuguese as usual had been first in Bengal. But they incurred the anger of Shah Jehan because they held aloof when he rose in arms against his father Jehangir. Once Shah Jehan was firmly on the throne he took his revenge, driving the Portuguese out of Hooghly, massacring the men and carrying off the women. The English crept joyfully into the perilous vacancy thus created.

There was soon well established at Hooghly a Bay Council, subordinate to Madras, having jurisdiction over outlying factories. Their letters and records are preserved and there are private journals of Streynsham Master and William Hedges. Master was selected in 1675 to restore order to the settlements on the east coast and he was a good choice. He was a born administrator and his journals paint a vivid picture of the kind of things that will go wrong in small societies everywhere. But behind all the quarrels and the pettiness is always the relationship with the Moguls, in which there is usually more than a hint of menace.

Aurangzebe had restored the poll-tax on unbelievers and this had to be compounded for. Presents to the Viceroy of Bengal and his subordinates were a continual trouble. There were presents to the Emperor as well, but bribery, like blackmail, is a dose that has to be not only repeated but increased if the symptoms are not to recur. By an expenditure of fifty thousand rupees, an order was obtained from the Emperor permitting the Company to trade on terms which would end all difficulties – but, needless to say, when the order came it could be interpreted by local officials in a sense quite different from that intended by the English, and it was just as necessary to give presents as before. In Patna, Peacock, the Chief of the Factory, was not sufficiently obliging and was seized, forced to walk through the town bare-headed and bare-footed and subjected to many other indignities before he paid up and was released.

Sir Josiah was not the man to put up with insult and humiliation; he declared war on the Mogul Emperor, and sent six companies of infantry and ten armed vessels to conquer India. After some fumbling, this expedition abandoned Bengal and with Job Charnock, Chief of Council in Bengal, fell back on Madras; now the Mogul began to feel the effect of sea power. Sir Josiah perceived, rather late, that he could make the Emperor feel his strength best by blocking his trade with China and the South-East. The Emperor gave in, granting permission for the establishment of factories in Bengal.

Job Charnock came back in triumph and founded a city that was to become one of the largest in the world. He was the rougher kind of Company's servant; he was not a man of good birth and education like Streynsham Master or Gerald Aungier, nor can he be credited with any great foresight or imagination. But he sticks in the memory, perhaps from something in the harsh syllables of his name but perhaps more truly because of the silent stubborn obstinacy that seems to have been his strength. He died in 1693, having 'reigned more absolutely than a Rajah, only he wanted much of their humanity'.

The seventeenth century ended then with all three Presidencies established. In the first years after 1608 the English had been a colony of traders, begging for the right to exist in Surat on sufferance; now the Governors of Madras and Bombay live in regal state with a navy, a standing army, a militia, judges and a mint. The servants of the Company are still mainly concerned with kerseys and calicoes; it is trade they are after. But already they are experienced in the diplomacy of the East; they are learning to be administrators in a small way, and every man among them is an occasional soldier.

There have been men among them of imagination, foresight and restraint; in almost any society Oxenden, Aungier and Master would have shone. Others, such as Pitt and Charnock, excel by the force of a stubborn gusto for mastery. Idleness and folly no doubt are there in plenty, and technical dishonesty, for you will not get incorruptibility for ten pounds a year. But most of it is the sanctioned dishonesty of the East, the commission that does not go beyond what is customary. It was no worse in India than in Whitehall.

They are quarrelsome, no one can deny it; a hot-tempered, full-blooded generation who eat too much meat for the climate and drink too much arrack punch and too much of the livery flavoursome wines of Spain and the Canaries. But the quarrels vanish and the ranks close when they are faced by Mogul or Portuguese and already they display the qualities that are to put this empire in their hands – a stubborn fidelity to each other and an obstinate tenacity of purpose; discipline; a preference on the whole for keeping their word. Above all, there is among them a fair number of that rare sub-species of man through whose character shines the sharp blade of decision, the steel of leadership.

3
WAR IN THE SOUTH

1 The New Century

During the first half of the eighteenth century, there was no great change in the way the English lived in India. Then, at the mid of the century, the wind blew a sharp and sudden blast that changed the face of nature. But in the meantime, says Hamilton: 'Most gentlemen and ladies in Bengal live both splendidly and pleasantly, the forenoons being dedicated to business and after dinner to rest, and in the evening to recreate themselves in chaises or palankeens in the fields, or to gardens.'

It was as well to live splendidly and pleasantly while you could, for Hamilton writes elsewhere: 'One year I was there and there were reckoned in August about twelve hundred English . . . and before the beginning of January there were four hundred and sixty burials registered in the clerk's book of mortality.'

The newcomer now usually began as a Writer on £10 a year, and could expect to rise to Factor on £20 in three or four years. Governors and Agents seem often to have come in direct. We have seen the case of Higginson; Master was another, but the most outstanding was Thomas Pitt, who for years had been the chief rival of the Company, a private merchant daring to trade in defiance of their monopoly, who at last became such a nuisance that the Court of Directors made him Governor of Madras — and a very good one he made, quite apart from begetting a line of Prime Ministers.

The young Writer had to look forward to three or four years of drudgery, if he lived so long. He was forbidden, throughout his service, to take part in private trade outside India. In his first year or two the Writer probably lacked either the capital or the knowledge needed for private trade inside India. On the other hand, he ate and boarded free; and in addition to his salary he had an allowance from the Company that was meant to cover the payments he must incur:

22

The Company's allowance is eight pagodas twenty-three fanams (that is, about three pounds ten shillings) a month, out of which the money paid for servant's wages, washing, candles and many other necessaries belonging to housekeeping together with the dearness and scarcity of provisions makes it as much as ever we can do to live upon that allowance.

This is part of a letter from a young gentleman in the Company's civil service, Robert Clive, to his father. He had to pay for his passage out and his keep on the voyage; he had also to furnish his rooms on arrival and buy clothes. It is clear that a young man was in great need of an indulgent father or a benevolent patron. But sooner or later he would find a means to start in private trade and then he would be rich before long.

In 1690, the Marathas sold the English as much land as would fall within random shot of a cannon fired from Cuddalore; the largest cannon in the Presidency was fetched at once and Fort St David founded. There was another important step in 1698, when the Mogul gave the English leave to fortify Calcutta and granted them in three villages the right to collect the King's share of the produce and to administer justice.

No sovereignty was claimed here. The English Company simply became a *zamindar*, or landholder in Bengal; it is a term that means something different in other parts of India and particularly in the Punjab. In Bengal it meant any intermediary with a right to collect the King's share. One of the English merchants became the zamindar; here is the description of his own functions by Mr Holwell:

The zamindar acts in a double capacity . . . the one as Collector of your Revenues, the other as Judge for all matters both civil and criminal, wherein the natives only, subjects of the Mogul, are concerned. He tries in a summary way, has the power of the lash, fine, and imprisonment; and in all criminal cases proceeds to sentence and punishment immediately after hearing, except when the crime (as murder) requires the lash to be inflicted until death, in which case he suspends execution of the sentence until the facts and evidence are laid before the President and his confirmation of the sentence obtained.

It is not pleasant to find that even in that age, callous to death and suffering though most men were, Englishmen should have whipped murderers to death because they had no legal power to hang them. The Mogul custom in the same circumstances was to mutilate and leave to die.

That they had become zamindars made no real difference to the relations of the English with the Moguls. The round of bribery and intrigue – into favour and out again – of procrastination, evasion and deceit – all that was unchanged; only the Emperor was weaker, his Viceroys stronger. And in Bengal, the tale of the Viceroys and their governors is the familiar sequence of idle debauchee alternating with merciless tyrant.

Meanwhile, the face of India is a melancholy sight. For once it is permissible to let oneself drift on the strong tide of Macaulay's rhetoric. He wrote of the forty years that followed the death of Aurangzebe:

> A succession of nominal sovereigns, sunk in indolence and debauchery, sauntered away life in secluded palaces, chewing bang, fondling concubines, and listening to buffoons. A succession of ferocious invaders descended through the western passes to prey on the defenceless wealth of Hindostan ... and every corner of the wide Empire learned to tremble at the mighty name of the Marathas.

He is exactly right when he goes on:

> Wherever the Viceroys of the Mogul retained authority they became sovereigns. They might still acknowledge in words the superiority of the house of Tamerlane; as a Count of Flanders or a Duke of Burgundy might have acknowledged the superiority of the most helpless driveller among the later Carlovingians. In truth however they were no longer lieutenants removable at pleasure but independent hereditary princes.

And this tendency to become hereditary and independent spread downwards; wherever he could, the collector of the King's share of the produce of the soil turned his assignment into a hereditary chieftainship.

2 The March to Arcot

It was in these conditions of growing chaos that war began in the South – war with the French. It is a war that for the general reader is apt to be both dull and confusing. The numbers of French and English are very small and the loss from disease high, so that the arrival of a ship from Europe with five hundred fresh soldiers for either nation is usually enough to sway the balance to their advantage; the Indian troops on either side were at this stage usually ready to change sides with the swing of the tide. The result is an uneasy see-saw of apparently overwhelming victory and calamity.

War broke out between France and England in 1743; the news reached India in 1744. There is no room here to follow the ups and downs of war's fortune in Madras; it must be enough to say that the first period, of open war, was indecisive, with the advantage slightly to the French; peace was signed in Europe and a period followed in which Dupleix, the French governor, tried to make himself master of Southern India by putting his candidates on two thrones, that of the Nizam or Viceroy of the Deccan and that of his nominal vassal, the Nawab of the Carnatic.

There was peace in Europe between France and England but in India there could be no peace short of complete victory for Dupleix. Each nation supported its own puppets. A time came when both Dupleix's candidates were enthroned. The English claimant to the Carnatic, Mohammad Ali,

Dupleix: the founder of British rule in India – for without the ambition of Dupleix the English would hardly have begun their career of conquest.

with some English soldiers, was besieged and heavily outnumbered at Trichinopoly. It seemed only a matter of time before Mohammad Ali and the whole force with him surrendered; there would be an end then of all pretence; the English would have no Nawab to fight for and they would have nothing to do but submit to the mercy of Dupleix.

It was now that a suggestion was put forward by Robert Clive, of the Company's civil service – for the second time turned temporary soldier. This was the moment, he suggested, to relieve the pressure on Trichinopoly by marching to attack Arcot, the capital of the Carnatic. The town was not strongly held and its new ruler, Chanda Sahib, the French candidate, could hardly stand by and see it lost. It was a suggestion of which the direct results lasted two hundred years and the indirect may last as long again.

Anyone can think of such a plan, but it takes faith in the future to find the men and decide that the thing shall be done. Mr Thomas Saunders, now President at Fort St David, was surrounded by enemies; the whole continental background was in hostile hands; at Trichinopoly Chanda

Sahib's troops outnumbered Mohammad Ali's by ten to one. But Saunders perceived the valour, the leadership, and the genius of Clive, a man not yet twenty-six. He heard Clive's plan and accepted all the deadly risk involved; with the unanimous support of his Council he scraped together for Clive's march every man that could be raised, leaving himself only a hundred English soldiers at Fort St David and fifty at Madras. For the expeditionary force there were two hundred English and three hundred sepoys, with eight officers, six of whom had never seen action, while four were young men in the civil service of the Company now commissioned for the first time. They had three field pieces for their artillery; a siege train of two eighteen-pounders was sent after them later.

The expedition marched from Madras on August 26, 1751; on the 31st Clive was within ten miles of Arcot, which was garrisoned by a force of about eleven hundred men. The garrison abandoned the fort to Clive without fighting, but he was no sooner in Arcot than he was besieged.

Almost at once, the thrust at Arcot began to have the effect intended.

Robert Clive, the Baron of Plassey. 'Brilliant in sudden danger & adversity, profuse, moody, recklessly generous, unable to endure himself or subsist in idleness ...'

Four thousand of Chanda Sahib's best troops left Trichinopoly and were joined on the march by reinforcements of French from Pondicherry. Clive was at first outnumbered by two to one, soon by ten to one and then by twenty and even forty. But his own indomitable resolution kept up the spirits of his men, British and Indian alike.

It was September, close, hot and moist; in red coats and tight stocks, heavy felt hats, belts and pouches, the men must have poured with sweat. Water was bad and short; food was short. There were nothing like enough men to man the walls; they had to go short of sleep. There was not much hard fighting but constant danger of death; Clive went the rounds with a sergeant by his side; on three separate occasions the sergeant was killed and Clive saved.

September dragged on into October. Things got steadily worse. But there were rumours that help was on the way. On the evening of November 13 a spy brought the news that the assault would be at dawn next day. 'But as our people were night and day on their posts we made no alteration in our disposition.' There were now eighty English and a hundred and twenty sepoys fit for duty.

The assault began before dawn. It was the tenth day of Moharram, the climax of the fast and of the mourning for Hasan and Husain. The attackers came on with a desperate enthusiasm, regardless of life, sure of a martyr's crown if they fell.

'The ditch before the breach to the north-west was fordable; and as many as the breach would admit mounted it with a mad kind of intrepidity . . . a number of muskets were loaded in readiness, which those behind delivered to the first rank as fast as they could discharge them . . . there were 12,000 cartridges expended during the action, which lasted not an hour, so it will be readily allowed we were not idle.' A little after day-break the enemy fell sullenly back, but fired all day at the fort and breaches, till in the middle of the afternoon they asked for a truce to bury their dead. At four in the afternoon they began to fire again and kept it up till two in the morning. Then the fire died down and in the morning they had gone.

Soon after came more 'agreeable news, which gave us unbounded joy when we heard Captain Kilpatrick was within a few hours' march'.

The siege was over. And not the siege only; other things too were over. The tale of the siege spread east and west, south and north; there will be no more turns of the tide now; now steadily comes flooding in the main. There is much hard fighting still to be done, but in ten years it will be the French who are confined to a few trading-stations, the English who have rich provinces at their feet.

The siege was over. The hour of the victory and the splendour of Dupleix was finished. It was goodbye as well to taffeties, ginghams, mull-mulls and muslins, indigo and saltpetre, vermilion, quicksilver and pepper. Not much longer would men aspire to be Warehouse-keeper or Purser Marine; councillor to a Government, plenipotentiary at a Prince's

Court – those would soon be the appointments on which their eyes were set. They would govern rich provinces and rule the affairs of men. But no one yet knew that. The day after Arcot was relieved, the sun rose on a discomfort no less torrid than the day before; the soldiers had still to find food, to look to their ammunition, to take care of their feet. They had a long way to go and there was a great deal still to do. But the change had happened all the same.

Sketch by Mrs Moss-King of children with several servants and a mounted policeman on the move from one camp to the next. Mrs Moss-King, who made this drawing and those on pp. 134, 179, 206 and 228, was the wife of an I.C.S. officer in the United Provinces; her son followed the same profession; his daughter married a third.

PART II
Traders to Rulers 1751–1798

4
THE REVOLUTION IN BENGAL

1 The Reversal of Roles

For a century and a half the English had been humble petitioners to the Mogul Emperors and their Viceroys. But within a few years of Arcot, all that was changed. When Mr Vansittart, Governor of Fort William, arrived at Murshidabad, one evening in 1761, it was the Nawab of Bengal, the Mogul Viceroy, who made haste to visit the English Governor at nine o'clock next morning. Already it was established etiquette that the Englishman should walk to the end of the hall to greet his visitor, should make him the offer of a ceremonial present, which would be refused as inappropriate from an equal, and should then lead him to a couch, where they would take care to be seated at exactly the same moment and side by side. Formally they were allies; in reality it was the Mogul who did as he was told.

The events which brought about this revolution are more dramatic than those which in Madras had led to the undoing of Dupleix. There is a flavour of the Arabian Nights in the contrast between the magnificence of Suraj-ud-Daula's prospects when he was enthroned, the sumptuous folly of his brief reign and the wretchedness of his end; there is much to pity in the decline of Mir Jafar and there is tragedy in the picture of Mir Kasim fighting against the march of events and a people too strong for him.

In England, Englishmen who had brought about this revolution were impeached, assailed with the most shocking imputations, held up to public obloquy in the House of Commons, in the Press, on the stage and in the novel. Anyone not wholly carried away by this torrent of detraction is left in the state of poised inquiry of a small boy listening to his form-master's guarded description of the orgies of a Roman Emperor. He wants to know what actually happened.

The last Viceroy of Bengal, Behar and Orissa who could truly be regarded as an independent Prince was Ali Vardi Khan. He was shrewd in

The Mogul Emperor in 1781 is reviewing the East India Company's troops. Outward respect is paid him but power has changed hands – and everyone knows it.

most things but not in his choice of a successor. He chose Suraj-ud-Daula, who took his seat on the throne with no need to fight an exhausting civil war, with no external enemies threatening invasion and with a full Treasury. But the unfortunate young man was notable only for ignorance and indecision. He believed there were no more than ten thousand persons in all Europe, and saw no reason why these aliens should live on any different terms from the rest of his subjects; they were merchants and moneylenders, no more, and ought to be subject to a capital levy whenever it suited their sovereign.

The English Settlement had grown to a city of four hundred thousand inhabitants; it was a City of Refuge not only for men but for money from all over Bengal, Behar and Orissa. All the richest Bengalis banked in Calcutta as the only place where property was respected. It was not unnatural that a spoilt young man should cast his eyes on so rich and unplundered a store. He seized the first occasion for a quarrel and in 1756 marched on Calcutta.

Calcutta was in no state to stand a siege. The fortifications were wretched, the garrison inadequate and the militia untrained. Even worse, there was no leader with the will to victory of Clive. There was a panic; most of the English, headed by the Governor, Roger Drake, fled incontinently to the boats without letting the garrison on the walls know what they were doing. Once in midstream they refused to come back for the companions they had deserted – less than two hundred English, of whom the senior was the same Mr J.Z. Holwell who had been zamindar of Calcutta.

Everyone knows what happened that evening of a Calcutta June at the time when the torrid dark falls and the heat, sullenly rejected by walls and floors, seems to grow thicker and staler than by day. One hundred and forty-six English were confined in the punishment cell of the fort, a room 'about eighteen feet long by fourteen wide' with only one small window; twenty-three of them came out alive next morning.

Those are Holwell's figures. He has been shown to be inaccurate but something of the kind did happen. It was not, however, deliberate cruelty on Suraj-ud-Daula's part; he had ordered the prisoners to be confined and did not take the trouble to see how it was done. Nor was it in a spirit of outraged vindictiveness that Clive and Watson led the expedition that was sent at once from Madras to recover Calcutta. That feeling of outrage about the Black Hole grew later, when the English took it for granted that they were the rulers of Bengal.

Clive and Watson had little difficulty in taking Calcutta. One night attack sent the Nawab scurrying northward and with no very serious fighting he was ready to sign a treaty. The main terms of the agreement were three; the English were permitted to fortify Calcutta and live there under their own laws and with their former privileges as regards customs; the Company were to be reimbursed for the goods and money lost in the looting of Calcutta; and Suraj-ud-Daula was to be the friend and ally of the English.

The Black Hole, Calcutta.
This is a reconstruction by an
artist, but something of the kind
did happen, though perhaps not
exactly as first described.

Fort William, Calcutta, in 1763, two years before Clive took over the Diwani of Bengal.

These terms are not vindictive. Clive was in fact blamed at the time, but for moderation not severity. But he must be judged in the light of the situation he faced.

There were two clear points at issue between the English and the Viceroy. Indian rulers were accustomed to take a levy of what they needed from the bankers and merchants who were their subjects, as King John had done from the Jews — and the English would not put up with that. There was also another point of the greatest consequence. Everyone knew that war was about to break out again with France. That was why there was an armament at Madras which could be sent so quickly to Bengal. But the council at Madras wanted it back; it was needed badly in the South. There were large French forces at Hyderabad and in war Madras would be threatened. Clive had no time to lose.

But he could hardly leave Bengal without dealing with the French settlement at Chandarnagar, where there were both French soldiers and French-trained Indian sepoys. Suraj-ud-Daula was as likely as not to join with the French as soon as Clive's back was turned. Clive offered the French in Chandarnagar an agreement to keep the peace in Bengal, but they delayed, saying they were not authorized to sign. News came at last that war had broken out in Europe; nothing remained but to take Chandarnagar.

The English did not yet feel strong enough to meet the combined forces of the French and Suraj-ud-Daula. They must therefore obtain the latter's consent before they attacked the French. Mr Watts, and later Mr Luke Scrafton, civil servants of the Company, were sent to Murshidabad on this delicate and dangerous mission. Suraj-ud-Daula was not stupid and he

34

would much prefer, if he must have the English in his dominions, to keep the French as a counterpoise. But he was himself threatened by an invasion from Delhi, and Mr Watts made 'artful use' of this danger, which he backed by a handsome present of money to the Nawab's secretary. By these means, he obtained a letter which could be construed as a reluctant assent to the attack on Chandarnagar.

Chandarnagar was taken; Clive wrote to congratulate Suraj-ud-Daula on the victory achieved 'by the influence of your favour'. But he needed more favour; there were other French factories.

Suraj-ud-Daula however still wanted the French as a counterpoise; he took into his service the refugees from Chandarnagar and formed them into a military company; he wrote offering alliance to Bussy who commanded the French forces in the Deccan. On this, Admiral Watson sent his famous letter telling the Nabob that if he continued to protect the King's enemies – that is the French – 'I will kindle such a flame in your country as all the water of the Ganges shall not be able to extinguish.'

There followed in the Indian camp a conspiracy against Suraj-ud-Daula. According to the *Siyar-ul-Muntakherin*, an account by a Mogul of a noble family who for many years held a place at court, it was spontaneous. 'His two principal Generals confederated with . . . other disaffected Grandees . . . in the scheme of oversetting Suraj-ud-Daula, whose character of ferocity and thoughtlessness kept them in continual alarms and whose fickleness of temper made them tremble.'

However it originated, the conspiracy came pat to Clive's hand. There followed Plassey, surely the most miserable skirmish ever to be called a decisive battle; Clive with eight hundred Europeans and two thousand sepoys faced a force estimated at fifty thousand and far superior to him in artillery. Mir Jafar, the leader of the confederated grandees and the

Watts and Mir Jafar. Mr Watts concluded on behalf of Clive a Treaty with Mir Jafar, one of the leading nobles of the Nawab of Bengal. At the battle of Plassey, Mir Jafar kept out of the fight and was made Nawab in his master's place. Mir Jafar is on the left, his despicable son Miran in the middle.

In 1765, Clive accepted from the Emperor the appointment of the Honourable East India Company as Diwan – that is, Chief Minister and in particular Revenue Minister – for Bengal, Bihar and Orissa. This was the biggest single step in the transformation of traders into rulers.

Nawab's chief general simply abstained from fighting – but it was enough. Suraj-ud-Daula fled to his capital, escaped by night with a selection of his favourite jewels and women, was recognized by a private enemy and handed over to the agents of Mir Jafar, who led him back to Murshidabad.

Suraj-ud-Daula was put down; Mir Jafar was put up. And there was nothing indefinite this time. The treaty stipulated the exact amount that must be paid to the English, together with fifty lakhs as personal rewards for the army and navy; all French possessions in Bengal were made over to the English, who were also given the right to collect the King's share of the revenue in certain tracts of land. Clive had pursued his way with his usual dogged pertinacity; he had let nothing turn him aside, he had not shrunk from intrigue and deception. He had rid Bengal of the French and for the English had won security to trade. Those had been his two objects, but he had also won much more.

To an Indian brought up in the traditions of Sanskrit and Persian literature, nothing could have been more incomprehensible than the systems of checks to absolute power which in England already existed in various stages of growth, and in America were soon to be set up in all the radiance of conscious intention. To the Indian, power was indivisible and lodged in the sovereign, whose will was absolute. But here was a power that could put down one King and enthrone another. It was clear now to every Indian where power lay. From Plassey onwards, a recommendation from the English became the only sure way to office and it does not need much imagination to see that once the English had recommended a man they would inevitably become involved in the affairs of their nominee.

Take, for example, the case of Ram Narain, a Hindu, the Governor or Deputy Viceroy of Behar. As soon as Mir Jafar was in power, he moved towards Ram Narain as though to inquire into his affairs. Ram Narain arranged for a forged document to be presented to him by his secretary at that unwary moment when he was 'duly seasoned with his dose of bang'. It was a guarantee to Ram Narain of life, property and honour; it confirmed him in his office without being called to any account. Mir Jafar agreed that his seal should be affixed. Clive was now asked to add his name; he supposed the document represented Mir Jafar's real intentions and he signed too. Mir Jafar could not remember what he had signed and grudgingly accepted the situation. From now onwards the faith of the English was pledged that Ram Narain should not be called to account. Whether they liked it or not, they were responsible for his administration of Behar.

Here it will be convenient to set down the steps by which the English acquired Bengal. Calcutta and the villages immediately around it came in 1698 with the grant to Job Charnock of the right to collect the King's share of the revenue. This was confirmed after Plassey. The Company were supposed to pass on to the Mogul authorities the King's share; they were zamindars, like hundreds of other semi-feudal collectors of revenue. To Calcutta was added after Plassey the district called The Twenty-four Pergunnas, in which the Company were also zamindars. This was 'Lord Clive's Jagir'. The next accession came when Mir Kasim was enthroned in 1760; he rewarded the Company by the assignment, free of revenue, of the provinces of Midnapore, Burdwan and Chittagong. Here they collected the King's share and kept it; for the first ten years, it brought a profit of about half a million pounds a year.

Then in 1765 came a much bigger step. On the Company's behalf, Clive accepted from the Emperor the appointment of Revenue Minister for Bengal, Behar and Orissa.

These were the first steps towards an Empire; now everything was ready for one of the worst chapters in English history. The English on the spot had, deliberately, and with the aid of force, both overt and diplomatic, of bribery and of intrigue, set out to attain two limited objects, to drive out the French and to make their own trade secure. They had been led further than they meant to go; they had wanted power but had not realized that it must bring responsibility. As for the Directors in England, they had been presented with an empire at which they looked with the incredulous elation, shot with sharp twinges of doubt, of a village grocer who has inherited a chain of department stores and is not quite sure whether they will pay him a profit beyond his dreams or drag him down to ruin.

2 One of the Worst

Let us shut down the telescope, lift into place the microscope and look at something small and wriggling from a pond, Mr William Bolts, one of the worst of the Company's servants.

William Bolts arrived in Bengal in the summer of 1760. He was not an Englishman – one is relieved to note – being the son of Dutch parents and born in Holland, but he had come to England when he was fourteen and had been an apprentice in London and later with an English firm in Lisbon. He was twenty-five when he came to India, having been for ten years 'regularly bred to business, almost from his childhood'.

He was soon able to enter into partnership with two members of Council, Mr John Johnstone and Mr William Hay. The firm traded in woollen goods, saltpetre, opium, cotton and diamonds, and was soon bidding for the right to collect the King's share of revenue from certain lands.

They gave advances for crops. In the months before harvest the peasant needs cash; if he sells his crop before it is cut, he sells low and at a discount and he will be charged interest. When he has handed over the whole crop, there will still be something owed. So he will promise to sell next year's crop and in the spring he will take another advance on worse terms than the first. He will be sucked dry, as a spider sucks a fly.

They gave advances to the peasants; they bought from Indian merchants at low rates, terrifying them by threats of force; they sold at high prices to the village shopkeepers, and they paid no duty on their goods.

Customs had been a grievance of the English from their first coming. A shipping of indigo, saltpetre or vermilion, such as Peter Mundy had brought down from Agra to Surat in 1632, might pay blackmail, tribute, or customs to a hundred petty chiefs on the way. It might become so ruinously expensive that the trade was not worth while. Such a cargo was not in competition with the grain, salt, cooking-vessels and the like which the native merchants might be carrying fifty or a hundred miles; it was fair enough that it should be exempt. To get this exemption had been an object of all the early embassies; it had been achieved by Surman's mission of 1715.

But there was then no question of internal trade in articles which were consumed in the country. And now it was noisily claimed by such as Bolts that not only the Company, not only the Company's servants, but the servants of the Company's servants, anyone who could show a pass with an Englishman's signature, could buy, sell or transport without duty, whatever he liked, wherever he liked. No one who paid duty could compete with such traders as these.

Mir Kasim saw it very clearly; he was a man of ability, energetic and outspoken. He had been made Nawab of Bengal by the English as Mir Jafar sank lower and lower in drug-soaked indolence. This is what Mir Kasim wrote to the Governor and his Council in May 1762:

And this is the way your Gentlemen behave; they make a disturbance all over my country, plunder the people, injure and disgrace my servants . . . In every village and in every factory they buy and sell salt, betel-nut, rice, straw, bamboos, fish, gunnies, ginger, sugar, tobacco, opium . . .

They forcibly take away the goods and commodities of the peasants, merchants, etc., for the fourth part of their value, and by ways of violence and oppressions they oblige the peasants to give five rupees for goods which are worth but one rupee.

Mir Kasim's evidence is supported by the better men in the Company's service.

In his first attempts to fight these evils Mir Kasim can only be admired. He instructed his governors to prohibit any trade with the English or their agents that was based on advances; to cash transactions there was no objection and indeed over these his officers would help. Mr Bolts and his partners protested indignantly and eventually their letters came before the Governor and Council in Calcutta. Messrs Hay and Johnstone as Members of Council took full responsibility for Bolts and retaliated with a fierce attack on Vansittart, the Governor of Fort William.

Vansittart was disliked in the first place because he was a Madras civilian. He had been brought in over the heads of the Bengal Council on Clive's recommendation as an honest man. And he was disliked too just because he was honest. He had recently been to visit the Nawab and had negotiated an agreement about trade. The right to external trade free of duty was confirmed, but on internal trade, whether the merchant was English or Indian, there was laid a uniform duty of nine per cent, while English traders were forbidden to give advances and were made answerable to the Nawab's officers. This was a fair settlement; but in Council the Governor had only a casting vote, and there was no one but Warren Hastings to support him. His agreement was denounced; to be fair to Indians was to be prejudiced against the English. The word went round that Vansittart was weak; he favoured the Nabob. The behaviour of Messrs Johnstone, Hay and Bolts was upheld by a resolution of Council and it was many months before the orders of the Directors reached Bengal and reversed the decision of Council.

Since the English would not pay duty, Mir Kasim's next step was to restore the balance by freeing Indians as well. All trade became free; all customs were abolished. He lost revenue, but his merchants could at least now compete with the English. But this was as shocking an infringement of the rights of Englishmen as the other. Vansittart and Hastings alone were of the contrary opinion.

They were overruled and the Council dispatched Mr Amyatt to visit Mir Kasim and compel him to tax his subjects for the benefit of foreign trade. And at this Mir Kasim lost all patience and in something of Macbeth's last mood began to wade deep in blood. Mr Amyatt was assassinated; Ram Narain, the former governor of Behar who had relied on Clive's guarantee, was tied to a stone and thrown in the Ganges; the grandees who had helped to overthrow Suraj-ud-Daula were executed, and at least one hundred and fifty English merchants and soldiers, unarmed prisoners at Patna, were slaughtered in cold blood.

It is time to bend the eyes once more to the murky progress of Bolts. Exonerated by the Council, he was reprimanded by the Directors; we next hear of him making a fraudulent attempt to avoid signing his covenant. Clive had brought back, on his third journey to India in 1765, strict orders that all the Company's servants were to sign covenants undertaking not to receive valuable presents from natives of India. This was one of the first; the last such covenant was signed in 1939. Frustrated in this, Bolts was next in trouble for a quarrel with Marriott, his Chief at Benares, over the spoils of some illicit transaction. Reprimanded again, he was suspended for evading transfer to Calcutta and was soon making what looks like a fraudulent charge against another of his seniors for eloping with his wife.

But that is enough of Bolts. He was not a nice man and he has served his purpose. There are, however, still aspects of the evil done in Bengal in those first years after Plassey which hardly appear in his career. One is touched on in the matter of the covenant. 'Presents', once given by the Company to the Mogul, were now given by the Mogul's Viceroy to the Company and its servants. When Mir Kasim's reign ended and the pathetic figure of Mir Jafar was brought out, shaken, dusted, and a second time enthroned, presents were promised amounting to £300,000 to the Company, £530,000 to the gentlemen of the Council, and £250,000 to the army and navy. In the eight years that followed Plassey, there were four enthronements of Nawabs, each accompanied by 'presents'. They amounted to over a million pounds every two years, a grievous charge on a revenue of two and a half million pounds a year.

Presents on this scale stopped when Clive came back to India in 1765. But there continued for some years an even worse drain. One of the Company's greatest difficulties had always been the argument that they were impoverishing England by draining the country of bullion. They had to export silver to pay for the goods they brought back from the East. But when in 1765 they began to collect the revenues of Bengal and Behar, they found a fund of silver to their hands. With this not only could they pay for the annual investment – the purchase of goods in India for England – but they could export silver to the East for the investment in China and Japan. From a total revenue of less than two and a half million pounds, Bengal was soon paying every year three-quarters of a million for goods sent to England and a quarter of a million for purchases in China. The remaining sum, of between a million and a million and a half, was spent on the civil and military establishments of the Company, the military taking about two-thirds.

One may doubt whether things were quite as bad as Macaulay thought but no one can study the evidence and deny that there were many and grievous wrongs. Fortunes were made by oppressive trade and sent home to England; corrupt and exorbitant presents drained the Treasury; there was a drain of silver to China and Japan. The author of the *Siyar-al-Muntakherin* writes of the English:

They join the most resolute courage to the most cautious prudence, nor have they their equals in the art of ranging themselves in battle and fighting in order. If to so many military qualifications, they knew how to join the arts of government; if they ... exerted as much ingenuity and solicitude in relieving and easing the people of God as they do in their military affairs, no nation in the world would be preferable to them or prove worthier of command.

There were many wrongs. But we are judging by high standards. These men were conquistadors; Genghis Khan and Tamerlane, Cortés and Pizarro, would have joined Clive in opening their eyes at his moderation. It is hardly to be wondered at that merchants suddenly entrusted with an empire should have enriched themselves; it is a slight comfort that though they displayed avarice, ignorance and indifference, they are seldom charged with deliberate cruelty or with malice. What is surprising is that along with such men as Johnstone, Hay and Bolts there should so soon have been such men as Vansittart and Hastings, Verelst, Shore, Grant and Duncan.

It was an age when in England, boroughs, votes and places were looked on as property, when political society was by nineteenth-century standards corrupt. But in the short space of the twenty years after the Revolution of 1758 there developed in Bengal a body of true public servants, men who in ability, industry and sense of duty were ahead of those in Whitehall and who exercised from the earliest age a responsibility that never would and never could fall to any professional public servant in England. It is pleasing to turn from one of the worst to some of the best and to observe that from the start there was someone trying to clean the stables.

3 Some of the Best

They came out young. Henry Vansittart was only thirteen, but sixteen was common. They were boys by our ideas when they came out as Writers in the Honourable East India Company's Service and first wrote H.E.I.C.S. after their names. They were boys who had said goodbye to their parents, for five or ten years at the least, perhaps for much longer, perhaps for ever. Their chances of seeing home again were not so good as those of a subaltern leaving for the trenches in the First World War.

It was a long voyage. Sometimes it was as long as eighteen months, sometimes it was only six. When at last they saw the surf of Madras and heard the gulls, it must have seemed to each that he had been a lifetime in that swaying, creaking wooden world, but once past the surf there came the beginning of a new life on shore.

There was not much of interest in the work at first; the young man was a

Writer; he copied letters; when a ship was in, he checked cargoes. But responsibility would come soon. Hastings, at twenty-seven, was Resident at Mir Jafar's Court, perhaps the second post in Bengal. And it was a staggering responsibility.

They were faced with a complex civilization, with thirty million or so of subtle and intelligent people, professing one or the other of two ancient religions whose sacred books the English could not read. Their law was strange to the English; their institutions were overlaid and obscured by the dust of invading cavalry and the mould of despotism in decay. To this vast mass of incomprehensible material a few of the English from the start bent themselves laboriously and set about the task of understanding, straightening and controlling.

Vansittart is usually described in the history books as a weak well-meaning man, a judgment not only crude but untrue. He became a close friend of Clive's and it was on Clive's recommendation that he was appointed President of the Council and Governor of Fort William, where he arrived in July 1760. He had fourteen years' service and was twenty-eight.

In Bengal, he found the Treasury empty, the income insufficient to meet the expenses and the troops unpaid. He came quickly to the conclusion that nothing would go right so long as Mir Jafar was on the throne. In October, within three months of his arrival, he went with a body of troops to see Mir Jafar at Murshidabad. His object was persuasion; the Nawab was to be induced to hand over power at once to Mir Kasim, his son-in-law, whom he would also nominate his successor. But he would not be induced. When this became clear to Vansittart he deposed Mir Jafar and put Mir Kasim in his place.

This was not the act of a weak man, but it was an offence against the baron of Plassey, who had taken so much trouble to set Mir Jafar up. It was followed by worse; Vansittart reversed Clive's policy with regard to Ram Narain the Governor of Behar, who had obtained Clive's guarantee by such dubious means. It was just such an act as would be classed as weakness and betrayal. Yet in the circumstances in which each man was placed at the time, Clive's support and Vansittart's repudiation seemed equally intelligible.

The background to Clive's actions in 1757 and immediately after was a Bengal in which the Nawab had been all-powerful. What was needed was some guarantee against irresponsible tyranny. But for Vansittart the whole situation was reversed. For three years no one had known who was ruler. Power lay with the English, but they would not govern. It seemed essential that someone should, and Mir Kasim had been chosen. His hand then must be strengthened and surely he could have only a semblance of power if his officers could defy him on the strength of a perpetual English guarantee. Vansittart refused to continue the guarantee and left Ram Narain to the mercy of Mir Kasim. The Council endorsed his action.

There were twelve members of Council. Council was supreme and the Governor had only a casting vote in the event of a tie. Vansittart had been humiliated and his policy reversed by Council when he attempted to make a fair settlement of the customs with Mir Kasim. It was not by any means a solitary instance. Everything was against him. Clive thought him weak because of Ram Narain; his colleagues called him weak because he stuck to his opinion that their views were unjust. The Directors, nine months away, dismissed three of his supporters in the Council and appointed his most bitter opponent, Ellis, to be Chief at Patna, now the nearest station to Mir Kasim's court. Ellis was violent, loud-mouthed and rude. He insulted and tried to bully Mir Kasim; finally, with no authority, he surprised the Nawab's garrison in Patna and by a *coup de main* took the town, only to lose it after a few hours and eventually to lose his own life in the massacre of Patna.

Clumsy blustering little Ellis was the occasion only for what was inevitable. There was no alternative now but to rule and to this conclusion the Company and Parliament were gradually brought. Vansittart's policy had failed; he retired and became Member of Parliament for Reading. His reputation grew after his return to England, he became a Director of the Company in 1769 and in the same year was appointed one of the three Supervisors who were to reform the whole government in India. The three Supervisors sailed from England in September, and from the Cape on December 27, 1769; they were never seen again.

If he was really only thirty-eight, as he is said to have been, Vansittart's life had been full enough. He had formed a plan for restoring Oudh to the direct rule of the emperor and helping him to recover Delhi, so that there would be not only an English Nawab of Bengal but an English Emperor — and a powerful one. In such matters, he had something of Hasting's vision, but lacking his tenacity he left India too soon, a brilliant disappointed man — none the less one of the first to be a public servant. He was the first Governor after Clive, the first after that reversal of roles by which the English became the dispensers of favours and the Moguls petitioners. And in that capacity he is by no means a man to be ashamed of; he had courage and ability and he did try to be fair.

Harry Verelst arrived in Bengal in 1750, being presumably sixteen or seventeen years old. By 1760 he was a member of Council and very decided in his views. He believed it was a mistake to elevate Mir Kasim and a worse mistake to abandon the guarantee to Ram Narain. He does not seem to have looked far ahead, but the great thing about Verelst is that he was a district officer before he was a governor; he was the first of district officers and the first of revenue officers. When Mir Kasim made a perpetual grant of the three provinces, Burdwan, Midnapore and Chittagong, it was decided to appoint an Englishman to collect the revenue, and from 1761 to 1765 Verelst was in charge of the province of Chittagong. In 1765 he took charge of Burdwan and in 1766 of Midnapore. He had thus a unique experience of revenue work. He was a good businessman; he collected more than had been collected before, but though this was his first object, it is clear that it was by no means all he thought of.

When Clive accepted the post of revenue minister to the Emperor, he had no intention of really collecting the revenue in any part of Bengal except in the 'three provinces' (or rather districts) already assigned to the Company. The administration of justice remained with the Nawab; the English took no responsibility whatever. This was Clive's 'dual system'; he stated it clearly enough and with some complacency.

Verelst supported the dual system in Clive's day but did not stick to it long after Clive had left him as Governor. He was proud of his three 'provinces', the districts of which he had been himself in charge. They were better governed than the rest and he wanted to extend the benefits they had received to the rest of Bengal and Behar. He and his committee therefore undertook in 1769 the 'very arduous task' of extending to the whole of Bengal and Behar the supervision by English officials which had now been tried for eight years in Burdwan, Midnapore and Chittagong. If there is any one point other than Elizabeth's charter to the Company at which the Indian Civil Service may be said to have begun, it is now.

There was to be a Supervisor to each province or district – thirty-nine altogether. He was in the first place to collect and trace a summary history of the province. Next, he was to prepare a rent-roll, with the areas in each district, and 'the method in which they are laid out and appropriated . . . The next task is to fix the ancient boundaries and divisions' – and so it goes on. All titles to land are to be investigated and the different kinds of land distinguished; the various amounts of revenue and cesses carefully set down, commerce regulated, justice administered. But the most important part of the instructions is the attitude they impress on the Supervisor-to-be:

> Amongst the chief effects which are hoped for . . . are to convince the Ryot [the peasant] that you will stand between him and the hand of oppression; that you will be his refuge and the redresser of his wrongs . . . that honest and direct applications to you will never fail producing speedy and equitable decisions; that, after supplying the legal due of government, he may be secure in the enjoyment of the remainder; and finally to teach him a veneration and affection for the humane maxims of our government.

Verelst died in exile and poverty. His life may perhaps be written one of failure, and it was many years before even part of what he envisaged was achieved. But by the intention of his instructions let him be judged.

5
SETTING UP AS RULERS

1 Warren Hastings

Whether it was the surf of Madras or the long reaches of the Hooghly that he had to face when he left his ship, the young Writer was greeted at last by an Indian agent, a *banyan*, who undertook to find him servants and a house, to lend him money, to buy him a horse. The agent must have looked at his employer with a speculative eye; if he survived the first two years, he would provide a stipend for life, but if he went to the graveyard within six months – and the chances were that he would – then those overdrawals, those bills for punch, fodder and saddlery, insensibly mounting month by month, all were lost. It was perhaps with more discernment than his English messmates that his agent that first morning cast an eye over the slight figure of Hastings; already a good agent would know that those who were stout of build and ruddy of hue did not last the longest and perhaps he would detect the glint of an obstinate determination not to die. But he could hardly have guessed that since Akbar no one of this stature had walked the Indian stage.

The sturdy violent figure of Clive – self-centred but unable to see himself, brilliant in sudden danger and adversity, profuse, moody, recklessly generous, unable to endure himself or to subsist in idleness, virile in action, emotionally feminine – this is a man you have met and would know again. Hastings is more elusive, a far subtler character.

A passionate absorption in his work was nourished by a deep, constant and unselfish love for one woman. Profoundly reserved to the world, he found complete release in letters to one person; to turn over the pages of Hastings's letters to his wife is to feel even now some shame at one's own indelicacy. He writes as a man who loves deeply but is utterly alone; in this marriage, the finer spirit is the suppliant. None the less, Hastings's love did not distract him but nourished his work. And with his capacity for love went two other outstanding qualities, an inexhaustible patience and a

45

Warren Hastings: since Akbar no one of this stature had walked the Indian stage.

readiness to accept personal humiliation if by that means he could gain his ends.

Hastings persevered in the face of a Council of which he was the nominal head, whose members outvoted him on every point, who undid every item of his work which they sufficiently understood, who heaped him with calumny. It was he who 'led and laboriously promoted the current business', combining 'the loose and incongruous opinions of the other members into a form which they might all approve, though foreign from my own'. This he did 'for the sake of despatch, from a conviction that even wrong movements are preferable to inaction, which is the death of public affairs'. One by one his enemies 'sickened, died and fled'; he outlived and outstayed them all until power was his once more and he could start to build again.

Industrious, tenacious, quick in decision, rich above all in a sense of the practical — it was by those qualities that he achieved what he did but it was not by those qualities that his name lives. He was remembered by Indians because he thought of Indians as human beings, because he usually liked them and treated them always with courtesy. Himself a good Orientalist with a considerable knowledge of Persian, he laboured constantly to convince the Directors that the people of India had laws of their own, that their customs should be respected. He thought of the rulers of India as men like himself who could be trusted if they were properly treated and who could be honestly disliked as equals if they opposed him.

Here are his views on the character of the Hindus: 'They are gentle, benevolent, more susceptible of gratitude for kindness shewn them than prompt to vengeance for wrong sustained, abhorrent of bloodshed, faithful and affectionate in service and submission to legal authority.' And, he went on, it was the duty of the English 'to protect their persons from wrong and to leave their religious creed to the Being who has so long endured it and who will in his own time reform it.'

All this is very different from the picture presented by Macaulay of the cold hard man swayed only by reasons of state. No one now regards Macaulay's essay as a true picture of Hastings. But two episodes must be mentioned; the execution of Nuncomar and Hastings's treatment of Chait Singh, the Rajah of Benares.

Nuncomar was a man who had been all his life an intriguer, an arch-suborner of false witnesses. He had long been an enemy; Hastings said afterwards: 'I was never the personal enemy of any man but Nuncomar, whom from my soul I detested.' A time came when Hastings was in a minority in Council, outvoted daily. And it was now that Nuncomar brought against him grave charges of bribery. They were false. But they were awkward, because the majority pretended to believe them.

Into this atmosphere fell suddenly the news that Nuncomar had been arrested for forgery, committed for trial and sent to gaol. Within three months he had been tried, found guilty and hanged. His guilt is beyond serious dispute. It is the execution that sticks in the gullet.

There is not a district officer but can remember some such tale. There is a born intriguer who will try to make a dupe of a new official – but if authority refuses to be a dupe, he will make trouble. He will quote phrases out of their context and appeal to higher authority against the monstrous tyranny displayed by his oppressor. A shrewd district officer rests confident in his own integrity; he takes no action; he waits. It is a situation on which he has given his juniors advice. 'Wait for him,' he has said; 'sit up for him in a tree; don't move or you'll frighten him; sooner or later your sights will be on him.'

That is what Hastings did with Nuncomar. He probably said no word – but someone brought to light a bond Nuncomar had forged for unlawful gain. He was hanged for forgery according to the law of England, but the bazars of Calcutta – to whom forgery was just as serious as parking in the wrong place – the bazars knew very well that Nuncomar was hanged for intrigue against the Governor-General.

And in the same way the affair of Chait Singh, Rajah of Benares, is hard to understand except in the light of what happens in a district. There is little evidence in the library or the study, but any district officer can guess why Hastings acted in what looks like plain contradiction of his character

47

and policy. Money was badly needed for a war; Chait Singh, richest of the Company's subjects, was asked for something beyond his fixed revenue. He refused, standing on the letter of his agreement with something less than customary politeness. Hastings went to his capital with a few sepoys, refused to see him, put him under arrest and deposed him. It looks from the library like a brutal exhibition of despotic power.

But it does not seem unreasonable to suppose that here too he was dealing with a familiar situation. At first there is nothing tangible, but hostility is there. Everyone knows it. Then there is something open, perhaps a small but deliberate discourtesy; if this is ignored, there will be something worse and then sooner or later more liberties and perhaps in the end riots and bloodshed. With such a man, a resolute ruler will take the first chance that comes and act at once.

Even so, even if Hastings knew that Chait Singh was secretly stirring up trouble, his action was one of the most ill-considered of his life. A statesman – and even a district officer, who is a statesman in miniature – must be concerned with how his acts appear to an audience. Hastings was unfortunate; his acts fall to be judged by three audiences, the people of Bengal, whom he seldom forgot, his countrymen and contemporaries in England, whom he sometimes ignored, and the blurred critical faces in the vast auditorium which fills as posterity is admitted.

But in spite of that arrogant and over-masterful passage in his life, Hastings lives by his moral fervour and his imaginative range. It was not that he was always right; indeed, he was often wrong. But he had a poetic vision of many deep truths. A vast empire had come into English hands 'by perilous and wonderful paths', but English power in India seemed to Hastings something alien and exotic, likely to be short-lived. He refused the blunt vigorous assumption that one culture was necessarily and in every way better than the other. The ideal he had in mind is clear to the view. He did not want Englishmen in the districts; he wanted to centralize all English influence in Calcutta and to keep there the persons of all Englishmen but traders.

'There is a fierceness', he said, 'in the European manners, especially among the lower sort, which is incompatible with the gentle temper of the Bengalee.'

But already the supervisors were settled in districts. Hastings believed that the name and the power of England were being used as the instruments of oppression.

The real cure for this was to improve the training and prospects of the supervisors, to help them to gain experience and establish a real control. Hastings preferred instead to recall them to Calcutta, to centralize control there, and to collect the revenue and administer justice through Indians.

He was wrong and he was fighting against the genius of the country. The way India wants to be governed, the way she feels to be naturally right, is not by centralized rules but by personal decisions, on the platform

3 Akbar with his son Jehangir and grandson Shahjehan. Akbar died in 1605.

4 View of Bombay, from Edward Barlow's Journal, 1703.

beneath the pipal tree in the village, on the threshing-floor of polished mud, on the balks between the rice-fields.

It was, strangely enough, corruption in England that prevented Hastings from doing the wrong thing. He could not abolish the district officers because to do so would interfere too sharply with the patronage of Leadenhall Street. To set down every detail of change would make only for bewilderment. It is enough to say that the district officers survived Hastings's attempts at centralization.

But Hastings as a man is greater than his opinions. He saw that it would be possible to achieve 'the dominion of all India' – but that, he added, was 'an event which I may not mention without adding that it is what I never wish to see'. What he did want was a British power in Bengal so strong that its influence was felt in every corner of India. Bengal was to be a base from which, by a series of treaties and alliances, indirect rule through Indian chiefs would be exercised, peace maintained, and 'a strong moral influence permeate the whole'.

The alliance with Oudh was the keystone of his arch; he would gradually have extended this system until it covered India. And Oudh is the perfect example of its weakness. The Kings of Oudh, once they could lean on British strength, had no more fears of insurrection and not much of external attack. They were encouraged in irresponsibility. Oudh became a byword for maladministration and corruption.

The Marquess of Hastings, Governor-General 1812–23, at a banquet in Lucknow in 1814, given by Nawab Ghazinddin Haidar of Oudh, after he had been given the title of King by the British. But the system encouraged irresponsibility: 'Oudh became a byword for maladministration and corruption'.

That he did not perceive the dangers of supporting Princes in irresponsible rule is one side of a medal of which the other is his trust in Indians and his wish to employ them in the districts, a point in which he was a century and a half before his time. And no one, not even Macaulay, has ventured to impugn his skill as a diplomat. Consider the skill, the patience and above all the courage, with which this lonely man concluded the Treaty of Salbai.

The Treaty was made when France and Spain were in arms to help the seceding American colonies. There was a real danger that the French might re-establish themselves in India; England was alone and hard-pressed. In a world so dangerous, the Governor and Council of Bombay had chosen to embroil themselves in an unnecessary war with the Marathas. The Bombay army was surrounded and forced to surrender, their commanders accepting ignominious peace terms for which they had no authority and which were immediately repudiated by Hastings. The memory of this disaster had not been wholly wiped out by the brilliant march across India on which Hastings had dispatched Colonel Goddard from Bengal; the Treasury was low in each of the three Presidencies; the French had a squadron off the East Coast; Hyder Ali from Mysore had attacked the Madras Presidency and was in alliance with the Marathas, the Nizam of Hyderabad was on the point of joining them, and it even seemed as though the five Maratha states would once again act as one great confederacy.

Hastings was faced not only by this impending onslaught of all the most formidable powers in India, not only by the usual dissension in his own Council but also by insubordination in Bombay and Madras. The gentlemen of Madras actually suspended from duty their agent at the court of Hyderabad for the offence of having 'betrayed the secrets of his trust to the Governor-General and Council of Bengal'. But with coolness and patience Hastings set about his solitary task of gently prizing apart from each other the enemies who opposed him.

He contrived to keep the Nizam neutral while he split the Maratha confederacy and brought its members one by one to terms. The Treaty of Salbai was signed in May 1782; it was based on instructions given in the previous November when Hastings was at Benares in the thick of the Chait Singh affair, faced by a local rising and in danger of his life. At such a moment he had been able to dictate the terms that were to be made with enemies who in combination were far stronger than the English.

The final verdict on Warren Hastings must be that of the House of Commons, pronounced in 1813 when he was eighty-one, eighteen years after his formal acquittal of all the charges brought against him. He was called again to give evidence in the place where he had suffered so long and so deeply. When he ended, 'all the members by one simultaneous impulse, rose with their heads uncovered, and stood in silence till I had passed the door of their chamber.'

This was not because he had made the Company the paramount power in India, nor because he had in his own words 'explored the wilds of peril and reproach'. It was not because he had treated the people of India with consideration and endeavoured to make all the servants of the Company do the same. It was because the House recognized the fervour of his spirit, the flame of purpose that shines in everything he wrote or said, the glow of his indefinable imaginative greatness.

2 Shore and the Land Revenue

It was 1769 when John Shore landed in Bengal. This was the year when Verelst gave the Supervisors of districts their excellent instructions; the beginning of an end to the confusion and corruption that succeeded Clive's revolution. By the time Shore left India, thirty years later, something like order had been achieved in Bengal. A settlement of the Land Revenue had been made; the district officer was firmly established as the basis of the administration; the civil service of the Honourable East India Company had become a true service, its functions reasonably clear, its branches established, the salaries and prospects of its members settled. Shore's life in India covers that period of settling down; incidentally, he was the last Governor-General till John Lawrence to be a covenanted member of the service.

Shore does not arouse warmth of feeling; there is no strong love or hate, there is no fire in the man. He was fair, he was thorough, he was

left, John Shore, Lord Teignmouth: Governor-General 1793–8. 'He was fair, he was thorough, he was painstaking, he was temperate, he was honest . . .' – but he was dull; right, Lord Cornwallis, Governor-General from 1786 to 1793. Cornwallis, the first aristocrat to be Governor-General, did much to establish a sound administration. But he did not understand Indian conditions.

painstaking, he was temperate, he was honest. Though he is often right where Hastings was wrong, his words do not vibrate with force, he does not live in the imagination as Hastings does. His conscience drove him unremittingly to duties that he found mildly distasteful. The strongest feelings of his life were a dutiful affection for his mother and a mild evangelical religion.

He was always honest – and it was not always easy. When he first landed, his salary was ninety-six rupees a year, while he paid one hundred and twenty-five for 'a miserable, close and unwholesome dwelling'. He wrote however:

> Rest assured, my dear Mother, nothing shall allure me to part with my honesty . . . Poor I am and may remain so; but conscious rectitude shall never suffer me to blush at being so.

After a year of drudgery, he was appointed in 1770, still only nineteen, to be Assistant of the Revenue Council of Bengal. The Chief was idle, the others were usually away on tour, and the burden of the Council's work fell on Shore. He tried revenue suits by his own authority and settled six hundred in a year; there were only two appeals from his decisions.

The term 'revenue suit' needs explanation. In India, by accepting the revenue for a plot a collector automatically bestows a title; gradually it comes about that the Collector of Land Revenue spends only a few minutes a week on seeing that collections are coming in to his subordinates, but many hours deciding disputes.

After two years of this life, Shore found himself in 1772 Assistant to a new Board of Revenue in Calcutta. Here he was in danger of being involved in the controversy of mighty opposites. The Council had been reduced in number to five and Philip Francis and his two colleagues had arrived from England, a majority who knew that they were right and that the Governor-General and everyone else in India was wrong.

Francis was not to be the last. It looks so easy from a distance; it is simple for a quick mind to decide in Whitehall that in India everyone is second-rate, steeped in luxury and idleness. Not that the recurrent scornful influx of the beautifully tailored has been a bad influence through the centuries; on the contrary, again and again it has forced the man who knows what he is talking about to reconsider his prejudices and defend and adjust them.

However much Shore wished to avoid controversy, he really had no chance. It was the question of the day. No one arranged places at dinner without considering who was a Hastingsite and who a majority man. And in controversy about revenue, Shore, already an expert, had to be involved.

There were two questions to be answered; if those could be settled, everything else would fall into place. The first concerned the zamindars, the second the actual tiller of the soil. Some thought zamindars were mere officials removable at will by the sovereign. At the other extreme was Francis, who, being unencumbered with information, thought it simple; the zamindars were proprietors.

The truth was that the zamindars' rights had originated in several different ways. Some were the descendants of officials to whom in lieu of a salary the Emperor had given the right to collect the King's share. There were others to whom the assignment had been made not as salary but as pension. Then there were mere farmers of taxes, while others were the descendants of chieftains who before the Moguls came had been more or less independent. There were also subordinate holders of rights sub-infeudated by the zamindars, and below them too other grades until at last, below layer upon layer of sub-sub-infeudation, lay, naked and despoiled, the tiller of the soil.

Nor was even his case uniform or simple. He and his fellows might be descended from those who once, long ago, constituted the old village brotherhood. Emperor or Viceroy would give a concubine's uncle or a favourite cook the right to collect the King's share from the brotherhood, who would gradually become tenants where once they had tilled in their own right. Then there was the village that had once been waste land, a sandy strip left desolate by the river's changing course, to which a zamindar had sent men to bring the land into good heart, lending them seed and bullocks and forgiving all rent for the first five years. Here the zamindar's capital, enterprise and energy had remade the land. The rights then were not simple. And they were complicated beyond belief because one man seldom holds one right. Here five brothers are joint heirs of the son-in-law of the original assignee. Here seven families, each headed by one of the seven grandsons of one man, hold shares of varying size, because there were three sons and the right to collect rent was first split into three and then − but it is needless to go on. The shares sometimes go into thousands. And tenant rights, too, are split between families and a tenant's holding is made up from many scattered plots.

To decide who was the zamindar and who the tenant was a matter of historical research, but to find out what the tiller of the soil actually paid as rent was like a criminal investigation to which the answer was guarded by two powerful trade unions.

Akbar and Todar Mal had been at pains to fix a fair King's share. But more had always been extorted and the peasant dared not tell the truth; he feared the lord on the spot more than the King in Delhi. As central control decayed, the zamindars became united in a determination not to reveal to the new government how much in fact they collected.

There was one theoretical check, the *qanungo*. He was originally an official, the King's watchdog on the zamindar. He was there to record the collections. But the post had become hereditary and a hereditary record-keeper inevitably became the ally of the zamindar.

This then was the complex situation with which John Shore and his contemporaries had to deal. It was a situation which cried out for understanding and swift action. What made it worse, the districts had been depopulated in the famine of 1770. The losses have been put at one-fifth of all the people of Bengal.

But even without the famine, the Directors would have been disappointed. The right to collect the revenue had been put up to auction; speculators had competed with zamindars for their own districts. The revenue was inflated far above a reasonable level and was sharply punctured by the famine. At every council meeting in Calcutta was read over a melancholy list of defaulting revenue contractors, of imprisonments and mounting debts.

3 Some Questions Answered

Shore in 1772 as Assistant to the Board was at the centre of controversy and it must have been he who first read and who presented to the Board the reports that came in from the districts. They are strangely interesting. In the first place, they all have a ring of honesty. In every case the writer seems to be giving genuine advice, seeking neither direct self-interest nor the favour of the Council. There is shrewdness and ability – that might have been expected – but it is surprising to find already so strong a consciousness of duty to the people governed.

Hear Mr George Vansittart, lately Chief at Burdwan. He recounts what has been done; the old bad system of passes free of customs signed by an Englishman has been abolished, duty is brought to a low and uniform level, new taxes on the tillers of the soil have been prohibited, and all these measures are salutary, but slow in operation. He can think of no quick way of raising the revenue; indeed, he would like to reduce rents.

George Vansittart sounds a gentle and amiable man. Others were ready to state their views more forcibly – Samuel Middleton, for instance, was definitely in favour of reducing rents provided care was taken that the benefit reached the poor labourer. Contractors, he goes on to say, can only fulfil their engagements 'by such an oppression of the ryots as must in the end prove destruction to the Company's revenues'.

P.R. Dacres too put down the poor returns to over-assessment and the famine; he writes of Jessore district that the peasants 'are taxed beyond what they can afford'. His remedy is the most sweeping anyone has yet suggested: 'Grant the ryots a total remission of the taxes which have been accumulating on their payments for these last fifteen or twenty years past: let a settlement then be made with the zamindars, fixing the rent to perpetuity.'

G.G. Ducarel, who had been Collector of Purnea, also wanted a permanent settlement 'upon an equitable valuation', while Hunt from Patna was another who thought the revenue too high. W. Harwood of

Dinajpur wrote vividly of the oppressions of petty revenue officers. N. Bateman of Chittagong tells the same tale and adds the pregnant observation that 'the injured find it easier to suffer than to complain'.

Shore was all his life at the centre of a society with urgent problems to settle and they were not settled quickly. It was in 1789 that Cornwallis announced the permanent settlement of Bengal and answered the question of who was the zamindar. Most of the district officers welcomed the settlement; almost to a man they were convinced that a long-term settlement was required. Confidence was needed more than anything. Shore himself believed that a settlement for ten, twenty or thirty years would have given as much confidence as the announcement of permanency and he was probably right as usual.

But when Shore left India, the question of how much the tenant paid was still not known with accuracy. It was, however, on the way to being known.

The position of the district officer was not assured. The keynote of the Directors' attitude to their officers in the districts had at first been suspicion, and the Council had not been far behind. Touring had been forbidden except for specially selected officers in special circumstances, and from 1773 to 1781 there were really no district officers. But in 1781 they were restored, though these new Collectors had very limited powers. It was in 1786, after Pitt's India Bill of 1784, that the district officer really came into his own. The Collector now became responsible for fixing the revenue in his district as well as for the collections. He had the power of a magistrate to arrest and imprison, but not to try, a criminal. He could settle what was later called a revenue dispute and he sat as a minor judge in civil suits, but criminal jurisdiction was still in the hands of Mahommedan officials; it was the excellent intention of Parliament to combine European ideas of justice with Indian procedure.

The withdrawals and restorations of power, the new schemes, the returns to old schemes, would make a book in themselves, but when all are forgotten it would be well to remember the words of Mr Thomas Pattle, writing from Lashkarpur in 1774.

'My ryots' he says 'reckon an easy and uninterrupted access to justice as one of the greatest blessings they enjoy.' 'My ryots,' he says. And he spoke for many of his successors when he added that for 'my ryots', 'I shall always feel a degree of partiality, and I trust that there is no impropriety in the avowal'.

This was the age of the American and French Revolutions; half the century had been spent under a Whig administration; Locke was still a prophet. But, against the spirit of Locke, the system which was developing in India combined executive and judicial powers in one hand. It was the tradition of the country that one man should rule; it was the way India liked to be ruled, but it was repugnant to liberalism and Whig views. For a hundred and sixty years, from 1786 to 1947 liberal principles and the practical needs of administration in India made an uneasy bargain, sometimes inclining one way, sometimes the other. Already, in the eighteenth century, a distinction was made between frontier districts, often under military Collectors, and the more settled areas. Already in the settled areas there is a judge distinct from the district or revenue officer – a concession to liberalism – but the revenue officer has power to arrest – a concession to convenience.

That question was to be opened again and again. Another was settled before Shore left India and never again became serious. His salary when he landed was not enough to rent his quarters. The obvious point that men must be decently paid if they are to be honest was made to the Directors time after time, and there were continual changes and experiments. On the whole, a contemporary of Shore's who was reasonably honest would have had to live in penury and debt in the early years of his service, to be amply recompensed in his later years if he survived. Shore himself at the end of ten years had saved nothing. He was less than thirty years in India, he was Governor-General, he was – as he seldom fails to mention – scrupulously honest; he retired with a modest fortune of £25,000. Many were ruined in their early years by irretrievable debts; some retired with far larger fortunes.

The old idea that trade was the main means of livelihood died slowly and at one time there was even permitted a commission of 1 per cent on collections of revenue. But salaries gradually improved, particularly those of the highest posts and gradually salary became the sole permitted income.

It does not follow that because salaries were improved most of the Company's servants immediately became honest. The older among them had been brought up under a system by which honesty was made almost impossible – and Johnstone, Hay and Bolts died hard. In England, rotten boroughs were bought and sold and all appointments were by influence, for which consideration was often received. Jobbery from England went on a long time; not only did politicians and directors nominate men to the service, they took a hand in appointments to actual posts. The Prince Regent, none less, wrote to Cornwallis for a post at Benares – and was firmly turned down. A succession of Acts of Parliament put an end to this, and the Act of 1793 laid down that all offices, places and appointments in the civil line under the degree of Councillor should be filled up from the civil servants of the Company, a provision that with modifications continued till the end.

While men in India were coming to terms with the complex scene that faced them, Parliament was trying to settle its own relationship to the new Empire in the East. The question was fiercely argued. Pitt stole the best of Fox's India Bill, re-dressed and passed it; North's coalition fell because of India; it was India that put Fox out for life. During the years of Shore's service, no one subject took up more of the time of Parliament than India.

The three great Acts of 1773, 1784 and 1793 made changes that were vital, gradually settling where power was to lie.

Hastings put one side of the case when he described his charge as: 'A dominion held by a delegated and fettered power over a region exceeding the dimensions of the parent state, and removed from it a distance equal in its circuit to two-thirds of the earth's circumference', from which he argued for an almost total independence. Burke put the other view: 'The East India Company,' he said, 'did not seem to be merely a Company formed for the extension of British commerce but in reality a delegation of the whole power and sovereignty of this kingdom sent into the East.'

And the body who delegates power must ultimately control it. Burke on this point and at that time was right and Hastings wrong, and Burke won. Parliament's supremacy was established. But Parliament moved slowly, too slowly perhaps. The Act of 1773 certainly did not go far enough. It established a Governor-General, but gave him so shadowy a control over the Governors of Madras and Bombay that he was little more than first among equals, and it did not even give him control over his own council.

Pitt's Act of 1784, of which the structure was to last fifty years, cleared these opacities to some extent. The Governor-General had now a real control of Madras and Bengal; his councillors were reduced to three covenanted servants of the Company and he was given (two years later) power to override them; in England a Board of Control was set up of six persons answerable to Parliament, two of whom were to be Ministers of the Crown. The Board of Control did not as a rule initiate, but it had access to all the Company's dispatches. It was a slow and clumsy dyarchy, but it worked; if a real disagreement ever arose, the Board could, in the last resort, pass a new Act; the knowledge of this was usually enough.

Thus by the time Shore leaves India, Parliament is supreme, commerce in the background; livelihood is no longer dependent on trade and pay is drawn automatically at the end of the month. And lesser things, the morning ride, the day in office, the competitive dinner-party, the ball at Government House, all begin to be established. Hours of work grew steadily longer; Shore wrote in 1787: 'I rise early, ride seven to ten miles and breakfast by eight o'clock; after that, business occupies my time until the hour of dinner, which is three.'

By 1795, however, the pace had grown hotter, and he writes to a friend in England: 'When you were in Bengal, the business was transacted between the hours of nine and two. At present, the interval of occupation in almost every department is between seven and four, and I doubt if there is more regularity in any Government in the world: and I will venture to say that there is as little peculation or sinister emoluments.'

Sir John Shore, a Victorian long before Victoria, was Harrovian enough to play cricket even in Bengal. He used his leisure to translate into English a Persian form of a Sanskrit exposition of the doctrines of *Vedanta*. He constantly slipped into his correspondence verse translations from the Arabic or imitations of Horace; his recreations were, in short, those of a scholar. He found time all his life for letters to his friends and when he could forget his conscientiousness must have had many endearing qualities. There is real affection beneath the conventional language of his ode on the death of his cousin, Augustus Clevland.

Here let us digress and read Bishop Heber's words written of Clevland forty years later. The Bishop is writing of the Sonthals, aboriginal hill tribes of Chota Nagpur:

> A deadly feud existed till within the last forty years between them and the cultivators of the neighbouring lowlands; they being untamed thieves and murderers, continually making forays, and the Mohammedan Zamindars killing them like mad dogs or tigers, whenever they got them within gun-shot. An excellent young man of the name of Clevland, Judge and Magistrate of Boglipoor, undertook to remedy this state of things. He ... punished all violence from the Zamindars. He got some of the Mountaineers to enter his service and took pains to learn their language. He ... established regular bazars at the villages nearest to them where he encouraged them to bring down for sale [the produce of their hills] ... He gave them wheat and barley for seed; he encouraged their cultivation ... And to please them still further ... he raised a corps of Sepoys from among them.

All this Clevland had done by the time he was twenty-nine. The Governor-General and Council of Bengal raised a monument in honour of his character and for an example to others, and he was one of the original sources for John Chinn 'who made the Bhil a man', in Kipling's story: *The Tomb of his Ancestors*.

Solemn, conscientious, a little heavy on the bridle-hand, Shore plods through his thirty years at the dogged stone-breaking trot of a battery wheeler. But he must not be mocked because he does stand for something good, for the new service and the end of Johnstone, Hay and Bolts. Hear him as Governor-General:

> When I consider myself the ruler of twenty-five millions of people ... I tremble at the greatness of the charge ... I consider every native of India, whatever his situation may be, as having a claim upon me; and that I have not a right to dedicate an hour to amusement further than as it is conducive to health and so far to the dispatch of business.

And he concludes: 'I look forward to the time when I must render an account of my commissions as well as omissions.'

He was not thinking of Parliament there. The Victorians – and Shore was essentially a Victorian – felt they were God's trustees for every corner of the world where they could plant the flag.

6
THE BACKGROUND TO THEIR LIVES

1 Hickey's Calcutta

If an Englishman in the reign of Queen Anne had been suddenly and miraculously transported from London to Calcutta, he would have had no real excuse for surprise at what he found. The society he came to would have seemed dull, provincial, pedestrian and behind the times; his fellow-countrymen would have seemed strangely oriental in habits of food, dress and speech, a company of merchants busy as a rule about cotton piece goods. But all this he might have foreseen.

In the later part of the reign of George III, however, the passenger by magic carpet would have been aware of an independence that was more than provincial, of a city with life of its own. Superficially, he would have found men more like himself in their habits than their grandfathers had been to his. Loose Indian clothes of cotton stuff were becoming yearly rarer in Calcutta, though they lingered on in Madras. Clothes followed the London fashions, usually some way behind and more garish than a London tailor would have permitted. Hickey's gay coats caused so much talk when he first went home that he had to discard them all. Indian food, too, was much less general.

But there was a new independence of outlook, a new self-confidence. We are made aware of the feeling in Warren Hastings's impatience with home authority and in the tone of the district officers' reports. It was there, too, in the life of the capital, in its lavishness, its insolence, its improvident defiance of the climate and of common sense and of the hard economic facts of retirement in England.

The visitor would also observe, and perhaps with some amusement, that in Calcutta social position in Europe was not forgotten but suspended and overlaid by a varnish of official rank, through which it still gleamed darkly. To him it would have seemed that the Company's servants were a mixed bag. There were cadets of noble families, such as the Honourable

59

Robert Lindsay, son of the Earl of Balcarres, who did extremely well out of transactions in salt, lime and shipbuilding and when Collector at Sylhet remitted the land revenue to headquarters in limestone, the principal article of his private trade. Another was the Honourable Frederick Fitzroy, a younger son of the Earl of Southampton, who came out a Writer at thirteen; Hickey at first supposed him 'what I had been myself in my early days, that is a complete pickle', but eventually records on him the sad verdict 'that there was more of sheer vice than boyish mischief in his pranks'. Since Hickey's boyish mischief included misappropriating cash from his father's office and sleeping with the nursemaid, it is hard to guess what Fitzroy did.

These aristocrats were the exception; the bulk of the Company's servants were uncompromisingly middle class. In the lower reaches, perhaps, was to be placed such a man as Sir George Barlow, at whom Hickey never loses the chance of a gibe. Hickey, a solicitor in private practice, was one of the world's great diarists. He says of Barlow: 'the son of a silk mercer in King Street, Covent Garden and nature had certainly intended him for nothing more elevated in society than a measurer of lute-strings from behind a counter ... His manner in society was cold, distant and formal. I do not believe he had a single friend in the world.' He was an able man all the same and honest; but he quarrelled with everyone worth making a friend of.

There were many from Scotland, as mixed as the English. The Scots were always to form a core to the service, sons of the manse, younger sons of the big house, sons of doctors or crofters, more industrious than the English, less aloof, hardheaded but emotional, more romantic at heart, but to the Indian indistinguishable.

Of the English in the narrower sense, the most numerous were men of the social position of John Shore, although of him too Hickey remarks that he was 'of low origin'. The Shores had been small landed gentry for two centuries at least and the objection seems to have been less to origin than to tastes; Hickey loved company and claret and always had the best of both, while Shore did not care for either. Perversely virtuous, obstinately middle-class, he spent his leisure mugging up Persian – and did not even pretend to be idler than he was.

The traveller just from London then would look round on a Calcutta of social differences which were not forgotten but ignored. Faced by the gulf in manners and thought that lay between themselves and their Indian subjects, between themselves and the rank and file of the British Regiments, the middle and upper classes in India closed together. Everyone called at Government House, everyone was asked to the Governor's Ball, everyone belonged to the Club; that was to be the rule and already in Hickey's day it was becoming accepted.

With this levelling up went a fashionable raffishness that imitated London not quite successfully. A man who in England would have lived soberly and respectably, as a lawyer or civil servant should, acquired in Calcutta the vices of the aristocracy; he learnt to keep a mistress, to give large parties, to sit up with Hickey, 'continuing our orgies until a brilliant sun shone into the room, whereupon we staggered to our palankeens . . . '

Mr William Mackintosh, who was in India for a few months in the time of Warren Hastings, describes with a touch of malice a day in the life of a Bengal Nabob:

'About the hour of seven in the morning, his durwan [doorkeeper] opens the gate and the viranda [gallery] is free to his circars, peons [footmen], hurcarrahs [messengers or spies], chubdars [a kind of constable], houccaburdars and consumahs [stewards and butlers], writers and solicitors. The head bearer and jemmadar enter the hall and his bedroom at eight o'clock. A lady quits his side and is conducted by a private staircase, or out of the yard. The moment the master throws his legs out of bed, the whole force is waiting to rush into his room, each making three salaams.' He is dressed 'without any greater exertion on his own part than if he was a statue'. Tea and toast are taken in the breakfasting parlour; 'while the hairdresser is doing his duty, the gentleman is eating, sipping and smoking in turns'. He goes to his office at ten and returns for dinner at two . . . 'with no greater exertions than these do the Company's servants amass the most splendid fortunes'.

This bears the same relation to life as a Rowlandson sketch. There is no exaggeration in the number of servants; when a man dined at the house of a friend he took with him two men to wait at table, the hookah-burdar who prepared his hubble-bubble, and all the running retinue − the mace-bearers, the palanquin-bearers, and a light screen of messengers and scouts. Hickey, who at that time was a bachelor, listed sixty-three when he left India − excluding Tippee and Gulab who are described as female servants and provided for more generously than the others. Many households would have employed a hundred.

It was not true however that two or three hours a day of attention to business were enough to amass the most splendid fortunes and it was definitely misleading to suggest that eight o'clock was a usual time for getting up. Already the morning ride was not unusual; already there were men who worked before breakfast; Shore talks of offices opening at seven.

It is possible already to distinguish the three main divisions of Anglo-India, the Company's civil servant, the military officer, and the independent merchant whom a later generation was to know as a box-wallah. There was perhaps more intermingling in Hickey's day than later; the civilian became inclined to withdraw from general society in Calcutta as his work grew heavier and as he came to spend an increasing amount of his service in the districts.

But there was no sign of withdrawal about Hickey's friend Bob Pott, a handsome, spoilt young man, who took to Hickey when he first saw him and won from him a real affection. Bob Pott was far from polite to people he did not find amusing, and his impertinence must have made more enemies than his good looks and laughter won him friends. He was the son of rich parents, ship-owners, and he had influence. He secured through Lord Chancellor Thurlow the nomination to the next vacancy as Resident at Murshidabad, the most coveted appointment in the service. But he could not wait till it fell vacant, and paid Sir John D'Oyly three lakhs of rupees, or about thirty thousand pounds, to retire at once. He spent recklessly 'on his palace at Moorshedabad', where some thirty guests sat down daily at two o'clock to a most sumptuous dinner and from which he drove abroad with a party of sixty light horse, 'dressed in rich uniforms and mounted upon beautiful Arabian horses', and where in short 'everything was in a style of princely magnificence'. Hickey makes no mention of his doing any work, though he probably did more than he pretended. At least he must have understood the language well, for he knew that the beggar to whom he laughingly threw a rupee was not thanking but cursing him with a torrent of gross abuse. Hickey did not understand this. Hickey was concerned with the English courts of law, which had jurisdiction only in Calcutta and whose proceedings were in English. Neither Jemdanee nor Kiraun, Gulab nor Tippee, taught Hickey so much of the language as the graceless Pott had learnt in court.

It was a small world, linked closer by marriage, almost weekly contracted by death, a world in which one of the principal recreations already was gossip about everyone else. You can read the gossip about everyone in Calcutta, about the reigning beauty and the bachelors supposed to be infatuated by her, not only in Hickey's memoirs but also in the outspoken, not to say scurrilous, pages of the *Bengal Gazette*, edited, when he was not in prison, by William Hickey's namesake, Augustus Hicky. If you put on a handsome coat and one evening went visiting at the house of that famous Calcutta figure the Begum Johnson, as like as not you would know everyone there and everything about them. You would certainly know that your hostess was the daughter of a Madras civilian, that she had been twice widowed in four years, had taken as third husband Watts, the diplomatic hero of Clive's revolution, and had been imprisoned by Suraj-ud-Daula when he attacked Calcutta. Her fourth husband had been the Reverend William Johnson, usually referred to in the *Bengal Gazette* as the Reverend Tally-ho – but he would not be mentioned at the Begum's house. He had sailed 'with a comfortable fortune' for England in 1788 – 'an event for which no friend of Mrs Johnson can be sorry'. She was to stay on in Calcutta for twenty-four years, keeping open house every night, a garrulous dark-featured old lady – for both her father and grandfather had married in India and her mother had an ominously Portuguese name. She did not die till the year of her triumph, when her grandson Lord Liverpool became Prime Minister.

You would not meet many Indians at the Begum Johnson's though. There were formal entertainments; Raja Nobkissen gave a dance in 1781 in commemoration of the birthday of Miss Wrangham, the reigning beauty, and thanked her as he said goodbye for having 'illuminated his house with her bright appearance'. But there is no trace of informal friendliness or equality. Hastings spoke of Beni Ram Pundit as 'one whom you know I reckon among my first friends', but Hastings was exceptional in every way and even Hastings could not ask the Pundit to dinner. The barriers of religious custom were probably stronger then than they were ever to be again; there were as yet no Indians who had accepted European ways. It was defilement for a Hindu to eat with an Englishman or even to touch him, while hardly any Muslim would drink wine in public or take the risk of eating meat which might not have been killed ceremonially by a Muslim. On the English side, there was not, I think, more than a slight consciousness of colour as a bar — and that mainly on the part of the newcomer; the constant use of the word 'black' was not, as a rule, derogatory but followed the model of Hindustani and of Elizabethan English. But it was less trouble to stick to people of one's own kind — how could you entertain people who would neither eat nor drink nor smoke with you?

A trivial world enough no doubt, and certainly one in which it must have been difficult for a woman to employ herself rationally. There was little or nothing she could do about the house or for her children; for long hours she was forbidden to stir abroad because of the heat; if she had no resources such as translation, sketching or music, she was lost indeed. But while this Calcutta life was something the merchant or the solicitor seldom left, it was already something to which the soldier and the civilian came back from long spells of loneliness. After three years at Burdwan or Chittagong, a man might well feel inclined for a little silliness. And there were others who turned in the evening to what Hickey called hard living simply because they had spent a day of uncomfortable steamy heat in exasperating work, much of it conducted in a foreign tongue and based on habits of mind that were only partly understood.

What is more, death was never far away. The funeral bells toll through Hickey's pages as steady as the hours in a cathedral close. And death was utterly unaccountable. No one knew that water had anything to do with cholera or mosquitoes with malaria. Much of the drinking water of Calcutta was drawn from the Lall Diggee, a large open pond in what later became Dalhousie Square, where one day (wrote a correspondent to the *Bengal Gazette*) 'I saw a string of parria dogs without an ounce of hair on some of them and in the last stage of mange plunge in and refresh themselves very comfortably.' The ignorance of the doctors was as ludicrous as tragic. 'After Sir John Royds had laid twelve days suffering under a cruel disorder and wholly insensible, the doctors gave up all hope of saving their patient.' Dr Hare went so far as to say: 'It is impossible he can survive two hours more,' whereupon all evening parties were cancelled and a Field Officer's party ordered to hold themselves in readiness

63

to attend the funeral. But Sir John disappointed them all. He was 'indebted to claret for his very unexpected recovery; during the last week of the disease they poured down his throat from three to four bottles of that generous beverage every twenty-four hours and with extraordinary effect.'

With doctors like that and death so close, it is not hard to understand the relaxation from the land revenue system of Bengal might often be frivolous. What is surprising is that in that improbable soil there should have flourished such leisure occupations as the concern of Sir William Jones, Halhed, Wilkins and half a dozen others with Sanskrit and Persian, with Hindu chess, music and chronology: that men tormented by heat, mosquitoes, ill-health and the frustration of their daily work, should have laid the foundations of the noble work of scholarship continued in the next century by the Germans.

2 A Country Station

One young officer in the judicial service, Mr Henry Roberdeau, has left a sketch of life in Mymensingh that will stand by itself for anywhere in Bengal and needs little change to fit any district in the North-West for some time to come. Roberdeau was posted to Mymensingh in 1801; he died there in 1808; his sketch was probably written about 1805.

Mymensingh, he explains, is about the size of an English county and the population is estimated at rather under two million. The Land Revenue is not so much as £90,000 sterling annually, so that each inhabitant may be supposed to pay less than a shilling a year, which Roberdeau thinks too little. It is twenty-five years since all the Company's servants thought the assessment too high. Twenty-five years of peace have made a difference.

'I get up between five and six,' writes Roberdeau, 'mount my Horse for a Ride, return about seven, bathe and dress for breakfast, to which I sit down about nine o'clock.' He was in court from eleven till 'four, five or six according to the season of the year. On leaving Court I take a Ride or drive or walk or lounge until the light begins to fade, when I dress for Dinner. I get into my Tonjon [a kind of palanquin] and go wherever Dinner may be and get to Bed again by eleven o'clock.'

There are in the station, four men, the Judge, who is also Magistrate and head of the district, the Registrar – Roberdeau – and the Collector and his Assistant. 'You will wonder how we can find conversation, considering the smallness of our Party, but our Evenings are, I assure you, very cheerful.' For the hot weather and rains – about eight months of the year – they have nothing to do but talk to each other. 'This dearth of Recreation is not however much felt because all Civil Servants in the country have business to perform and that business must be done ... However to speak generally, a Country life in India is dull, gloomy,

Sportsmen relaxing in tents after a day's shooting: 'our evenings are, I assure you, very cheerful'.

spiritless and solitary . . . '

In the cold weather, however, there is some diversion; the country abounds in game, and expeditions of all kinds are made. Hog-hunting is the first sport, 'and is thought very fine, in as much as the animal is fleet, wild, savage and resolute to the last extremity . . . There is something grand in first rousing a Boar, for the grass being as high as your Horse's Belly, you cannot see the game until you are close upon it. When he perceives his danger he gives a loud grunt and sets off as hard as he can go. Tally ho! You ride after him at a strong gallop and by keeping this pace you soon blow him . . . It is not until he gets tired that . . . the Boar turns and charges and this is the moment to deliver the Spear . . . '

Dinner is now much later, between half past six and eight. Except on Sundays and holidays lunch makes too much of a break in business to become general. Water is 'the universal drink', though milk and water is sometimes taken; Roberdeau has milk and water instead of tea for breakfast. The wine is always claret; 'a pint of port would throw a man into a fever and Madeira is too strong to be drank freely'.

There is no market in the country to supply eatables; you buy and fatten your own 'deer, oxen, sheep, calves, kids, ducks, geese, rabbits, etc.' Middling-sized roasting fowls are twenty to the rupee – about a penny each – a sheep can be had for a rupee, and an old ox for three or four, but they all have to be fattened before they come to the table. Bread is made at home and so is butter from your own cow.

There are no brick houses in the district except the jail and those of the half-dozen officials. Thatch and dried mud does for the rest. Even the

Englishmen live in what are really stationary tents, tents which have run aground on low brick platforms. They are 'Bungalows, a word I know not how to render unless by a Cottage. These are always thatched with straw on the roof and the walls are sometimes of Bricks and often of mats . . . To hide the sloping Roofs we put up a kind of artificial ceiling made of white cloth . . . ' There are 'curtains over the doorways to keep out the wind and . . . I have two Bungalows near to each other, in one of which I sleep and dress and in the other sit and eat'. 'Bed in the hot weather is dreadful, sometimes not a breath of air and we are obliged by the musquitoes, to sleep behind curtains.'

Roberdeau and his friends are quite cut off from Indians. He writes: 'You are aware that the Natives will not eat or drink with us nor partake of anything from our Tables; do not therefore imagine any black faces at our Dinners.'

The Judge is also the magistrate; it is he who is district officer and head of the district and not the Collector. Later – from 1831 – it was the Collector who was also the Magistrate and who became the executive head of the district. In Roberdeau's day, the head of the district had two functions; he was a civil judge and also a magistrate. In his civil capacity, the Judge administered Hindu or Mohammedan law; he had a Pundit and a Qazi to expound the law and assist him, but his was the decision, both as to fact and law.

For serious crimes, the judges of the Courts of Appeal from time to time resolve themselves into separate criminal courts, called Courts of Circuit, which visit each district twice a year and there deal with the criminal cases committed to them. The Circuit Judge is helped by a Muslim Law Officer, who gives a written opinion, both as to guilt and punishment; if the Judge of Circuit agrees with his Law Officer he gives orders for the sentence to be carried out; if he disagrees he refers the whole case to a superior Court in Calcutta.

These are the more serious cases. For lesser crimes the District Magistrate can himself punish with up to six months' imprisonment, a fine of five hundred rupees or thirty strokes on the back with a cane – much the powers of a second-class magistrate, which a young man in the twentieth century would be granted after about one year in India. Liberalism is strong here; no officer resident in the district can give more than six months' imprisonment and there is not much room for tyranny.

But there is one proviso – and one may guess that an energetic District Magistrate made use of it. 'He may confine any Person, however, of a notorious bad Character for any period of time until such person can give good security for his future good behaviour.' Here was the origin of that provision of the law that was always to be so strange to eyes fresh from England, the point beyond which liberalism never advanced in its struggle with orientalism. A notorious bad Character! The Magistrate decides what is good security; and in a district where the police are efficient no respectable person will offer security for someone the Magistrate considers a notorious bad character.

The district officer still had no regular police force, but two hundred and fifty armed irregulars who performed the duties later given to armed police and jailers; that is to say, they guarded convicts, jails, treasuries, record offices and the like. 'They are', wrote Roberdeau, 'in general a worthless undisciplined set of Scoundrels very different from the Regular Troops which are brave, honourable and obedient.'

The armed police were merely guards; they did not catch criminals, and Roberdeau says nothing about the arrangements for police administration proper. Such as they were, these were based on the village watchman, who for thousands of years had been the servant of the village community. They allowed him some grain but it cannot have been often that he received any cash payment. He usually came from one of the lower castes; he was always poor. His real power depended on the character of the man he reported to. This had been a Mogul official, usually the zamindar. Cornwallis, however, abolished the feudal powers of the zamindars and made the watchman responsible to police officers who were called *daroghas*. Each was in charge of a part of a district called a *thana*, but they seem to have had no trained regular constables. They answered to the Judge and District Magistrate, to whom they must deliver a criminal within twenty-four hours of arrest.

'In the *outward* forms of religion,' Roberdeau writes, 'Englishmen are rather lax, indeed except in Calcutta all devotion must be private, and which is surely as acceptable.' Indeed in Madras, the church was used for storing bags of rice, which had to be cleared away for the funeral of Eyre Coote. Eighteenth-century paganism lingered on in India and only slowly gave way to the absorption in religion of Shore and his Victorian successors.

Roberdeau's sketch of a country district ends with a character of the Englishman in the East, as misleading as all generalizations are apt to be, but no doubt true of many:

An Englishman in India is proud and tenacious, he feels himself a Conqueror amongst a vanquished people and looks down with some degree of superiority on all below him. Indolence, the disease of the climate, affects him with its torpid influence ... A cool apathy, a listless inattention and an improvident carelessness generally accompanies most of his actions; secure of today, he thinks not of tomorrow. Ambitious of splendour, he expends freely ... Generosity is a feature in the Character ... bring distress before his eyes and he bestows with a liberality that is nowhere surpassed ... In the public Character, whatever Calumny and Detraction may say to the Contrary, he is minutely just, inflexibly upright and I believe no public Service in the whole world can evince more integrity.

That was the claim. Of course, there were exceptions, but they were few and once they had been common.

Not much need be added to its outward life to turn Roberdeau's Mymensingh into a small station of Kipling's day. A separate Judge was still to come and the Magistrate would once more be Collector as well; the Superintendent of Police, a Canal Engineer and perhaps another for Roads and Bridges; a railwayman, perhaps a Forest Officer, would complete the familiar little circle. In the kind of life the civil servants of the Company lived there would be only one big change before the opening of the Suez Canal brought more English women and more frequent leave. Minor changes there would be; oil lamps would take over the duties of candles, there would be more ice, there would be soda-water and topis would replace top hats. An earnest evangelical religion would take the place of Roberdeau's mild rationalism; as Arnold's teaching spread out-wards from Rugby, the Englishman's day would come to be governed by exercise and it would become essential to health to add to the morning ride an evening game of polo, tennis or rackets, followed if possible by a swim. But none of these changes made to the district anything like so much difference as the reunion of executive power in the hands of the Collector and the general introduction of camping.

Until that happened, the administration was dead. No one at head-quarters knew what was happening in the villages. There was much crime of which no one ever heard and the people were afraid to report. The Judge-Magistrate sat at headquarters 'in a kind of vacuum' and dealt with the cases that came to him. But the system would spring to life when he had to go out into the fields and decide who had paid his rent and who had not, whether Lokhe Nath had ploughed this field himself or let it to Gangu Chamar. That would happen when the Magistrate became Collector again and men began to camp.

The first sniff of wet straw from the floor of the canvas bathroom behind the tent; the first sip of smoky tea; the kiss of the pillow on your cheek, cooler than in a bungalow and perhaps slightly moist with dew; above all, the first morning ride from camp with the scent of sugar-cane cooking at the corner of the field, the tops of the tall feathery grass still silver with dew – one by one each remembered scent and sound peeled away one layer of sweaty saline incrustation, the deposit of eight months of irritated wrang-ling and intrigue. Within three or four days, you were a different man. The people of your district were no longer cases to be got through, no longer tiresome creatures always making work by their absurd inability to agree. They turned suddenly into human beings who would squat on the ground and tell you their troubles, people childish no doubt, cunning but simple, laughable, stubborn, affectionate people, callous and gentle, cruel and compassionate, people for whom you too felt a real affection as you sat on a string cot in the village street and drank buffalo milk in which sugar had been stirred by a dirty finger. It was an affection that would survive the next hot weather, though it might lie dormant beneath the parched and dusty surface of the sun-baked soil. It was from camp, not from Indian mistresses, that some of the English learnt what India was like.

But this was not yet. Minutely just, inflexibly upright, that was all Roberdeau claimed to be so far.

3 The India Shore Left

It is time to stand back from the detail of lives such as Roberdeau's and Hickey's, to rise high enough in the air to see all India at once and compare it, on the day in 1798 when Wellesley arrived, with the India Clive had left.

From such a height, the Great Mogul is lost to view; we remember that he is there in Delhi, an old man, blinded, listlessly holding a tarnished sceptre in trembling wrinkled fingers. The Afghans have swept down to Delhi more than once and each time have washed back in a contemptuous undertow, esteeming the throne not worth the keeping or distracted by trouble at home; they still threaten from the north, a terror to peaceful folk. The Sikhs are as yet hardly stirring. To the east of Delhi are the ill-governed dominions of the Nawab-Vizier of Oudh, immersed in the most trivial amusements of despotism, but contriving always to find the annual subsidy for the English Company. In the south, Tippoo Sultan in Mysore, with his father's ferocity but none of his wisdom, alternating between sadistic foppery and bouts of Muslim fanaticism, is constant only in his wish to be rid of the English, while the Nizam of Hyderabad, prince of a country larger than Spain, wonders uneasily whether it is more to his interest to be the ally of the English or of the Marathas.

It is these two powers, the English and the Marathas, who fill in the chinks and hold together the fragments of Mogul masonry which survive in the composite rubble of India. The Marathas still pay a nominal allegiance to their old king, the Raja of Satara, but he has now become a ceremonial figurehead. Power passed long ago from the Raja to his five principal officers, each now the head of a state; first among these five was once the Peshwa, originally the Brahman Prime Minister, but now it is Scindia of Gwalior who is the most powerful.

The Maratha strength coils and twines round all the northern part of the Nizam's territory, reaches across India to threaten Madras and hold Orissa, sends long tenacious tendrils north to grip Delhi, Agra and Bundelkhand, surrounds the proud states of Rajputana. The English dominions are not so impressive. Their fief of Bengal and Behar is all that makes a show on the map; Madras itself is almost too small to be seen from this dizzy height and the British hold is not strong on the Northern Circars, nor on the new districts taken from Mysore; Bombay is quite invisible. But the English are stronger than they seem on the map. Oudh is really the Company's for the taking; Rohilkand, beyond Oudh, will be theirs within five years; the Carnatic they can have when they want it. And even the Marathas reckon that the numbers of every one of the Company's battalions should be multiplied at least by ten before an account is cast up and the decision taken to fight.

Looking down then on India at the turn of the century, one might picture the Afghans, the Marathas, or the English gaining dominion over the land. But the Afghans had never made any attempt to administer their conquests and surely in the end victory is likely to be with the power that pays its soldiers and keeps its peasants on the land. By that measure, there can be little doubt who will get the mastery.

The Maratha state was in its essence predatory; outside the Maratha homeland, there was no administration but simply tribute. The ruler had to pay the Marathas a fourth of what he collected. So long as there were fresh conquests every few years, the confederation hung together, but as soon as expansion ended, it was in danger.

Within Maharashtra, the home country of the Maratha people, the system of administration suited the people. As in the north, there was a district officer responsible for everything; he settled the King's share of the harvest, he collected it; he was responsible for order.

It worked, provided there was a strong ruler and a good supply of honest, energetic and able district officers. But by the end of the eighteenth century, none of these was forthcoming and the five Maratha states were fighting against each other as often as against any prince outside the confederacy.

As to the English, if you turned your gaze first on Madras or Bombay, you might not have felt much confidence in the future. Madras had stood still. She had made none of Bengal's progress because she had not, till thirty years later than Bengal, been forced to administer provinces and learn by experience how to do it.

The English advance to power had begun in Madras, but once the French were beaten things had begun to go wrong. The English had put on the throne of the Carnatic Mohammed Ali, a man of great charm of manner. He came to live in Madras instead of his own capital, Arcot, and here lived like a prince, entertained royally and whenever he needed money mortgaged a district to one of the Company's servants, usually at 36 per cent interest.

This is no place to follow the tortuous and unsavoury ramifications of the Nawab of Arcot's debts. It is enough to say that he kept the game on foot for nearly fifty years, surviving three inquiries by the Court of Directors and one in Parliament; Parliament imposed a settlement of all his debts but by the time of his death, they stood once more at thirty million pounds. Nothing can be said in extenuation; almost every servant of the Company in Madras was involved in the scandal, the worst being the notorious Paul Benfield. He had come out as an engineer in the

Company's service and surely holds a record that will never be beaten, having been dismissed the service after six years, reinstated, suspended, reinstated a second time, suspended and sent to London to answer charges, reinstated a third time, and finally dismissed, just eighteen years after he joined, with a fortune of half a million. The most shameful part of the whole business is that the sufferers were the people of the districts pledged by the Nawab as security.

So for the present Madras was damned and lost, engulfed in corruption. But there was new life already in the districts and she was soon to take the lead again, going ahead just because she had been backward when Bengal made the permanent settlement. For the moment, however, to sail to Madras is to go back to the middle of the eighteenth century, and not only in administration but in manners. Indian clothes and food linger on here among the English; private trade is far more general far longer. But there is less luxury than in Bengal, partly because money is not come by so easily and partly because good living is more difficult to arrange.

The Madras custom of arresting and imprisoning the Governor survived very late, successors of Sir Edward Winter, who did it a hundred years earlier, confining Lord Pigot and allowing him to die in captivity.

If Madras was provincial, still more so was Bombay. Cornwallis could not see why there should be a Governor with a Council at all; a small mercantile station with a commercial resident was all, he thought, that was needed.

Bengal, however, is another story altogether. Progress has not only been rapid; it has been irresistible. The chief actors themselves have been swept along by its force. Clive had seen the whole Mogul world at his feet and had dreamed of an India governed by the Crown, but the Directors would not have it and he had fallen back on the 'dual system', that is, government by Indian puppet rulers. Hastings told the Directors: 'All the arts of policy cannot conceal the power by which these provinces are ruled.' But even he shrank from direct control and tried to rule the country by Indian subordinates, controlling them by a centralized authority in Calcutta. That too was abandoned and at last direct rule by British officers had become general.

And now, in 1798, two generations have lived in Bengal without seeing an invading foe; the famine of 1770 is far away and already it begins to look as though the Government had been too easy with the zamindars when they made a settlement with them for ever. Grain is cheap; the cultivator is less wretched than he was thirty years ago and he has become aware of a new idea, that men are ruled by law, not by the whim of a ruler.

The rule of law has been introduced, and a service has been created to administer it. There is something like a civil list and appointments familiar to the ears of today. The men who hold them do not trade and are paid a salary on which they can live and save money if they take the trouble – but the odds are still against their retiring to enjoy their savings in

England. The Company still carries on trade but the Commercial Department is the least important and men go to it for life and have nothing to do with the revenue and justice of the country.

These first civil servants were chosen on the nomination of one director, a system theoretically indefensible but in practice by no means a bad one. The only training they received was a year or more of employment as copyists, which did little but give them time to settle down, after which they were appointed to a post and learnt its duties as they carried them out.

The Company's servants already consider that no public service in the world can evince more integrity; they pride themselves that they are 'minutely just, inflexibly upright'. They have already included in their number men such as Clevland who made the aboriginal a man; Tilman Henckel, Collector from 1781 to 1789 of the district of Jessore, whose inhabitants were so grateful for his fatherly care that they made an image of him and worshipped it; or Jonathan Duncan, sent to Benares to end corruption among the English but adding to that a private war of his own to stamp out the practice of killing unwanted daughters.

There are others, no doubt, as flippant as Bob Pott and young Fitzroy; there are still men in the Bolts tradition who are merely gross, selfish and greedy. But Roberdeau stands for the majority and for him it was enough to do his duty and no more; the idea is not yet general that the English are in India for God's purpose. Pride in the service is born but in its infancy; it is still rare for the peasants to speak of an Englishman as their father.

But the time is coming. The period of corruption is over; the period of experiments is coming to an end and will be done with when all executive power is back in the Collector's hands. Then comes the flowering, the highest peak perhaps in the lofty range of what the English have done, when a handful of our countrymen, by the integrity of their character and with not much else to help them, gave to many millions for the first time for many centuries the idea that a ruler might be concerned with their well-being.

PART III
The Golden Age 1798–1858

7
THREE GREAT MEN

1 Munro and the Peasant Settlement

You must fly over India if you want to see how it is put together, not in an aeroplane but in the mind. From a train it flashes by too quickly; by bullock-cart, it takes too long.

Fly from West to East, along the broad band of flat country that lies below the Himalayas. Come to the ground every three or four hundred miles and talk to the people, see what they eat and look at their fields.

You begin over windy plains of wheat, where the men might be Italian except that they are bigger than Italians, where people eat wheat and milk and butter, and meat when they can get it. Fly on towards the East, a faint jagged arabesque of snowy dome and icy peak on your left, and now the rivers run the other way, towards the rising sun, and you are still over plains, very flat, sprinkled here and there with plump square pincushions of glossy green which are groves of mangoes. Fly on all day till you come down in the evening in a country where wheat is unknown, where rice and fish are what the people eat, where there are boats instead of bullock-carts. At each halt, you have met men a little darker and shorter than the last, but beneath a different colouring, the shape of their features did not seem so very foreign, and the languages they spoke were all dialects of one tongue that was cousin to Latin.

But if you had turned to the South, the Deccan, there would have been a change at once and you would have flown over a tangle of hills and forests, rocky rivers and gorges, ruined forts on red sandstone crags, temples with onion spires and little lakes, a country of red rocks, red gravel and dark green foliage, sharp and garish after the almond-green and almond-buff plains of the North. And you would have come down among a strange people, among Brahmans with the arched nostril, the sharp-bridged nose, of the temple carvings, among labourers with the heavier features and darker skin of the aboriginal, among people whose many tongues were as

75

incomprehensible as the clucking of hens or the conversation of squirrels.

The foundation is the same, the village brotherhood, in a dozen different forms, hidden here by the obliterating cruelty of conquest, there by natural disaster and resettlement, but surviving somehow, reappearing in one dress or another, Tamil, Telegu, Kanarese or Maratha. Almost everywhere, there is a headman and a village committee; there are village servants, there is usually a record-keeper and a watchman.

All the same, it was a confusing scene that confronted the Company's servants at the end of the eighteenth century when they first began to acquire districts to be administered. And the state of the villager was worse in the South than in the North. Akbar's rule had not reached so far as this. There had been no attempt for half a millennium to set on every field a fair yearly price. In most districts it had been simply a matter of what could be wrung from the peasant; rents were collected with whips and pincers. For centuries, five main kingdoms had fought each other over the peninsular part of India and there was no peace yet. For the peasant, the sight of strangers was always matter for dread and it made little difference to him whose horses ate his fodder, whose men burnt his thatch, whether what they took was loot from an enemy or taxes from a subject.

Because there had been no secure rule within human memory, there was no network of collectors of the King's share, as in Bengal. Here and there, feudal chiefs were found, known as *poligars*; they were not as a rule officials become hereditary, but more often condottieri who had been

Fort St George, Madras, was the first territory on the mainland where the English claimed sovereignty. There was no harbour; ships anchored offshore and coming ashore through the surf was always a hazard.

able to establish independence against an overlord.

In this South India, the Presidency of Fort St George was responsible until nearly the end of the century for a small area round Madras itself and for the Northern Circars and for no more. Absorbed in making what they could from the Nawab of Arcot and in wars with Mysore, the Governor and Council for long made no serious attempt to administer their possessions.

But the tide turned. A moment came for a step forward towards a sound way of ruling India, comparable to one of those steps forward in the evolution of a species, when a variant begins to occur and to drive out the unimproved pattern. The giraffe with a longer neck soon ousts the old type; in the South, the leap forward produced a group of men of whom even a people who have had their share of great men may still be proud.

When Cornwallis's Mysore War – the Second – came to an end in 1792, certain districts were taken over from Mysore; one of them was called the Baramahal; it is now Salem. This district had to be settled; Cornwallis, a man of sturdy common sense and unusual honesty of character, found that the civilians available from Madras knew the languages or the customs of South India hardly at all. But men of the first quality were available from the Madras Army and Cornwallis chose soldiers, putting Captain Alexander Read at the head of the district, with Thomas Munro, a lieutenant, as one of his assistants.

Read was a most unusual man. Munro wrote that he had: 'a master whose conduct is invariably regulated by private honour and the public interest. These, and an unwearied zeal in whatever he undertakes, constitute the great features of his character.' He goes on to speak of Read's 'intimate knowledge of the language and manners of the people and happy talent for the investigation of everything connected with the revenue'. Every word might have applied just as well to Munro himself. And for the next thirty years the story of Munro's doings tells in itself how the service and its work developed.

Munro, who in 1791 was thirty years old, now began a life which was to last for sixteen years. He writes in a letter:

I go from village to village with my tent, settling the rents of the inhabitants; and this is so tedious and teazing a business that it leaves room for nothing else – for I have no hour in the day that I can call my own ... One man has a long story of a debt of thirty years' standing contracted by his father. Another tells me that his brother made away with his property when he was absent during the war; and a third tells me that he cannot afford to pay his usual rent because his wife is dead, who used to do more work than his best bullock.

This was written in 1795, three years after the districts had been ceded; already the people were crowding round a ruler who would listen to them, just as they would still crowd a hundred and fifty years later.

Sir Thomas Munro, one of the four great heroes of the Golden Age. He worked all his life for the direct settlement of taxes with the cultivator, hearing disputes till far into the night. 'A stern countenance, a piercing eye . . .' but there was a warm benevolence beneath.

It was a land of small cultivators; there was no one between the peasant and the Collector. Munro all his life remembered this district; to him it was the archetype, and his memory of it changed the administration of South India. Writing to his father in 1795, he explained how he thought the country should be managed. In the first place, Collectors must know the language of the people. Next, they must be well paid, and by that he means at least four thousand pounds a year. Finally, a reduction in the revenue and a long settlement will, with the natural fertility of the soil, greatly increase the prosperity of the people – who will then be able to buy English goods.

He stayed seven years in the Baramahal, which he surveyed completely and for which he fixed rents that were lower than Tippoo's. But greater exactness in accounting and less corruption meant that just as much was collected as before and more of it reached the Treasury.

Munro believed that the King's share was fixed too high all over India – and he was right. This was because the English began with the idea that the books of the King from whom they took the district showed a true revenue. But neither Tippoo nor any other Indian ruler had ever expected so much as his books showed. For centuries there had been no assessment of what the land could fairly pay; all that was fixed was what in the jargon of today would be called a target – and, what with corrupt and idle officials, what with perennial war, insurrection and civil commotion, what with plague, drought and famine, a target that was not often hit. But the English expected to hit it every year. It took them a long time to learn that if the King's share was to be collected regularly and efficiently it ought to be less.

From the Baramahal, Munro went as joint secretary to the Commissioners who were to draw up the treaty that followed the Third Mysore War. This was in 1799; here he made two lifelong friends, Arthur Wellesley and John Malcolm. Next, he went as Settlement Officer and Collector to another new district, Kanara, on the West Coast. But he did not take kindly to Kanara, which had to be pacified by force. Munro had no troops at his disposal; he had instead a number of 'peons' – a word which literally means a footman, the pawn of chess. 'My peons in the neighbourhood of Jumlabad have defeated a party of the enemy and taken some prisoners,' Munro says casually in the course of a letter. The enemy were the overflow of the war; parties of Tippoo's disbanded soldiers had taken to brigandage. They did not stop the work of settling the revenue which went forward at a prodigious pace: 'From daybreak till eleven or twelve at night,' Munro wrote to his sister, 'I am never alone except at meals and these *altogether* do not take up an hour. I am pressed on one hand by the settlements of the revenue and on the other by the investigation of murders, robberies and all the evils which have arisen from a long course of profligate and tyrannical government.'

Kanara was a very large district; 'I cannot go the rounds, by any road, under six hundred and fifty miles,' and since his camp cannot move more than ten miles a day, that is sixty-five days of the year – and it was difficult country with no roads fit for wheeled traffic. Munro said he was working so hard to get away from Kanara, but it was more from an incorrigible inability to leave a thing half done or badly done. That, with a sturdy common sense and an invincible fairness of mind, are his first qualities; he possessed these three prosaic virtues in such good measure that they make his character heroic. There was indeed more than a slight resemblance between Munro and his friend Arthur Wellesley. Neither stopped to ask why a thing should be done; each saw what he had to do and went straight

After the Third Mysore War and the capture of Seringapatam in 1793, Cornwallis annexed half Tippoo's territories, which opened the road to Munro's settlement with the peasants. Here Tippoo's sons are handed over as hostages for the execution of the Treaty.

at it by the simplest way. Neither had the least doubt that his work was good.

Munro wrote:

> The people . . . whoever be their rulers . . . are . . . indifferent whether they are under Europeans, Mussulmans or their own Rajas . . . they consider defeat and victory as no concern of their own but merely as the good or bad fortune of their masters; and they only prefer one to another as he respects their religious prejudices or spares taxation.

Munro brought Kanara 'into such a state that it may be managed by anybody' and handed it over to two assistants, civilians he had trained. It was split into two now, as being more than any one man could manage. He went on to the districts ceded by the Nizam in 1801. Here he stayed seven years, with four civilian assistants; the area was 27,000 square miles and later became four districts. It was almost the same tale again. It was his custom when he was not in camp, which was seldom, to stop work at half past four in the afternoon, to dress for dinner, while an assistant read to him. He would dine at five and sharp at eight he would be again receiving petitions and his night court would be open as a rule till midnight. Next morning as soon as it was light he would be out of doors, pacing to and fro in discussion with whoever had come to see him.

Here in the Ceded Districts, it was not quite the same tale because at first there was added a much sharper conflict with poligars who under the Nizam had made themselves almost independent. If they were wise enough to submit, they were allowed to retain estates in which they collected rent, but they must give up their feudal powers of justice, their armed retainers, all the tattered shreds of sovereignty. It was the work Henry VII of England did; Munro had sometimes to use artillery and dragoons, but most of it he did with three thousand peons, and in the intervals of his main work of settling the Land Revenue.

In 1807, he went on leave; he had landed at Madras in 1780 and had earned it. The first part of his life was over; he was not again to have charge of a district. The period of high office and controversy comes next, but in the new period as in the old Munro saw every problem from the point of view of the district officer.

The air was full of controversy. In 1798, the Governor-General, Wellesley the elder, with his usual imperious certainty, had ordered the Government of Madras to adopt the Bengal system as codified by Cornwallis. He was determined to waste no time arguing with those whose interest it was to obstruct. He had some justification; Madras was to all appearance hopelessly behind Calcutta, and the work done by Read and Munro was not yet visible.

In Bengal, it had been argued that there could be no improvement unless the King's share was fixed in perpetuity with a zamindar who by this means would become just like a Whig landed proprietor in England.

But in Madras there was no zamindar to settle with. Zamindars would have to be created, and they were created by the simple means of auctioning the posts to the highest bidder. It is hard to understand how any sensible man could have agreed to anything so inept and iniquitous. The one saving grace was that the Directors cautioned the Government of Madras to go slowly, which was as well, because in Madras the system simply did not work. The bad harvest of 1806–7 convinced even the system's supporters that it was not a success. It was agreed to go no further and now the debate began between two systems which had at least the merit of being native to South India.

Munro's we know already; the Collector assessed the King's share which every field could reasonably pay and every year let out to each cultivator as many fields as he wanted. The alternative may be called Hodgson's. John Hodgson, at least ten years younger than Munro, was a Headquarters man; when he left the service, in 1823, of thirty-one years, he had been only four in a district, and all in one area, the Jagir.

Hodgson had found in the Jagir a strong corporate village life, and he proposed therefore that the settlement should not be with individuals and based on individual fields, but with the village as a whole. The committee of shareholders would enter into an agreement, for three years, or ten years, or preferably for ever, and they would decide what each man should pay.

It sounded convincing enough and the scheme was introduced, but it did not work well. Under Munro's system, each cultivator every year made a personal agreement with the Collector; it was quite another thing to make promises for the whole village for three years ahead and committees of co-sharers were frightened of the responsibility.

Now came one of Parliament's periodical reviews; the Fifth Report of the Select Committee of the House of Commons was published in 1812, and it came down uncompromisingly in favour of Munro. The Committee believed that the Collector could and should be the best safeguard of the interests of the peasant, that when he dealt direct with the peasant he would get to know what was happening and what a man could fairly pay.

Munro had won; the Committee's report settled that question and Munro was sent back to Madras to introduce his system everywhere. From now onward, the settlement in Madras was made direct with the peasant. Munro had had the backing of most of the district officers, many of whom had been trained under himself and Read, and his victory was the triumph of the district officer. Henceforward he was not to be a distant guide, but in close contact with the peasant, the father and mother of his people, controlling everything that happened so completely that a time came when the child felt the control irksome and wanted his own way.

Munro was not, however, one of those who believed nothing would go right unless controlled by British officers. All his life he protested against this idea: 'More European agency', he wrote, 'is recommended as a cure for every evil. Such agency is too expensive; and even if it were not . . . it is in many cases much less efficient than the natives.' He goes on to rebut the idea that 'the natives are too corrupt to be trusted', arguing that if they are trusted and properly paid they will respond just as the English did when their allowances were raised. He argued therefore for Indian judges and village *panchayats*, village committees to which he would give the powers of petty courts to try small offences. 'Foreign conquerors', he added, 'have treated the natives with violence and often with great cruelty, but none has treated them with so much scorn as we, none has stigmatized the whole people as unworthy of trust.'

The Third Maratha War came and he begged to be allowed to become a soldier again after a quarter of a century away from the parade-ground. He was given the rank of Brigadier-General but very few troops; he advanced into an enemy district, raised troops to complete his brigade, dealt with the enemy, settled the Land Revenue and left behind him as he advanced a civil administration already established and proceeding smoothly. He became Governor of Madras; he was Governor for five years and he regarded his province as a larger district.

His views on young civilians must be remembered. To them, when he was Governor of Madras, he said:

> The junior civil servants of the Company have a noble field before them. No men in the world have more powerful motives for studying with diligence, for there are none who have a prospect of a greater reward and whose success depends so entirely on themselves . . . language is but the means, the good government of the people is the great end.

And again:

> The advantage of knowing the country languages is not merely that it will enable you to carry on the public business . . . but that by rendering you more intimately acquainted with the people, it will dispose you to think more favourably of them.

Beside this must be set his view of the future:

> Our sovereignty should be prolonged to the remotest possible period . . . Whenever we are obliged to resign it, we should leave the natives so far improved from their connection with us, as to be capable of maintaining a free, or at least a regular, government amongst themselves.

Munro had carried South India forward from the eighteenth century into the nineteenth; he had come to a world of sloth and corruption, he left when he died a body of young men whom he had trained himself, Read the younger and Ravenshaw, Cochran, Thackeray, and Stodart, men in whom any administration in the world might feel pride. But the last word on Munro shall be left to a contemporary, another Scot, Mountstuart

Elphinstone; who after a first meeting wrote of his:

> strong practical good sense, his simplicity and frankness, his perfect
> good nature and good humour, his real benevolence . . . his activity and
> his truthfulness of mind . . . he is delighted with those things that in
> general have no effect but on a youthful imagination. The effect of these
> last qualities is heightened by their contrast with his stern countenance
> and searching eye.

2 Malcolm and Central India

Munro had seen a new age before he died. The red of British districts, the
pink of British allies, had spread over the map; the Company was
unquestionably the first power in India. It was recognized now that the
Company's servants must rule the districts the Company had taken over
and men wondered how long it would be before the whole country was in
their hands.

Much of the change had taken place during the seven years of the
Marquis Wellesley's administration. His conquests, merely in terms of
size on the map, can be compared with those of Napoleon and lasted much
longer. He had immense energy and immense capacity for detail; everything was centred on himself. But he could have done nothing without the
Company's servants, a team of trusted agents, brilliant young men, of
whom some had started as soldiers and some as civilians.

What Wellesley did can best be understood by simplifying drastically
and considering his treatment of his two main allies and his two main
enemies.

His two principal allies were the King of Oudh and the Nizam of
Hyderabad. Each paid an annual sum to the Company for the upkeep of
certain troops which were to be maintained for his protection. In each case
Wellesley demanded the cession of territory which would provide for ever
for the upkeep of those troops. The pound of flesh was to be taken where
the Marquis chose; it completed the encirclement of Oudh, it shut off the
Nizam from the sea and from Mysore. The King of Oudh was not only to
cede territory but to disband all his own troops as well.

The two principal enemies were Tippoo Sultan of Mysore and the
Marathas. It is difficult to see how war could have been avoided with
either. Tippoo Sultan hated the English and to them he was an ogre more
hateful even than Bonaparte. Wellesley ensured, by careful preparation,
sound planning, and choosing the right men, that the force brought
against him should be overwhelming, that the inevitable war should be
ruthless, quick and therefore merciful. Tippoo was crushed and killed, his
dominions reduced to half their previous size, and on the throne was
placed a ruler of the Hindu dynasty from whom Tippoo's father had
usurped it.

Richard, Marquess Wellesley, Governor-General 1798–1805, the eldest brother of the Duke of Wellington, was known as 'The Glorious Little Man' to his close circle of subordinates. As imperious as Curzon, he extended British influence over two-thirds of India.

The Maratha states were essentially predatory; Warren Hastings by the Treaty of Salbai had kept them in check for twenty years but war had to come. The Nizam's Chief Minister told John Malcolm in 1802: 'If they mean to keep their lawless bands together, they must lead them to plunder ... These Maratha gentlemen need a lesson and we shall have no peace till they receive it.'

Their lesson began at Assaye, administered by Arthur Wellesley; it continued at Laswari, the culmination of Lake's brilliant campaign in the north. The Marathas were at the Company's feet when the Directors decided to recall Lord Wellesley and reverse his policy.

But the face of the map had been changed and it had been changed by Wellesley. 'I can declare my conscientious conviction,' Lord Wellesley wrote, 'that no greater blessing can be conferred on the native inhabitants of India than the extension of the British authority, influence and power.' But unfortunately, while he acted on his conscientious conviction, he justified his acts by arguments which were really untenable and when argument failed he fell back on turkey-cock indignation. Bullying is never pleasant to watch and it is with distaste that one must regard the manner of

Wellesley's diplomacy. All the same, there can be no doubt that his swiftness was merciful, that for instance much human misery in Central India would have been prevented if he had himself been allowed to conclude the war with the Marathas that began with Assaye.

As it was, Wellesley's work was left to be completed by the Marquis of Hastings. Cornwallis came out in 1805 to undo Wellesley's work; the English withdrew from Central India. The patched-up peace lasted for ten years, but they were years of unimaginable chaos and lawlessness. Each year, as the rains came to an end, the Rajput or Maratha chief looked to his harness and sharpened his sword; he called up his vassals, mounted his horse and rode off to see what he could bring back on his saddle-bow. Those who by old age or infirmity were prevented from taking the field themselves kept gangs of marauders, 'as poachers in England keep dogs', said Sleeman. These Pathan mercenaries, known as Pindaris, at first attached to the Maratha states, later set up on their own, each as a chief without a state, dependent on plunder as a sole means of livelihood.

In the Pindari War from 1817 to 1819 Lord Hastings set out to end these gangs. But it was impossible to kill the dogs without a quarrel with the poachers. So the Pindari War became the Third Maratha War; it ended with the annexation of great tracts of land in which there was now to be peace, while even in the dominions which were to remain with the princes it was established that there was to be no more moss-trooping.

'The native chiefs', wrote Sleeman some years later, 'feel like squires forbidden to chase foxes.' Bishop Heber, in 1825, found men hoeing their crops each with a spear stuck in the ground by his side. All was peace now, they said, and the bad times had gone — but they were sure to come again. 'A few years ago,' a peasant told Sleeman in the 1820s, 'I could not have gone a hundred yards from my village without having the clothes ripped from my back.' And to Tod another said: 'Who durst have passed this spot eighteen months ago? They would have killed you for the bread you had about you; now you may carry gold . . .'

This kind of evidence could be continued endlessly; a country the size of Spain, France and Germany had been pacified, and men felt a deep relief.

It is to Malcolm and Elphinstone that most of the credit must go for settling the Maratha country, though both learnt from Munro. Both were Scots; indeed, of this great four only Metcalfe was English in the narrower sense.

Malcolm was one of seventeen children and when his father fell suddenly into financial trouble it became necessary to settle as many sons as possible. The Directors of the East India Company were doubtful whether they could commission a boy of thirteen. 'Why, my little man,' said one of them playfully, 'what would you do if you met Hyder Ali?' he being the father of Tippoo and the ogre of the moment. 'I would draw ma sworrd and cut off his heid,' replied the candidate, and was commissioned

INDIA BEFORE
WELLESLEY 1795
British Territory
Carnatic „ „

at once with acclamation.

Till he was past twenty, he enjoyed himself unreservedly; he got into debt, as a young man should, he became a fine horseman and rubbed off the awkwardness he had brought from Eskdale. But soon after twenty he began to feel the urge of ambition; he began to spend his leisure with a Persian grammar, he began to hope for staff appointments. Ambition was always a part of his character in a sense it never was in Munro's or Elphinstone's. It was a frank open ambition; he courted service and he admired power, but he would not flatter a power he did not admire. His ambition was that of the boy who wants to be captain of the eleven and head of the school; he was known as Boy Malcolm, and he was always the big able boy who is good at everything, but who is not quite grown up because everyone has always liked him, because everything has come easily to him.

He was appointed Assistant to the Resident at Hyderabad, but before he reported for duty he was summoned to Calcutta by Lord Wellesley. 'I wish to see you . . .' wrote the Governor-General, 'it will be advantageous to the public service that you should thoroughly understand my opinions.' At Government House, he was at once in a congenial atmosphere. He became one of the Government House set.

The Governor-General's ideas were exactly those which Malcolm had hoped to find. It was with a genuine delight that he recognized a vigour and forthrightness that matched his own, and though there was always an element of awe in his regard for 'the Lord', or 'the glorious little man', as the set called him among themselves, there was undoubtedly affection too.

Employment came soon; in the Mysore War, Malcolm was the Governor-General's Agent with a force commanded by Arthur Wellesley. Soon after this came his Persian Embassy; he was thirty-one when he set out on this mission, with a train of five hundred assistants and servants. In Persia he was an immediate success; he had a fine imposing appearance and a good seat on a horse, a ready laugh and a tongue that was quick to that kind of humorous fooling flattery in which at a Persian court it was a fashionable game to compete — and above all he had presents.

There followed a series of confidential and delicate missions; 'send Malcolm' became a catchword among the set. He was sent, for instance, to Bombay to smoothe ruffled plumes after the murder of the Persian ambassador — and he smoothed them with such Wellesleyan magnificence that the Persians said among themselves that at this price the English were welcome to kill ten ambassadors. He was Private Secretary to the Governor-General; at thirty-four he was Resident at the Court of Mysore. But he did not have much time for this task; he was again deputed as political adviser to Arthur Wellesley, this time in Lord Wellesley's Maratha War, and he was engaged in negotiations with the Maratha chiefs till Lord Wellesley left India.

But the sky was obscured by a cloud, nothing less than a difference of opinion with the Lord. Scindia had been defeated and negotiations were in progress for a peace. Both Malcolm and Scindia's representative thought that the fortress of Gwalior was to be restored to Scindia. Malcolm believed that this was in accordance with the Lord's views.

But the Lord had quite different ideas. Malcolm was given a very sharp scolding. 'Lord Wellesley is excessively angry at your conduct . . .' and much more to the same effect. Malcolm wrote: 'I am perfectly heart-broken by these communications,' and he was not thinking only of his career. There was a close bond between the Lord and his ambassador and there was real pain on both sides over the difference. This intimate, this curiously emotional, relationship with Wellesley explains the disappointments of Malcolm's later career. He was identified, in the eyes of the Directors and the Ministers, with the magnificence of his master. That was why, when Lord Minto, alarmed by Napoleon's alliance with Russia at Tilsit, sent Malcolm again to Persia, those at home hastily appointed an ambassador from the Court of St James. Obviously a King's ambassador trumped a Governor-General's and though there was no doubt in anyone's mind that Malcolm was twice the man Sir Harford Jones was, and much better liked by the Shah, he had to come back. All he achieved was some consolidation of British interests in the Persian Gulf.

In the Third Maratha War, Malcolm was Agent to the Governor-General in the Deccan and Brigadier in the Force advancing against the Pindaris. Those were the days in which it was still possible to be a diplomat in peace and a soldier in war. Malcolm won a battle, resumed his diplomatic status and parleyed with the enemy, threatening, if nego-tiations became too slow, to turn soldier again.

After the peace, he took over Malwa, a network, an archipelago, a Milky Way, of small states and estates, each claiming some ill-defined shreds of sovereignty. Here was indescribable confusion; it was a land of Rajput chiefs who had been overrun and ground up piecemeal by the Maratha conquests; it had been the ideal breeding-ground for Pindari gangs. As for the peasants, if their condition was to be pitied in other parts of the peninsula, it was worse here.

Malcolm had to hunt down and catch the leaders of the Pindari gangs who were still at large. Next he must make a settlement with the various chiefs. He determined: 'to alter nothing that can be tolerated, to distrust as little as possible, to attend to usage more than reason, to study feelings and prejudices and to make no changes but such as I am compelled to do.'

Here was no brilliant reform, no rationalization of a political map on to which the little states seemed to have been 'shaken as if from a pepper-pot'. But it worked. 'The fellows that I was hunting like wild beasts are all now tame and combine in declaring I am their only friend,' he wrote, and again: 'The peasants ... actually have reappeared in thousands, like people come out of the earth, to claim and re-cultivate lands that have been fallow for twenty years.'

They came because Malcolm restored order, because of his name and fame and because he was ready to see them. He had the knack of putting a point in the vivid phrase that a peasant understands. To a Bhil tribesman who, after a long tale of woe, begged him for justice at once, here and now, on an oppressor who had not been heard in answer, Malcolm asked:

'Why do you suppose God gave me two ears?'

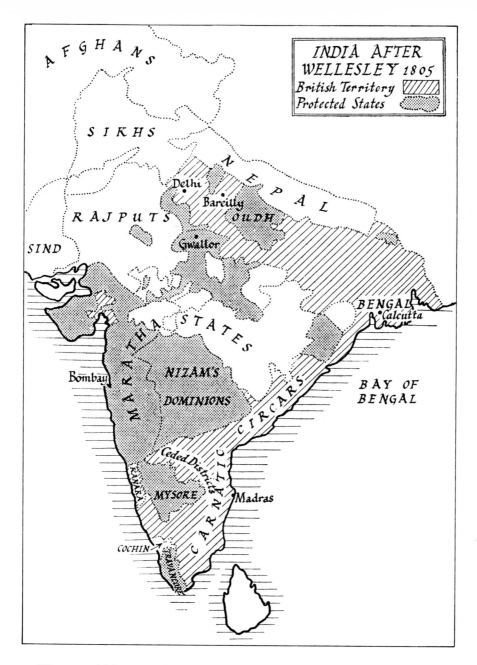

That would be enough; it would carry instant conviction where half an hour's explanation would have produced only a sullen bewilderment. It was an answer which ought to have been taught to every young man entering the Company's service.

'I often wish you were here,' Malcolm wrote to his wife, 'to enjoy the blessings I obtain from the poor inhabitants, who all continue to refer their happiness to me; and it joys my heart to find myself . . . restoring great provinces to a prosperity they have not known for years.'

This was Malcolm's great task; these were his greatest days. Meanwhile, Elphinstone was performing a similar task in the country round Poona.

3 Elphinstone and the Marathas

Admiration is the feeling with which one looks on Munro and Malcolm, but it is a dull creature who can read or write of Mountstuart Elphinstone without affection. It would be with trepidation that the young officer sat down to breakfast opposite the stern countenance and searching eye of Munro; it might be with a sigh for the boisterous health and robust high spirits of his companion that an older officer sat down with Malcolm; but breakfast with Elphinstone would have been all pleasure. A companionable silence would be possible; there is wit in his face and in all he wrote or said, but there is no cynicism or spite or self-seeking; he can be detached, humorous, resigned to the inevitable, and yet enthusiastic as a boy.

He was born in 1779 and landed at Calcutta in 1796. He was first employed at Mirzapur and Benares, where he spent most of his time reading Latin and Persian. But he made friends. There was a Sanskrit scholar, Mr Samuel Davis, as Chief at Benares, while near by at Ghazipur, his brother James was under H.T. Colebrooke, the father of Elphinstone's future biographer.

Colebrooke invites a digression. He was disturbed by the uncertainty of Hindu law; the opinions obtained from Brahmans were vague or contradictory and repelled his exact mind. He set to work to learn Sanskrit in order to read the ancient texts himself and became in a sense the first great European scholar in that tongue, for he went much deeper than the pioneer, Sir William Jones. He was a judge-magistrate, and a conscientious one, for he had 'to hear from 300 to 500 causes a month'. But with many other pressing duties he found time to leave a formidable list of learned works, mostly on the Sanskrit law with excursions into ancient Hindu astronomy, a masterly survey of Indian husbandry, and accounts of the religious beliefs of the Jains as well as of the ancient Hindus.

Elphinstone was soon appointed to the Residency at Poona and marched there by way of Hyderabad, taking nearly a year on the way, learning a good deal of the country and reading voraciously – reading Persian, Greek, Latin and Italian poets, Indian history and politics, English philosophy, English poets – always reading. At Hyderabad, Kirkpatrick was Resident; he had a Persian wife and dyed his fingers with henna; at a visit to the Nizam, 'Kirkpatrick behaved like a native, and with great propriety'.

At last Elphinstone reached Poona and here he learnt his work. But there was not much time for routine; almost at once there broke out a war between Holkar and the Peshwa, which led in the end to the Second Maratha War. Malcolm was to be political adviser to Arthur Wellesley, but Malcolm went sick; Elphinstone took his place and was present at Assaye, riding by the General's side throughout the battle.

In a letter to his friend, Strachey, he describes a day of the camp-life that followed as they pursued the beaten enemy. 'The tent-pins rattle and I dress while they are striking my tent ... ' There is breakfast before the general's tent; 'it is bitter cold and we have our great-coats on. At half past six ... we mount and ride.' They reach their ground later in the morning; 'the General lies on the ground and we all talk till breakfast is ready. Then we breakfast off fried mutton, mutton-chops, curries, etc.' The middle of the day is spent by Elphinstone in arranging his 'harkaras' – a word which

Mountstuart Elphinstone, Governor of Bombay 1819–27.
'Detached, humorous, resigned to the inevitable, yet enthusiastic as a boy ...' no one can help loving Elphinstone. Yet he was also the most far-sighted of rulers and predicted with considerable accuracy the end of British Rule.

can mean either messenger or spy – 'and sometimes I talk politics and other privitie with the General'. Later, he dresses and goes to dinner, 'and we all talk about the march, and they about their former wars and this war and Indian courts and politics'. And he adds, most characteristically: 'I have enjoyed – I mean relished – society and study and business and action and adventure, all according to their several natures.'

A little later in the campaign, at the siege of a fort, he writes: 'Breakfasted with Kennedy and talked about Hafiz, Sa'adi, Horace and Anacreon. At nine I left him and went to the trenches . . . I went up to Colonel Kenny, said I heard he was to lead the storming party and that if he would allow me I would be of his party. He bowed and agreed.' There is a long and spirited description of the storm which reminded Elphinstone of the third book of the *Iliad*. 'And after one gets over the breach one is too busy and animated to think of anything but how to get on.'

At the noble age of twenty-four he was the Lord's representative at the court of the Bhonsla; but instead of Malcolm's eager adulation for the glorious little man, Elphinstone displays an amused, a critical, disrespect that was not without admiration. 'Old Villainy', he calls him in his intimate letters; there is a clean, dry sparkle to Elphinstone, like the best champagne. He was the younger son of an old Scottish barony, and for the next importation, Lord Minto, he felt the familiarity of a Border neighbour, writing home with amusement of the doings of Gibby Elliott.

He went on leave to Calcutta in 1807. Here there were 'such lots of women and laughing and philandering that I was in heaven'. Then came the sinister pact of Alexander and Napoleon at Tilsit; Malcolm left for Persia, Elphinstone for Afghanistan, and Metcalfe for Lahore, each commissioned to get as much and give as little as he could in the way of a defensive alliance to protect India against Napoleon.

Not much in the way of diplomatic triumph came of his embassy, but it did produce Elphinstone's history of the Kingdom of Cabul, which was long the standard work. He had been encouraged by the example of Malcolm, who in the course of a crowded life found time to write a history of Persia and a history of Central India as well as a collection of Persian fairy tales and the life of Clive which occasioned Macaulay's essay.

Elphinstone came back to be Resident at Poona and now had leisure both to read and to write. He rode ten or twenty miles every morning and did a bodily exercise known as the *kasrat*, spent the morning on public business, lunched at two on 'a few sandwiches and figs and a glass of water' and about three began to work on his Afghans. He was a man who revelled in the stress of circumstance when it came his way but who never courted it.

Elphinstone was always shrewd in his judgment of men. He regarded Malcolm as one of the best of men, in spite of his 'noise and egotism', and wrote of him: 'Malcolm certainly has wise and enlarged views of policy, and, among them, the kind and indulgent manner in which he regards the

Sir John Malcolm was long known as 'Boy Malcolm' because of his high spirits and enjoyment of life. He was a favourite of Wellesley the Governor-General and a friend of Wellesley the Duke. He was both soldier and administrator and wrote A History of Persia *and* A Life of Clive.

natives (though perhaps originating in his heart as much as in his head) is by no means the least.'

It was this indulgence of Malcolm's that led to the most dramatic episode in Elphinstone's life. Malcolm was the chief political officer in all that led up to the Pindari and Third Maratha Wars. He could thus override Elphinstone's opinion; he went to see the Peshwa Baji Rao, who persuaded him that he was a loyal friend who could be trusted. Elphinstone knew better, but he was overruled; troops were taken away from Poona.

Elphinstone, left with a handful of Indian troops at the heart of the Maratha confederacy, knew how hard it would be to win if the five Maratha powers combined. He had seen Assaye; he knew how easily that field might have been lost by any other general. And in that war only two of the five Maratha powers had been engaged. Now the five must be kept apart; the Peshwa must be kept neutral so long as there was any hope of a treaty with Scindia. If one went against the English, both would go.

The Peshwa Baji Rao was tortured by fear and indecision, urged by hatred to attack the English but confused by the fumes of indolence and debauchery and bewildered by the conflicting counsel of soothsayers and astrologers. To be near him was to be in the presence of a tiger cornered in a ravine.

Elphinstone kept perfectly still; a British battalion was on the way, any moment news might come from the north that the treaty with Scindia was signed; meanwhile he would not move hand or foot. He would not order his few Indian troops to stand to; he would not move them or the Residency staff to a more defensible position. Baji Rao continued to collect and arm troops; the inhabitants began to leave Poona before the coming massacre of the British.

News came one night to the handful of English in the Residency that the Peshwa and his advisers were debating whether to attack at once before help came. A little before midnight on October 28 came intelligence that 'their guns were yoked, their horses saddled, and their infantry in readiness'. Elphinstone stood on the terrace, listening to the uproar in the Peshwa's camp. Everyone would know if he ordered the troops to stand to; it might be just the spark that would touch off the mine. In the end: 'the motive which had hitherto prevented preparation determined Mr Elphinstone to defer it some hours longer'.

The noise died down; the attack was not made that night. Next day, Elphinstone directed that the troops should be put under orders that made surprise impossible; the day after, a British battalion marched in. Baji Rao had missed his chance; it was a week later that he made his attack. The Residency was abandoned and was soon ablaze: 'We went to observe the enemy. The sight was magnificent as the tide rolled out of Poona . . . Everything was hushed except the trampling and neighing of horses and the whole valley was filled with them like a river in flood . . . I now . . . sent an order to move down at once and attack . . . Soon after his whole mass of cavalry came on at speed in the most splendid style. The rush of horse, the sound of the earth, the waving of flags, the brandishing of spears, were grand beyond description but perfectly ineffectual.' At one stage, 'I own I thought there was a good chance of our losing the battle . . .' but in the end 'we found ourselves alone on the field and the sun long set'.

There cannot have been many battles that have been personally directed by a man with no military rank, nor many in which the leader of so small a force has recorded so much aesthetic pleasure at the onslaught of his assailants.

When this war was finished, there came the settlement of the Peshwa's country, now annexed. 'Officers will be forthwith appointed', ran Elphinstone's proclamation, 'to collect a regular and moderate revenue on the part of the British Government, to administer justice, and to encourage the cultivation of the soil.' He saw it as his task to 'prevent people making laws for this country until they see whether it wants them'.

He believed that the old Maratha system had worked well enough when there were good officers and integrity at the top. Disputes about property were referred to a panchayat, which is to say a committee of arbitration. What had actually happened was usually known to the arbitrators and public opinion in the village acted upon them strongly.

Criminal justice was erratic but that was what the people expected. Malcolm, travelling in this country before it was annexed, once came on a party of soldiers escorting a bound prisoner. There had been a highway robbery at a spot a little further along the road; they were taking the young man there to cut off his head. 'And how did they know he was the culprit?'

Oh, they replied, he probably knew nothing about it. But they had orders whenever there was a robbery on this stretch of road to catch a young man from the district and execute him on the scene of the crime; it worked very well, there had been far less robbery on the road since these orders had been passed.

Strange justice, but perversely preferred to the English courts, to the stamps, the petitions, the lawyers, the judge-magistrates and the courts of circuit. Everywhere, in Central India and the Deccan where the English became rulers, there seems at first to have been relief. There was peace now and good order, no more troops of horse on forays for what they could get. But there was also a fear which Elphinstone was anxious to allay, that the English courts would come with all the apparatus of the Bengal regulations. To keep out the regulations, Elphinstone made his own simple rules.

All power – except of capital punishment – was vested in the Collector, who was also Magistrate, Judge and head of the police; under him were the old Maratha officials known as *mamlatdars*, who were magistrates and collectors of the revenue. The *patel* or village headman was retained and encouraged; the panchayats were reformed and regularized. The laws of evidence and procedure were made simple; the trial was arranged with a view to publicity, known principles, and speed, retaining, however, one principle of English law – acquittal when there was any doubt of guilt.

But punishment was clear and rigorous. When a plot was detected among the Brahmans of Poona to murder all the Europeans, Elphinstone did not hesitate to order the ringleaders to be blown from guns, observing that this method of execution 'contains two valuable elements of capital punishment; it is painless to the criminal and terrible to the beholder'.

Method and system, in short – but not too much of either – were introduced where they had never been known before.

During this time he wrote that he did not think 'our Indian Empire' would be long-lived, and added: 'The most desirable death for us to die of should be, the improvement of the natives reaching such a pitch as would render it impossible for a foreign nation to retain the government; but this seems at an immeasurable distance.'

The news came that he was to be Governor of Bombay. He was by no means elated; he had been cured of ambition long ago, his brain was too fine, his temper too philosophic, his humour too astringent, to take pleasure in power or success or adulation for their own sake. Malcolm, a spirit not so fine, was bitterly disappointed. But he was still tainted with the magnificence of Wellesley, and he had to wait for Bombay till Elphinstone had done with it. All the same, there was no bitterness towards Elphinstone; they wrote to each other of what had happened with true friendship, a true greatness of soul.

8
CHAOS TAMED

1 What Kind of Men

What kind of men were they, these men who went out to rule India for the Company, who proclaimed peace and tamed chaos after the Maratha Wars? Pictures of some of them we can frame from the dusty old books, the faded photos, the memoirs for private circulation. And by looking at some of those pictures, we can judge the truth of some caricatures.

We may discard the 'savage old Nabob with an immense fortune, a tawny complexion, a bad liver, and a worse heart'; he really belongs to the previous century. But there is a caricature that everyone knows, and drawn by someone with knowledge of the subject. William Makepeace Thackeray's grandfather had been a Bengal civilian and his father and his father's three brothers were in the Company's service in Madras. Still, Jos Sedley is a caricature, though there is no denying that a great deal about Jos was apt to be true.

'He was as lonely in London as in his jungle at Boggley Wollah' – and there have been others whose eye brightened when it fell on someone who would listen to conversation about India. 'There was a girl at Dum-dum, a daughter of Cutler of the Artillery, and afterwards married to Lance, the surgeon . . .'; that was the opening with which Jos sent his father to sleep after dinner, and although it is malicious, it is malice with a point. That is how we do talk and always have talked. When you have lived a long time in a small world it is a little difficult at first to enter into general conversation. To talk about the things that have interested you so long is to be a bore, so perhaps you try not to be a bore and keep quiet and then you are dull.

Men rather stolid and mediocre, then, their lightness of touch and gaiety deadened by solitude, perhaps a little over-concerned about food and drink and their consequence in the eyes of the world – that is one kind of picture for which there is support. By its side may be placed some words of Malcolm's about the Secretariat officer, the sedentary civilian; 'I do not

Bishop Heber, who travelled across India 1824–5 describing the men he met; he wrote that the service of the East India Company was 'one of the best within an Englishman's reach'.

think there is a human being . . . I dread . . . half so much as an able Calcutta civilian . . . some good but abstract maxims in his head, the Regulations in his right hand, the Company's charter in his left, and a quire of wirewove foolscap before him.'

That is one side of the coin; on the other are Malcolm and Elphinstone and the assistants who nobly supported them – men always ready to listen to a peasant and to right a wrong, men half the day in the saddle, spending what leisure they found in writing histories, as Mark Wilks did of South India and Henry Pottinger of Sind, men witty, generous, and hospitable, a band of brothers nobly emulous.

Read of Malcolm's delight when he asks where he is and is told by a villager: 'In Munro Sahib's kingdom'; note the pleasure of Mark Wilks when he records a tale of how peasants threatened with injustice retort that they will complain 'to their father' – meaning Munro; read of Malcolm's young men in Central India, of the assistants trained by Sleeman to hunt the Thugs, read the letters written to and by Henry Ellis, Edward and

Richard Strachey, John Adam, the generation who came next after the great quartet; and from all this comes a picture of men above the common stature of mankind, striving to tame chaos.

There seem to be two races, then, the Malcolms and the Sedleys. But were they all Sedleys, those who were not the giants? What in fact was the general level? The best witnesses are newcomers and two of the best of these are Heber and Jacquemont.

Bishop Heber travelled across India, from Calcutta to Bombay in the years 1824–5. It was he who found the memory of Clevland so green forty years after his death, there being every year a meeting at his monument and 'a religious spectacle in honour of his memory'. The Bishop is amiable and intelligent, a strange figure in a land still fierce and turbulent, through which he moves with unruffled courage. He made ceremonial gifts of lavender-water to his more exalted callers and moved into the wildest country with the observant tolerance he would have shown at a meeting of the Mothers' Union in the village hall.

He called on the Nawab Shams-ud-Daulah of Dacca and was 'gratified by seeing the humane (for it was even more than good-natured) respect, deference and kindness which in every word and action Mr Master showed to this poor humbled potentate'. The Bishop's next host was Mr Warner, a man of sixteen years' service. He had 'a very well-furnished library', including a dialogue from an ancient Arabic manuscript containing a dispute between a Christian monk and certain learned Mussulmans.

Mr Warner told the Bishop how things happen in an Indian court, how a man who has been knocked down and beaten by two others will spin a tale he almost comes to believe of a hundred men who left him for dead. He told the Bishop a great deal about gang robbery and about the protection often given by a large landowner to a gang who pass as peaceful citizens. Mr Warner sounds amiable, industrious, intelligent and interested in his profession.

At Dinapore, the Bishop's host was Sir Charles D'Oyly; he was, wrote the Bishop, 'the best gentleman artist I ever met with'. His drawings of the contemporary scene are certainly pleasing and his 'Tom Raw the Griffin' is still amusing, though the plates, rather in the manner of Rowlandson, are on the whole better than the verses. He did not rise high in his profession and sounds a witty, idle, agreeable fellow.

At Benares, the Bishop was the guest of Mr Brooke, who 'has been fifty-six years in India, his manners singularly courteous and benevolent, and his tone, in speaking Hindostanee or Persian, such as marks a man who has been in the habit of conversing much with natives of high rank'. Here he was told of an incident that was to become sadly familiar: 'the two religious processions of the Mohurrum and the Janam Asthami encountering each other, the Muslim mob killed a cow and poured her blood into the sacred water. The Hindoos retaliated by throwing rashers of bacon into the windows of as many mosques as they could reach . . . both parties took to arms, several lives were lost, and Benares was in a state of uproar for many hours till the British Government came in with its authority and quelled the disturbance.'

When the disturbance was over, it remained to purify the holy river. 'All the Brahmins in the city amounting to many thousands, went down in melancholy procession, with ashes on their heads, naked and fasting . . . to the river and sat there, their hands folded and their heads hanging down, to all appearance inconsolable.' But after two or three days of fasting, a hint was given that if the magistrates would go down and beg them to eat once more perhaps they might relent. 'Accordingly all the British functionaries went to the principal bathing-place, expressed their sorrow for the distress in which they saw them, but reasoned with them . . . ' and at last after much bitter weeping it was resolved that Ganges was Ganges still. 'Mr Bird, who was one of the ambassadors, told me that the scene was very impressive and even awful.' But an observer unused to India might perhaps have found that a smile mingled with his awe at the spectacle of haughty foreign rulers pleading with their subjects to spare themselves further mortification.

The Bishop left Bareilly and made for the hills. At Shahi, the first stage out, he found Mr Boulderson, the Collector of the district, 'encamped, in the discharge of his annual duty of surveying the country, inspecting and forwarding the work of irrigation and settling with the zamindars for their taxes'.

Tom Raw the Griffin presents his letter of introduction. A 'griffin' was a newcomer to India, who was always a subject for mockery. The artist, Sir Charles D'Oyly, was himself in the Honourable East India Company's Civil Service, and sounds 'a witty, idle, agreeable fellow'.

The comfort of Mr Boulderson's tent impressed the Bishop. The Bishop felt that such luxury would be very cumbrous for himself but recognized that Boulderson was differently placed as he 'spent so much of his time in the fields' that some comfort was not unreasonable. 'I believe we parted with mutual regret; his pursuits and amusements were certainly very different from mine' – for he was an enthusiastic sportsman – 'but I found in him a keen temper and an active mind, full of information respecting the country, animals, and people, among whom he had passed several years.'

In Kumaon, the Bishop found that 'the British Government was most popular' and that 'we are still really regarded as the deliverers of the people from an intolerable tyranny'. He came to understand something of the affection the English who have served there have usually felt for the land between the jungle and the glaciers, for the people who live there and for the country itself, a people brave and humorous as soldiers, faithful as friends and servants; a land of swift thunderous rivers and clear brooks on stony beds, of mighty gorge and precipice, of ridge on broken ridge shaggy with dark forest. Some of this Bishop Heber saw and something he learnt from Mr Traill.

Mr Traill first went to the hills in 1815, when the Gurkha tyranny of which the people still talk came to an end. He had become Commissioner in 1817, and with one brief absence, stayed there till 1836. He carried out the first survey; sketchy indeed it was, and sometimes the records he left were a sad puzzle to his successors, but he was right to get it done quickly. He wanted to know how many villages there were in his kingdom, what the fields could reasonably pay, where the peasants thought the boundaries ran between one village and the next.

Mr Traill's men went from village to village and wrote down where the boundaries lay. His authority was absolute. If Mr Traill sent orders to a village community that a road was to be made to the next village, the shareholders would turn out and make a track passable for mules and loaded men. That was how the first roads were made. There were no wheeled vehicles.

Bishop Heber, of course, could not guess that more than a hundred years later the people of the hills would set finality on discussion with the words: 'It was so in Traill Sahib's day.' What he does say of him is this:

'It is pleasing to see on how apparent good terms Mr Traill is with all these people. Their manner in talking to him is erect, open and cheerful, like persons who are addressing a superior whom they love, and with whom they are in habits of easy, though respectful intercourse. He says he loves the country and people ... and he has declined ... several situations of much greater emolument for the sake of remaining with them.'

Bishop Heber left Kumaon and went south through the plains towards Agra. His picture is not all rose-coloured. He heard in Agra that the French officers who served there with Perron under Scindia, though often 'oppressive and avaricious', were of more 'conciliating and popular manners than the English Sahibs'. He speaks of the 'exclusive and intolerant spirit' of the English, their 'foolish surly national pride'; 'we are not', he goes on, 'guilty of injustice or wilful oppression, but we shut out the natives from our society and a bullying insolent manner is continually assumed in speaking to them'.

Mention must be made too of Captain Tod, not yet the author of the *Annals and Antiquities*, 'whose name appears to be held in a degree of affection and respect . . . highly honourable to him and sufficient to rescue these poor people from the often repeated charge of ingratitude'. And at Baroda there was Major Walker, who, like many before and after, waged a war against the murder of unwanted daughters, and was rewarded by 'the most affecting compliment which a good man could receive, being welcomed on some public occasion by a procession of girls of high rank who owed their lives to him, and who came to kiss his clothes and throw wreaths of flowers over him as their deliverer and second father'.

The Bishop wrote to the father of some boys whose future he had been thinking of: 'the service is still one of the best within an Englishman's reach, affording to every young man of talent, industry, and good character, a field of honourable and useful exertion.' He adds that: 'Drunkenness is almost unknown in good society' and is 'regarded with much disgust and dislike by the majority'; 'connection with native women, though sadly common among the elder officers of the army, is among the younger servants by no means a fashionable vice.'

It would be hard to think of a traveller whose character makes a sharper contrast with Bishop Heber's than that of Victor Jacquemont. A rationalist and an agnostic, Jacquemont is gay and pointed where the Bishop is mild and amiable; his wit plays over the English with admiration, affection, envy, contempt – but with laughter when he most admires and liking when he most despises.

'The English', he wrote, 'who inspire so much respect in the natives of India by their power, strength, wealth and morality (always true to their word, upright and just ninety-nine times out of a hundred) who . . . receive from them so many Asiatically servile demonstrations of respect and submission . . . are the only European people that do not take a pleasure in these marks of respect. They esteem themselves too highly, they despise the coloured races too much, to be flattered by their homage.' Where the Frenchman would think himself the first, the Englishman, he goes on, would regard himself as alone.

That is true. But any implication that the French would manage better Jacquemont denies, pointing out to French friends in Pondicherry that in a French possession the salaries of eight Englishmen would be divided between fifty or a hundred Frenchmen. The English, he always considered, had an *habileté gubernatrice* in which the French were lacking;

and he never wavered in his opinion that English government was a great benefit to the people of the country. But he went on:

> Some officials desire the Government to apply itself to the task of elevating a polished, literate educated class, enriched by the exercise of its talents, above the level of the people as a whole . . . They say openly that English supremacy in Asia cannot be eternal, and that it is a duty to humanity to prepare India to govern herself by raising the moral and intellectual capacity of its inhabitants thro' a liberal education . . . one often hears this language even on the lips of officials of the English government . . . If I thought that the foundation of English schools . . . would hasten the fall of English power . . . I would certainly close those schools, for I have a deep-rooted conviction that no national government would secure them the benefits which they owe to the English government: peace both external and internal and equal justice for all.

But his moods changed rapidly and he is sometimes sharply sarcastic about the Englishmen he meets, about their way of life and their large salaries, indignant that they should run into debt, in humorous despair at their neglect of the emotions. And he writes after one dinner-party: '*Les femmes anglaises sont exactement comme si elles n'existaient pas . . .* ' while at Poona, he can hardly contain himself: 'The stupid creatures! The idiots!' he cries.

At Benares, on the other hand, he writes: 'These are no vulgar Nabobs . . . the conversation during the evening will be both solid and elegant . . . English hospitality is splendid as a rule . . . ' and he was charmed by Simla, finding it added an extra flavour to a truffled pâté of hare from Perigord to eat it in the middle of the Himalayas. He stayed with an ex-gunner, a political officer, Captain Kennedy, who has 'a hundred thousand francs pay', commands a regiment of mountain chasseurs, the best corps in the whole army, and 'discharges the functions of a collector, acting as judge over his own subjects, and, what is more, those of the neighbouring rajas, Hindu, Tartar, and Tibetan, sending them to prison, fining them, and even hanging them when he thinks fit.'

Jacquemont went on into the Punjab when few Englishmen had been there and into Kashmir, where, he says, no European had been but Moorcroft, 'whose principal occupation was making love'. 'One has to have travelled in the Punjab to realize what an immense benefit the domination of the English in India is to humanity. What misery eighty million people are spared by it!' He ardently desired to see the English carry their frontier to the Indus, but complains in the same breath that they do not anglicize their people as the French would gallicize them. He rhapsodizes over Mhairwara, a part of Malcolm's Malwa, where he found 'a people of murderers, now changed into a quiet industrious happy people of shepherds and cultivators', but the mood changes again. 'I am an

English gentleman,' he writes, 'that is to say, one of the most brilliant animals in all creation. I have left the joys of Europe, the charms of family life, behind me; I have said farewell to my friends to come and live in this dog of a country. *Ergo* by way of compensation, I have the right to excellent food, drink, clothes, lodging, carriages, etc. And if my pay is insufficient, I shall run into debt in order to cope with this necessity.'

Jacquemont forgets satire however when he writes of William Fraser, one of the commissioners for part of the Delhi territory. Fraser must have been nearly twenty years older than Jacquemont, but they felt an attraction for each other at their first meeting. To Fraser, wrote Jacquemont, the most keenly enjoyed of all emotions is the excitement of danger and he has a mania for fighting, but because of his humanity will never kill a man; 'whenever there is a war anywhere, he throws up his judicial functions and goes off to it'. He is always the leader in an attack and has 'two fine

William Fraser who killed eighty-four lions and had 'as many children as the King of Persia'. He was Resident in Delhi, where he was murdered in 1835, almost certainly by a young noble whose guardian he had been and whom he had sharply reproved.

Victor Jacquemont, an engaging young Frenchman in search of scientific information, followed Bishop Heber's footsteps seven years later and comments on the English he met 'with laughter when he most admires and liking when he most despises'.

sabre-cuts on the arms, a wound in the back from a pike, and an arrow in the neck which almost killed him'. 'His mode of life', wrote Jacquemont, 'has made him more familiar, perhaps, than any other European with the customs and ideas of the native inhabitants. He has killed eighty-four lions, mostly on foot and on horseback and has had quite a lot of his hunters eaten. He has six or seven legitimate wives, but they all live together, some fifty leagues from Delhi and do as they like. He must have as many children as the King of Persia, but they are all Moslems or Hindus according to the religion and caste of their mammas.' Jacquemont stayed a long time with Fraser, but at last the time came for parting, and a long-drawn and emotional parting it was.

Make allowance for Heber's kindliness, his reluctance to think evil; take Jacquemont at his most critical, when his host's rich dinners are taking toll of a stomach that has grown used to griddle cakes and milk — and you will still be left with a feeling that many of the Company's servants were not quite like Sedley.

2 Bombay

Cornwallis, it will be remembered, had thought Bombay did not need a governor; he did, however, send a good one, and just when he was needed. Bombay began to expand just when Jonathan Duncan arrived, and at the same time became increasingly important in connexion with the Red Sea and the Persian Gulf. Duncan had come to India two years after John Shore in 1772; he was, like Shore, a solid creature, upright and incorruptible, righteous and just, not at all like the brilliant young men of the set who ruled India under the glorious little man.

In 1788, Cornwallis sent him to Benares as Resident to clean up corruption. Seven years he stayed at Benares, fighting the scandal of illegal gain among the British, and the practice of killing unwanted daughters among the Indians – and incidentally finding time to found and encourage the Sanskrit College. In 1795, he went to Bombay as governor. He died there in 1811, having stayed sixteen years.

His first duty in Bombay had been to find the supplies that Arthur Wellesley's army needed. Then there was new territory to settle, and he was faced with many small chiefs, whom he recognized as sovereign princelings. They became princelings, not princes; they did, on the whole, as they were told.

In Kathiawar Duncan found that the custom of killing daughters was as general among certain castes as it had been near Benares. The reason was the same; women of the higher Rajput castes cannot marry into a lower sub-caste nor within their own; there are few marriages they can make and for these a substantial dowry is needed, while to be single is to be unchaste and a disgrace. Disgrace or expense, one or the other, is on the way when a daughter is born and to a Rajput death is better than disgrace. So the child is destroyed soon after birth.

It was difficult to know how to deal with such a problem but first in Benares and later in Kathiawar, Duncan induced chief after chief, one by one, to sign a solemn covenant with the English Company, denouncing the practice and promising to give it up. The covenant was broken more often than kept but gradually, year by year, the custom became less frequent.

Jonathan Duncan was 'a simple-minded man of enlarged benevolence,' wrote Kaye. Malcolm too wrote of 'the worthy Jonathan' with the good-natured contempt of a young and brilliant man. To Malcolm he seemed old-fashioned but there was nothing old-fashioned about the stand he made against killing babies and against dishonesty in Benares.

Duncan died in 1811. It was not till 1819 that Elphinstone became Governor, and he too remained a long time, handing over to Malcolm only in 1827. His two main achievements in Bombay were the codification of the laws and his encouragement of education; of the first it is enough to say that a code was prepared under his direction, a long dusty thankless toil of which the results lasted forty years. But education was more controversial. Two questions constantly discussed in India at this time were 'colonization' and education. Should we import large numbers of Englishmen to settle in the waste lands? Or should we continue the old policy of keeping out all Europeans not employed by the Company? And were we to educate the natives and if so, to what degree, in what languages, and with what object?

It is hard to see the question of education with the eyes of our ancestors. In the first place, it was their general belief that sound government meant leaving everyone alone unless they hurt each other. In England, it was only slowly and reluctantly agreed that the state had a duty to see that its citizens could read and write. That was the business of parents or voluntary bodies such as the Church. It was not till 1833 that the reformed Parliament doubtfully voted £20,000 as a grant from national funds for teaching the people, and until 1856 no attempt was made by the state to control the way the money was spent.

There was another difference from today, almost as important. We know now that we of the West are over-concerned with the material, bogged deep in the lusts of the flesh, lost in the miasma of sex and the cinema, eaters of beef, drinkers of strong water, impure and unclean because we use paper in the toilet and clean our teeth twice with the same toothbrush. That, we are told, is how we seem to Indians. And most intelligent people from the West are ready to believe that we might learn much from the East. Even the least inquiring knows that Hinduism in its higher reaches has a spiritual message that can lead to saintly lives.

But our ancestors did not think the East more saintly than the West. They speak with almost unanimous abhorrence of a religion which sanctified burning women alive, throwing young children to crocodiles, suffocating sick old people with mud and marrying little girls to old men. They saw people who kept women like hens, penned together for life in dark and crowded quarters; they saw people who believed it was more offensive to Heaven to kill a cow than a fellow man; it seemed to them that a religion which countenanced such practices degraded and misguided its followers.

If they went slowly, it was not because they had any doubt that their own learning and religion were superior to those of the Hindus; it was because they believed that impatience would defeat its own ends. Almost everyone believed that as education spread the obvious superiority of Christianity would be recognized and there would be wholesale conversions.

Elphinstone was cautious enough at first. But soon after he reached Bombay he became President of a voluntary society which had the education of Indians as its main object; within a year he was making grants to that society from public funds – thirteen years ahead of England – and within three years he could write in his private diary of 'extensive plans for the education of the natives'. 'I am perfectly convinced,' he wrote, 'that without great assistance from Government, no progress can be made . . . ' And he went on to outline 'the principal measures required'. Better teaching and more schools; more books; encouragement to 'the lower order of natives' to use the schools made available to them; and much more

– fourth, fifth, sixth and seventh. There were to be prizes, standard examinations, offers of employment. 'It is difficult', he wrote, 'to imagine an undertaking in which our duty, our interest and our honour are more concerned.' Early marriage, debt, apathy to all improvement – 'there is but one remedy for all this, which is education'. But religion must be kept out of the schools or the Brahmans would be frightened.

Elphinstone was always in favour of the greater employment of Indians, he was always against colonization, which would mean that 'the people of India would sink to a debased and servile condition . . . resembling that of the Indians in Spanish America'. So he would now educate Indians to a stage when they might 'superintend a portion of the district, as European assistants do now', rising perhaps even to be collectors and judges, 'and it may not be too visionary to suppose a period at which they might bear to the English nearly the relation which the Chinese do to the Tartars, the Europeans retaining the government and the military power, while the natives filled a large portion of the civil stations and many of the subordinate employments in the army.'

Not many can have foreseen the future with such strange accuracy as Elphinstone, who guessed exactly how we should govern India just a hundred years after he wrote. He handed Bombay to Malcolm and left India with the eagerness of a boy at the end of term, looking forward to travel in Greece and Italy, to leisure for books and talk with friends.

Elphinstone's keen intellect belonged more truly to the inquiring rational atmosphere of the eighteenth century than to the nineteenth and nothing could be more foreign to him than the dogmatic certainty of some of his evangelical successors. His attitude to the universe was one of a delicate and considerate reverence; he seemed almost to respect the privacy of the Almighty. He wrote of 'a doubt whether it is not presumptuous to pray at all, whether you can instruct omniscience even as to your wishes, and whether you can increase the bounty of perfect benevolence. But prayer is useful for its influence not on the Deity but on the suppliant.'

Elphinstone went, Boy Malcolm came; he was a generous open creature and it was unthinkable that he should give way to that petty form of self-assertion that changes everything a predecessor has done. The morning ride, the public breakfast, the rest of the day till dinner secluded in business – all the externals were continued, but not the wit, the learning or the selflessness.

Malcolm's time in Bombay was largely taken up by a quarrel with the Supreme Court. This consisted of three English judges; it administered English law, undiluted, and it was meant to apply within Bombay island and to the European Servants of the Company. The Court, however, claimed a wider jurisdiction – and the judges knew nothing of Indian law or custom. To Malcolm it was simply a question of 'who shall henceforward be deemed superior in the Deccan . . . I shall not remain a week to

have the government over which I preside trampled upon nor the empire
to the prosperity of which the efforts of my life have been devoted beaten
down, not by honest fellows with glittering sabres, but quibbling quill-
driving lawyers . . . '

He was vindicated, upheld by the Court of Directors on every single
point and three years later when he left India, he too was ready to go at
last. Even Boy Malcolm had had enough. He was a great man in a different
way from Munro, Elphinstone and Metcalfe; he had the same qualities,
and in the same proportion, as a hundred other officers of the empire-
building days – energy, high spirits, good humour, justice, honesty,
quick wits, the power to command men and be obeyed – but he had more
of each. That was all.

3 Some Evils Ended

To murder an unwanted daughter, to burn a widow alive, to throw a child
into the river among crocodiles or sharks – these were things that to the
servants of the Company seemed wicked. But these cruel deaths were
inflicted in the name of a religion in which the subjects passionately
believed, while the rulers thought it a mischievous superstition.

Everyone agreed that the English should not use their position as rulers
to interfere with the religion of the people. Their government was
founded on tacit consent; wherever they had taken sovereignty, within a
few months the English magistrate could go anywhere in the district
unattended, alone among a million of his subjects. This was because they
preferred him to any other possibility; that, surely, must be because he
did not interfere with their religion.

But what about acts done in the name of religion which to a Christian
seemed neither more nor less than murder? Take one example, from an
area the size of Wales, mountainous country in Orissa. Here the plains
were inhabited by Hindus, but in the mountains was an older race, people
darker and squatter of feature, who had been driven up into the hills when
the Aryan invaders came, people still primarily hunters, much given to
drunkenness and to worship of strange godlings. Many of these tribes
made a habit of particularly cruel human sacrifice.

The victims of these Khond sacrifices were kept in comfort by the
villagers, as men keep and fatten pigs – but the pigs do not know what
death they are going to die. The Meriah – the victim – had to be bought
with a price, paid in kind. Once bought, the Meriah might be kept for
years a servant of the village, well treated; but sooner or later, to end a
drought, to banish caterpillars or locusts, he would be sacrificed.

The rites would last two or three days. The victim, mercifully drunk,
was tied; there were dances, there were anointings of his head and
strange prayers; he would be carried round the village bounds; on the

second or third day the climax would be reached. They killed in different ways in different tribes; but in all forms of the sacrifice, strips of flesh must be torn from the victim to be buried in the fields or slung on a pole above the stream that watered the crops; in all forms the victim was made drunk; in one he was suffocated in pig's blood before the dismemberment began.

Of these habits the English did not at first become aware. In 1836 the first report was sent in by Russell of the Madras Civil Service; he wrote at length, reciting the facts. He concluded:

> We must not allow the cruelty of the practice to blind us to the consequences of too rash a zeal in our endeavour to suppress it . . . Are the government prepared to engage in an undertaking which . . . must lead to the permanent occupation of an immense territory and involve us in a war with a people with whom we have now no connection and no cause for quarrel, in a climate so inimical to strangers and at an expense which no human foresight can foresee?

No, he thought, we must use moral influence rather than power to end the evil.

The Government of Madras agreed and were against the use of force; when they authorized Captain Campbell to go up into the hills, they gave him strict orders that his escort was to be used 'exclusively for the protection of his person'.

Captain Campbell, however, was a man prepared to take risks. He began by summoning the chiefs and leaders of one part of the country. He spoke of the horror in which the Great Government held human sacrifice. And what was the use of it? Were their crops better or their men stronger than among the tribes who did not sacrifice human beings?

The chiefs retired to talk it over among themselves. Campbell waited in anxiety for their reply. He had gone too far for anything but the use of force if they were obdurate — and that was against his orders. And it would lead to long guerrilla campaigns in fever-haunted mountains, burning villages, arrows at dusk, men hanged on trees.

At last they came back. It was what they had always done. They had thought it was right. But now they were subjects of the Great Government and they must do as they were told. If the earth refused its natural increase — 'it is not our fault. It is on the head of the Government. We will give up the sacrifice of men and kill animals instead; to the goddess we shall say: "Do not be angry with us: vent your wrath upon this gentleman, who is well able to bear it."'

It was done; in that area at least the back of the thing was broken. There were set-backs of course, but only once did Campbell have to fire. The Khonds brought in the Meriahs they had bought and handed them over, for, as they said, if they kept them in the village, the temptation might be too much for them. Campbell was in these hills for sixteen years, during

which time he rescued one thousand five hundred and six Meriah pros-
pective victims — already bought and paid for.

The Khond country stretched into Bengal as well as Madras. Here too
the government was cautious but here too there were men on the spot who
were ready to go beyond their instructions. Bannerman, for example,
arrived on one occasion in the nick of time, when the victim was bound
and the whole village drunk. He was lucky to get away without loss of life.
As much was done too, by Miller, Hicks, Macpherson and many others.

It is an example of what was happening all over India. Everywhere, but
particularly in the South and the Centre, there were odd little pockets of
old animistic religion, customs of sacrifice to the forces of destruction.
And since no animal is so valuable as man, in times of drought or
pestilence a human victim would sometimes be found. There was the rope
sacrifice in the Central Himalayas, in which the victim had, it is true, a
sporting chance of escape; both the Todas of the Nilgiris and the Banjaras,
who carried loads all over India, drove herds of cattle over children half
buried in the sand; in one Burmese district a living child was taken round
the village and a finger cut off at each house before the victim was at last
killed by repeated stabs. These were outside Hinduism or on its fringes;
but at Tanjore a male child was sacrificed in the Saiva temple every Friday
evening until British rule forbade it; in Bastar in 1830 the Raja sacrificed
twenty-five men together at one time.

Probably at least once every year in the first half of the century someone
had to wait anxiously like Campbell to see whether persuasion and bluff
would win or whether he would have to fight.

The custom of burning widows alive was a more difficult problem. It was
widespread, it belonged to the higher castes of Hinduism, it was believed
passionately to be a road to Heavenly beatitude. It arose from the Hindu
belief that for a married woman her husband is her god on earth; it was
preserved by the general opinion that no one can live alone and chaste; it
was fed by the natural jealousy of a man who does not wish to leave behind
a young and beautiful woman as a plaything for someone else; it was
spread by economic interest, for who wants to support a useless mouth?
But no apologist has been able to suggest why, even if the widow must die,
she should die painfully.

The oldest Hindu scriptures, the *Vedas*, do not command the practice
and though undoubtedly very ancient it was not general in Vedic times. It
is the *Shastras*, which are much later, which glorify it, and even the
Shastras say that the act must be voluntary.

There is nobility in some tales of Rajput suttees. Sleeman, with no
authority but his own, forbade the practice in his own district. A Rajput
noble died; his widow sent word to Sleeman that, though her husband's
body had been burnt without hers, she considered herself dead. She had
built a second pyre and would burn herself on this as soon as the English

magistrate gave permission to her spirit to depart. Meanwhile she would sit by the side of the river and neither eat nor drink.

Sleeman went to see her. He told her the practice was not enjoined by the Hindu scriptures. She smiled and pointed to the sky, where she could clearly see her husband's spirit and her own side by side. She was dead already and her body could feel no pain. She waited only for the Englishman's permission to go.

He resisted till the seventh day and then gave in. The pyre was lighted and she walked once round, then stepped in and sank down among the flames without a cry, as though reclining on a luxurious bed.

That is the noble side; there are many examples of it in Tod. There was the Rajput warrior who in the midst of his marriage ceremony received the call of his feudal overlord. He went at once to war and next day was killed in battle with the wedding garland still fresh on his breast. She, virgin, bride and widow, her flowers as fresh as his, without a tear or cry caused the pyre to be built, lighted it and died.

Such women expected of their men a courage as indomitable as their own. Tod has another tale of a chief who, after fighting all day against hopeless odds, towards evening rode for his castle, blood-stained and weary. The gate of the fortress was barred; he beat on the heavy doors and called to the men on the walls above. At last a message came from his wife. Her husband would never leave the field of battle defeated and alive; the man at the gate must be his ghost. She had ordered her pyre to be lighted. There was nothing left for him to do but go back to meet his enemies. He mounted and forced the unwilling horse to turn; in the evening light, the wind towzled the flames above the dark ramparts as he rode away.

To defy pain and death so completely must be admired. But in most of its forms, and particularly in Bengal, suttee was sordid and cruel. All the evidence goes to show that, in nine cases out of ten, the woman in Bengal went to the flames in fear and horror. As her husband lay dying, fear was added to the sense of loss; sleepless from watching, exhausted by hysteria, the moment he passed she had to face persuasive relatives, anxious priests. Her death would bring honour to all her family; her husband would earn aeons of blessedness with her in a heaven of their own, he being released by her pain from the burden even of such sins as killing a cow or a Brahman. Flaccid with grief, she had only to raise her hand, to loosen her hair, to break a bangle; the tired gesture was enough, she had consented. It became the duty of a Hindu to see that she died.

In Bengal, she was usually tied to the corpse, often already putrid; men stood by with poles to push her back in case the bonds should burn through and the victim, scorched and maimed, should struggle free. She could hope for no pity from her own people. There is a case reported when a woman did succeed, in the dark of a rainy night, in escaping from the pyre and hiding herself among some brushwood. But they found her. Her son dragged her out and in spite of her pleading tied her hand and foot and threw her back into the flames.

This was the evil that faced the Company's servants. In a small area, it was easy; Madras had forbidden the practice a century and a half ago, but in those days all that need be done was to take the wretched woman a few miles over the border. It was a very different matter when the English dominions grew. Brooke prevented a suttee in 1789 by force; James Elphinstone rescued a twelve-year-old widow in 1805; Sleeman could forbid it in his own district, Charles Metcalfe throughout the territory of Delhi. But even Metcalfe, when back in Calcutta on the Governor-General's council, was for long doubtful about total prohibition.

Wellesley was advised that prohibition would cause a mutiny in the native army. In 1813 orders were issued which were meant to check but in fact encouraged suttee. A widow must not be burned without permission; an Indian police officer must be present and must certify that she was not drugged, that she was not a minor or pregnant, that she went willingly. This set the stamp of acquiescence on something previously done with a consciousness of official disapproval; officially recorded burnings for Bengal, which were 378 in 1815, rose steadily to 839 in 1818.

It was not till 1829 that widow-burning was prohibited in the Bengal territories, Madras and Bombay following six months later. That was because Lord William Bentinck was the first Governor-General who was prepared to take the risk of provoking a general cry of religion in danger.

The advice given by the Company's servants in the long-settled districts had in the main been for abolition. One, more emphatic than the rest, wrote: 'I look upon this inhuman practice as one tolerated to the disgrace of the British Government; it is even abominated by the better sort of natives themselves and nowhere is it enjoined by Hindu law . . . '

At last, the hateful business was forbidden in British territory and there was no flaring up of popular feeling. But though it was finished as an institution, it was never quite done with; suttee was something always to be watched against. I have had two letters from living officers who were concerned in cases of suttee in the 1930s.

In the States, there was no general prohibition but the pressure brought to bear by the Paramount Power steadily increased until it became out of the question. But the change came slowly. The number of women burned alive at his funeral had in many states been the criterion of a prince's success in life; the number of empty guns fired when he visited the Governor-General was a tame substitute. Eighty-four women died with Raja Budh Singh of Bundi; sixty-four with Ajit Singh of Jodhpur, and numbers in the neighbourhood of twenty were usual.

From 1833 onwards, the opportunity was usually taken, when a state required any favour, of including in the treaty or covenant some clause about suttee. There are a hundred stories that will never be told of risks taken to prevent a suttee, risks of stirring up riots and losing life, risks of

5 above, 'An Indiaman in a Fresh Breeze', by Charles Brooking. Brooking, a promising marine painter, died early, in 1759, of 'injudicious medical advice'; 6 below, 'An English Officer Arrives in India, c. 1820.'

7 *Shahjehan, grandson of Akbar, ordered the execution of all his collateral male relatives when his father Jehangir died in 1627.*

incurring rebuke for exceeding authority. The thing came at last to an end. Of the numb misery with which each helpless creature went to the slaughter there remains for visible sign only perhaps the figure of a stone woman crouching at the feet of a husband of stone, or perhaps the more moving testimony of a red handprint on the frame of a door. For as she left her home, the woman on her way to death dipped her hand in red pigment and laid it flat on the doorpost or lintel. The print of that small lonely hand remains but nothing else.

Suttee was in some way part of Hinduism. This could not be said of the practice of sacrificing children in the river. A wife would vow her first child to destruction, trusting that thus appeased the gods would grant more. The child would often be kept till it was seven or nine years old; then it would go to the crocodiles of the Ganges or the sharks at Sagar Point. It was encouraged by the Brahmans; it was forbidden absolutely by Lord Wellesley.

More difficult to control was the treatment of the old and sick. It is accounted virtuous to die on the banks of the Ganges – and all rivers partake in some degree of the sacredness of the Ganges. Therefore when an old woman seemed likely to die, she was hurried to the water's edge. But there is no coming back from that journey; those who recover are beyond hope of blessing. There was a village not far from Calcutta for those who had refused to die and it was easier for all to aid the spirit in its passing by ladling Ganges water into the sick mouth and if that failed by stuffing nose and mouth with Ganges mud. And lepers, too; it was simplest to bury them alive.

All these things were forbidden but people do not change their ways because a man hundreds of miles away has signed a paper; it will depend on the way the district is run.

One more evil must be mentioned in more detail. There had always been stories of travellers who were strangled by Thugs, but the mysteries of that murderous society were closely guarded and they left no survivors. Again, it was Lord William Bentinck who gave orders which ended the Thugs. Sleeman was for most of the time in charge of the operations; he had a dozen young men working under him, mostly soldiers turned political with a few civilians.

The first step was the most difficult. But once a member of a gang had confessed, then others of the gang would usually hurry forward to gain a pardon and gradually the doings of that group would be cleared up. It was slow laborious work. A gang would set out in the autumn; they would come back in the spring, having murdered anything up to a thousand travellers.

They would camp near a town or a large village; one or two chosen men would go to the shops and wander about the streets. As soon as they saw a small party of travellers they would move nearer and seize on some chance of getting into conversation. The talk would slide round to the dangers of the road and heads would be shaken at the folly of travelling without a sufficient escort. The travellers would speak cautiously of joining parties for safety; the stranger would be reluctant but in the end the two parties would ride on together. Never, the travellers would think, had they met such good company. But a night would come when the company would seem even better than usual, the tales told with more gusto, the jokes more ready and the laughter more uproarious. Then suddenly the leader would cry in a loud voice: 'Bring the tobacco!' and clap his hands as though to summon a servant. And that clap would be the last thing the travellers heard on earth. In a few more minutes their bodies would be stripped naked and tumbled higgledy-piggledy into a grave already dug; a few more and the grave would be filled and the senior gravedigger would be dragging a thorny bush over the sandy soil to hide all traces.

The killing was done by a handkerchief, a square of cloth, in one corner of which was knotted a silver coin consecrated to the goddess Kali. The knotted coin made a grip for the left hand; the free end went round the victim's neck, then a quick twist, and in skilful hands the victim would be dead before he reached the ground.

The Thugs *were a secret society who believed they had been entrusted by the goddess Kali with the duty of murdering travellers. More than four thousand were brought to trial; some had personally strangled hundreds. These men were photographed in prison where they had been set to making carpets.*

It was not just plain crime for gain. Destruction of life was the first object; the booty was the devotee's earthly reward, granted him by the goddess. The Thugs believed that they were carrying out a divine mission and that as a reward a heaven of their own would be reserved for them. One Thug told Meadows Taylor that he had personally murdered seven hundred and nineteen people and that he would no doubt have reached a thousand if the government had not caught him. His only regret was that he had not killed more.

There was excitement and adventure in rounding up the Thugs – but there was plain slogging hard work when they were caught. It was the task of Sleeman's young men to build up a list of the members of each gang and a narrative of the incidents in which that gang had been involved in each hunting season for the last ten or fifteen years. In court a discrepancy in the evidence would be taken as a sign of innocence. It must all be pieced together. The judges must have clear, corroborated, uncontradicted testimony, because they stood for the rule of law as against the individual whim that had ruled before.

Between 1831 and 1837 more than three thousand Thugs were convicted. It would be a fair guess that there had been at least ten thousand operating before Sleeman's net drew tight. Forty or fifty gangs; perhaps twenty or thirty thousand travellers killed every year. It is guesswork, but that is the kind of figure.

The thing was ended. This evil was completely stamped out and the craft forgotten; it was done by long monotonous hours of questioning, by the laborious comparison of a hundred reports.

But of course it is open to anyone today to argue that the servants of the Company were on the wrong side, that they should have thrown in their lot with Kali and Siva and kept down the population, which is now certainly far too large.

9
BECOMING A SERVICE

1 Metcalfe and the Supreme Post

Charles Metcalfe is the last and probably the greatest of the great quartet. He is the last in time, having landed at Calcutta, not yet sixteen, on January 1, 1801. He is also the most difficult to understand.

Munro and Malcolm have the simplicity of characters in Thackeray; Elphinstone, with his Renaissance zest for scholarship, action, society and war, though more complex, we feel we know; but it would be a bold man who claimed to have plumbed the majestic pessimism, the liberal realism, the lonely magnanimity of Metcalfe.

He was English, in the narrower sense, an Etonian of the Etonians, armoured, as the three Scots were not, by an isolating crust of convention and social ritual. His mother made no secret of her preference for his elder brother Theophilus and no doubt that added to his loneliness. A half holiday at Eton was to him an opportunity for translating Rousseau, for reading Gibbon, Ariosto, Lucan, Homer and Juvenal. There is no hint of boyish mischief; Metcalfe never took any delight in swift motion or the use of his body. He was, however, not without friends and does not seem to have been unhappy at Eton.

He came to Calcutta, not quite sixteen, with introductions to everyone and was soon an intimate at Government House. In spite of 'an ugly phiz', he had an attractive manner and made friends; he was soon recognized as one of the inner set, one of the true rulers of India. But he was lonely.

Of course he became a diplomatic or political officer. He started as assistant to the Resident at the Court of Scindia, 'King' Collins, an autocratic eccentric who did not like being argued with. But his failure to get on with Collins was not regarded as a blot. He became Political Assistant to Lake, and won the general's confidence by volunteering for a storming-party at Dig.

Assistant at Delhi, he complained that Seton, his chief, did not give him

Charles Metcalfe in 1812, aged 27, became Resident at Delhi and administered an area the size of Wales in which he abolished capital punishment and flogging and forbade slavery and the burning of widows. He acted for nearly two years as Governor-General – and would have made a better Governor-General than his successor, Lord Auckland.

enough to do. Seton was conscientious, kind, modest and unassuming, but no deputer of authority. 'He rises before the day and labours until the middle of the night. He does not move out; he takes no exercise and apparently no food.' His administration was mildly inefficient and it was certainly a relief to Metcalfe when in 1808 at the age of twenty-three he was sent as Envoy to Ranjit Singh in the Punjab.

His mission was part of Gibby Elliott's triple diplomatic move against the Corsican bogey. Malcolm in Persia, Elphinstone in Kabul, Metcalfe in Lahore, each had a difficult task, each having been instructed to get something for nothing. But Metcalfe had the most difficult of all, because Ranjit Singh was a man who can be spoken of in the same breath with Akbar. In spite of his drunkenness, few men have equalled his courage, his perseverance or his political vision. His two great pieces of wisdom were his refusal to quarrel with the English and the tolerance for Muslims that enabled Muslim vassals to fight for him. Against this hard-riding, hard-drinking, lustful, shrewd barbarian was pitted young Charles from Eton, a complex, introspective creature who kept a diary and noted in it thoughts on self-love and duty, sin and suffering.

Charles came out of it with great credit to himself. He did not get the alliance against Napoleon, but he had given away nothing, maintained a firm front, and made it perfectly clear that Ranjit Singh's empire was not to spread to the east bank of the Sutlej. What is surprising, he had won from 'the wily and unscrupulous Sikh' a kind of ironical and affectionate

Ranjit Singh: the founder of the Sikh empire in the Punjab, 'a man who can be spoken of in the same breath with Akbar ... his two great pieces of wisdom were his refusal to quarrel with the English and his tolerance for Muslims ...'

regard. That, however, was a thing that did again and again happen between Englishmen and Indian; it came of recognizing the situation and perceiving that it was not without humour; it could not live long in the air of moral indignation.

Metcalfe's Victorian biographer does not mention his three Eurasian sons, of whom the eldest born in 1809, the year in which this mission ended. That Metcalfe had for seven or eight years an Indian wife or mistress is beyond doubt; that she was a Sikh of good family, perhaps even a connection of Ranjit Singh's, is conjecture. But no one knows what became of her.

Seton went to Penang as Governor; Metcalfe at twenty-seven became Resident at Delhi. The Resident was in theory a diplomat at the court of the Mogul Emperor but in fact Metcalfe was administrator of an area about the size of the six northern counties of England. At the same time he was political agent in charge of relations with a network of states that were rather less than independent.

The Delhi administration under Metcalfe was the most enlightened in the world. In England men could be hanged for a forty-shilling theft; the United States permitted slavery for another fifty years. But there was no hanging in Delhi and no selling of slaves.

Capital punishment was ended by Metcalfe as a matter of principle; he was convinced of the fallibility of all human judgment and in particular of verdicts in Indian courts. And since sentence of death once carried out cannot be revoked he preferred not to inflict it. He forbade the slave trade and the burning of widows; he collected swords and spears, beat them literally into ploughshares and returned them to the owners. He first discouraged and then stopped flogging, for he rejected the vindictive aspect of punishment and was sceptical about reformation. The great thing was to put the criminal where he would not be able to disturb society again; his sentences of imprisonment were therefore severe when guilt seemed tolerably certain. Instead of whipping boys from criminal tribes caught picking pockets, he sent them to a camp where they were taught a trade. But it is really shorter to say simply that in most of his penal theory he was a century ahead of his times.

Revenue rose from about forty thousand pounds in 1807 to about one hundred and fifty thousand in 1813. That could happen only where peace was felt to be secure. The King's share which Metcalfe took was always light, and in the course of his settlement he became sharply critical of the permanent settlement in Bengal. He judged by what he had found near Delhi; he believed that the cultivator should be regarded as the proprietor and the zamindar was really a representative of the government, falsely made a proprietor by Cornwallis. But it had not been quite the same in Bengal.

He governed Delhi his own way, using a code of his own. One feature of his system became general over all those parts of India recently acquired; he would have none of Cornwallis's division of judicial from executive, he would have no one glued to his chair in court or office. The man who collected the revenue was also responsible for order, he was policeman, magistrate and judge.

Metcalfe was King of Delhi from 1811 till 1819. He left for two appointments in Calcutta; he was to be both Private Secretary to the Governor-General and Secretary in the Secret, Foreign and Political Departments, with the salaries of both posts – just under ten thousand pounds a year, with no income-tax and at a time when a pound would buy a good deal. He was thirty-four.

From Private Secretary Metcalfe went to Hyderabad as Resident, not without a wistful glance at Delhi; there was something that appealed to his lonely melancholy in the vastness of the dusty plains that lie round Delhi, in the brightness of its pale windy skies, in the sense of fallen greatness that it must bring to the least sensitive. But he went to Hyderabad, where he found things not much better than they had been near Calcutta in the days of William Bolts.

At first, the Nizam had borrowed money to pay the troops from the house of William Palmer; later, the house of William Palmer paid the troops and recovered what they had spent — plus 25 per cent — from the villages mortgaged by the Nizam. The peasants sank deeper in misery, but the officers got their pay and did not trouble their heads how it came. Europeans paid from Hyderabad revenues received a house at the expense of the state, and free servants in addition to their pay. Worst of all, Residency officials, even Russell the Resident himself, were said to have shares in William Palmer & Company. It was a bog of corruption, of which the smell, Metcalfe said, was sickening. He fought a lonely fight against the house of William Palmer, and set about the steady and systematic cleansing of the administration.

He met with no support from the Governor-General. One passage from one of Metcalfe's letters must stand for many. Charged with hostility to Chandu Lal, the Nizam's chief minister, he wrote:

It is very true that I think ill, in the highest degree, of the spirit of his internal administration; that I groan for the devastation inflicted on the country by his merciless extortions; and that I cannot love his heartless recklessness of the miseries of the people confided to his charge. I mourn also for the reproach attached by public opinion to the British Government as if it countenanced the criminalities which its support alone has given him the strength to practice.

Lord Hastings does not come out of the story well but Metcalfe had the support of the Council, and in the end the Directors were on his side. He went again to Delhi; he came back to Calcutta as Member of Council; he was nominated successor to the Governor-General and deputy in his absence. But though he did not go back to England for thirty-seven years he never lost himself in the Indian scene. To his aunt, who resigned for her son an appointment in India, he wrote, approving of her act: 'Why doom him to transportation from everything dear to him?'

All speak of his gracious and sweet disposition; he seemed happier now than in his younger days. But it was not that he liked society any better; dinners, balls, the whole round of meeting people was to him always a tedious loss of time. If he seemed a little more at home in the world than once he had, it was because: 'I live in a state of fervent and incessant gratitude to God for the favours and mercies which I have experienced . . . The feeling is so strong that it often overflows in tears and is so rooted that I do not think any misfortunes could shake it.'

Metcalfe's life is too rich, too complex, for this small-scale map, but some of his opinions must go in. On the question of whether the Government was bound to continue to his descendants a grant of land made to an individual, there occurs this superb widening of the whole discussion:

Our dominion in India is by conquest; it is naturally disgusting to the inhabitants and can only be maintained by military force.

It is our positive duty to render them justice, to respect and protect their rights, and to study their happiness. By the performance of this duty, we may allay and keep dormant their innate disaffection; but the expectation of purchasing their cordial attachment by gratuitous alienations of public revenue would be a vain delusion.

This is realism. At the same time, he did not doubt that the Company conferred a benefit by taking territory under its rule. But it was folly to expect gratitude when memories of anarchy had faded.

He was against interfering in the affairs of native states. He extended this principle to Persia and Afghanistan with whom 'we should be on the most friendly terms that will not lead to war with Russia'. And again: 'You may depend upon it that the surest way to draw Russia upon us will be by our meddling with any of the states beyond the Indus.'

Those were always Metcalfe's views. If they had prevailed, the worst chapter in Indian history need not have been written. It is the worst because it records actions the most unrighteous as well as the most disastrous. But by then Metcalfe had left India. He had been adviser and deputy to Lord William Bentinck, with whom on most subjects he had agreed; he succeeded Lord William provisionally as Governor-General, he was strongly recommended for permanent appointment by Lord William and by the Court of Directors. But the Cabinet clung to the convention that the highest post in India should go to a noble lord from England.

It was not a bad convention as a rule. The great argument in favour of Cornwallis, the first noble lord, was that he did not have to make his fortune. That argument no longer had much force, but Sir John Shore and Sir George Barlow had both been too subservient to authority in England. A fresh mind – if sufficiently powerful – will come to Indian problems free from clogging detail, free from long-established prejudices as to what can be done and what is impossible, while a man who has held cabinet rank in England can get his way in London better than an obscure exile, however able.

Metcalfe however was overlooked simply because the ministry would not forgo patronage. A Tory ministry made a Tory appointment. A Whig ministry cancelled the Tory, and changed to a Whig. George Eden, Lord Auckland, was appointed. Metcalfe, who had been two years Governor-General, gave way to him with a good grace, and took up the lieutenant-governorship of the North-Western Provinces. But he had by now fallen from favour with the Court of Directors. He had, while acting as Governor-General, passed a measure freeing from censorship the English-written press. Bentinck, Metcalfe and Macaulay had been agreed but Metcalfe was Governor-General when the Act was passed and it was at

Metcalfe that the Court's anger was directed. The governorship of Madras fell vacant; they did not appoint Metcalfe and the reason was the Press Act. He would not, he said, serve on in disgrace; he resigned, going on to be Governor of Jamaica and Governor-General of Canada.

Lord Auckland remained. He had a reputation in England for ability, he had a mild and amiable good nature. In India, however, he was bored. Invested with the empire of Tamerlane and Akbar, made suddenly heir-at-law to Kubla Khan and Prester John, he was bored. Charged with the destiny of millions, moving in a magnificence at which he mildly chafed through a countryside stricken by famine, among children dying of starvation, he was bored.

Lord Auckland was a humane man. It may be that he was appalled by the horrors of the famine and dismayed at his own ignorance and impotence. It may be that he concealed his wretchedness behind an emotion that seemed more appropriate to his birth. That is an interpretation more charitable to the man than to take his boredom at its face value; it does not, however, raise his reputation as a Governor-General. Either Metcalfe or Elphinstone would have known what could be done.

The famine cannot be attributed to Lord Auckland. Not so the Afghan war. Lord Auckland refused the friendship of the strong and able Ruler of Afghanistan and invaded his country, in order to put on the throne a pretender who had been three times turned out by his people. There were many widows and orphans, Indian, Afghan and English, as a result of this policy; while, with no shadow of justice, Auckland plunged Afghanistan into four years of misery, saddled India with a bill for fifteen million pounds, and involved British armies in the most complete Asiatic disaster they were to suffer until exactly a hundred years later in 1942.

Lord Auckland was left a wide discretion and he always spoke of the decision as his own. Kaye believes he was manoeuvred into it by his Secretaries but the theory does not seem to me tenable; in any case, no Secretary would have manoeuvred Metcalfe. Here was a man morally and intellectually out of his depth.

It was January 1842 that Dr Brydon reached Jalalabad, fainting from wounds, hunger and exhaustion. He was the sole survivor of the force that had accepted terms at Kabul. Another army had to be raised, another expedition had to go to Kabul, another war be fought, to put right the results of that cruel wrong. There were more widows, more orphans, but the widows were mostly Afghans this time. None of this would have happened if Metcalfe had been Governor-General.

2 Fort William and Haileybury

Elphinstone and Metcalfe were the kind of men who would educate themselves however they were placed – and there were others. 'I have found', wrote Lord Wellesley in 1800, 'the officers of the Secretariat to possess the industry of clerks with the talents of statesmen', but their education had been cut short at the age when it began to be most valuable; their first year in India had usually been spent in the 'menial, laborious, unwholesome and unprofitable duty of mere copying clerks'. He therefore decided to set up in Calcutta the College of Fort William for their education. He did not propose the measure; he made his decision and set it in hand, blandly informing the Court of Directors that their 'early support ... will tend to give animation and spirit to the new Institution'.

At this college, every young man appointed to the Company's service was to spend three years. Newcomers, Lord Wellesley pointed out, were anyhow little use to the administration for the first three years. They would learn Indian history, law and Oriental languages, but their general education would not be forgotten and the course would include ethics, international law and general history. The discipline and administration were to be on the lines of a college at Oxford or Cambridge and the staff included orientalists of considerable distinction. It was all running smoothly by the time the Directors heard of the project.

The Court of Directors were determined not to be bullied; the glorious little man found it necessary to record his 'unqualified contempt and abhorrence of the proceedings and propensities of the Court of Directors'. The Directors had their way; the College of Fort William was whittled down to a school of oriental languages for Bengal alone.

The front façade of Old Haileybury. The East India College, Hertfordshire, opened at Hertford Castle in 1806 and moved to Haileybury in 1809. Here the young men who were to be servants of the East India Company received a 'liberal education' including 'political economy', taught here by Malthus and not yet taught at Oxford or Cambridge.

But in the course of contesting the Governor-General's arguments, the Court of Directors accepted some of them and committed themselves to a college in England. 'The East India College, Herts', opened in 1806 at Hertford Castle and moved to Haileybury in 1809; it lasted just fifty years.

There was a good deal at Haileybury that was borrowed from Fort William. The subjects taught were divided into 'Orientals' and 'Europeans'. The Orientals were mainly languages; it was a two-year course divided into four terms and in the first term a beginning was made with Sanskrit, to which Persian was added in the second term and a third language, usually Hindustani, in the third term.

'Europeans' included the classical languages and mathematics, and there was law, both general and Indian; what was less to be expected, there was great emphasis on political economy and general history, then hardly taught in the older universities. Malthus was the first professor in these subjects and held the chair till he died thirty years later; he was succeeded by Mr Richard Jones, whose book on 'Rent' expressed considerable differences from Adam Smith, Malthus and Ricardo. He was a brilliant lecturer; his pupils listened with breathless attention.

Haileybury was something between a public school and a college at Oxford or Cambridge. The students lived in small bedsitting-rooms, a combination of cubicle and study. The day began about seven, when 'an aged bedmaker came in, lit the fire and disappeared. Then came the scout who filled the bath with cold water, laid the table for breakfast, cleaned the boots and made as much noise as he could in order to awaken the sleeping student. Gradually we got up, dressed, put on cap and gown and hurried off to chapel at 8.' Back to breakfast, 'ingeniously balanced on the tongs before the fire', curried soles being a great favourite; the morning was packed with lectures and the more conscientious spent the early hours of the afternoon writing up their notes, but there seems to have been no 'tutorial' in the Oxford sense. There was no regular lunch – that meal being still mainly a feminine flippancy – but beer and bread and cheese were to be had at the 'trap', that is, the buttery.

There were fives and cricket and rowing and some managed to hunt. In the afternoon some went off to play games, 'the fast men on dogcarts to play billiards at Hertford or Ware, or perhaps to slip up to town by train for the afternoon, and the steady men to take a solemn constitutional along the roads'.

Dinner was in Hall at six and evening chapel at eight, after which 'the steady men went to their rooms and read far into the night'.

In most respects Haileybury was like any other college of the time. Discipline was lax, but so it was at Oxford and Eton. But the distinguished men who taught at Haileybury had difficulties from which their colleagues elsewhere were free. The course lasted two years, but the age-limit for admission was from fifteen to twenty-two; they had to face boys who should have been still at school sitting side by side with young men who might have taken a university degree. The lower limit was raised to seventeen in 1833 but there was still too great a gap between the eldest and the youngest. Some attempt, however, was made to keep men up to the collar. There was an examination in every subject every term and every student was graded. There were prizes; the Directors came down in a body twice a year – 'Di's Day' it was called – and there were speeches and prizes and pats on the back. It was very much a family affair, since every young man must know at least one Director well enough to have been nominated and many had fathers, uncles, or godparents in the Court. If a young man was 'too idle or too stupid' for the Civil Service, he was nominated instead to the cavalry, for which nothing so vulgar as training was required. About one-fifth of the Haileybury students fell by the wayside; four-fifths entered the Company's Civil Service.

It was argued that finding the best students could safely be left to the conscience of individual Directors; everyone knew the importance of choosing a young man who was able, industrious, had reasonably good manners and would do credit to his nominator. But not everyone took the trouble he might have done and Macaulay hit on a device which he thought would save the Directors' patronage and yet introduce the competitive principle. There were to be four young men nominated for each vacancy and a competitive examination to decide which was the best. This became law in 1833, but it only lasted a year.

Everyone agreed that there should be an interview in which pleasant manners and social background would count for something; everyone agreed that some intellectual standard was needed. At last a decision was reached in favour of open competition. This was in 1853, by the last Government of India Act which concerned the Company – seventeen years before the home Civil Service was opened to competition. It would have been possible to keep Haileybury, simply making entry competitive, but Haileybury, in that incarnation, was ended in December 1857. It was coincidence that this was the year of the Mutiny.

There were to be many more changes; some believed the competitive examination should come on leaving school, after which two years should be spent on probation at a university, while others thought selection should be after the normal university education, when a degree had been taken. This view won in the end but both experiments were tried.

Haileybury had fostered a close family spirit; because of Haileybury, the Indian Empire was administered by men who knew each other and strove together in the friendly spirit of the cock-house football match. They trusted each other and worked for the Company, the Queen, the team, what you will, but not exclusively for themselves. No doubt the close ties Haileybury knit were useful while the empire was expanding, but perhaps the work of the college was done by the middle of the century; perhaps in the second part of the century a less exclusive, a more open-minded, ruling caste was needed.

The course should have been longer, three years at least. Far too much was crowded into two years. And certainly the professors might have done much more to interest the students in the life they were to lead and the work they were to do. But the best men always spoke with respect of the mental training they had had at Haileybury, far wider, most of them believed, than they would have been given anywhere else, while Haileybury men, in spite of their clannishness had a remarkably detached point of view when they arrived in India.

Coming from comfortable homes, most of them connected with the Directors of the Company, most of them were found to be on the side of the tiller of the soil, surprisingly few believed in supporting an enlightened aristocracy who were supposed to look after the peasant and whose interests would coincide with those of the Government. And it is by the outlook in India of Haileybury men that Haileybury must be judged.

3 Thomason and the North-West

Even before Haileybury began, there was a spirit among the men who ruled India which survived till the end.

It is not easy to define. Their profession encouraged idiosyncracies because it put them where they were alone among men of an alien race, isolated by religion, food, custom and above all by responsibility. There were men among them who were industrious, men who were idle, men devout and men indifferent, bent scholars in Sanskrit and cheerful sunburnt men whose leisure was spent shooting tigers and spearing hogs.

Charles Trevelyan, brother-in-law of Macaulay and grandfather of George Macaulay Trevelyan the historian, 'was an Indian civilian through and through'. He became Governor of Madras.

But there was in them all a combination of two qualities usually antagonistic.

There is a consciousness that they have a great task and that they belong to a service. But there is also an independence of outlook, a readiness to criticize and to state an opinion, however unfavourable to authority. There are always one or two who are permanently in opposition, sharply critical; the staidest pillars of the regime are sometimes in disagreement and usually say what they think.

One side of the coin was put clearly by W.S. Seton-Kerr, speaking in 1864 about the new men, the competition-wallahs, who were replacing the Haileybury men. He had won prizes at Haileybury and done well in India. 'We shall be content', he said, 'to be far surpassed in talent if we are only equalled in integrity and honour. I trust . . . that from the first they will act steadily on the sure and simple maxim that we are bound to govern India in trust for the natives and for India itself.'

Already, then, they were a caste of guardians, of trustees. But they were individualists and usually ready to speak up against injustice. Charles Edward Trevelyan, for instance, went his own way all his life. In India, he began by discovering that his immediate chief was corrupt. He exposed him; he stuck to his guns through the long dreary inquiries that followed; the man was removed from the service. Trevelyan became Metcalfe's favourite assistant, he was Secretary to the Board of Revenue; later he became Assistant Secretary to the Treasury in London and came back to India as Governor of Madras. He married Macaulay's beloved sister Hannah and was the father of George Otto Trevelyan, and the grandfather of George Macaulay Trevelyan.

Charles was an Indian civilian through and through. He adopted certain pet reforms and worked until his views were heard. He was the father of free trade within India; he worked all his life for the education of Indians; not being able to persuade the authorities to pay for an improvement in the street planning of Delhi, he paid for it himself and the area became Trevelyanpur. He was also 'a great master in the most exciting and perilous of field sports, the spearing of wild boars . . .' But he had no small talk 'even in courtship'; his mind was full of schemes, wrote Macaulay.

Trevelyan, however, carried his independence too far when he was Governor of Madras; he disapproved of the financial reforms which the Government of India was about to introduce and said so; it became necessary to recall him.

There is intellectual detachment, too, though of quite a different kind, in the attitude of a more typical man, Samuel Wauchope, who became the special commissioner in Bengal for the suppression of dacoity – that is, robbery by gangs. On a man being brought before him who was accused of dacoity, Mr Wauchope 'heard him out and then laughingly replied that the story was doubtless a very good one but that it was not good enough for him'. He went on to mention that this same man had been arrested under another name in such a district, under a third name in a third district, that his real name was yet a fourth and the nickname used in the gang to distinguish him from another dacoit was a fifth – 'and by that nickname Mr Wauchope called him'. At this the man confessed all: what he found most frightening and surprising was perhaps less the knowledge than the laughing detachment with which it was displayed.

Independence and detachment of outlook were then the distinguishing qualities of the Company's civil servants. Independence of outlook does not usually occur without some material security; by now the Company's civil servants were reasonably well provided for, the young civilian being already, as mammas told their daughters, a match worth 'three hundred a year alive or dead'. An annuity scheme had been introduced; when he retired, with twenty-five years' service, the Company would buy him an annuity of £1,000 a year. And his widow would be entitled to the celebrated three hundred. Everyone, then, was comfortably provided for, no one would be turned out of the service except for grave misconduct, incontrovertibly proved; men could afford to speak their minds.

There seem also to have been rebels in almost every generation who expressed opinions critical of the regime. F.J. Shore, the son of Sir John Shore, was such a rebel. He had twenty years' service when his papers were printed in book form in London in 1837 over his own name.

There are about fifty articles of varying length. 'Suppose a few African merchants received permission from the English government to erect a factory somewhere on the South Coast of England,' Shore begins and it is clear at once how the argument is going to develop; the Africans gradually get possession of the whole country, they decide that the English are never to be trusted, that the Africans are the only people fit for the higher posts.

Shore does it very well; he assailed the whole system that existed before 1833, when some of his criticisms were met; but his sharpest language occurs when he is assailing the boorishness of those who display contempt for a man because of his colour. It was the more wounding because Indians themselves attach such importance to shades of complexion.

What Shore attacked is hateful, and no honest person could deny that it existed throughout the whole time the English were in India. Shore gives the impression that consideration and good manners to Indians were in his day the exception; from Bishop Heber, on the other hand, one would gather that, at least among the Company's civil servants, it was bad manners that were the exception. The truth, no doubt, is that on the whole bad manners were due to ignorance and that as a rule British soldiers, subalterns in royal regiments on first arrival, and Calcutta traders were the worst offenders because they knew the least. Shore speaks of young officers using such expressions as: 'I hate the natives,' or 'I like to beat a black fellow,' which they would certainly not have dared to do in the presence of Malcolm or Elphinstone; nor can one imagine such words used before Bird, Thomason, Trevelyan, or the Lawrences. The odious thing seems on the whole to have been rather worse in the 1840s and 1850s than in the 1820s and 1830s, perhaps because the Company's position was growing steadily stronger; perhaps because the English were becoming intoxicated by power. But a deeper reason was perhaps a dislike among the less educated English for the official doctrine of trusteeship and jealousy of the increasing education and employment of Indians.

The point for the moment, however, is that Shore said what he thought and criticized every aspect of English rule. He wanted smaller districts, with one Englishman to supervise and inspect a number of courts in which Indians would preside; he wanted every Englishman to know more of the language and customs of the people and the idlest to work as hard as the most conscientious; he wanted more employment and better pay for Indians. Munro, Malcolm, Elphinstone and Metcalfe agreed with all these points and the Act of 1833 went far to meet them.

Akbar had seen that the problem for any ruler of India was to settle what was the King's share of the produce of the soil, to take enough to provide a solvent Treasury, to leave in the peasant's hands enough to keep him on the land, at work and reasonably content. The English in Bengal had seen the same and they too had put land revenue first. Like Akbar, the English needed money; like Akbar, they perceived that a ruined land was against their true interest. But they were puzzled; they could not find an *owner* of the land. They decided that he who paid the revenue was the owner.

This caused some injustice in Bengal; it was worse when English rule spread to the North-Western Provinces, later the United Provinces. Here there seem to have been three main kinds of injustice unwittingly done by the English.

Sometimes an Indian subordinate would pocket the Land Revenue which a man had regularly paid, write him down a defaulter, cause his lands to be sold and buy them himself, through a cousin or connexion.

Another was even simpler. Low-paid Indian officials were sent out with instructions to write down both the owner of the land and the contractor who actually collected the revenue from the tiller of the soil. But here there was no contractor. A man collected from his own peasants. 'Are you the one who collects the dues?' was all that Nasar Ali would ask. 'Yes?' And down would go the name in column two – 'contractor'. The first column where the owner's name should be, would be blank for a year or two and then unobtrusively a new name would appear but no one in the village would see the owner or know of his existence. Then Nasar Ali would retire and soon afterwards the fictitious owner by a deed of gift would transfer the village to Nasar Ali.

Much the same thing would happen where there had been a brotherhood holding the village jointly. Their names would go down as cultivators and no more; for years they would know nothing of how they had been entered. Then one day they would discover that there was a name in the first column, the name of someone they had never heard of, who had become their overlord and the owner of land that had always been theirs.

All this happened to a people who were simple and illiterate, who had been used to expect very little of either Heaven or man. They did not think it was any use complaining and they usually said nothing.

There were three preliminary attempts at a settlement – but the old records were misleading, the new subordinate officials were untrained, there were not enough reliable supervisors. Newnham, however, Collector of Cawnpore in 1813, sent in many reports of careful inquiries into injustice. They were not, however, easy to put right. It was easier to go by the record.

Four years later in 1817, Mr Robertson, as Judge of Cawnpore, gave a number of decisions against the records and in favour of men he thought wronged. But the Court of Appeal reversed his decisions one after another. They had nothing solid to go on but the records. Robertson, however, a man 'with an eager sense of justice', wrote – irregularly – direct to the Government and a Commission was appointed to inquire into all transfers of property during the first ten years of British rule. It was not easy to put things back as they had been but the principles for a new settlement were clearly stated in the Commission's report in 1822 and were never to be substantially changed.

It was in 1832 under Robert Merttins Bird that the great settlement of the North-West began. It was to last in each district for thirty years, when it would be revised. Bird carried out between 1833 and 1840 operations which affected twenty-three million people in an area about the size of England. He was not only to settle what was the King's share but to decide where the boundaries lay between one village and the next; to define and record all the various rights of all who hold land; to prepare a record of the fields and of the rights of every cultivator; to reform the village accounts; and to provide a 'system of self-government for the communities'.

What was new about Bird's work was the method and the speed with which it was done. The *patwari*, the village accountant, now became a government servant. His records were taken as a starting point by the staff of the settlement officer, who made a new record. The new record was checked by the assistant settlement officer; and every villager was given an opportunity to see it or ask questions about it; if he objected to anything he could file a complaint without cost. A percentage of the entries was checked by the settlement officer himself.

Sleeman wrote only a few years earlier that 'we might almost as well attempt to map the waves of the ocean as field-map the face of any considerable area in any part of India'. But this is what Bird did in the North-Western Provinces. A trigonometrical survey fixed certain points, from those points there spread a simpler field survey by triangulation, a system for which the only essential instruments are a measuring chain and a pair of compasses. I have made maps with it myself and within a village it is astonishingly accurate.

At one stage it looked as though the survey would have to be given up as too slow and expensive. Bird had a conference with Henry Lawrence, one of his surveyors; Lawrence asked for an increase in his low-paid staff, whom he would train and with whom he would undertake to survey 3,000 square miles in a season instead of one thousand. So the speed was trebled at a trifling extra cost.

The survey and the field maps Bird completed; he made a record of the rights he believed to exist which was a great advance on anything there had ever been before. But he was not entirely successful in settling what share of the produce of the soil should be the King's. It had always been the intention to settle 'leniently', and it was assumed that the cultivator needed about half the produce of the soil to feed himself and meet his expenses. If the King's share was fixed at a third, a sixth would be left for the zamindar. This was lenient, by Mogul standards. But English collections were much more regular than in Mogul days. Bird found an assessment that was too high and managed to lower it. But he was not allowed to go far enough. The assessment of what the land could pay and the proportion taken − one-third of the whole − were both still too high. The proportion was reduced in the 1850s by John Russell Colvin to one-quarter of the whole; it came down eventually to one-sixth.

On the other hand, waste land brought into cultivation after the settlement paid no revenue for thirty years and this was generally enough to make the settlement a fair one. It was too high to start with but, on the whole, it worked. And it would be hard to exaggerate the effect it had of producing a peaceful and law-abiding population. Men for the first time had some confidence in the future.

Bird directed this settlement but he could not be in every district at once; he worked through district officers and settlement officers. He chose young men. 'Where he reposed his confidence, he did so without reserve. He received the opinions of those employed under him with respect; looked after their interests, defended their proceedings and fought their battles as if they had been his own.' His young men speak of him each 'with the faith of a disciple and the love of a son, and seldom mention his name without an inward genuflexion'.

It was Bird more than anyone who made the post of settlement officer what it became. There were long hours of work, there were long months in camp. But disputes were decided before a settlement officer without cost; there were no court fees, no pleaders, no recording of evidence and no expensive witnesses, no underlings to be tipped. The whole affair was decided after discussion with both parties in the presence of the villagers.

Almost every settlement officer found that his heart went with his labours. Many a man kept till his death the settlement report that he wrote

James Thomason: he died in 1852 while still in office as Lieutenant-Governor of the North-Western Provinces, but before that he had mapped and settled the taxation of this great area and 'improved every branch of the administration'.

in his thirties, a printed volume as long as an ordinary novel, even without the tables of crops, soils and percentages. But his heart would be in the introduction, describing in loving terms the country and people where he had been so happy, turning joyously aside into long dissertations on race, language and custom, dwelling on the angle of a jaw-bone, on a phrase or rite recalling Homer or the Bible.

This is a simplified account of what happened in the plains of the North-Western Provinces. In the hills – Mr Traill's hills – settlement was with the village brotherhood in its purest form. In Madras and Bombay, thanks to Munro, it was direct with the peasant; in Bengal it was with the zamindar, which there meant a large landowner. Behar was still part of Bengal and in the whole of Bengal the settlement was permanent while in the North-West it was for thirty years. There were a hundred local variations, but they could all be described in terms of difference from the North-West.

James Thomason, who succeeded Bird in charge of the settlement operations, was at first employed in or near Calcutta; he was a secretary to government before he had been ten years in the country. But he decided that he must know for himself what happened in a district; he resigned his secretarial appointment and the flesh-pots of Calcutta and went to be Magistrate, Collector, Opium Agent and Settlement Officer of Azamgarh, which is about a hundred miles from Benares.

Every man loves the first district in which he serves and the first of which he has charge; with Thomason, the two were one, for he learnt his district work as head of the district. He was happy in his married life in Azamgarh, almost for the last time, for his wife died not long afterwards, he was six months in camp every year, hard at work on his settlement. Many years later, he wrote: 'Hurrah, hurrah, for old Azamgarh!'

Thomason succeeded Bird in charge of settlement affairs; he went on to be Lieutenant-Governor of the North-West Provinces; he was ten years Lieutenant-Governor, dying suddenly while still in office at Bareilly in 1852. He was worn out, worked to death.

Thomason belongs to another generation than the great quartet and in nothing more clearly than in his religion. To Munro, Malcolm, Elphinstone and Metcalfe, each in his own way, religion was a private view of the universe, essentially undogmatic. They belonged to the eighteenth century. But Thomason and those who followed him were evangelical; their doctrine was explicit and exclusive; there was one truth only, eternally revealed; it was a matter of intense conviction, never far from the conscious mind. Thomason did not read Theocritus but Hooker and Jeremy Taylor; he read sermons. Convinced that the secular power must not be used for the spread of Christianity, he still always felt his conscience challenged by the millions of heathen who surrounded him.

Religion is the mainspring of all he did. Thomason was delicate, very tall but slight, and his back had been injured in a riding accident when he was still young. He had none of Malcolm's abounding physical energy; it was a belief in God's purpose and a sense of his duty to God that drove him to wear himself out.

Thomason lost his wife before he became Lieutenant-Governor; all seem to have been impressed by his selflessness and by that tenderness for others that sometimes follows loss. He carried it into official work; everyone felt that his own special interest was Thomason's. He was the father of public works, in particular the Grand Trunk Road, the Ganges Canal, and the Engineering College at Roorkee which still bears his name.

He was continually travelling about his province; every officer was aware of a friendly personal interest and an acute knowledge of every detail of a district officer's work. His praise was generous and his condemnation was felt to be deserved; he knew exactly what were the special interests and what was the right post for each officer. His success as a trainer received painful recognition; when the last great wave of conquest took the English forward into the Punjab, it was to Thomason that the rulers of the Punjab turned for men. They took nineteen of his best.

He improved every branch of the administration; to him, however, the first was that which had always been first with every great Indian ruler, the settlement of the land revenue.

The tenure of land and collection of land revenue is a subject obscure, technical, fascinating to a few, of vital importance to millions. Thomason made the principles clear. His instructions remained the handbook for settlement officers for many years and was the basis for all later work; it was possible even in the Punjab to start where Thomason left off. In a settlement, he wrote, there are two tasks, one administrative, to decide how much the King should take, the other judicial, to make a record of rights. And bringing the record of rights a little nearer perfection was made by Thomason a continuous process. He believed that nothing else, except a just assessment, would contribute so much to the happiness of the people; it was one of his main objects, always in the forefront of his mind, clear in the forefront of his instructions to Collectors.

Thomason's work continued Bird's; it was not final, it was still far from perfect, as both knew. 'How far short have I fallen in the fulfilment of God's will . . .' But in the fifty years between the British entry into the North-Western Provinces and Thomason's death at Bareilly – just the length of Akbar's reign – land tenures that were in a state of chaos had been analysed and sorted; there was to be no more argument about principles or definitions. A field by field survey had been made and against every field had been entered the name of the cultivator, the crop sown, the rent paid, and the name of the person, or more usually group of persons, who took the rent and paid the Land Revenue. The village rights and customs had been put in writing. As well attempt to map the waves of the ocean, Sleeman had written, but it had been done, at least over one great arm of the sea and the network was spreading over the whole.

Mrs Moss-King's sketch of Robert Moss-King's camp in Gonda (Eastern U.P.), 1875.

10

BEFORE THE DELUGE

―――――◇―――――

1 The First Half of the Century

By 1842, the map has changed since 1798. Up to the Sutlej, there is either
the red of British districts or the lumps of undigested pink which stand for
protected states. Beyond the Sutlej lies the Sikh empire. Ranjit Singh had
begun as the chief of one of the many warring clans which one by one he
had overcome, by battle, cunning or bribery, until his empire stretched
from the Khyber to the Sutlej and northwards over Kashmir. The Sikhs
are a sect of reformed Hinduism; they profess a rule of life which rejects
the many castes and the many gods of the Hindus, but Sikhism is a
military order as much as a religion. It is the nature of the Sikhs to fight;
they had fought the Moguls at first and latterly they had fought each other
with almost as much enthusiasm. Ranjit Singh brought them together and
held them together but, when he died in 1839, the Punjab began to seethe
and boil; soon it would boil over and there would be war. For the moment,
the disintegrating empire of Ranjit Singh confronted across the Sutlej the
new empire of the English.

This empire, an agglomerate mass of districts directly ruled and states
indirectly guided, was governed by three groups of Englishmen who were
chosen in three different ways. There were less than a dozen in the top
posts who came to India for the first time in middle life after a moderately
successful career in England. The rest of the rulers, who did not yet
number a thousand, were either civil servants of the Company, usually
educated at Haileybury, or had been educated at Addiscombe, Haileybury's military counterpart, had come to India as young officers in the
army and had then been specially selected for civil employment.

Those who began as soldiers supplied most of the men employed in the
States on semi-diplomatic duties and most of the men for special tasks,
such as the suppression of Thuggee. There was as yet no separate police
service and there were barely enough trained civilians for the regular posts

135

as district officers, judges and secretaries, so that for any special task it was a matter of downright necessity to call on the army. The soldiers strike one as less liable than the pure-bred civilians to fall into a rut or become pedantic; perhaps fewer of them took the broad detached view that was common to the best of both kinds. Neither side could claim a monopoly of courage or ability, of hard work or devotion to duty.

The civilian spent much of his early life alone. The soldier did not as a rule come to civil employment till he was older; his youth had been passed more gregariously, he was more used to society and as a rule better versed in the agreeable art of talking about nothing without embarrassment or fatigue.

The civilian was encouraged from the first in a sturdy independence. No Colonel would see that he did not run into debt; no one would guide him in the first case he tried. He would simply be told to try it, with no more help than the law he had learnt at Haileybury, the Hindustani he had picked up at Fort William, and an Indian clerk who spoke no English. That first case would be a slow and puzzled affair; the wretched litigants would be kept at headquarters while the young man slowly mangled his way through evidence that two years later would not keep him an hour. It is a slow way to learn, but perhaps the best. It taught not only the way to try a case but a sovereign contempt for all professional mysteries. It had been said of the eighteenth-century civilians in Madras that 'no member of Council would hesitate, at a pinch, to take command of a company of foot, to read a sermon, or administer a dose of physic'. That was still true of almost everyone in the service, but to the list should now be added: 'to lay out a road or a canal, design a jail or build a house'. Every district officer was his own engineer as well as his own policeman.

The idea that personal power can be limited by law was still strange to India; the English had brought the idea with them but they compromised with the oriental; they modified the rule of law by a kindly personal despotism. Even in the twentieth century there was to be one district officer who after carefully reading through a new Act was to write decisively in the margin: 'This Act will not apply in this District.' And it did not.

The district officer then was accustomed to give orders. Not so the political officer, whose more difficult task was to keep his head among the splendours and the barbarities of an oriental court; to judge when he must, and how far he might, interfere; to persuade and advise, to know when to ignore and when to stand firm and not budge. Tod of Rajputana achieved such influence that many of the rulers of Rajputana would ask him, as a friend, to adjudicate in disputes as though he was the Raja himself.

Tod felt for the Rajputs an affection and an admiration that were far from unusual; he was in fact only one of the many Englishmen who have given a generous championship to the people in whose country they have served.

Troops in those days were more widely scattered than later; at the headquarters of even quite small districts there might be a company of native infantry; at the headquarters of the larger districts there would almost certainly be at least a battalion. The social life of the Company's servants in such places was very like small town life in England, but more isolated. It would be seventy, eighty or a hundred miles to the next station; the railway was being talked of in the 1850s – indeed, work had begun – but in Northern India, travel was mainly by horse-drawn vehicle, though palankeens were still used at night. There were transport agencies which arranged stages. It was known as 'travelling dawk'. The stages were nine or ten miles; you might get through to the next station in a day, 'travelling dawk', but it would be a day of discomfort.

For a longer journey, those who valued their comfort travelled in their own carriage with riding horses in attendance to vary the monotony. Charles Crawford Parks was posted in 1826 from Calcutta to Allahabad; he had never before been away from Calcutta and he and his wife felt a good deal of trepidation about the move. However, they started on November 22; they travelled about fifteen miles a day and reached Benares, some four hundred miles from Calcutta, five weeks later on Christmas Day.

It is Fanny who leaves an account of the march; the journal she wrote for her mother, with sketches, paintings, recipes, oriental proverbs, accounts of suttees and of visits to the *zenana*, is the cream of all such books. Charles emerges as a placid figure, intelligent but not ambitious, regarding with mild amusement the enthusiasms of his wife, as she turns from Hindu mythology and Persian proverbs to the draping of a *sari*, from botany to ice-making or the strange ways of the servants.

'Our marching establishment consisted of two good mares for the Stanhope, two fine saddle Arabs for ourselves, two ponies, and nine hackeries [bullock-carts] which contained supplies and clothes, also a number of goats . . . We travelled by the Grand Military Road, riding the first part of the stage and finishing it in . . . the Stanhope.' The heavy luggage went by boat up the Ganges.

They travelled in the early morning, resting in the middle of the day at a dak bungalow. 'They are built by government and are all on the same plan; at each a *khidmutgar* [a man who waits at table] and a bearer are in attendance.' In the evening, Charles took out his gun after quail and partridge, snipe and pigeon; Fanny as a rule went too and 'enjoyed it very much'. A horse runs away from a bear sleeping in the road; a servant at a dak bungalow steals a silver spoon; there are suttee-tombs and temples; it is all interesting. There are *fakirs* with withered arms and nails growing through the backs of their hands – but Fanny is an expert in religious mendicants; she finds out all about everything she sees.

At such places as Allahabad, Benares, or Bareilly, there would be Assembly Rooms, where sometimes there would be dances and private

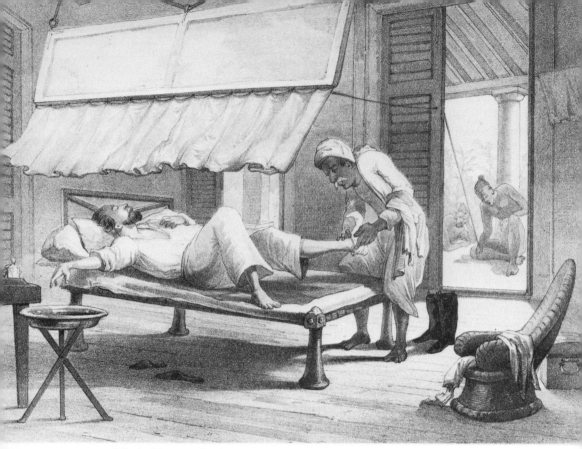

'The bed is a wooden framework on four legs'; everything in the bedroom is severely functional but there is a man to take off your socks! And another to pull the cooling punkah. Kipling has a story of a bull-terrier who growled in the punkah man's ear if he fell asleep.

theatricals. In the smaller stations these festivities would occur less often, while where there were no troops of course they were out of the question. That meant in about half the districts where a civilian might be sent; the soldier's small station is large to the civilian. In a station small by civilian standards there would be the Judge, the Collector, who was also the Magistrate, his junior the Joint Magistrate, a doctor — and that would be all. The engineer and the policeman were still to come; the Collector performed their functions himself. The padre would come perhaps once a month, but those four would be the station. It was necessary to endure each other, even in the hot weather.

Curry and Rice is a satirical picture of a medium station, first published in 1854; the drawings are better than the text, and the people in it are types, but they are well-chosen. The judge, old-fashioned in his clothes and untidy, is 'so desperately absorbed with his official duties that we see but little of him'; he plays the violoncello in a quartet — his only recreation; he has been in India thirty-two years and does not want to go back to England at all. But he is hospitable and kind to subalterns; everyone likes him.

The Collector, too, talks shop; give him a chance and he will lecture on 'settlements – revenues – land-tax – decrees – jails – crops – remissions – duties – salt – police –' and much more. He is rather dull – but 'his Moselle is sparkling and light'. The Joint Magistrate, his junior, fancies himself as a sporting man and is knowing about horses and dogs; 'he is a bit of a dandy, curls his hair, cherishes the rudiments of a moustache'; he listens to complaints with the *Delhi Gazette* in his hand, he has a poor opinion of his seniors; 'nothing comes amiss to him . . . he would with equal willingness preach an extempore sermon at a moment's notice, undertake a Protestant discussion with the Pope and all his Cardinals, or with equal promptitude and despatch, prepare a work for the press on heresy and schism, heavy gun drill and the plurality of worlds'.

As to the women, it was true that many had not enough to do because their interests were trivial. There were not many who were as unfailingly busy as Fanny Parks, preserving the skins of birds and setting butterflies; keeping up her archery and riding; making vocabularies from the thieves' slang of the Thugs, sketching and learning to play Indian musical instruments. Her only complaint was that she was far too often interrupted by eruptions from the farmyard and disputes among the servants, but

The Judge's Wife. The lady makes the most of her tasks, measuring out, and locking up; the servants obey her, in patient deep disdain.

she had brought this on herself by learning the language.

Bungalows up the country were more elaborate than the thatched tents run aground of Roberdeau's day. The most common kind was a square building, with a deep veranda on each side; it had a central room, with a dining-room and three or four bedrooms opening on to the verandas. In the hot dry months, the house became a fort against the sun, every opening closed; outside there were half-a-dozen coolies, almost naked, drowsily throwing water on screens of scented grass, or pulling the cord of the swaying punkah.

In the Joint Magistrate's house or the bungalow shared by four subal-terns near the mess – the bachelors' quarters – everything is severely functional: half-a-dozen hammock-like chairs with arm-pieces prolonged so that weary legs can be propped up on them; perhaps a tiger-skin, a few panther-skins on the floor, a few antlers on the wall, a rack of hog-spears. The bed is a wooden frame on four legs, with no headboard or footboard, strung with coarse tape. There is no mattress, but a cool reed mat to lie on; a brass bowl on three bamboos, a metal uniform case and a wooden chest bound with metal, a folding table, a straw chair, a small mirror – that is the bedroom furniture. No pictures, no curtains, no drawers, bare whitewashed walls; a striped cotton mat on the brick floor.

The Parks at Allahabad had fifty-seven regular servants besides twelve or fourteen extra in the hottest weather for punkahs and keeping moist the grass screens. The list includes a man to wash and another to iron; two tailors; a lady's maid and assistant; eight bearers, originally meant to carry the palankeen, but since palankeens are now seldom used, one is a valet and the rest dust the furniture and pull the punkahs. There is a cowman, a shepherd, and a man who looks after 'the fowls, wild ducks, quail, rabbits, guinea-fowl and pigeons'; a gardener and two assistants; a coachman, eight grooms, eight grass-cutters, and a woman to grind grain for the horses. There are even two carpenters on the permanent establishment; the total of fifty-seven cost about two hundred and ninety pounds a year.

Take it for all in all, it is a life which to English eyes was a strange mixture of inconvenience with luxury. Luxury no doubt for a man to have the socks rolled on the feet with no effort on his own part, for a woman to have her hair brushed for half an hour every evening; but was it worth the dust, the cholera, the lack of privacy, the heat and its effects? Even Fanny Parks sometimes thought it was not.

But a good deal had been done in the half-century. Immense territories had been assimilated and were no longer preyed on by bands of roving horsemen; suttee was forbidden, Thuggee finished, gang-robbery reduced. The peasant knew what he had to pay. And the Company was no longer a group of traders but a corporation for the purpose of governing India under the direction of Parliament; they had lost their monopoly of trade in 1813 and in 1833 ceased altogether to be a trading concern.

Something else of great consequence had happened in 1833. The policy of employing Indians in positions of trust had been proclaimed as a matter of principle. Cornwallis had tried to exclude all Indians from positions of responsibility but it was impossible. In a minute of November 5, 1829, Butterworth Bayley pointed out that of every twenty original suits instituted in civil courts, nineteen were settled by Indian officers. Now the facts were admitted and the policy announced of associating Indians with Englishmen in an administration based on English law.

The positions that Indians were now to hold were responsible and important although subject always to supervision. Civil causes were now tried in the first place by *Munsifs*, that is, subordinate Indian judges of various grades; in the North-Western Provinces in 1849, over forty-five thousand suits were tried in the first instance by Munsifs, only twenty by European judges.

This was for civil disputes, that is suits about property. Indians were not yet judges in criminal cases, but as deputy magistrates they might have power to sentence to three years' imprisonment, which was the limit of the Englishmen's powers as a magistrate too. But there was no question yet of equality; they could not be members of the covenanted service.

It was once customary to extol British justice as a priceless gift to India; recently it has become the fashion to write of it with disparagement. Both views are one-sided. There was almost universal relief in the early days of British rule when peace and order replaced anarchy; there was nothing but praise for the suppression of the Thugs and the reduction of gang-robbery. That feeling of relief, understandably, wore away; the dissatisfaction that gradually took its place had not much to do with modern liberal values. Mogul justice had had its admirers. Its methods are illustrated by a tale told by Bernier in the seventeenth century. He called on a Mogul officer whom he already regarded as a friend. Two criminals were brought in. The officer at first took no notice but after some time, he raised his head and addressed them each with a simple statement of fact: 'You committed highway robbery with violence at such a place on such a date.' There was a pause but no reply. One was sentenced to have his hands and feet lopped off, the other to be disembowelled, both to be left in a public place to bleed to death. They were taken away, dictation continued.

This kind of justice was admired because people felt so strongly the need for public order. When the English first came, their methods were usually milder than the Mogul's but less intermittent, swift enough and sufficiently informal. An inquiry was held, usually in the village of the crime; it was held by the ruler – the Indian word means the man who gives orders. When he was satisfied, he gave an order and it was carried out. There was not much dissatisfaction in those first years with British criminal justice.

But in the regulation districts – the older acquisitions – criminal justice had already grown formal; there were lawyers and men were encouraged to plead innocent even when everyone knew they were guilty; gradually the business of producing witnesses had become a contest, a trial of strength and cunning between the police and the friends of the accused.

At first there was no time to deal with cases properly. This was largely because insufficient use was made of Indian magistrates. From 1833 onwards, however, there was a great improvement in criminal justice and most people acquainted with the working of criminal justice in India would agree that in the great majority of cases the person prosecuted actually was guilty. In more than half the cases prosecuted he would be found guilty, while not once in ten cases was an innocent person convicted. This was much better than anything that had happened before.

There were also private prosecutions, often hardly criminal at all; a man does not become a criminal because he has a quarrel with a neighbour over cattle straying into his sugar-cane. From the start, far more of them might well have been left to village committees – as Munro had hoped they would be.

Roads were in their infancy, but palankeens were giving place to wheeled vehicles and progress was being made. The next few years were to show great advances – the Grand Trunk Road from Calcutta to Peshawar; the Bombay-Agra road; the Bombay-Calcutta road – over three thousand miles of metalled surface, a thing new to India, all these were in progress.

Canals for irrigation were needed even more than roads; canals could reduce the area of a famine; roads and railway could bring grain from outside. Now the Western Jumna Canal, four hundred and fifty miles long, was watering five thousand villages, the smaller Eastern Jumna was complete, and work was in progress on the Ganges Canal, which was to be twice the length of the Western Jumna and irrigate four times the area. When the Ganges canal was finished the system would be the most extensive in the world.

But in spite of progress it is no use pretending that the Government of the Company was liked. Sleeman believed the Indian States should always be kept in existence; the contrast between their ill-government and the orderly administration of British India would serve as a reminder of past anarchy. But few people are governed by reason. As soon as they had forgotten the bad old days, men in the British districts began to look regretfully across the border at the turbulence, the confusion and the excitement of the State. They found life dull in British India, where the Company provided no fireworks and no sanguinary contests between wild beasts, where the business of collecting revenue was a dull monotonous grind. In a State, revenue collection combined the excitement of a sweepstake in reverse and a bullfight in a small Spanish town. The demands of the revenue collector would be resisted, often with loss of life; nothing was predictable and it was all much more fun.

Most Indians would agree that there had been progress in the half century; but no Indian, surely, could fail to be aware of something a little chill and clammy near his heart when he regarded the conquerors who were bringing his countrymen so marked a progress in things they would hardly have chosen for themselves. The colour and danger of the old fierce, merciless India, the intoxicating possibility of jewels and slave-girls beyond counting one day and on the next of death, pashed to bloody rags at the feet of an elephant – all this was being filmed over by a viscous monotony of precedents, regulations and law suits.

And there was a deep and subtle danger in the attitude of his new rulers to himself. The great Englishmen of the last century had taken the country, its people and their ways with a noble openness of mind; Warren Hastings had been content 'to leave their religious creed to the Being who has so long endured it and who will in his own time reform it'. That could not be the attitude of Thomason. Honoria Lawrence, a woman whose human love was deep, whose religion was warm, ever-present and living, spoke for the best men of her generation when she wrote: 'There is something very oppressive in being surrounded by heathen and Mahommedan darkness, in seeing idolworship all around.'

No doubt there were still many district officers who talked to the peasant as easily as Sleeman did, to the Raja as frankly as Tod; but it is hard to believe there can be real freedom of talk between those they regarded as pagan and men who were so sure of the truth as Thomason and Henry Lawrence. And if there seems a coldness in the attitude to Indians even of men so great as these were – men whose lives were literally given up to service and who fervently believed that all they did was for the good of Indians – it is not surprising that something worse should have arisen among lesser men, that there should have been people who talked about niggers and danced quadrilles on the platform before the Taj Mahal. But among these I do not think there were many civil servants of the Company.

In the 1840s, then, an observer from another planet, looking at the settled districts, might have been inclined to suppose that an alien, bureaucratic greyness was settling on the gorgeous Orient, that revolution and cataclysm were over. But if he looked forward to the frontier and forward in time, he would see at once that nothing could be further from the truth.

2 The Titans of the Punjab

Now comes a time of swift heroic action. It is the decade and a half of the Sikh wars and the Mutiny, when Titans move in the North-West of India, when two or three dozen men toil with fierce nervous energy at tasks more than mortal.

Speed and an unnatural tension are the notes of all they do; there is no pause for rest, no thought of ease, no time now for such prophetic meditation as had nourished Elphinstone. All is struck off at white heat. 'His mind and body', wrote Kavanagh of Henry Lawrence, 'were always in a state of tension and both alike were denied proper rest.' 'We have agreed', wrote John Lawrence, 'not to recommend any leave unless men are sick. Every day is of value and the best officer cannot work too hard or too long.'

These men were enlisted in a Holy War, fighting beneath the watchful eye of a Heavenly King. Theirs was a simple faith; they did not ask questions. They did not doubt that the hand of God sustained them in all they did. To Edwardes, the Mutiny seemed a national punishment because the English had withheld Christian principles from the people. 'It was not policy', wrote Montgomery, 'that saved the Indian Empire to England and England to India. The Lord our God, He it was.'

These men of more than mortal stature were knit together by their work, by their fierce restraint and by their puritanical religion. 'What a loss have we sustained in our ever dear friend [Sir Henry Lawrence] ...' wrote Edwardes to Nicholson, 'how his great purposes and fiery will and generous impulses and strong passions raged in him ...' 'Tell him I love him as dearly as if he were my son,' said Honoria Lawrence to her husband of John Nicholson as she lay dying.

Few of these men were married; they speak constantly of their mothers in terms as emotional as they use of their religion. Passion blazed in them and was harnessed to work and to bodily rigour. Marriage before middle-age was an infidelity. Still, there *were* marriages; there were deaths too among the wives and many among the children. A woman who married into the Punjab Commission had taken a step as decisive as entering a convent. She and her children became camp equipment, jolted in bullock-carts and on the backs of camels, exposed to dust, sun, heat, cholera, malaria, moving always from tent to bungalow and back again, gypsies without a home beneath the stars. They must expect hard wear and a short life and in the end, if they survived, years of deadening, anxious separation.

No doubt they were hard men to live with, sometimes a torture to themselves and to those near them. But they were dynamic; there is a size and force to them. Without their taut strung emotions they would not have achieved what they did. What that was can perhaps never wholly be understood because there was something about it miraculous. Even an imperfect understanding is only possible against the swiftly-moving political events which began with Lord Auckland's unrighteous Afghan War of 1839 and did not end till the Queen's proclamation after the Mutiny.

The Afghans rose and drove the English back from Kabul and for a little it seemed as though the star of the Company had set. The effect of the disaster, in a land so ruled by the stars and by the concept of *iqbal* –

8 above, *Procession of an Indian Prince. It is a religious procession but the Residency staff attend; by the middle of the century there were those who thought the Government should not give any countenance to the heathen;* 9 below, *A Nautch Party – dancing girls and musicians – performing in a European mansion c. 1820. This became less and less common as the nineteenth century wore on. But officers would go to see a nautch party arranged by soldiers or police.*

10 above, *Cornwallis's army on the march in 1791 during the Third Mysore War. The mountains rising suddenly from the plain were a feature of all the wars in the South;* 11 below, *The Roorkee Aqueduct, part of the headworks of the Ganges Canal, which in 1854 completed the most extensive irrigation network in the world.*

Sir Charles Napier, the conqueror of Sind, 'rough-tongued and hot-tempered, dogmatic, cynical, shrewd and honest'.

predestined good fortune – can hardly be exaggerated. Pollock carried British arms to Kabul – but they were then withdrawn. The plain fact was that the English had failed to do what they set out to do.

The Kabul war came to an end and Lord Ellenborough annexed Sind, in the mood, said Elphinstone, of 'a bully who has been kicked in the streets and goes home to beat his wife in revenge'. The conqueror himself, Sir Charles Napier, rough-tongued and hot-tempered, dogmatic, cynical, shrewd and honest, a man who put an edge on all he said, called the annexation 'a very advantageous, useful, humane piece of rascality'. He was right; its only justification was the belief that the inhabitants would be better off under British rule than under their Amirs. Henry Lawrence, Outram, all the best servants of the Company in India, considered it unjust.

Napier wanted the people's welfare and could not bear to wait for it. He wanted swift justice – and his subjects got it. He would have no red tape or formalities, and he had a gift for convincing repartee. Everyone knows his answer to the Brahmans who pleaded that suttee was a national custom: 'My nation also has a custom. When men burn women alive, we hang them ... Let us all act according to national customs.'

After Sind came the two Sikh wars, and these could by no English act have been avoided. Ranjit Singh had died in 1839; he left no son of undoubted legitimacy, sound mind and mature age. There followed an interlude of murder and intrigue, one wretched assassination following

145

General Sir James Outram received by the Raja of Travancore. Outram was romantic where Napier was shrewd and realistic; they were temperamentally incompatible and Outram expressed his strong disapproval of the annexation of Sind and also of Oudh.

another, the army becoming a kind of Praetorian Guard, greedy, irresponsible and powerful, who acclaimed the highest bidder Chief Minister or Regent. The final move, long feared and anticipated, was an attempt to unite the Sikhs by war; without the formality of alleging a grievance, in 1846 they crossed the Sutlej, advancing into country known to be under the Company's protection.

There was hard fighting; the Sikhs were beaten and the British forces – mostly the Company's sepoys of the Bengal Army – moved forward to Lahore. By Asiatic standards, the terms were moderate and the Sikhs themselves were astounded at the forbearance of the English in leaving them a kingdom at all. It was Lord Hardinge's intention to preserve a Sikh state that would be a buffer but not a menace; the bulk of the Punjab proper was to remain under the sovereignty of the boy Maharajah, Dhalip Singh.

There was also to be an indemnity of a million pounds, but there was no money in the treasury at Lahore to meet it. A tributary chief, Gulab Singh of Jammu, offered to pay the indemnity in return for Kashmir. The offer was accepted and the throne of Kashmir was sold.

The Maharajah Dhalip Singh's mother was a woman of low caste who had entered Ranjit Singh's harem at a stage in his complicated maladies which made it unlikely that she would bear him a child. With the assistance, however, of a water-carrier – or so it was rumoured – she had produced Dhalip Singh; she now proposed to govern the Punjab through her paramour.

When the terms of the treaty had been carried out and the time came for the English to withdraw, the leaders of the Sikh tribes felt deep apprehension. They begged the English to remain.

Lord Hardinge replied that English bayonets could not stay to enforce the orders of such a man as the Queen's favourite. They would stay to keep order on behalf of a Council of Regency, which would act under the guidance of the Resident; otherwise, they would go.

The offer was accepted, and the rule of the Titans began. Sir Henry Lawrence was Resident while his young men – Herbert Edwardes, John Nicholson, James Abbott, Lumsden, Reynell Taylor, George Lawrence, Vans Agnew and Arthur Cocks – scoured the country, advising, exhorting and from time to time firmly, and without any authority, taking things into their own hands. 'The protection of the people against the oppression of the Sikh Collectors will be your first duty,' wrote Lawrence to Nicholson.

The doings of Herbert Edwardes in Bannu are the best illustration of what happened in those days. The Afghans had ceded Bannu to the Sikhs but neither had ever administered this high desolate valley, where every man went armed and no one had ever willingly paid a tax. Every three years, the Sikhs sent an army to punish the Bannuchis for their failure to pay tribute; they lived on the valley, burnt the crops they did not eat, carried off the cattle and brought back not a third of one year's revenue.

The time came to send out another of those punitive expeditions. Sir Henry Lawrence agreed, but on condition that a British political officer went too and tried to make a peaceful settlement. The Sikhs smiled and agreed; Herbert Edwardes set out, the only Englishman with an army of Sikhs, recently defeated. He was not even in command. But he began by enforcing an order that the army must pay for everything.

This transformed the situation. The Bannuchis were astonished by an army that did not plunder; they came and talked. They sold provisions to the army. Night after night, they came to Edwardes's tent and sat talking to him about the terms on which they might agree to pay revenue peacefully. In the end, he went away without his agreement but he had promised to come back for a longer stay and next year, when he came for three months, he achieved miracles. They dismantled their forts; they agreed to pay a reduced land revenue and he began a field-to-field survey that would lead to an accurate assessment. Finally he decided that they needed a legal code, and wrote it one night. He turned it into Persian next day and made a beginning of administering his code single-handed. The Political Adviser became judge as well as financier, tax-gatherer, commander-in-chief, engineer and legislator – Moses as well as Napoleon.

Even Edwardes himself seems hardly to have realized quite how miraculous his achievement was. He was alone among these people who obeyed him because of the certainty with which he spoke to them, because of the intensity of his moral fervour. But he did wonder where this

Sir Herbert Edwardes, who was one of the 'Titans of the Punjab', the band of young men who surrounded John and Henry Lawrence. He achieved miracle in Bannu, whose wild inhabitants he persuaded to be taxed But he became fanatical after the Mutiny, and wished to give no recognition to either Hinduism or Islam.

outpouring of energy and goodwill would lead.

To the Sikhs, too, there was something unreal about the Regency. They could respect a master or an enemy who would treat them with the uncompromising harshness they themselves dealt out to their subjects. They could not understand victors who held their hands in the moment of victory, these allies who interfered with their customs. The Second Sikh War was a rebellion headed by the Sikh Army, supported by dissident barons. It interrupted Edwardes's work in Bannu and the work of a dozen more like him, Abbott in Hazara, Lumsden among the Yusufzai, John Nicholson at Rawalpindi. It interrupted John Lawrence in the Jullundur country, where with the help of Cust, Scott, Barnes, Lake and Christian a summary assessment that 'added from fifteen to twenty per cent to every man's income' had been made within six weeks of annexation. It was an interruption, but a short one that cleared the air.

The rebellion began with the murder of two of Henry Lawrence's young men, Vans Agnew, a civilian, and Anderson, a political lieutenant. There was again some very hard fighting; when it was over, there were no more compromises that the Sikhs would find difficult to understand. In 1848, the Punjab was annexed and ruled.

In this second phase in the Punjab, government was by a board of three members. They were served by a commission of seventy-nine covenanted and commissioned officers, among whom were all Sir Henry's young men, mostly military politicals with a sprinkling of civilians, while John's preference on the whole was for civilians from the North-West. But there was not much feeling between Haileybury and Addiscombe. There was too much to do.

Sir Henry Lawrence was the President of the Board, his brother John as the second member had revenue and finance in his portfolio; the third member, who at first was a civilian, Charles Mansell, was responsible for judicial affairs. Mansell was succeeded by Robert Montgomery from the North-West, Thomason's brother-in-law, who described himself as 'a regular buffer between two high-pressure engines'.

The Lawrences had much in common. Both were men of immense energy, of strange controlled passion, both were deeply religious. Both were essentially rulers of men, each, though in a different degree, inspiring warm affection among his subordinates. But there were great differences between them.

John had the clearer and the harder head; plunged almost as soon as he arrived in India into the tangled responsibilities of district administration, he had the ruthlessness of a conscientious busy man who must deal with the most important things first. He would not debate a proposal for long without thinking of what it would cost. Cost on the other hand would be one of the last things to occur to Henry. In Henry there was an innate romanticism, an introspective quality, and later, he had been a survey officer observing the habits and feelings of the people without responsibility for the revenue.

The two men put the emphasis on different ends of the balance. John's emphasis was on fear, Henry's on love; John's on what you must pay for what you want − Henry's on the ideal whatever it costs; John's on the rule of law, Henry's on the good of the individual. But it was a difference of

left, *Sir Henry Lawrence*, right, *John Lawrence. Both the Lawrence brothers were great rulers of men but Henry put his emphasis on the good of the individual and respect for Indian ways. John Lawrence was a man of fierce energy and instant decision. Duty for him was a stern daughter of the voice of God. He was a Leveller, who had no time for old ways if they got in the way of progress.*

emphasis not of principle. Ferocity and kindness alternate in John Lawrence's famous proclamation to the people of Kangra when they showed signs of joining in the Second Sikh war:

> What is your injury I consider mine: what is gain to you I consider my gain . . . If your lands are heavily assessed, tell me and I will relieve you: if you have any grievance, let me know it, and I will try to remove it . . . if you will excite rebellion, as I live I will surely punish you. I have ruled this district three years by the sole agency of the pen and if necessary I will rule it by the sword . . . Tell those who have joined the rebellion to return to me, as children who have committed a fault return to their fathers, and their faults will be forgiven them . . . In two days I shall be in the midst of you with a force which you will be unable to resist.

That is John's voice, clear and resonant; it rings with the language of the Bible and plays on the primitive emotions of the Old Testament, fear, fatherhood, forgiveness. Henry, in Lucknow ten years later, on the eve of the Mutiny, wrote: 'Time is everything just now. Time, firmness, promptness, conciliation and prudence.' But he could be as bold and as ferocious as John. The long-awaited outbreak came at last; as Sir Henry sat at dinner, they heard the sound of musketry which they had been expecting. Sir Henry went out on to the steps and stood waiting for his horse; the Indian officer commanding his escort of sixty sepoys came and asked if he should load. 'Oh, yes, load of course,' said Sir Henry without a moment's hesitation. The escort stood in line, facing the group of officers on the steps. They loaded and brought up their muskets; 'every heart but his beat faster'. He cried out: 'I am going to drive those scoundrels away: . . . take care to remain at your posts and allow no one to enter my house else when I return I will hang you.' And with that he rode off, without a glance to see if he was obeyed.

The Company's servants seemed naturally to become either protectors of the poor or protectors of the noble. John, like most civilians, was a protector of the poor; he saw the peasant wringing a hard life from the soil and believed the Government should care for him alone and should not trouble a tender heart about nobles who had done little more than collect revenue. The country could not support both busy European officials and idle Asiatic chiefs.

Henry felt no man should lose because the English had entered the country. He was always tender for those who had been granted estates free from revenue in return for some service to the state. 'He thinks we treat these classes harshly,' said John. 'I think we have been very kind. I cannot see the political value of such allies as these.'

No one can doubt that John was the abler man and that Henry must have been trying to his superiors. But while both were leaders, each with the power of inspiring a band of devoted followers, it was Henry, hot-tempered till the end, quick to lose his temper and to ask forgiveness,

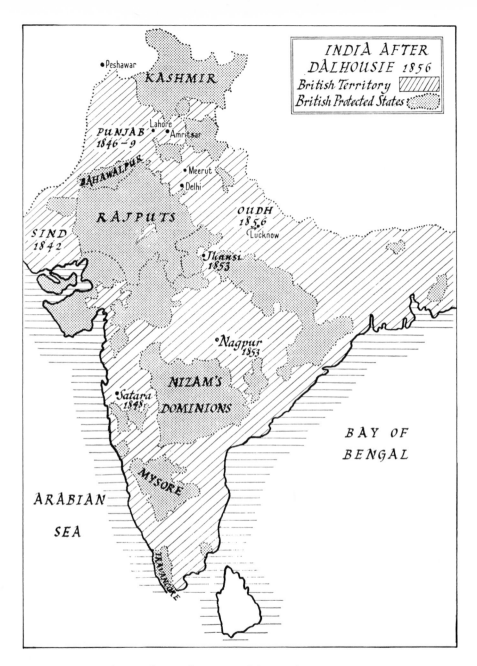

India After Dalhousie 1856
British Territory
British Protected States

Peshawar

KASHMIR

PUNJAB
1846-9
Lahore • Amritsar

BAHAWALPUR

Meerut
Delhi

RAJPUTS

OUDH
1856
Lucknow

SIND
1842

Jhansi
1853

Nagpur
1853

NIZAM'S
DOMINIONS

Satara
1848

BAY OF
BENGAL

MYSORE

ARABIAN

SEA

TRAVANCORE

Henry, warm-hearted, passionate and inconsistent, who inspired a love warmer and more widespread. There is a brooding look on Henry's face; something of the saint, the poet and the prophet burned behind his eyes. When he left the Punjab, his progress was like a funeral procession. All who knew him and worked for him loved him; at the end, in Lucknow, the English soldiers of the 32nd (the 1st Duke of Cornwall's Light Infantry) broke into cheering whenever he came near them and the four who were to carry his body for burial at the last uncovered his forehead and kissed it one by one.

There was nothing of the poet about John. Plain John Lawrence was a man of facts, of immensely hard work, of detailed knowledge. His ideal was 'a country thickly cultivated by a fat contented yeomanry, each riding his own horse, sitting under his own fig tree and enjoying his rude family comforts'. He believed in keeping the peace and lightening taxes. 'One lakh given in the reduction of assessments and making people comfortable in their homes is better than three lakhs given to Rajas,' he said.

No one gave himself so utterly to his work. All his time was given to it and he was impatient of time wasted. He was intolerant of discussion or argument; he wanted the facts, briefly; he would understand them quickly and make up his mind at once. A line scribbled in the margin of a paper usually conveyed his orders.

There is an unconventional view of him, recorded fifteen years later by John Beames, a hard-headed and sensible young man who married early. He wrote:

> The signal services rendered by this great man have caused him to be regarded as a sort of popular hero and it will seem almost blasphemy to say a word against him. But . . . by those who served under him he was intensely disliked . . . He was a rough, coarse man, in appearance more like a navvy than a gentleman. His ideal of a district officer was a hard active man in boots and breeches, who almost lived in the saddle, worked all day and nearly all night, ate and drank when and where he could, had no family ties, no wife or children to hamper him.

He seemed a governing machine, but a machine is driven by stored energy and the heat was tremendous. In his official report on the Mutiny, he writes: 'There is a judge over both them and us. Inasmuch as we have been preserved from impending destruction by His mercy alone, we should be merciful to others, reflecting that if He were to be extreme to mark what we have done and still do amiss, we should forfeit that protection from on High which alone maintains us in India.' Therefore there should be an amnesty for all not guilty of murder who had fought against the English.

A man who wrote state papers in such words as those was not to be shifted from what he thought right by any clamour. He came in the end to see that there was something to be said for some Indian princes. But to the end it was the peasant for whom he cared.

Dalhousie believed that the Punjab was ruled the better for the difference between the brothers, but a time came when a choice had to be made between them. Dalhousie chose John, who all along had been more in his confidence, being of a temperament more like his own. Henry went as Resident to Rajputana, to him a backwater after the Punjab. Before he left

Lahore, he and his wife knelt together in prayer for John's success in the Punjab; the brothers became better friends once more, but Henry in spite of many good resolutions never quite forgave Dalhousie.

Things were not so bad that they could not sign a unanimous report on their administration. It is an official document; there is much left unsaid. Edwardes's doings in Bannu are barely mentioned, nor is there much about Nicholson who administered Bannu so effectively that a religious community was founded in his honour and lasted at least ten years after his death. There is so much to say that eloquence is not needed. Hear for instance the Board's idea of justice:

> The Board desire that substantial justice should be plainly dealt out to a simple people, unused to the intricacies of legal proceedings. Their aim is to avoid all technicality, circumlocution and obscurity; to simplify and abridge every rule, procedure and process. They wish to form tribunals where every man may plead his own cause, be confronted face to face with his opponents, may prosecute his own claim or conduct his own defence ...
>
> With a force of 11,228 men, a difficult Frontier has been guarded, 500 miles long, inhabited by a semi-barbarous population, and menaced by numerous tribes of hostile mountaineers ... With a police force of 14,000 men, internal peace has been kept from the borders of Sind to the foot of the Himalayas, from the banks of the Sutlej to the banks of the Indus, and this when a disbanded army of 50,000 men had mingled with the ranks of society.

Behind this frontier, court-houses, jails, treasuries had been built, roads, canals and bridges.

Land revenue was as always the backbone of the administration. The Sikh rulers in two-thirds of the country had collected direct. The crop was in theory divided, the most primitive form of collection, the state usually taking from one-third to one-half. For this system, a cash revenue was to be substituted. Throughout the province this was fixed at between twenty and thirty per cent below the Sikh rates. The first assessment was hasty; it was capable of much greater refinement, to allow for differences in the quality of land, in the expense of irrigation and much more, but on the whole it was not a bad one.

Whether the people would really like their advancement – that was not a matter the Board discussed in their report. The test, however, was to come. The Board was ended and John Lawrence ruled alone, but there was little change. Tireless energy and deep good will were part of his being; he demanded the same from all his subordinates. Prompt reward, swift punishment, low taxes, peace, roads, canals – those were the stones with which he built – with which the Board had built. And when the flood rose and the stream beat vehemently, the building stood.

11
THE MUTINY

—————◆—————

1 Why It Happened

In the tale of English rule in India there has so far been more reason for
pride than for shame. What has been surprising has been not so much the
lapses into corruption or harshness as the speed with which it has become
an established principle that the country must be governed for the good of
its inhabitants. But an interlude comes now at which no Englishman of
intellectual honesty can look without embarrassment and unhappiness.

It is a matter for unhappiness that the thing should have happened at
all. It is a matter for shame that the revolt should have been suppressed
with such indiscriminate ferocity. This last can be understood. The
English were in the proportion of one to four thousand, and their lives
were in danger; it was not a situation in which anyone was likely to be
discriminating. But to understand is not to excuse.

It is believed by many today that the Mutiny was a national rebellion; it
has also sometimes been argued that it was a purely military rising with no
political significance. The truth is somewhere between the two and to
understand this it is necessary to consider the curious nature of the sepoy
army and its history.

The infantry of the Bengal Army – and it is not the armies of Madras or
Bombay with which we are concerned – was recruited largely from
Hindus of high caste, usually Brahmans and Rajputs; their caste rules
were respected by their officers with scrupulous tenderness. There is
surely something paradoxical about a professional soldier in a mercenary
army who will not eat meat, yet there were whole battalions who were
vegetarians. It is surely strange to find a soldier who will go to death at his
officer's order, who will rescue him under fire, but who will throw away
his food and starve if the same officer's shadow falls on his cooking-pot. All
this was true of the Bengal Army.

The rules for Rajputs were only slightly less elaborate than those for

Brahmans. And caste is infectious; even Europeans became tainted. Indian Muslims are subject to restrictions unknown to the Koran or to any Arab. But Brahman, Rajput and Muslim could in an emergency be induced by good officers to forget many ritual absurdities, which in peace might be elevated by competitive sanctimoniousness until they became necessary to salvation.

It was a mercenary army. It was not from patriotic motives that the sepoy enlisted, but because the army was his hereditary profession, because it brought him an adequate livelihood together with social position, consequence, and honour. The sepoy was a landowner; he went on leave with a man to carry his bundle; even on a campaign there were five followers to one fighting man. He was proud of himself and of his profession. He had a fierce pride in the colours of his regiment, which − if he was a Hindu − he worshipped yearly with the same rites the peasant used before his plough, the smith before his tools. The regiment was a close hereditary corporation, in which son succeeded father, knit together by blood, religion and a deep emotional feeling for the colours.

It was a mercenary army, officered by foreigners. They were not only foreigners but of another faith and the personal habits of officers and men were so widely different that each regarded those of the other as disgusting. All the same, between those foreign officers and their Indian soldiers there often sprang up a confidence and affection of which both English and Indian may well feel proud. It was something that could survive long marches through burning deserts and icy mountains, sieges on starvation diet, torture and the threat of instant death. Indeed, it throve on such fare as this. But forget that the army was a living organism, treat it as a dry skeleton, sit at a desk and look at returns of strengths, send away the officers he knew to other regiments − and the sepoy's confidence would wither. And once his affection was gone, once his confidence had withered, his fidelity to that far extravagance, that shadow of a name, that abstract nothing, the Company, was liable to shatter at a breath, at a whisper, at a hint from the bazar of some imagined peril.

So far, however, his fidelity had been something for wonder and admiration. The sepoys had fought and died for the Company because it had fed them and paid them in peace and because they trusted and admired their officers. But mutinies had been known. There had been Buxar in 1764, there had been Vellore in 1805, there had been Barrackpore in 1824. There had been several mutinies in the 1840s, when Sind was declared a British province. These arose from a characteristic piece of financial pedantry; the sepoy's reward for victory was the loss of his foreign service allowance. The Company's flag flew over Sind instead of the Amir's; foreign service allowance, therefore became 'wholly inappropriate'. But Sind was no closer than it had been to the sepoy's home, the air and water were as strange and harsh as before. The sepoy was always particular about air and water; he did not after all ask for very much of anything else.

In almost every case of mutiny, it was possible to trace the same pattern. There were usually two predisposing factors and then some immediate occasion, which might be trivial.

There was almost always something from outside, nothing to do with the regiment. It might begin with a feeling in the villages; men would come back from leave with news of a bad harvest or perhaps a revenue assessment that was too heavy. They would be unhappy. Then would come a malicious rumour. The English had all been killed in the Crimea; the troops were all going to be forcibly converted to Christianity – something like that. This came from a political source – a dispossessed prince, a communist cell; it was deliberate subversion from outside.

With good officers whom the men knew, none of this would matter. The officers would hear the tale, talk to the men and laugh at the rumour. But if there was no one with the regiment but subalterns fresh from Addiscombe and senior officers transferred from another corps, then the thing would fester and the men grow more and more ripe for mutiny until a touch would set it off. They might be ordered to carry out some new fatigue or wear some different dress, something quite trivial. If there was a real unhappiness, subversion from outside, and poor officers within, almost anything would be enough.

India was held more by bluff than by force. In a district of a million Indians there would often be one English magistrate only, but there were Indians on whose support he could rely, because most people did not find English rule intolerable and because they believed that there was English strength somewhere in the background. That strength was light. In the 1850s, the total of the Company's armies was rather less than three hundred thousand fighting men, of whom as a rule some forty-five thousand or a few more were English troops. There were more than two hundred million natives of India. There might be one English soldier to every five Indian soldiers – and one soldier, fair or dark, to every six hundred civilians. The balance was kept, so long as there was confidence in the star of the Company. The word men use again and again is iqbal; it means predestined good fortune.

In the years before 1857 much happened to shake the confidence of the civil population. It had been Lord Dalhousie's sincere belief that he ought not to neglect any chance of acquiring territory, because British rule was for the benefit of the inhabitants. Whenever a ruler died without direct male heir of the body, his state was annexed. There were therefore disappointed heirs, bitter against the Company, ready to pass on any lying and malicious rumour. And there were other rulers who feared that their turn would be next.

There were also men from all over India, once large landholders, who felt themselves aggrieved by the policy of the new generation of British, mostly protectors of the poor. And everywhere there were the Brahmans who began to scent the danger to their ascendancy that 'progress' threatened.

Education in western science, western medicine, railway trains and telegraph-wires — all were dangers to the Brahman system. And to these insidious assaults, the English had now begun to add legislative interference. Suttee was the first step; then it had been made legal for Hindu widows to re-marry; now a convert who had changed his religion was to be allowed to inherit property. Convicts in the jails were being made to feed in messes instead of each man separately. No one knew what might come next. In part, the Mutiny was a reaction of obscurantists against social change.

Then came news of the disaster at Kabul; the English could after all be beaten. Next there was garbled news from the Crimea.

Unease was in the air; it was widespread among the civil population; there were plenty of enemies to whisper in the sepoy's ear. And there were not many good officers who knew their men still with the regiments. For years, it had been the aim of every ambitious man to get a staff appointment, and this meant every better paid post. Who would not rather be Edwardes in Bannu — King, Prime Minister and Commander-in-Chief — rather than a subaltern in cantonments, inspecting cross-belts and ammunition pouches for two hours before breakfast, and yawning away the rest of the day beneath a ragged punkah in a shabby bungalow with the plaster peeling off the walls? For years there had been a drain of the best men to other posts, and those who stayed behind felt themselves mediocrities. Nor was that all. Promotion was too slow, commanding officers were too old and their powers were being reduced, battalions were constantly amalgamated, officers reshuffled.

With this weakening of the regimental officer went something common to all the English in India. Religion had become intolerant and dogmatic, racial pride more exclusive. Now it was the right thing to be as English as possible in everything. The overland mail brought letters only a month old; the steam navigation companies brought out young ladies for the cold weather; there were station book clubs and amateur theatricals as well as hog-hunting, polo and shooting; altogether, there was plenty to do that was more amusing than 'listening to the garrulous old subadar'.

And among the sepoys themselves there were reasons for discontent. There was a feeling that now there were no more worlds to conquer; everything in India belonged to the Company and so no doubt the army would soon be disbanded — or sent to conquer Europe. Then came something more specific, the General Service Enlistment Act of 1856. This meant that in future all recruits must swear on their enlistment that they would cross the sea in ships if they were ordered. To cross the sea was pollution to an orthodox Hindu; no Indian soldier could eat salt pork and ship's biscuit. Up till now, the sepoys had been bound to serve in India only; they were within their rights if they refused to sail to Rangoon or Persia. No general straight from England could be expected to regard such a situation without impatience.

In the same year, 1856, came the annexation of Oudh, the chief recruiting ground of the army. The country had been grossly misgoverned for years, but every Prince in India felt himself unsafe when he learnt that fidelity was not enough, that he must also be enlightened and public-spirited, a kind of glorified municipal commissioner. More important still was the sepoy's loss of prestige in his village.

He had been the servant of the Great Company in a state where no one else expected justice; if he had a boundary dispute or a question of succession, he would tell his tale to the Resident or his Assistant. The Resident need not hear the other side – in fact, he must not; the other party was a subject of the King of Oudh. God had given the Resident one ear only; he would go to the King or his minister and demand justice for the oppressed sepoy. No minister would quarrel with the Resident over anything so easy to grant as the decision in a village quarrel. But when Oudh became British territory, the Resident turned into a Chief Commissioner with the normal equipment of ears; he must listen to both sides now and the sepoy's consequence fell away.

The sepoy had, then, cause for anxiety when the greased cartridge story began to spread. Cartridges for the new Enfield rifle had to be heavily greased; they had to be bitten to open the end and release the powder. The Company's army was now to be re-equipped with these rifles. It had all been arranged by specialists of the Ordnance department, to whom it had naturally never occurred to think of the sepoy army. The grease was half of it tallow, which came from animals of all kinds including both pigs and cows. The grease was plentiful; the muzzle of the weapon was smeared with it after loading. On the lips of a Hindu cow's fat would be an abomination for which there is no parallel in European ways of thinking; it was not merely disgusting, as excrement would be; it damned him as well; it was as bad as killing a cow or a Brahman. To a Muslim pig's fat was almost as horrible.

The cartridges were in the ordnance depots. They were being prepared for issue to the troops when the news broke. It did not take long to reach the officers; on January 24, 1857, the danger was reported to the Government. The 25th was a Sunday. Orders went out on the 27th; the greased cartridges from the ordnance depots were to be kept for British troops and the sepoy was to grease his own with beeswax and vegetable oil; the rifle drill was changed and the greased cartridges were now to be broken with the fingers.

It was too late. The tale had spread quickly and grown in the telling. The English had planned to break the sepoy's caste, thinking they would then find it easy to make him a Christian as the only refuge left him. They had not only greased the cartridges, they had mixed the ground bones of bullocks with the flour; they had polluted the sugar.

None of this would have been believed thirty years ago. No one in his senses would then have thought the English could possibly plot to convert their soldiers to a creed they hardly seemed to hold themselves. All that was changed now. The prevailing tone among the Company's servants was earnest and evangelical. More and more of them had begun to feel it a duty to convert others.

There were mutinies in Bengal in the early part of the year; there was no general attack on officers. In May, eighty-five men at Meerut refused cartridges − not the offending variety. They were sentenced to long terms of imprisonment; a punishment parade was held at which the sepoys were drawn up in lines, commanded by the guns of British artillerymen and the sabres of a regiment of British dragoons. The eighty-five were stripped of their uniforms, the irons were fastened on them by smiths on the parade-ground.

It was a long business, taking several hours. It seems to have filled the remaining sepoys with a burning sense of injustice and convinced them that they really were to be forced to use something that was against their religion. On Sunday evening three regiments broke open the jail, murdered as many as they could of their officers, their wives and children, and made for Delhi. Here there were no British troops. Here too the Indian troops rose and massacred their officers, their wives and children. The Mutiny had begun.

2 The Savagery on Both Sides

It was not done in cold blood. It was done in panic fear, in an irrational frenzy. Meerut was in all India the station strongest in British troops. If the thing had been thought out, it would have started anywhere but there. It was done in panic fear, brought to a head by the parade on Saturday morning. They had long talked in the lines at night of the plots hatched against their religion, but that Saturday night they must have planned in stammering haste, fright and anger contending for mastery. Their decision, if they had stopped to think, was suicidal. There was a regiment of British cavalry, there was a battalion of infantry − riflemen, an important point, for the sepoys still had muskets − and there were guns; the English in Meerut were in numbers almost as strong as the Indian, they were better armed, and they had immense prestige. No one could have guessed that they would be so ineptly commanded. No one could have foretold that the mutineers would be allowed to complete their forty-mile march to Delhi without being brought to battle.

They were beyond reason, they were desperate. And once a jail had been broken and an officer killed, there was no turning back. They knew there was no mercy to be expected and, to make sure that every man should be bound to his leaders by fear of the rope, those who were in the thing most deeply incited the rest to spare no one, to destroy any life that might remind them of their own guilt.

There were no British troops in Delhi. When it was realized there was no pursuit from Meerut, the officers in Delhi too were attacked and murdered, usually with their wives and children.

The other risings did not follow instantaneously. The news spread and in almost every station where there were Indian troops there came a period of tense waiting; English and Indian alike were frightened and furious. Between Barrackpore, near Calcutta, and Agra, a distance of nearly eight hundred miles, there was only one British battalion. At a hundred stations in between, a handful of English, sometimes one or two, sometimes a score, watched Indian squadrons and battalions; the Commissioner or Collector met the military officer commanding the station every day in anxious debate. The civil officer was in almost every case distrustful of the sepoys and anxious to take precautions at once, while the officer of the sepoy army was almost always sure that he could trust *his* men to the death. Sometimes the civilian had his way and precautions were taken which convinced the sepoys that they were about to be attacked; sometimes the soldier went on trusting until he was shot in the back.

The Sixth at Allahabad were a regiment whose officers had always taken a friendly care of their men and a keen pride in their fidelity. The men seemed to return the officers' feeling; they reported strangers from the bazar who made seditious approaches to them, they demanded to be led to Delhi against the rebels. A model regiment, they received the thanks of the Governor-General at a special parade; they greeted the Commissioner's praise with ringing cheers. That same night they rose and murdered their officers.

This was one reason for the relentless fury with which the English waged this war. The sepoy had been a friend. Suddenly the friend had become a murderous and irrational enemy and the English too ceased to reason.

It was partly the suddenness of the treachery, partly the murder of English women that roused such a frenzy of hatred. Men of any race would wish to punish the slaughter of their women, but the English were roused to a special pitch of passion. The Victorian Englishman had raised for himself an ideal picture of womanhood, based in part on poetic convention and no doubt often sentimental, but it was held with all the force that could be banked up by sternly repressed instinct. It sprang from the truth that women are weaker than men and more often in pain and that to treat women with consideration and respect is more truly human than to treat them with cruelty and contempt. To hear that the women of his own race, to whom he himself gave so chivalrous a precedence, had been treacherously slaughtered reached the centre of the English officer's being, the

Brigadier-General James Neill was a leader of great energy and courage who believed it his duty to inflict merciless vengeance on all mutineers for the massacres at Cawnpore.

very heart of his emotions.

Inevitably there arose stories that English women had been violated and mutilated. Careful inquiry indicates only the case of Miss Wheeler, the Eurasian daughter of General Sir Hugh Wheeler, who was carried off from Cawnpore as the mistress of a sepoy. But the stories were believed. That was why John Nicholson wrote to Edwardes: 'Let us propose a Bill for the flaying alive, impalement or burning of the murderers of the women and children at Delhi. The idea of simply hanging the perpetrators of such atrocities is maddening.' Nicholson was normally a merciful man, but in the Mutiny he forgot what he had been, he and many others. A few kept their heads and exercised some restraint – Canning, John Lawrence, John Peter Grant – but many thought as Nicholson did, not only in India but in England.

Here are General Neill's instructions to Major Renaud, who led the force which was intended to relieve Cawnpore:

The villages of Mubgoon and neighbourhood to be attacked and destroyed; slaughter all the men; take no prisoners . . .

All sepoys found without papers from regiments that have mutinied who cannot give good accounts of themselves to be hanged forthwith . . .

Futtehpore to be promptly attacked, the Pathan quarters to be destroyed, all in it killed; in fact make a signal example of this place.

Those who followed Renaud and Havelock found that 'human beings there were none to be seen ... the blackened ruins of huts ... the occasional taint in the air from suspended bodies upon which the loathsome pig of the country was already feasting ... all these things combined to call up such images of desolation and blackness and woe as few ... would ever forget.'

For mutineers there was no mercy; they were hanged or blown from guns and not much time was wasted on trial – sometimes none at all. The mutineers, however, were guilty in law of an offence punishable with death; there was no sniff of legality about the slaughter of many males of the civil population at Allahabad, Cawnpore and Delhi. Both at Cawnpore and Delhi there is good evidence that the bazars had had quite enough of the mutineers and of anarchy. They wanted the rule of law again and were glad to see British troops. But not for long. The English soldier has never made much difference between one brown skin and another; he was in no mood at all to discriminate now. Nor were the Punjabis. 'To the troops (Native and European alike) every man inside the walls of Delhi was looked upon as a rebel worthy of death,' wrote Roberts, describing how he saved a group of money-lenders.

Part of the feeling was due to tales of crimes the sepoys had not committed. What they had done was bad enough, though it was strangely mixed with instances of devotion. Sometimes a sepoy would risk his own life to save an officer who had been kind to him; often villagers or servants at great risk protected escaping parties.

The tale of Cawnpore became notorious. The garrison after a long and gallant resistance surrendered to the Nana Sahib – the adopted son of Baji Rao, the last Peshwa, who had now proclaimed himself the Peshwa. It was to him the surrender had been made – and on the clear condition of a free passage to Allahabad by boat for all the survivors. When the garrison reached the landing-stage, they were surrounded and shot down. It was no accident; it was carefully planned.

Many women were killed there, but some were saved, making some two hundred all told. They were kept in privation and great discomfort; but they were not actively ill-treated till the last. When, however, Havelock's column drew closer and the Nana knew that he must fly, he gave orders that the two hundred English women should be killed. The mutineers who formed their guard were ordered to fire on them through the windows. They refused to obey; butchers were sent in with knives. Next morning the bodies were dragged out and thrown in the well.

Neill, left in charge by Havelock, saw the room where this massacre had taken place. Before he had seen it, when he had only heard what had happened, he had written: 'I can never spare a sepoy again. All that fall into my hands will be dead men.' Now he saw the room. 'Ladies' and children's bloody torn dresses and shoes were lying about and locks of hair torn from their heads. The floor of the one room they were all dragged

Massacre in the boats, Cawnpore. After long resistance, the few British still alive at Cawnpore surrendered on the understanding that they would be given free passage by boat down the Ganges to Allahabad. But when they reached the boats they were shot down.

into and killed was saturated with blood . . . Who could be merciful to one concerned? . . . I wish to show the natives of India that the punishment inflicted by us for such deeds will be the heaviest, the most revolting to their feelings, and what they must ever remember.' He passed orders that 'every stain of that innocent blood shall be cleared up and wiped out previous to their execution, by such of the miscreants as may be hereafter apprehended, who took an active part in the mutiny . . . Each miscreant, after sentence of death is pronounced upon him, will be taken down to the house in question under a guard and will be forced into cleaning up a small portion of the blood-stains; the task will be made as revolting to his feelings as possible and the Provost-Marshal will use the lash in forcing anyone objecting to complete his task. After properly cleaning up his portion the culprit is to be immediately hanged.'

It will be noticed that the men Neill caught he tried; he tried them for mutiny. 'Unless he can prove a defence, he is sentenced to be hanged.' Neill set his face against indiscriminate vengeance on a whole nation, but he assumed that all mutineers must be held guilty of the massacre of the women. He was sure of the guidance of God. 'I will hold my own, with the blessing and help of God. I cannot help seeing his finger in all this – we have been false to ourselves so often,' he wrote.

Fear of a stronger people whom they did not understand had turned in the sepoys to hatred, panic and murder. Deep hidden in English hearts too had glowed a tiny spark, never revealed or admitted, fear of a people far more numerous; that too had flamed up in uncontrollable hate when the despised and feared rose treacherously and laid beastly hands on English women. Against this sombre background shine many strange and deeply moving acts of tenderness and fidelity, such as that of the sepoys who stayed true to Henry Lawrence and defended Lucknow for eighty-seven days. There were many more but they were exceptions. Merciless savagery on both sides was the general rule.

3 The Civilian in Hindustan

In the South, all was quiet. The Madras and Bombay armies did not mutiny. There was no disturbance among the people. In Bengal proper and in the Punjab, a grip was maintained and the country never wholly lost. Indeed, in the Punjab, the work of the Lawrences had been such that they could not only hold the country but spare armed men for Delhi. But Hindustan – that is Behar, Oudh and the North-Western Provinces, roughly from Patna to Delhi, that long stretch which contained only one British regiment – Hindustan was lost.

Even here there was no general rising of the people. When the troops had killed their officers and looted the Treasury, sometimes a local chief would put himself at their head, as the Nana had done at Cawnpore. Kunwar Singh in the country east of Benares, Khan Mohammad Khan in Rohilkand, made themselves Viceroys for the Emperor in Delhi. Some landowners joined them, some believed the star of the English would rise again. Most believed that English rule was ended and scrambled for what they could get. There was indiscriminate massacre and confused fighting between chiefs and villages. The peasants were often in sympathy with the mutineers; perhaps more often still they were indifferent, as they usually were to a change of ruler. Sometimes they despoiled and murdered English fugitives; sometimes they slaughtered to destroy the evidence of their guilt; just as often, villagers and landowners saved lonely English families, fed them and hid them, sometimes to their own danger.

Eighty years later men would come with grubby fragments of yellowing paper; 'June, 1857: This is to say Nubbee Bux of village Ajnore gave water to me to-day when I was escaping with two children from the mutineers at Bareilly. Mary Smith, wife of Captain Henry Smith, 89th N.I.' He risked his life to do it. A mutineer would have shot him without scruple. And it would seem to the great-grandson of Nabi Bakhsh in 1937 a betrayal to keep his son out of the clerkship for which there were fifty applicants.

But though the rising was never general, the country from Patna to Delhi was lost because the key points were lost. There was a treasury at the headquarters of each district; everywhere in Hindustan the mutineers made sooner or later for the treasury, the civil administration ceased to work, and the people took to fighting among themselves. But the mutineers did not always come at once. There was first a time of waiting.

Henry Tucker, Commissioner at Benares, will stand for those who had to wait and watch troops who might still be saved from rising. He was fortunate in his companions, Frederick Gubbins, the judge, and Lind, the magistrate, two who 'exerted themselves with great skill to maintain the peace of the city, now patrolling with parties of troopers, now persuading Bunyas to lower the price of corn'. 'Mr Gubbins and Mr Lind agreed with me,' wrote Henry Tucker, when certain soldiers suggested retiring to a fort eighteen miles away, 'that to show any open distrust would cause a panic, the bazars would be closed, and both the troops and the city would be up against us. We therefore determined to face the danger without moving a muscle.'

Tucker did not possess any weapon but a riding whip and rode every evening, with his daughter, to the most exposed places, 'fearless and confident, saying to himself: "The Lord is my rock, my fortress and my deliverer; the God of my rock, in Him will I trust."' He kept his head when not many were kept, writing early in June for power of life and death for every civil magistrate, adding that he would prefer this to martial law. 'I do not think', he said, 'that the greater proportion of the military can be entrusted with the power of life and death. The atrocious murders have aroused the English blood and a very slight circumstance would cause the Natives to be shot or hung. I would therefore much prefer retaining the powers in the hands of those who have been accustomed to weigh and value evidence.' But already in Calcutta the acts had been passed which made possible just that outbreak of lynch law which he had foreseen and feared.

Herwald Wake at lonely Arrah, between Patna and Benares, had another problem. There were no troops at Arrah, and this was the district of Kunwar Singh, the rebel Chief. But a few hours' march away at Dinapore were three battalions of native infantry, who rose on July 25 and marched for the treasury at Arrah.

Here were Wake, the magistrate, and fifteen other civilians of various grades, with fifty Sikh military police, sixty-six men all told. They defended themselves for eight days in a small bungalow, usually used as a billiard room, against a besieging force of two thousand five hundred sepoy bayonets and about eight thousand local volunteers who had joined Kunwar Singh. They were under fire almost continuously for the whole period; one relieving column was defeated and driven back; a second, about two hundred strong, eventually relieved them on August 3.

The defence of the little house at Arrah is one story from one district: there were half a hundred districts in the North-West and Oudh and Behar from which came tales of death and danger and escape; there can hardly have been one civilian whose life was not in peril a dozen times that summer. Most had to leave their districts; sometimes they found in another district work such as organizing supplies or restoring some kind of order. More often they became moss-troopers. Bax-Ironside, Joint Magistrate at Ghazipore, rode with a troop of twelve hog-spears, who were in the force that relieved Arrah; Richard Oldfield, an Assistant Secretary to the Government at Agra, and Phillips, Joint Magistrate at Etah, were with Prendergast's Mounted Volunteers, a troop of twenty who charged three hundred rebel cavalry, losing five killed and nine wounded. Wallace-Dunlop, Magistrate at Meerut, founded and led the Khaki Risala, the Dusty Squadron, a force in which Commissioners rode knee to knee with Assistants, with officers who had lost their regiments, plate-layers who had lost their railways, faithful Indian troopers and clerks from the Divisional Headquarters. They patrolled the district, keeping it clear of mutineers and keeping the road open to the Ridge at Delhi.

John Cracroft Wilson, Judge of Moradabad, showed no less courage than Henry Tucker in that first anxious period when the loyalty of the sepoys still hung in the balance. When all was lost at Moradabad, he made for Meerut and there organized a small force of former native officers of Irregular Cavalry, with whom he roamed the country rescuing English fugitives. He had, said Lord Canning, 'the enviable distinction of having by his own obstinate courage and perseverance saved more Christian lives than any man in India. He did this at the repeatedly imminent risk of his own life.'

Loyd, Magistrate of Hamirpur, and Donald Grant his Assistant, were invited to come into Banda and join a stronger party there but they refused. Loyd had no illusions about the one company of Indian troops in Hamirpur who were, he said, 'as ready to cut our throats as they can be' and if mutineers come from elsewhere 'will turn on us like wolves', but he raised some local auxiliaries of whom he had hopes and the people of Hamirpur 'are all for us though if a shot was fired they would keep to their houses'. He wrote a letter to his wife, who was in England, on May 28, saying that it 'truly, unless God in his mercy interferes, may be my last!' Cawnpore, further north, had gone; Allahabad went on June 6. Loyd was still in Hamirpur on the 13th, when mutinous sepoys from outside arrived and his one company rose. He and Grant escaped across the river under a heavy fire of musketry but on the 15th went back to the district and were fed by friendly villagers, until they were betrayed by a goatherd, brought bound to Hamirpur and shot.

Ten years later an officer on tour in Hamirpur found Loyd's name still remembered. Men pointed to wells, steps down to the river, banks to store water for irrigation, as the work of Loyd Sahib. He had been a good district officer. He wrote before he died a paper, noting the few rupees he owed his Indian landlord for his bungalow and directing that his watch should be given as a present to his head reader. In his last letter he had written: 'Kiss my dear Babes for me and tell them how necessary it is for the youngest as well as the oldest to live daily to God ... '

Mackillop, Joint Magistrate of Cawnpore, volunteered during the siege for the supremely dangerous task of fetching water. There was no cover at all near the well and there were besiegers always posted, by day to watch it and by night to listen for the creaking of the tackle; there were always guns trained on the well and loaded with grape. Mackillop was Captain of the Well for a week, which was longer than anyone had hoped; as he lay dying, he asked that the lady to whom he had promised a drink for her children should not be disappointed.

That is a sparse handful of names. It would be easy to find many more, easy, too, if there was room, to give many examples of Indians who risked or lost their lives for Englishmen. I have said nothing here of those on the lonely heights, Colvin the Lieutenant-Governor at Agra, Henry Lawrence in Lucknow and his Financial Commissioner, Martin Gubbins, brother of the Gubbins at Benares, nothing of Spankie who held Saharanpur and Keene who held the Doon. There are many more left out. The civil servants of the Company were picked men, a corps of officers, and they lived in a time of national greatness, of strong and simple emotions. It is not surprising that they should have displayed a high sense of duty and unselfishness, some of them outstanding powers of leadership, all of them unflinching courage. It is not surprising; they would have put it themselves that they were unprofitable servants; they had done that which was their duty to do.

4 The Civilian in the Punjab

The Punjab held. It was a new province, still appreciative of benefits received; there had been a good harvest; it had been brilliantly administered by men specially chosen – and with painstaking, self-destructive energy; it was, besides, much less under Brahman ascendancy than Hindustan. Perhaps most important of all, the Punjabis hated the Hindustani sepoys who had conquered them.

The Punjabis, whether Sikh, Jat, or Muslim, had made the British fight harder than anyone else. They had been beaten, and as a whole felt no resentment against the English, whose prowess in battle and subsequent generosity they recognized. But they did resent the swaggering airs of sepoys from Oudh, men they felt they could have eaten alive if it had not been for British leadership. The Punjabis had been disarmed; the sepoy dared to ruffle it in the streets of Lahore and they dared not drive him out. But they did not like him. The rulers of the Punjab shared some of these feelings.

There were two unwritten rules in the Punjab service. There must be no hesitation. Show a bold front, take the offensive at once, a blow in time saves nine – that was the first commandment. And the second was this; because the junior must not wait for support, the senior must back him up. With confidence, one can rule a million. Every officer must be sure he will be supported.

The news of the rising at Meerut reached Lahore on May 11. John Lawrence was at Rawalpindi and Robert Montgomery the Judicial Commissioner was in charge. At Lahore were one royal regiment of British infantry and two troops of horse artillery manned by 'the Company's Europeans'. There were also three infantry regiments of the line and one of cavalry from the Company's native army, all with proud records and colours heavy with battle honours. Montgomery went at once to the Brigadier commanding the station. All agreed; on the morning of the 13th all four sepoy units were disarmed. They were taken completely by surprise and made no sign of resistance – indeed, they could not for they were drawn up in column, gazing straight into the muzzles of the guns.

That was the pattern for the Punjab. It was followed up by disarming parades at Ferozpur and Peshawar and 'before the sepoys had time to recover from these blows . . . all outlying treasure had been brought under proper custody'. John Lawrence was a little doubtful about Montgomery's swiftness, though of course he supported it in public. But he wrote privately to Edwardes: 'The misfortune of the present state of affairs is this – Each step we take for our own security is a blow against the Regular Sepoy. He feels this, and on his side takes a further step, and so we go on until we disband or destroy them, or they mutiny and kill their officers.' Not all perceived that tragic dilemma.

That Lawrence saw it so clearly did not, however, make him hesitate. He made it a matter of policy to replace men from Hindustan by Punjabis and to raise local levies. But the Punjabis waited to see whether the star of the English would rise again. 'Men remembered Kabul,' Edwardes wrote of those first days. 'Not one in a hundred could be found to join such a desperate cause.'

Very soon – on May 21, only eleven days after Meerut – the Hindustani troops mutinied at Nowshera, twenty-four miles from Peshawar, and it became necessary to decide whether it was possible to send British soldiers to Nowshera while five battalions of sepoys under suspicion remained at Peshawar unguarded. Edwardes consulted Nicholson and Cotton; they had to think of an external danger, too, for they held the gate of India. Edwardes and Nicholson took the risk; they disarmed four of the five Hindustani corps, many of whose English officers in profound shame and misery threw their own swords and spurs upon the muskets and sabres of their men. 'As we rode down to the disarming,' said Edwardes, 'a very few chiefs or yeomen of the country attended us and I remember judging from their faces that they came to see which way the tide would turn. As we rode back, friends were as thick as summer flies and levies began from that moment to come in.' It was a triumph for the policy of the risk taken by the throat.

That policy was continued. Among the first batch of deserters recovered was the Subadar-Major, the senior native officer, of the 51st Regiment; he was hanged in the presence of all the troops in Peshawar, including his own corps. The 55th mutinied at Hoti Mardan and fled, with their arms, colours and treasure. Nicholson hunted them ruthlessly down; he killed a hundred and twenty, captured a hundred and fifty and scattered the rest.

Even Nicholson wrote: 'I must say a few words for some of the Fifty-fifth prisoners.' Lawrence concurred. 'They were taken fighting against us and so far deserve little mercy. But on full reflection I would not put them all to death. I do not think we should be justified in the eyes of the Almighty in doing so. A hundred and twenty men are a large number to put to death. Our object is to make an example to terrify others. I think this object would be gained by destroying from a quarter to a third of them . . . These should be shot or blown away from guns . . . The rest I would divide into batches, some to be imprisoned ten years, some seven, some five, some three. I think that a sufficient example will then be made . . . the sepoys will see that we punish to deter and not for vengeance.'

A parade was held of armed and disarmed troops. In the presence of all, forty men were blown to fragments at the mouth of guns. 'Thousands of outsiders had poured in from the surrounding country to be spectators of the tremendous ceremony.' Every form of ceremonial pomp was used; guns boomed a salute as Brigadier Cotton rode on to the parade-ground. Every deliberate detail of inspection and review, every peal of trumpets and rattle of arms, made the conclusion more weighty, more considered and more terrible. After that parade, the people of Peshawar had no more doubts; the handful of men who at such a moment and in the face of such odds had dared to do that, and with such imposing, such insolent calm, would assert their iron will on Hindustan.

There was one British soldier to every three Hindustanis and to every two thousand warlike Punjabis. Every officer in the Punjab believed that the only freedom of which the people of the country had been deprived was freedom to murder and oppress each other, to burn widows and torture peasants. Every officer believed that the English would in the end restore their rule; if the Punjab stood fast, it would not be long before that day came; if the Punjab went, the whole country would have to be reconquered slowly and bloodily. Therefore the Punjab must now be held at all costs.

It was no time to be squeamish. Men were hanged for seditious conversation. There were cases when government servants were hanged for 'having failed in their duty to the State', not for a positive act but for being lukewarm. 'The Punjab authorities adhered to the policy of over-awing, by a prompt and stern initiative . . . and would brook nothing short of absolute, active and positive loyalty. Government could not con-descend to exist upon the moral sufferance of its subjects,' wrote Cooper of Amritsar, a claim more insolent, more superb, than perhaps any made in history.

That same Cooper was responsible for the most extreme example of severity I have found. It is not a pleasant tale, but in fairness it should be told. And the attempt must be made to understand feelings on both sides.

Until Delhi was recaptured from the mutineers – which was not till September 14 – it was touch and go in the Punjab. Very few Sikhs from the Punjab proper came to the colours till Delhi had fallen. No one was sure how long the Punjab troops and police would hold fast; there were large numbers of Hindustani troops disarmed who if they escaped would no doubt increase the strength of the mutineers in Delhi.

At Delhi, a small British force on the Ridge watched an army of mutinous sepoys of at least five times, and sometimes nearer twenty times, their numbers. The great states; the Bombay army; Nepal, Hyderabad, Dost Mohammed in Kabul – all watched Delhi for the result. Still Delhi did not fall. John Lawrence had seen from the first the importance of Delhi; at last he decided it was Delhi or nothing. Taking the Frontier on trust, holding the Punjab with his left hand only, John Lawrence shifted all the strength he could muster to the Ridge. He sent every man and gun. He held the Punjab by a shred of faith that a stray shot might sever.

This was the English side. The left hand had to hold. On the other side, it is not hard to imagine the calculations of the disarmed sepoys in Lahore; their brothers were fighting in Delhi, but they had no arms and it was hardly safe to move. But every now and then any rational reckoning-up would be blown to the winds by a gust of fear. They had committed no fault but they were not trusted with arms. They were under suspicion – and in the Punjab in the summer of 1857 men were sometimes hanged on suspicion.

Early in July, the disarmed 26th Native Infantry broke from Lahore and fled; they killed a Major and two warrant officers in the going. They turned north, as if they meant to hide in the hills and make their way gradually eastward to their homes. They entered Amritsar, Cooper's district; they were attacked by a force of Sikh villagers under the *tahsildar*, a subordinate magistrate. They were unarmed, and weak from want of food. About a hundred and fifty were killed by the quarterstaffs of the villagers. About two hundred and fifty took refuge on an island in the river.

Cooper arrived in the evening with thirty Sikh troopers, and another thirty Muslims whom he did not regard as reliable. The mutineers surrendered peacefully and were bound; he got them ashore by means of two leaky boats and conveyed them to the nearest police-station, six miles away, where they were locked up for the night. He was the only Englishman present and it was no mean feat.

Cooper had meant from the start to finish them off and had made arrangements for immediate execution. Some more were captured during the night, bringing the number in the lock-up to 282. In the morning he began to carry out his intention.

'Ten by ten the sepoys were called forth. Their names having been taken down in succession, they were pinioned, linked together, and marched to execution, a firing-party being in readiness.' The number executed had arrived at two hundred and thirty-seven when the remainder refused to come out of the bastion where they had been imprisoned. It was supposed that they were planning a rush, but 'behold! they were nearly all dead. Unconsciously, the tragedy of Holwell's Black Hole had been reenacted ... Forty-five bodies, dead from fright, exhaustion, fatigue, and partial suffocation, were dragged into light.'

Cooper had been no more aware than Suraj-ud-Daula that his prisoners were dying, but Suraj-ud-Daula has never been regarded as a model ruler. Cooper had deprived these men of liberty and was responsible for their lives. They had surrendered 'in the insane belief' that they would be given a trial. He made sure, one may assume, that his horse was fed that night and even a condemned prisoner is entitled to as much care as a newly bought litter of pigs.

Cooper in his account argues that 'had the 26th Native Infantry escaped, or even had their punishment been less terrible and instantaneous, the whole of the disarmed regiments would of a certainty have followed their example ... their extermination probably saved the lives of thousands.' So spoke Dyer seventy years later. But the man on the spot is concerned with the local situation and with that only. He is not entitled to act on his own authority from mere impatience or because he wishes to force higher authority into something he suspects would be refused sanction.

The men were technically mutineers and their lives were technically forfeit, but when before has every man of a mutinous regiment been executed? As to expediency, what Lawrence had written of the 55th at Peshawar was still true; ten men executed at Lahore in the presence of the troops would have had a more deterrent effect than two hundred in an obscure village. And there was a note of gloating triumph in Cooper's telling of the story that is sickening. Lawrence backed him up in public because it was essential to back up a junior but to the end of his life Lawrence spoke of Cooper's account of what he had done as nauseous.

One must feel pity for those two hundred and fifty men, starving, wet and exhausted, hunted and terrified, dragged out to death. One must feel shame that an Englishman could have fallen to the depths of flippant brutality that Cooper displayed. But it remains true, that six or seven thousand British had to keep their hold on fourteen million warlike people and yet find strength to recover Delhi; if there had not been such men as Lawrence and Montgomery in the Punjab, if they had faltered or shown fear, the bloodshed would in the end have been far greater. They saved India; Delhi fell in September, and from that day onwards everyone in India knew what the end would be. The bluff held good; men began to come over to the winning side and now, 'friends were as thick as summer flies' once more.

INTERVAL

―――――――◆―――――――

The three hundred and fifty years the English spent in India make a story which unfolds itself like an Elizabethan play in five acts. The first sets the scene and shows them as traders. In the second they transform themselves into rulers. In the third, the hero – who is not one man but a thousand – appears to be at the height of his glory, but the contradiction in his own character and the conflict in the whole situation are already apparent; he has triumphed for the moment but the conflict is unresolved. The fourth act will show a hardening of the elements of strife. And the last act shows the result, which has in it triumph as well as tragedy.

The Mutiny was neither an end nor a beginning but an interruption. It was inspired by people for whom progress was too fast, by priests and princes who did not like to see their old world melt. Those who supplied this inspiration were not themselves organized, but they acted dispersedly on the one organized source of power, the Bengal Army. And in that there were already at work just those ingredients which were always to be found when there was trouble in that Army, officers who did not know their men, discontent at minor incidents of military life, the soldier's loss of prestige at home in the village. The result was a reactionary outbreak of force, defeated by force, but symptomatic of a deeper disorder that was not to declare itself frankly for years to come.

The Mutiny then was an interruption. Nor was there anything new about the direct assumption of responsibility by the Crown which followed it; Lord Granville in 1813 had said in Parliament that 'the British Crown is *de facto* sovereign in India'. Each of the great Government of India Acts, in 1813, 1833 and 1853, had asserted a little more clearly the sovereignty of Parliament. All that happened in 1858 was the final extinction of a corporation through whom sovereignty had once been exercised, but over whom parliamentary control had been progressively strengthened.

The first English in India were petitioners for leave to trade. But they found it necessary to have cities of refuge in which they could be secure from the power of Indian monarchs to impose from time to time a capital levy on merchants in their dominions. This necessity, together with an obstinate determination not to play second fiddle to the French, led to the astonishing twenty years between 1740 and 1760, by which date the English had ceased to be petitioners and had become the first power in India.

Presented with absolute power there were many among these merchants who used it as a cynic might expect. But that shameful period did not last long and soon we have Verelst as Governor-General instructing his District Officers to be patient, accessible and sympathetic and Pattle confessing with some embarrassment his 'partiality' for the people of his district. In another twenty years there is Roberdeau already superbly claiming to be 'minutely just, inflexibly upright', a member of a Service without rival for integrity 'in the whole world'.

Then came the golden age of Elphinstone, Metcalfe and Munro, men who used absolute power for the good of those they ruled, who rejoiced in a battle or a hog-hunt and yet could meditate on philosophy and think of the past and the future as part of history, who already looked ahead to the end of our rule. The pace increased and there came in their stead Thomason and the Lawrences, and their followers such as Edwardes or Taylor, who wrote that 'there was a glow of work and duty round us in the Punjab such as I have never felt before or since', unresting men who worked at white heat, who gave all they had to their work and who yet, by the side of that earlier generation, seem humourless and dogmatic. It was in their time that the interruption came.

Elphinstone and Munro had pondered constantly on what would happen when 'the Natives were so far improved' as to be capable of self-government. In the generations before and after the interruption, that was forgotten in the absorbing task of perfecting the system of rule by Guardians. Then, as the system became technically more and more efficient, the problem of how it was to end became more and more insistent. It had now to be settled by what process the English should 'take the glory of their achievement as their reward' and leave this Empire which they had built with so much blood and so much expenditure of vital force. That is the last act.

This is a book about the men who ruled India, about what kind of men they were. Go to stay a night with a certain kind of English family and a portrait or a book will come out from the lumber-room, a sword or a writing-desk or a bundle of letters; he served in India, they will tell you, and gazing at the fading sepia of the photograph or the long sloping characters of his hand, you try to picture the man and what he did, what he felt about his part in life and his fantastic exile in an empire seven thousand miles across the sea. You can learn a little of his outward habits and what he achieved — but to understand fully these must be set against a background as complex as the score of a symphony.

There is the will of England, political control from Westminster, alternating in the fourth act between the kind of views represented by Gladstone and Morley and those of Disraeli and Joseph Chamberlain. Liberals and Conservatives had much in common, but the emphasis was different. One party had more faith than the other in the ability of Indians to govern themselves eventually. Both believed that the English were trustees, but in a different sense. To one it seemed inevitable that the wards should come of age and right that the trustee should train them for responsibility; the other was less sure that for a long time to come there would be much lightening of the White Man's Burden.

This party conflict in England was the sign of an inner conflict between profound but simple ideas. The English believed in personal liberty for themselves, and in their own country were steadily moving towards a wider distribution of political power. But they were confused about whether this tendency should extend outside the island; were the people of the Empire their brothers, or not of the same clay?

English ideas were confused, and those which prevailed for the moment in Parliament were asserted with less and less attention to views from India. This was bound to happen; steam, the electric telegraph, the Canal, brought England nearer; the Press and the vote spread interest in India and brought responsibility home to Parliament. As London tried to tighten control on India, so Simla tried to tighten on the provinces and the provinces on the district officer. At the same time, individual officers were far more certain of England's imperial destiny, far more conscious of the lead given her by industry and sea power. There was then a growing rigidity, a hardening of the arteries, an increasing uniformity, a sense of superiority and a lack of human sympathy, more red tape, more office work, less of the old direct human rule of one man which India had always understood.

That was one strain in the music. But there was another. There was always far more understanding between individual Englishmen and individual Indians than appeared from outside. The men of the service were chosen and trained on Plato's principles as Guardians who would rule in the light of their own vision of what was right. Such a system aims at producing confidence and certainty, virtues in a ruler which may degenerate into arrogance towards the ruled. But this confidence turned at least as often to an easy and humorous disregard for authority. As the system grew stiffer, character became more and more what saved it, the character of individual district officers, choleric, eccentric, warm-hearted men, who did not always pay attention to Government orders.

The visitor to India, such as James Bryce, in 1888, might find the men with whom he dined in Simla hard-working, able but unimaginative. But his host was probably a man who had had his first step as an Under Secretary. A good Under Secretary is patient and industrious; he makes suggestions but is submissive if they are treated with scorn; fire and imagination, burning zeal, anything at all unEnglish, are qualities that it may well be politic to suppress.

But it is not so in a district. The young District Magistrate in a lonely district is monarch of all he surveys and can be as unEnglish as he likes, provided he has sense enough to keep his ebullience out of his fortnightly reports. And in fact the system did produce plenty of men whose fads provided just that warmth the centre lacked, men with hobbies they enjoyed which happened very often also to be something the district needed.

On the whole the nearer men were to each other, English or Indian, the kindlier they felt. It was in Calcutta or Simla, or in the long vacuum of the Northern hot weather, that thoughts turned sour and stale and men spoke of 'the natives' with dislike, contempt, or even a touch of unconscious fear. Impossible, once the smell of canvas and smoky fires was in your nostrils, a horse between your knees on a dewy morning, or walking home in the darkness through the wafts of rich scent that eddy slowly round the village − impossible then to think of Sohan Singh or Mohammad Khan in such terms as that! No, he was a man − a man to be circumvented in some nefarious plot, to be encouraged by promotion or reward, or simply helped because you liked him − but in every case much more real than that shadowy and usually hostile abstraction the Government.

Attitudes, however, were changing throughout the fourth act. Like Elphinstone, Thomason had believed that education would solve all problems. But by the 1880s, when the 'educated Indian' was a reality, he became a rival and it was easy to be irritated by his airs of adult independence. At the same time, far from meekly accepting all that Western education offered, Hinduism had turned back to its own traditions and for a time was inclined to defend even institutions such as child marriage and caste. Nationalism turned defiantly Hindu, and more and more educated Indians were in varying degrees nationalist at heart.

There was a growing contrast, then, between the ideal of an India held in trust, and on the other the reality of despotic power. It was an odd kind of despotism, because its distinguishing principle was the delegation of power. Almost from the day he arrived in India, a member of the Guardian caste was given authority which anywhere else he could hardly have attained with less than twenty years' experience; he felt confident that he would be supported and that what he did would be understood. And he too must learn to delegate if he was to get through the day's work. The result was a great economy in the number of despots needed and less rigidity than might have been expected. It was despotism tempered by economy − and also by the despot's liberal upbringing.

This is a book about men, not about systems or philosophies. No generalization is true about all these men. And yet there is a change, as the centuries progress, a change of profound importance, which affects most of them. Hawkins and the Elizabethans believed that the hand of God was active about them; they made no more question of His lively presence than did the Muslims or Hindus around them. The Victorians of the fourth act in this long play lived in a world of doubt; it was the age of Darwin, Tennyson and Matthew Arnold. An assertive note creeps into the voice with which most men speak of the Almighty. They protest rather loudly that they are doing the Lord's work. And they are inclined to stress that masculine austerity in the God of the Old Testament that distinguished Him most sharply from the many-armed divinities of the Hindu.

In the fifth act, the period of reform, this tendency changes again. Religion in this period is seldom mentioned. But the moral framework within which each man proceeds is distinctively Christian; it insists on the value of the individual. As to dogma, this is not a word that has a pleasing ring to men who have spent their lives trying to prevent the bloodshed that is likely to follow the clash of hostile creeds. A handful of professed agnostics, a handful of the orthodox, you would find; most, if questioned, would admit to accepting the fundamentals of Christianity but to some scepticism as to the detail of ancient dogma and to a feeling that man is here to do what he can in this world rather than prepare for the next. With that change came less sense of a mission, but also less sense of strain in dealing with people of other creeds.

Early in the new century the first steps were taken in a process that would hand over power to Indian parties responsible to an electorate in India. To many of the Guardians the pace seemed too swift, but to many politically minded Indians it seemed too slow. In theory, the wards were learning how to manage their own affairs; in practice they were fighting to get control at once. To the Deputy Commissioner, engaged in efforts to prevent people killing each other, utterances from London or Delhi seemed often fantastically unreal; this contrast between tactical and strategic aims is one reason why the man on the spot sometimes appeared hostile to the declared policy of his country. But though there were different views about the right pace, almost everyone was agreed that trustees cannot go on when the ward has come of age and no longer wants advice.

The last part of the story is one, then, in which against a background of growing complexity in the business of government, a caste of Guardians who had been amateur despots transform themselves into a modern civil service, indigenous and answerable to a legislature. While they did this, they had to carry on a surreptitious, intermittent and undeclared civil war with the people to whom they were handing over power and whom they were supposed to be training for responsibility. At the same time they could never lose sight of their first task, which was to preserve order, to keep chaos at bay.

The growing bitterness between Hindu and Muslim is one feature of the last act. The two religions are alike in one respect only, that for their devotees they affect every aspect of life – clothes, food, attitude to the family, sacred books, language, mythology. At best they can be oil and water, but historically Islam had been the faith of conquerors. For a hundred years the two creeds had lain down unwillingly together beneath a yoke alien to either. The suggestion that the yoke might soon be removed was itself enough to bring both to their feet in wary but hostile surmise. One stream of nationalism became militantly Hindu, one dogmatically secular; Islam remembered the valour of past generations and realized with shock that her sons were unfitted for the new warfare of ballot-box and competitive examination. As the end grew nearer, strife increased and the chance became almost daily less that unity would remain as England's one indubitable gift to India.

At the same time a revolution was taking place in ideas of what a government ought to do. As little as possible – that had been the classical answer in the nineteenth century. Now that was changed and a government was expected to develop, to stimulate, to encourage, to originate. And for this kind of government, the despotism of a foreign caste, however benevolent, is not really suitable. Simla had been more socialist than Westminster in the last century; in this it fell behind in that function of government which initiates and develops. It was a pity that the departments handed over to Indian ministers in 1919 were those concerned with this new aspect of administration – education, local government, the 'nation-building' services. They came to be regarded by the Guardians as secondary to the old main business of seeing that chaos did not come again. To the Guardians they were frills. To the nationalist they became immensely important and he came to take for granted finance, police and defence, the essential pillars of the state.

There is much to regret in the way the end came. But that the end could not have been longer delayed, that it was the fulfilment of the best part of what the English had stood for – of all but unity – hardly one of the Guardians would have denied. In a final assessment – perhaps a hundred years from now – the awakening of India's spirit which took place in the nineteenth century will have to be weighed and a balance struck. In the scale will be set all the best that India acquired from contact with England – a liberal and rational approach to human institutions, a sense of the individual's value and yet of his duty to the state; in the other scale must come the lack of self-confidence bred by alien rule, the lack of realism encouraged by an alien educational system, the instinct to resist even a reasonable suggestion because it came from the patronizing, superior West.

Here then are the last two acts in the story of the Guardians. Here are the Guardians, selected and trained now on more Platonic lines than before, being, as Plato says, 'brought up from their childhood to imitate whatever is proper to their profession and to model themselves on brave, sober, religious and honourable men'. The words are Plato's, but they might be Dr Arnold's: 'if he'll only turn out a brave, helpful truth-telling Englishman and a gentleman and a Christian, that's all I want', was the meditation of Squire Brown, as he said goodbye to Tom on the morning he left for Rugby. But it was with some surprise that in the fifth act the Guardians suddenly perceived that they had in fact been creating freedom, that all they had been doing wrote their own death-warrant. Yet from beginning to end, they seem the same men; with all their differences, there is something in common to them all. They think their own thoughts and do their duty in their own way − and it is a way of which no people need be ashamed.

Mrs Moss-King's sketch of Rahim, the bearer, playing with Carleton, later Sir Carleton Moss-King.

PART IV
The Guardians 1858–1909

12

AFTER THE MUTINY

1 A Liberal Conservative

It would be absurd to pretend that the Mutiny was not of importance to the way Englishmen and Indians came to look at each other. On the other hand, it is easy to make too much of it. The Mutiny happened in Hindustan, the country between Patna and Delhi, and hardly anywhere else. For the Punjab, Bengal and Sind, it was a time of great anxiety, but for those in the South it was quite remote. Even in the North, after a very few months things on the surface were almost as they had been. In the districts round Delhi, the instalment of land revenue that fell due in the summer of 1857 was paid in part that autumn and the winter instalment was paid as usual.

Bitterness of course remained. The civilian seems on the whole to have recovered more quickly than the soldier, both more quickly than the trader or planter. Alfred Lyall, two years out of Haileybury, had been in the thick of the fighting, had killed a man in battle, had hanged sepoys afterwards. But he could feel no animosity against villagers who 'thought we were all gone and reverted to the fashion of their forefathers'. 'In spite of all that has happened,' he wrote in November 1858, 'I take immense interest in the natives of India and like to be constantly among them.' And Lord Roberts, years later, remembered that racial hatred very soon began to go as Englishmen remembered the fidelity of servants and villagers, of the Hindustani sepoys who fought with Henry Lawrence in defence of the Residency at Lucknow, of the Punjabis with whose help Delhi was taken.

On the English side, the sharpest rancour remained among the traders and planters, and in England *The Times* and *The Spectator* were impressed by the civilian's inordinate bias in favour of 'the native', the fact being that the civilian saw Indian villagers every day and knew that they were people. He really had no time for bitter memories – not at least when he was in camp, riding every day among the young green wheat and tall

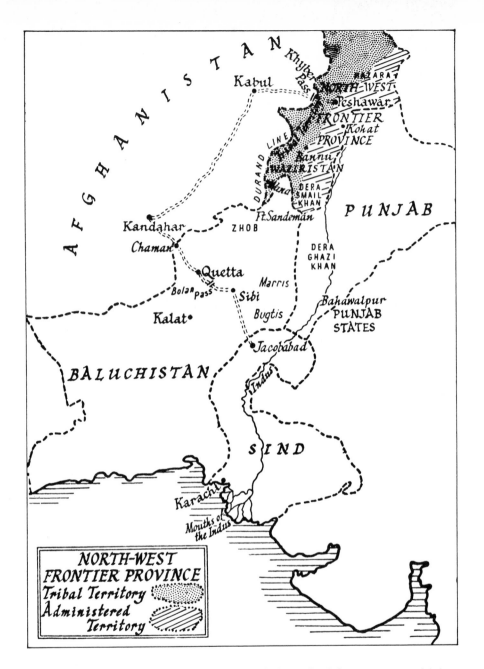

NORTH-WEST
FRONTIER PROVINCE
Tribal Territory
Administered
Territory

sugar-cane, listening to grave long-winded rustic debates, sympathizing over a crop damaged by locusts or a well that had been maliciously spoiled.

The Indian view of the English, however, is much more a matter of speculation. All one can say with confidence is that it is wrong to attribute to 1860 the emotions and arguments of 1920. Asia is careless of human life, used to stern measures, respectful of power. It is my guess that in the

184

Queen Victoria in 1893, with her Indian servant. The Company's servants had long regarded themselves as servants also of the Queen. She came to feel an affection and concern for her Indian people, often strangely reciprocated.

villages there was some anxiety to display repentance, not much hatred and no sense of injustice but an awed and rather chilled fear of the English in general, a gloomy acquiescence in the inevitable. But the fear did often lift like morning mist for the cultivator who met his district officer strolling near his tent with a gun under his arm.

Bitterness on the Indian side was stronger among some of the princes and nobles and the more educated, but it was not so much on account of the ruthless suppression of the revolt as at subsequent slights and rudeness. G.O. Trevelyan has a story, almost inconceivable to anyone who knew India in the next century, of a planter lashing out indiscriminately with a hunting-crop at a group of Indians who had paid to come on to a race-course and had had the effrontery to stand in a good place for the finish.

There were also many decisions that appeared inevitable to everyone in the 1860s but which had become a grievance to Indians by the 1920s; in the army, for instance, all gunners were in future to be English. That seemed natural enough to Indians at the time; it was a frank sign of distrust. It came to be a sign of insincerity only when the English professed to be making the Indian Army into the weapon of a new dominion.

Nor did the change from the Honourable East India Company to the Crown make so much difference as might have been supposed. The Company's servants had long regarded themselves as servants also of the Queen; for long the Court of Directors had been more a convenience to Parliament than an independent body. Their place was now to be taken by the Council of India, who were to be 'neither the masters nor the puppets but the valuable advisers to the new Minister'. The majority of the Council were to be former servants of the Company or the Crown, so that the seasoning of experience would be stronger than before, but to the men in India it did not seem that there was much difference between the Court and the Council.

The most disturbing change was the introduction of competitive examinations in 1853. It seemed to the older Haileybury men that the 'competition-wallahs' belonged to a new race. They were bookish hobbledehoys who fell off their horses, misunderstood Hindustani and made silly mistakes about the ways of the country. But, seen from a distance, there does not seem so great a change; the old hand had always made fun of the 'griffin' – the new arrival – for just these mistakes and many of the first competition-wallahs had fathers or brothers in the service.

It is all the same significant that the most outstanding figure of the ten years after the Mutiny had none of the dogmatic certainty of John Lawrence and his school but looked back always to Elphinstone as the hero of a golden age. Bartle Frere came to India in 1835 and there is a pleasant picture of him learning his work: 'Young Frere was always seen sitting on the carpet by the side of Old Narsopant Tatia, for whom he entertained the highest respect, and whom he used to call by the respectful name of Kakaji [elder uncle].' He was soon assistant settlement officer and later settlement officer, when he came directly under the Revenue Commissioner. 'Since I have been working with Williamson, working himself, and making me work, as hard as we well could, he never once said or wrote a word to let me know he was master . . . It is true that this is the best way

John Jacob, who made a lasting peace on the Sind Border. He founded the Sind Horse; he built a city, roads, railways and canals.

of getting work out of people, but it is not one man in five hundred who does so . . . ' It was, as a matter of fact, to be a tradition of the service, one that Frere learnt from a good master and himself helped to fix.

From settlement and revenue work he went in Lord Dalhousie's time to be Resident at Satara. The Raja died and Frere fought hard for his wishes to be followed and his adopted son recognized as heir. But Dalhousie was adamant and the State was annexed. Frere had to administer the territory which he thought had been unjustly acquired. He refused the offer of troops; he could manage without them. And he did. On paper, the most noteworthy development of his reign in Satara was the introduction of municipalities, the first in India, committees who collected funds and kept the towns clean; but it is not less important that when he left 'the grief of both Europeans and natives was evident . . . I saw men of both nationalities in tears . . . '

In 1850, Frere succeeded Sir Charles Napier as Commissioner in Sind. Here, too, he started municipalities, and fought great battles with Bombay on behalf of the port of Karachi. When he left Sind, he had convinced the Secretary of State that 'Kurrachee and not Calcutta is the natural port of the Punjab'.

He had done a great deal more than that. He built roads, railways, post-offices, travellers' bungalows, above all canals. In the older parts of India the use of postage-stamps was opposed on the grounds that the country was not yet sufficiently advanced. In the newest and least developed province, Frere printed his own stamps and devised without sanction a postal service.

But canals and roads came before anything else. A network was gradually spread over the country; a sample was the work carried out in the frontier districts, where Jacob 'cleared and laid out 2,589 miles of road . . . furnished with 786 masonry bridges, 88 of which, across navigable canals, were passable by boats of the largest size'.

John Jacob had begun his work under Napier, but most of it was done in Frere's time and the bond between them was one of trust, friendship, and admiration on both sides. The Sind frontier is the southern end of the chain of mountains and desert that make the North-West Frontier. Jacob's work lay at the junction of these two sections, where the people of Sind confront tribesmen, Baluch and Afghan, wild moss-troopers who until now had lived by loot, men among whom the blood-feud was the only justice known. From their stony and icy heights, it had long been their custom to raid the plains of Sind, carrying off camels, cattle and goats by the ten thousand.

Here Jacob made his headquarters, in a sandy country below the mountains, where the heat in summer is as intense as any man has to endure on the earth's surface. He built houses, planted trees, covered the country with a network of roads and canals, while with two regiments of irregular horse – the Sind Horse – he so chastised the raiding tribesmen that he brought peace to the border.

Frere gave him a free hand and saw that he was disturbed as little as possible. 'I must have no courts-martial or articles of war,' Jacob wrote to Frere. 'I want no lawyers among my men, neither do I wish to govern them by force or fear. I . . . will govern them by appealing to their higher, not to their basest, attributes.' In fact the punishment on which he relied was to turn a man out of the regiment; it was felt so bitter a disgrace and deprivation that no other was needed. Though most of his men were from Hindustan, their fidelity in the Mutiny was never doubted. Every man was inspired with his commander's spirit. Instant readiness for action, unshakable tenacity in pursuit of lawbreakers – these were the watchwords.

The same spirit lived in all Jacob's men, English or Indian alike. The English officers were not expected to take leave; both their private fortune and their pay were spent on the regiment or on the new town. They scorned fans and ice; they endured the heat without mitigation. The few huts with which Jacob began grew in seven years to a town of seven thousand inhabitants, with a laboratory, engineers' and carpenters' workshops, a large and valuable library. Surrounding the town were miles and miles of irrigated cultivation, where once there had been desert.

With Frere's backing, Jacob made a lasting peace on the Sind border, 'converting the murderer and robber into a harmless and industrious peasant', and Frere always believed that if the principles used on that frontier had been accepted further North, the Punjab border too could have been settled. No Frontier officer will assent to that belief, but it was strongly held in Sind.

The first difference was that in Sind Jacob was Deputy Commissioner of the frontier districts as well as commandant of the Sind Horse, whereas in the Punjab the Political Officer did not command the troops. This was in accordance with Frere's lifelong belief that in India there should be one head only to whom power is delegated. No specialized department should make any arrangements in the district that were not subject to the district officer's comment and control. The best system for India, Frere thought, was 'a good vigorous despotism, in which the risks of tyranny and arbitrary oppression are minimised, one in which the despot is accessible, when every man sees, knows, and can appeal to his own despot'.

The second great difference in frontier policy was even more far-reaching. The Punjab made the tribe responsible for any breach of the peace. If a raid took place and the tribe did not make immediate amends, the crops and villages of the tribe were burnt. This, argued Frere, was not only unjust in itself but put the tribe in an economic position from which the only escape was another raid. In Sind, the actual raiders must be followed up and either killed in fight or captured.

Again, Frere and Jacob strengthened the hand of the Khan of Kalat.

Their troopers did not hesitate to pursue a criminal into the Khan's territory, but when he was captured they would hand him over for justice, while they behaved across the border as civilized troops should in the territory of an ally. Again, the Sind authorities would not permit tribal warfare and forbade anyone on British territory to carry arms without a licence; most rigorously they forbade any form of private vengeance. Justice was in the hands of the Khan on one side of the frontier, of Jacob on the other. To plead a blood-feud was so far from extenuating murder that it was taken as proof that the crime was premeditated.

In the Punjab frontier districts, on the other hand, the customs were almost exactly opposite. Every man bore arms by right, the tribes were encouraged – Frere believed – to avenge offences committed against them by other tribes, the authority of the Amir was denied and troops never crossed the frontier except to inflict punishment, which was directed not against individuals but against the tribe and was therefore indiscriminate.

To all this, the Punjab frontier man would reply that Sind methods could not be applied to different people in different country, but Frere was never convinced. He particularly disliked indiscriminate punitive raids.

During the Mutiny, Frere's part was not unlike that of John Lawrence. The people of Sind remembered the misrule of the Amirs; here, as in the Punjab, there was no general disaffection. But there were units of the Bengal Army in Sind and no one could feel unshakably certain about the Bombay regiments. Frere held the province; he organized a supply line into the Punjab and postal lines both into the Punjab and across the desert to Agra and Calcutta; he dealt with the mutinies that did occur, he checked others before they reached a head. In July, he had only one hundred and thirty-nine effective British bayonets at his disposal for the whole of Sind. For four months he never passed a night without being disturbed by dispatches, 'often three or four times in a night', yet he was always able to lie down at once and go peacefully to sleep. He was able to spare troops for the Deccan and would have sent some to the Punjab if they had been accepted. His letters are always calm, cheerful and confident at a time when there was much hysteria. His belief in God sustained him, as it sustained the Lawrences, but it was a quieter belief and less exacting for other people.

It was not a time for hesitation and Frere did not shrink from executing the ringleaders of the risings that occurred in the 16th and 21st Native Infantry. But even here there was something characteristic. Finding on one occasion that a gallows had been put up before a trial began, he gently but firmly insisted that it should be taken down; the issue must not be prejudged. And before long he succeeded in persuading the General that courts-martial should consist of native officers. They were 'even more prompt and as severe as the European court', while the troops were made much more clearly aware of what was happening and convinced of its justice.

The heart of his political creed is expressed in a letter he wrote immediately after the Mutiny at a time when there was much controversy among Indian officials about the attitude the Government ought to take towards Christianity. Herbert Edwardes – once of Bannu – had come to believe that the Mutiny was a divine chastisement for the sin the English had committed as a nation by accepting a compromise with false religions. He wished to observe no Hindu or Muslim holidays, to refuse all recognition to caste, to teach from the Bible in all schools. Frere disagreed altogether: 'Let the Government of this world keep the peace and do justice and mercy to the best of its power, and rule the people so that peace and plenty prevail throughout the land, but let not Government presume to dictate to the meanest of its subjects what he shall believe . . . ' This was tolerance in the true line of descent from Warren Hastings, Elphinstone and Metcalfe. All Frere's utterances bear the stamp of that majestic dynasty, a liberal recognition that it is wise to be conservative about Indian society, to support Indian institutions, to admit Indian nobles and professional men to a share of power, to foster an upper class of Indians with an interest in the continuance of the régime. He disliked 'a policy which puts all real power into the hands of European officials and European colonists and treats the natives as at best *in statu pupillari* . . . to be governed . . . according to our latest English notions of what is best for them.'

Frere became the close friend and constant adviser of Lord Canning. He believed that Dalhousie's policy of refusing to recognize adoption and of annexing a State to which there was no direct male heir was regarded as an interference with Indian custom and unjust. He believed it had been a main cause of the Mutiny and was still a source of uneasiness to all chiefs and princes. His views were accepted; they were embodied in Queen Victoria's proclamation, the Princes were assured the right to adoption – and the States were petrified for ninety years. At the time, hardly any Indian could have been found who did not think this just. That the settlement proved an obstacle to progress sixty years later was a development which no one then foresaw or could have foreseen.

Frere, in agreement with Canning, was largely responsible for introducing an important step in constitutional progress. He proposed a widened legislative council, representative but not elected, its proceedings being public and the members being nominated by the Government from non-officials, European and Indian, with legislative bodies framed on similar lines for the provinces. An Act to this effect was passed by Parliament; three Indians became Members of the Viceroy's Legislative Council; in Bombay, Sir George Clerk, an intimate friend of Frere's, appointed four Indians. It was an important first step.

From Calcutta he went back as Governor to Bombay. 'You ask why I am always thinking and talking of irrigation,' he wrote to one of his children. 'If you had seen men's bones, as I have, lying unburied by the roadside, and on entering a village had found it untenanted by a living person, you would understand why.' He was a regular correspondent of Miss Nightingale, who wrote to him in 1860 after he had left Bombay: 'Bombay has a lower death-rate on the last two years than London, the healthiest city in Europe. This is entirely your doing. If we do not take care, Bombay will outstrip us in the sanitary race. People will be ordered for the benefit of their health to Bombay.'

Lord Canning was succeeded as Viceroy by Lord Elgin and he by John Lawrence. Frere welcomed Lawrence with an offer of loyal co-operation, in which he never failed, but there were great differences between them. John Lawrence was the first of the levellers, those protectors of the poor who had little respect for Indian institutions and the old order, who believed that hereditary chiefs kept the light of the sun from the poor peasant. Frere on the other hand belonged to the school of Elphinstone and Henry Lawrence, men whose reforms would never be radical, who thought rather of individuals than of systems and wished no one to be the worse for British rule. There were too their clearly expressed differences on Frontier problems. Both, however, were men of size enough to respect each other and there would not have been much controversy if John Lawrence had ruled India as well as he had ruled the Punjab.

Sir Bartle Frere, a liberal conservative of whom his biographer wrote despairingly that he seemed too good to be true.

Unfortunately, he came to his last spell of Indian service without the elasticity to learn new ways. He had been to the Punjab exactly the 'good vigorous despot' of Frere's ideal; he had been prompt, laconic, accessible; generous in delegating power to his chosen subordinates, he had always backed them up and had known what was happening in every district.

No one could have the same detailed knowledge of everything in India, but he tried to govern India as though it were the Punjab. And finding the old informal flexible Punjab system would not work, he fell back on rigidity, on hard and fast rules and no exceptions.

There were differences too over foreign policy, with which Frere was directly concerned only in respect of Aden and the Persian Gulf. In the Gulf, Frere spoke up for 'the duty and responsibility of protecting general commerce'. Lawrence, however, wanted 'to confine our labours, as a rule, to the suppression of piracy on the high seas'.

This was part of his general foreign policy of 'masterly inactivity', of 'keeping within our shell', which to Frere seemed 'a tempting sort of policy that looks safe and cheap', but which was really selfish, timid and short-sighted.

Frere, it will be seen, was deeply conscious of the destiny of Victorian England to police the seven seas and in a hundred ways to use her influence for peace and for the suppression of evils. In 1867 he left Bombay, after thirty-two years without furlough, but he does not entirely leave the Indian stage. He was a more than usually active and valuable member of the Council of India and there are glimpses of him working out a health plan for the whole of India – 'It is a noble paper – and what a present to make to a Government! . . . God bless you for it!' wrote Miss Nightingale – reforming the administration of the British Army, working always at articles, speeches, minutes. And his Indian training, surely, was responsible for the action he took on two occasions when he was dispatched on missions for the British Government.

He was sent to Zanzibar with the object of inducing the Sultan to end the slave trade to Arabia. His instructions were not very precise, and when the Sultan politely refused to do as he was told, Frere told him that in future British naval vessels would stop the transport of slaves to or from his island. The Cabinet was taken aback but after some hesitation accepted what had been peacefully accomplished. The trade was ended. A politician or a diplomat trained in Whitehall would have waited for further instructions; the Cabinet would have hummed and hawed; it may well be that another thirty thousand slaves would have reached Arabia if Frere had not done what he thought right.

Governor of the Cape Colony and High Commissioner for South Africa, he once again acted in perfect simplicity, as he would have done had he been a district officer, confident that his Commissioner would back him up. But that is another story.

Sir Bartle Frere is a man of whom his biographer wrote despairingly that he seemed too good to be true. That too is the impression made by a calm brow, the steady jaw, the forthright gaze. But there is no smack of priggishness about his quiet faith in God, his complete lack of selfishness. He was deeply loved. 'I have never known his like' – 'I loved him as a father' – 'I never spoke to him without being the better for it' – those were the phrases used of him by all who knew him. But the quality which gave worth to his great gifts was moral stamina. He judged every question by his own standards, which were absolute and admitted of no compromise. He did not consider whether his views would please his superiors or magnify his own importance but whether they were right. There cannot have been many periods in the world's history when it has been possible to rise to the highest posts in a public service by the unfaltering practice of such a principle as this. Nor could any other service in the world have given the opportunity for so prolonged and independent an exercise of such high responsibility as had been Frere's.

2 Clodhopping Collector

The Mutiny was over; things settled down. In the letters and biographies of the 1860s and 1870s, English administrators do not often betray a feeling of insecurity. They belonged to a service which gave them an assured position and the right to be themselves. In his district, the district officer was supreme; if he had a normal allowance of tact and intelligence, rather more tenacity of purpose and the good luck not to be transferred too often, he could get his way sooner or later in most things that he undertook. His work was extremely varied; there was plenty of it but most of it was interesting. He had the respect of the people among whom he lived. His pay never seemed quite enough for the education of eight or nine children in England, but he had the prospect of an annuity on retirement or a pension for his wife if he died.

Even if he distinguished himself in no way at all, if he never became any more than a 'clodhopping Collector', his life would not have been a bad one. He could probably count to his credit roads, bridges, a school or two, a hospital or canal, perhaps the field maps of a district. These were solid achievement, something beyond the day to day business of settling disputes, preserving the peace, keeping the wheels smoothly running. If, on the other hand, he had emerged from the ruck, there was hardly a limit to what he might do; he might find himself advising on war and peace, framing a country's budget, making plans that would affect the happiness of millions; he might govern a province the size of Great Britain.

In Madras and Bombay, a man went out to a district on arrival, but a Bengal man still had to pass language examinations in Calcutta. John Beames has left a detailed account of his first months in Calcutta in 1858 and 1859. He lived in a boarding-house, where he shared a sitting-room

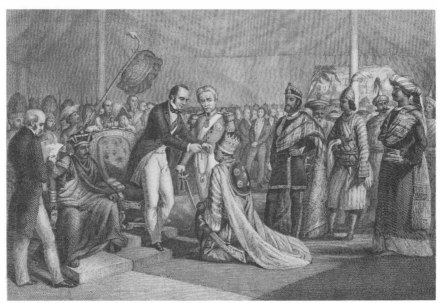

Durbar at Cawnpore after the Mutiny. Lord Canning, who had been Governor-General throughout the Mutiny, was strongly in favour of reconciliation afterwards and is here seen confirming the rights of leaders who had been loyal, and bestowing decorations. He was known as 'Clemency Canning' – meant as a reproach but a proud title today.

with a friend; they rose early, at five or soon after, drank tea on a balcony in their pyjamas, and about six went to ride. 'At seven we came in and got into pyjamas again. Many of our old Haileybury friends would drop in and our cool shady veranda was full of men drinking tea, smoking, reading the papers or letters, talking, laughing and enjoying themselves.' After breakfast, two hours' work on languages was supposed to follow, then calls on ladies, then lunch.

Beames writes with irritation of this idle life. He learnt very little. What was worse, many men fell hopelessly into debt and were crippled for the rest of their service. There were still young men who remarked complacently that they had 'turned their lakh' – that is, accumulated a debt of £10,000. Others, lonely no doubt in a strange land, fell into arms which were stretched wide to catch them and made unhappy marriages. John Beames was engaged to a girl in England, which was unusual; in his innocence he did not even know that he was being pursued in Calcutta. 'I suppose I was a very green conceited young prig,' he writes.

When at last Beames escaped from the College of Fort William, he was posted to the Punjab and, having reached Lahore, to Gujrat seventy miles away on the road to Peshawar.

He drove the seventy miles to Gujrat over unmade roads, jolting, lurching and bumping, as fast as a wild driver could urge relays of half-broken ponies. It was bitterly cold; Beames had been used to Calcutta for a year and had only Calcutta clothes. He was 'almost frozen through' when at last, after hours of 'the agonizing bumping and the piercing cold', the driver put him down in the small hours, 'bewildered and aching in every limb', at 'a little lonely post-house'.

Next day, his first step was to find the Deputy Commissioner. This was Major Herbert Adams of the Guides. He gave his Assistant breakfast, and then 'ignoring in true Punjab style the possibility of anyone being tired or wishing to do anything but work', strapped on his pistol, made Beames do the same, and led the way to court – 'a large, long and not very hideous building in the middle of a plain'. '"This is your court," he said, "and these are your clerks; now go to work," and before I could open my mouth to ask him a single question, he had left the room.

'"These are the cases on your Honour's file – what are your orders?" asked a young Musulman in beautiful Delhi Hindustani with many courteous periphrases. I said, as by instinct, "Call up the first case," though what I was to do with it I knew as little as the man in the moon . . .' The plaintiff and defendant both 'spoke Punjabi, of which I could not understand one word . . .' but the clerk translated into Hindustani as they spoke and Beames wrote in English a summary of what they said, 'so I got on wonderfully well . . . I went to bed intensely tired but very much interested in and pleased with my day's experience'.

Beames, who was an unusually good linguist, soon learnt to speak Punjabi fluently. And by degrees 'all the native nobility and gentry of the district came to call on me and finding I liked their society, used to drop in of an evening and sit talking for hours. With their swords across their knees they would tell me long stories of their adventures in war and foray.'

Adams was succeeded by Hardinge, whom Beames liked better and of whom he always speaks with affection. 'We were in the saddle by five in the morning and worked on horseback for two or three hours, riding about inspecting police-stations, roads and bridges and public buildings under construction, tree-planting, ferry-boats, settling disputes about land and property between villagers, and such-like business.' As Beames was generally in court from ten to six, this made a stiff day, but the administration was simple. 'There was no law in the Punjab in those days. Our instructions were to decide all cases by the light of common-sense and our own sense of what was just and right.'

Two years after he had left England, his fiancée followed Beames. They met at Bulandshahr, near Delhi, in a friend's house and were married there; the bridegroom says nothing of any trepidation on either part though – after two years apart and a journey half way round the world, after crossing Egypt and sailing down the Red Sea, after three weeks' weary travelling from Calcutta, after *dak-garis* and *dak*-bungalows, meeting now among strangers and in so strange a world the young man to whom so much had happened since she saw him last – she, surely, must have passed some anxious hours.

It was a happy marriage, though it included disappointments. Beames had to ride in twenty miles from camp to headquarters; his wife rode with him and there was a miscarriage. Later, Mrs Beames lost her first live child ten days after its birth, owing to injury to the head, caused, Beames believed, by the carelessness of a military surgeon whom he describes as idle and drunken.

Here pause to think for a moment of the Victorian girl, ignorant of her own body and often ashamed of her instincts, alone with the young husband she hardly knows and who is usually as ignorant as herself, thousands of miles from home, surrounded by people utterly alien in upbringing. The gossiping servants, the wondering eyes of villagers, the publicity that in tent life is inescapable for every act of daily routine – all this must have been repugnant to her, even when things were at their smoothest.

And things were seldom smooth for long. Civilians were always moving and seem to have taken no account of the seasons. In his unpublished memoirs, Colonel Henry Urmston, soldier Deputy Commissioner in the Punjab, speaks of a journey made with his young wife from Mainpuri near Cawnpore to Peshawar, some five hundred miles. It took three weeks, in the burning heat of June, and was nearly all accomplished in a litter carried by men in relays; they did thirty or forty miles a night and were supposed to rest by day, but often at dawn there were still twelve miles to go before the resting-place – twelve miles of jolting, over tracks that in the latter part were rocky and precipitous, under the searing sun. Their first child was born less than two months after that journey.

Beames and his wife were not to spend all their life in the Punjab. He was a man of forthright opinions, which he did not hesitate to express; he did not like John Lawrence and no doubt said so. Perhaps he was also felt to have married too soon, while his dislike of soldier civilians was open and strongly expressed. He thought the soldiers had had to intrigue and fawn for civil employ – and said so. It is not surprising that he was transferred.

Beames was at once aware of differences when he arrived in Behar, still part of the Presidency of Bengal. 'In Bengal, before you could issue an order, you had to find a section of an Act or Regulation empowering you to do so. In the Punjab you did so because you thought it was the proper thing to do . . . ' But simpler methods were soon introduced.

A new service was coming into existence, the Police. There was a new Act, the Police Act of 1861, which introduced a uniform system that was gradually to be extended to the whole of British India. The old system had been based on the *darogha* or station officer, a man who was answerable for about twenty square miles of country to the District Magistrate. It was the darogha's own business to enlist and discipline his force of a dozen or half-a-dozen *barkandazes* – literally lightning-throwers, gunmen, the forerunners of constables. Except when the district officer was actually in his area, the darogha was very much his own master.

All this was now to be changed. To each district there was to be a

Superintendent of Police, with deputy superintendents and inspectors. The darogha did not disappear, but he became a sub-inspector subject to regular training and frequent inspection; his constables too were to be trained men and government servants. It was obviously an improvement, for the Magistrate had never had the time to look after the police properly.

The Superintendent had to be a man of parts. He had to recruit, train and discipline his men, build up their physical strength, their self-confidence and their integrity; he must also be a shrewd judge of his officers. He had to leave them to act on their own responsibility, he must not stifle their initiative but must encourage them by constant praise, yet they must live in dread of his censure, must know that they would be detected if they lied to him or tried to conceal a tyranny.

Half the crimes reported to the police in India are fabrications; they are meant to get someone else into trouble or to provide a defence for some anticipated counter-charge. There is in common use a Hindustani word for exactly this process. Before he acts, a man will prepare his defence and make his witnesses word-perfect; the moment he has finished battering his enemy on the head he will hurry his witnesses to the police-station and lodge a complaint against the victim for a premeditated assault. The police officer has to decide whether there is a genuine crime, who is the criminal and whether he can produce proof that will satisfy a judge. The judge or magistrate will then have to decide whether he is confronted by the true criminal and true evidence, by the true criminal and bogus evidence, or by a criminal and evidence alike irrelevant to what happened.

The Superintendent of Police has to reckon what the judge's or magistrate's reaction will be. He needs to some extent the judicial mind. He needs the detective's mind. He must be a trainer. His men must fear him without being frightened.

This new arrangement began while Beames was in Behar and he has a good deal to say about the attempts of the old-fashioned darogha to conform to the new pattern of a smart young officer of the Royal Irish Constabulary. It was as though Dogberry had been suddenly posted to Scotland Yard. He describes 'a good specimen of the class . . . a tall portly Mohammedan, grey-bearded, with a smooth sleek look, crafty as a fox, extremely polished in manner, deferential to his superiors, but haughty and tyrannical to his inferiors. With his huge scarlet turban laced with gold, his sword hung from a gold embroidered baldric, spotless white clothes and long riding boots, he bestrode a gaunt roan horse with grey eyes, a pink nose, and a long flowing tail . . . The old daroghas,' he goes on, 'were often splendid detectives and they certainly knew all the criminals and suspicious characters.'

Beames was District Officer at Champaran, the home of indigo-planters; the planters expected the District Magistrate to dance to their tune. Beames was not a man to shrink from a fight but 'it was not', he says, 'from mere lust for power that I insisted on being master in my own district ... but because the district was a sacred trust delivered to me by Government, and I was bound to be faithful to that charge. I should have been very base had I from love of ease or wish for popularity sat idly by and let others usurp my place and my duties.'

The indigo-planter's hold on his *ryots* carries one back to the worst days of the eighteenth century. The planter let land to peasants on condition that they agreed to pay rent and to grow indigo on a quarter of their land. This they must sell to him. He gave them an advance which he was careful they should never repay in full. Thus they were his debtors as well as his tenants.

Soon after Beames came to Champaran one of these villagers rebelled. The planter sent men who besieged him in his hut. The man and his family could not even go to the well for water. After two days, he escaped by night, eluding the watchers; he lay hidden till daylight, then made his way to Beames and told his story. Beames decided that this was wrongful confinement under the Indian Penal Code and issued a summons against the planter. The planter 'who was as great a coward as he was a bully' paid compensation and ceased to molest the peasant.

In these years after the Mutiny, there was sharp feeling between planters and the servants of the company. There was the case of Rudd, who on the most trivial provocation beat and shot dead a shepherd on the estate where he was employed. The English press clamoured for mercy on the sole ground that Rudd was 'white'. But he was hanged. At this stage, the Lord Chief Justice of Bengal, fresh from England, was uncompromisingly for the planters, while the civilian magistrates and judges, the Haileybury men, like Beames, were usually on the side of the cultivator.

Pugnacious, arrogant if you like, outspoken, swift to condemn, Beames was warm-hearted, steadfast in friendship and love, honest and courageous, hot in defence of the oppressed. Later, in Orissa, where he spent the greater part of his service, he found the orders of the Government of Bengal harsh and oppressive. There was a tax on salt and orders against illicit salt-making and smuggling. But in one part of the district an old woman had little more to do than step out of her hut to pick up the salt for her morning rice. She of course would be dragged fifty miles to court and fined; the smuggler on a large scale could never be caught. Beames disobeyed the orders of Government; he would not have such offences punished and he would not reward the police for bringing them in. He was called sharply to order, took the chance and said what he thought. After long correspondence, the rules were changed; such people were exempted.

Beames shows no interest in shooting or pigsticking, spending his leisure instead on his *Comparative Grammar of the Modern Aryan Languages of India*. This was unusual and, although outspokenness and independence were general in the service, Beames did carry them further than most. All the same, Beames was in many ways a representative district officer.

'I was in fact called upon to act and not to act at the same time,' he says on one occasion, 'a false position in which Government is fond of placing officers by way of shuffling off its own responsibility, a regular Secretariat trick.' The average district officer says something like that very often and inveighs with equal vigour against instructions which leave him no discretion. No one else understands his district; 'the Government' wastes his time by interfering.

Beames is contemptuous of tours by Lieutenant-Governors, which are expensive, encourage the great man to think he knows something when he is utterly ignorant, and leave the district officer with heavy arrears of more important work. It was during such a tour that he committed his worst escapade as an *enfant terrible*, making a speech – late at night – in unmistakable parody of the Lieutenant-Governor, Sir Richard Temple.

Temple was always Beames's *bête noire* but then he does not care for Lieutenant-Governors as a class; his modified praise goes only to George Campbell, a vigorous and outspoken innovator. It is amusing to recognize Beames's Lieutenant-Governors in the verses of 'poor witty Frank Bignold, my predecessor at Balasore, a brilliantly clever man but so unpunctual and unmethodical as to be the ruin of any district that might be in his charge'.

> When Halliday held merry sway,
>   And fiddling was in fashion,
> My Stradivarius I would play
>   For music was my passion;
> Nor hushed my string till Grant was king
>   And indigo unquiet
> Then boldly rushed into the ring
>   The champion of the ryot!
>
> *For this is law that I'll maintain,*
>   *As ably as I can, Sir,*
> *That whatsoever king shall reign,*
>   *I'll be the rising man, Sir.*

Halliday was the first Lieutenant-Governor, appointed in 1853 to relieve the Governor-General of local administration. John Peter Grant was Canning's right-hand man in the Mutiny, and was always champion of the under-dog. After Grant came Beadon and Bignold continues his parody of the Vicar of Bray:

> When Beadon on the dais sat,
>   I shifted my position,
> Collecting sheep and oxen fat
>   To grace his exhibition . . .

Then came Grey and Bignold's 'Rising Man' goes on:

> When Beadon's day had passed away
>   And Grey assumed his station
> With pen in hand I took my stand
>   On the Higher Education . . .
>
> In framing rules for primary schools,
>   In rural exploration,
> My active mind shall seek and find
>   Congenial occupation . . .

Beames, himself a man of energy, approved of George Campbell, a reforming Punjabi, but Campbell's energy made Bignold sigh for the day:

> When 'neath the punkah-frill the Court reclined
> When Court clerks wrote and Judges only signed;
> Or, lordlier still, beneath a virgin space
> Inscribed their names and hied them to the chase.

As a rule he is good-tempered enough, but Bignold becomes bitter, as Beames does, on Richard Temple, of whom he wrote:

> A portent he in hero-worship's line
> Himself adorer, prophet, priest and shrine;
> And who can better an ovation claim
> Than he whose proper hands prepare the same?

Beames had first met Sir Richard in the Punjab when the great man had taken the credit — according to Beames — for a bridge of boats built by his newly arrived junior. He had come in more recently for a good deal of criticism in the service over a scare of famine which proved very expensive. The famine was averted, but to the rank and file of the service in Bengal Temple's prodigality was shocking. Beames wrote:

He set aside the opinions of Sir George Campbell and the Collectors of the afflicted districts and followed his own unaided judgment. In his usual theatrical way, he rode at the rate of 50 or 60 miles a day through the districts, forming as he said an opinion on the condition of the people and the state of the crops . . . He would sit down at night after one of these wild scampers and write a vain-glorious minute in which he stated that he had that day fully examined such and such tracts and come to the conclusion that so much grain, usually three to four times as much as was really wanted, would be required to feed the people.

But though Temple was not liked by district officers, he had had a knack

Sir Richard Temple was Finance Member as well as Foreign Secretary; he held charge of the Central Provinces, Bengal and Bombay. Yet this brilliant man was not admired by his juniors who regarded him as self-seeking and over-ambitious.

for catching the eye of his seniors. He was at Rugby under Arnold before passing out first from Haileybury; he went to the North-West in 1847 and did some settlement work at Muttra and Allahabad; he caught the eye of Thomason, and was among the picked men sent on to the Punjab. He caught John Lawrence's eye and was secretary to the Punjab Board and later to John himself, drafting the great reports of the Punjab administration; with less than ten years' service he was Commissioner of Lahore.

He caught the eye of Dalhousie and of Canning, and went to the Government of India as assistant to the Finance Member; he went on special missions to Burma and Hyderabad and in 1862 was the first Chief Commissioner of the Central Provinces. Municipalities, dispensaries, primary schools, district boards, dripped from his pen; he created, built, endowed, set up and vivified. He went everywhere and saw everything.

Two of the most important posts in the Government of India were Finance Member and Foreign Secretary. Temple held both. The first post in the Political Department was Resident at Hyderabad. Temple held that. He held charge in succession of three Indian provinces, the Central Provinces, Bengal and Bombay.

Yet the judgment of his juniors on this brilliant man was harsh. There is an intimate verdict, not necessarily that of history, often short-sighted, often far from the public's, pronounced by the men of his own profession on every member of a service who reaches high rank. Among Englishmen, that verdict sometimes forgives stupidity, is suspicious alike of brilliance and of unremitting industry, often admires idleness if backed by wit. But it is merciless towards self-seeking, hypocrisy and insincerity. A dash of those qualities must have been mixed with much in Temple that was admirable.

3 Man of Letters

Alfred Lyall was an almost exact contemporary of John Beames, but two men similarly educated could hardly be less alike. Except to close friends and the people he loved, Lyall did not reveal himself easily. To some, indeed, he might seem distrustful of his own powers and judgment, indecisive because he saw both sides of almost every question, too much a poet to be an administrator, too much a scholar to be a statesman, too diffident of himself, his interests too diffuse, to win complete success in any field. But he kept his doubts for his letters and his poems; his work was decisive enough. He did not win the love of all who served under him as Thomason or Henry Lawrence did. But those who did know him felt an affection which was quite free from hero-worship. What they admired was the man himself; it was because of his ability to smile ruefully at himself that they loved him. When he retired, the same qualities made him sought after by people in London who would not have cared for the society of John Lawrence or Richard Temple.

Alfred Lyall was seven years at Eton, going on at eighteen to Hailey-bury. He was posted to the North-Western Provinces and arrived in 1856, the year before the Mutiny. He seems to have enjoyed those first months before the storm broke. 'I have only one chair of my own and but three teacups,' he writes, 'but I have two horses and four guns.' He rejoiced too in the leisure the first year often gives for reading. Shakespeare, Herodotus, Cervantes, Gibbon, came first in his list.

All this was swept away by the Mutiny. Lyall joined the Khaki Risala, the Dusty Squadron, with whom he saw a good deal of mixed fighting. He had a horse shot under him, he killed a man in battle; he seems to have lost himself in the moment to an extent that for him was never again possible. There could be no two sides to this question; it was life or death. He need think no more but must ride, eat, sleep, take cover and shoot before the other man. He looked back afterwards to those four months in the summer of 1857 as the best in his life.

He married a wife who excelled 'in every muscular sport'. One pictures her not always understanding him with her intellect but perhaps for that very reason giving him the support he needed, simply by her comely unquestioning presence. In 1864 they were at Agra, then capital of the North-Western Provinces. They were enjoying a round of dinner-parties and Cora's triumphs at archery and croquet, when the news came that Lyall was chosen to go to Temple's new Chief Commissionership in the

Central Provinces. It meant promotion and there could be no refusal. The young wife with her baby must pack and be off at ten days' notice on a journey which took three hot and dusty weeks.

He missed the society of Agra as much as she did; there was nothing of the Puritan in Lyall's make-up and he believed that too much work was a mistake. He was unashamedly civilized. 'I cling like a pagan', he wrote about this time, 'to youth and strength and the flying years.' Yet he wondered about 'the importance of the human race'. 'My real sympathies are not with a pushing go-ahead administration like Mr Temple's.' 'I wish ... I could whip up more of the enthusiasm which others seem to feel.'

He had an understanding of the Indian at once realistic and poetic. 'I have been much refreshed lately by talking with Raja Dinkar Rao', he writes. Gwalior's Premier had assured him 'that the natives prefer a bad native government to our best patent institutions, and I know he is right'. He was in total disagreement with the 'universally prevalent belief that education, civilization and increased material prosperity will reconcile the people of India to our rule.'

That is realism; his understanding of what an Indian might feel was intuitive and poetic. It is there in his poems again and again. His old Pindari, remembering the coloured days of his youth, dreams:

> ... Of a long dark march to the Jumna, of splashing across the stream,
> Of the waning moon on the water and the spears in the dim star-
> light, ...
> Then the streak of the pearly dawn − the flash of a sentinel's gun,
> The gallop and glint of horsemen who wheel in the level sun,
> The shots in the clear still morning, the white smoke's eddying wreath;
> Is this the same land that I live in, the dull dank air that I breathe?

It might be supposed that holding such views Lyall would inevitably lose the confidence of such a chief as Temple. But he was too profound an agnostic to express disagreement; Temple might after all be right. Lyall

Sir Alfred Lyall. Foreign Secretary, Lieutenant-Governor of the North-Western (later United) Provinces, Alfred Lyall was in the succession of Elphinstone and Frere. Far-sighted but a gradualist, he saw both sides of every question. He was poet and man of letters as well as administrator.

did his work and did it excellently. At thirty-three he was permanent Commissioner, with four of his seniors under his orders and a salary of three thousand pounds a year. At thirty-eight, he was appointed Home Secretary to the Government of India. But in his letters he expresses his distrust of his own abilities, his hankering for scholarly leisure enlivened by witty conversation.

He left the Government of India for a spell as Agent to the Governor-General in Rajputana; it ranked as the second post in the Political Department, but there were moments when Lyall felt on the shelf. All the same, Rajputana stirred him. 'The whole feeling of the country is mediaeval,' he writes, 'the Rajput noblesse caracoles along with sword and shield, the small people crowd round with rags and rusty arms . . . I am afraid we do not altogether improve the nobles by keeping them from fighting.' And he was deeply aware of the isolated life of the English round him and the contrast with Indian life at the foot of the hill, where the cattle are dying from want of forage, 'where you may see gaunt hard-looking men come riding in across the sands on camels with their matchlocks and water-skins slung beside them.'

He was four years in Rajputana, going back to the Government of India as Foreign Secretary in Lord Lytton's administration. He suited Lytton well, being admirably adapted by temperament to put every point of view to an impulsive man who was naturally too quick to take decisions; they became not only colleagues but friends.

As Foreign Secretary, Lyall's main preoccupation was the North-West Frontier. He perceived that the Frontier 'can be considered as a question of border management, affecting merely the peace of our frontier districts'. And 'secondly, in a larger aspect, with regard to the defence of India against attack by a foreign European power'. Whichever aspect they were considering, men were inclined to fall into two rigid schools. The close border men would let the enemy advance through difficult mountain country, harassed by the Afghans; the forward policy men would meet them in the passes. Lyall always believed that St Petersburg, not Kabul, was the place to talk to Russia, and that a firm understanding with Russia would halve the problems of the Frontier.

He went on to be Lieutenant-Governor of the North-Western Provinces, characteristically looking back over his shoulder and feeling out of things as a provincial governor, lonely in his grandeur and condemned to deal with domestic policies which he found on the whole boring. But it was equally characteristic of him to enjoy his new life before long. 'I like the old familiar up-country life of rising early, taking long rides, and seeing all sorts and conditions of natives,' he writes from Lucknow, and coming back from a conference in Simla to Naini Tal, the summer capital of his provinces, he wrote: 'Simla itself has, after Naini Tal, a suburban and shoppy aspect; the woods and crags and lake of my petty capital are more to my mind.'

He had always believed in the diversity of India, which he, like Bartle Frere, pictured as a congeries of states and provinces, differing from each other in their needs. It followed that he thought the provinces should be left alone as much as possible, and he cultivated something of the district officer's jealous irritation at the ignorant interference of a central authority. But he conducted his warfare with an armanent few district officers could command. His irony was famous and he taught the Simla secretariat to address the North-Western Provinces in the mood of an experienced terrier approaching a hedgehog already on the defensive.

It fell to Lyall to introduce to the Provinces Lord Ripon's proposals for local self-government. There were already, over almost the whole of British India, committees for each district who were supposed to advise the District Magistrate about roads, education and bridges. Members were nominated by the Government on the advice of the District Magistrate and it was usually sufficient for him to explain his proposals swiftly in the vernacular to a silent but attentive committee. The members would bow their heads. 'As the Presence orders,' they would say.

Lord Ripon in 1882 suggested smaller committees, with smaller areas, four or five to a district, the members all to be elected and one of them to be chairman.

Lyall spent a good deal of time on this subject; the Punjab in general agreed with him and Lord Ripon accepted their advice. The district board remained, with the district officer as chairman, but the other members were elected instead of nominated; the sub-divisional boards were introduced, but they were to be subordinate committees of the main board. It was a step, a cautious step, towards self-government and there was another step, not quite so cautious, in the municipalities.

Next in importance to the development of local self-government was the Oudh Rent Act, one step of many that were taken to protect the tenant against an unscrupulous landowner. In Oudh, the *taluqdars*, chiefs descended from Mogul officials, had been confirmed after the Mutiny in their vast estates, but it was a slow and laborious business to discover and register the rights of the sub-proprietors and tenants below them, a pyramid of intermediaries between the soil and the Treasury. Gradually they were discovered and gradually the position of the tenant was strengthened.

One other incident of his six years as Lieutenant-Governor must be mentioned. An Englishman in India could until 1883 claim to be tried only by another Englishman, but by the 1880s at least one Indian covenanted civilian was a District Judge and another was a District Magistrate. Lord Ripon proposed to sweep away the racial distinction by what was known as the Ilbert Bill. Provincial Governments were consulted; Lyall acquiesced as a matter of course in the justice of the proposal. But the proposal looked rather different in Behar or Bengal, where there were planters, some of them with uneasy consciences, all aware that a false accusation by a disgruntled tenant can easily be made to sound true. There was an uproar in the Calcutta press. The measure inflamed sharp racial feelings, at a time when the emergence of a Westernized upper class of Indians made the situation very delicate. Lyall changed his view on deeper reflection, believing that it had been inopportune to introduce the bill at that juncture; there was for a short time a coolness between himself and Ripon.

Lyall's time ended; he felt he had been able to help in some 'important steps towards a kind of provincial autonomy'. He did not believe that voting or Parliamentary institutions were likely to help Indians in any foreseeable future. He did believe – as how many had before – that Indians ought to hold more responsible positions. He had appointed the first Indian to the Allahabad High Court, writing privately at the same time: 'I want to push on the native wherever I can, our only chance of placing Government here upon a broad and permanent basis.'

He left India and for fifteen years served in London on the Council of India, where he stood always for the devolution of power to provincial governments and for a progressive foreign policy based on an understanding with Russia.

The last words on Lyall must be those of his pupil and biographer Durand, who is speaking of 'his quick warm sympathy for the chiefs and peoples of India . . . His consistent teaching to us younger men was not to be hasty or hard, above all never to be contemptuous, but to recognize and admire all that was admirable even in those who opposed us . . . he always saw the amusing side of it, even if a man had got under his guard.' If all Englishmen had been like Lyall, the English would perhaps never have been in India at all; empires are not made by men who see both sides of a question. But there would have been fewer who wanted the English to go.

Mrs Moss-King's sketch of bullocks in the compound. The enclosure round an I.C.S. officer's house was frequently several acres and he often grew some fodder for his horses, see p. 228.

13
THE GUARDIANS

1 The First Years

In the fifty years that follow the Mutiny there was not much change on the map. The only addition was Upper Burma. Ruling Princes came closer under the Viceroy's control but there was no change of principle. The only hint that India was one day to be governed by Indians lay in Lord Ripon's Local Self-Government Acts and the slight enlargements of the Legislative Councils in 1893.

Most Englishmen still felt that the best government was that which interfered least with its subjects. To prevent foreign war and domestic strife, to keep famine and pestilence at bay, to let wealth grow naturally in the hands of the people, that was the ideal. Today, critics blame the Victorians for not moving faster, but they themselves often thought that the pace was too hot, and that the Government of India had gone far on the road to socialism; it had come gradually to own railways, to sell salt, to provide schools, to make rum and carpets.

India was ruled from above by a picked aristocracy whose ideal was a light but benevolent administration. It was strangely like the most celebrated of all ideal systems. Plato had entrusted his Republic to a class of guardians specially trained and chosen. They were to be persuaded that the god who created them had mixed gold in their composition to distinguish them from the common people; the older men among them were to rule over the younger; they were not to become householders and cultivators instead of guardians and were therefore to own no property. They were to settle disputes, trying to ensure that everyone kept what he had, kept his place and performed his proper function. In India, the four original castes of the Hindus, sages, warriors, traders and menials, were not unlike Plato's, and the new caste of English Guardians had only to be added at the top. They certainly believed there was something in their composition that distinguished them from the people they ruled; they were forbidden to own land in India or to take part in trade; they were governed by their elders on very much Plato's principles.

This new aristocracy was headed by a Viceroy who did not belong to the caste, chosen from outside its ranks by the English cabinet. It might have been supposed that English statesmen would vie eagerly for the throne of Akbar and Aurangzebe. But one man had his eye on the Foreign Office, another did not like to leave his hunters and partridges. Between Dalhousie and Curzon there was no Viceroy who might have held the Foreign Office or the Exchequer in England. Those who came between found themselves caught up in the current of the system and sometimes swam across it but never against it.

'I never tire of looking at a Viceroy,' wrote Aberigh Mackay in 1880, describing The Great Ornamental. 'He is a being so heterogeneous from us! ... He, who is the axis of India, ... lisps no syllable of any Indian tongue; no race or caste or mode of Indian life is known to him.'

The Viceroy was advised by a Council of five or six members, of whom three or four belonged to the caste of Guardians. He was also advised by a Foreign Secretary, while from the provinces came the opinions of the Lieutenant-Governors and Chief Commissioners, all of whom must belong to the caste. The Viceroy himself, perhaps the Commander-in-Chief, probably the Governors of Madras and Bombay, possibly the Finance Member of Council, a High Court Judge or so in the Presidency towns – these were the exceptions. The rest of the administration was in the hands of the caste.

Plato believed the best could only be obtained by careful breeding and his guardians were to be born from selected parents. The English recruited their Guardians by open competitive examination. But Aberigh Mackay in 1880 could still write of 'the thorough-bred Anglo-Indian, whose blood has distilled through Haileybury for three generations and whose cousins to the fourth degree are Collectors and Indian Army Colonels'.

The competition had been devised in 1853 by Macaulay's committee. It was based on the principle that 'the civil servant of the East India Company should have received the best, the most liberal, the most finished education that his country affords'. But there was some fear that the young men who entered by examination would not be sufficiently 'high-spirited' – by which both Plato and Jowett meant 'good at games'. This was eventually provided for by a *viva voce* which might give the high-spirited young man a long start.

In all this, India was many years ahead of England, where entry to the civil service was still by patronage. The competition took place in a large number of subjects – English, Greek and Latin, French, German and Italian, Mathematics, Science and others. A candidate might offer as many as he liked, a premium thus being set on the ability to get up a subject at short notice and remember enough of it to give the impression of

12 above, *Government House, Calcutta, 1824. Built by Marquess Wellesley in a
strangely prophetic resemblance to Kedleston, the home of Curzon, the Governor-General
who of all the long line resembled him most closely in character; 13* below, *Calcutta from
a point opposite Kidderpole, 1826. Ships and palaces and a swarming populace –
Calcutta, the creation of the English, took many English lives.*

14 above, *Temples on the road to the Shwe Dagon Pagoda, Burma, 1827. Burma was foreign to India in culture and religion but became an appanage of the Indian Empire;* 15 below, *Suttee – our ancestors' spelling of* sati – *meant the burning of a widow alive on her husband's pyre. It shocked the English but they were slow to interfere with a custom sanctioned by religion. It was made illegal throughout India in 1829.*

A young man at work in court. Whatever he did later, a young man in the Civil Service spent much of his time like this. The clerk reading to him is his peshkar – *or bringer-forward – and the order in which cases came forward gave him great opportunities. The scene changed little in a hundred years.*

knowing more. This is a useful accomplishment for a public servant, but it is not admired by scholars; in 1906 the number of subjects was limited and cramming became less valuable. At first, the competition was held at eighteen or nineteen and was followed by two years at a University; as a result of Jowett's interest Oxford had more than her share and at one time as many as half were at Balliol. But it was argued that it was easier at twenty-two than at nineteen to guess what a man would be like at forty. Further, Indians believed that their prize scholars had a much better chance at twenty-two of competing with Englishmen in English. And this view eventually prevailed; the examination was held after a normal university course. But whether chosen at nineteen or twenty-two, the young man, when he came out to India, was a University man and usually a classical scholar. Subalterns were inclined to find him conceited, lively young ladies to tease him because he was solemn.

There was no longer a period of dissipated boredom at the College of Fort William. A young man for a northern Province landed at Bombay, went straight to his district and within three weeks or a month was told to try a case. Alban Way arrived in India towards the end of 1890 and on January 21, 1891 wrote to his mother:

> Thursday was for me a momentous and eventful day. On that day, I tried . . . my first case. The prisoner was accused of stealing twenty-nine stalks of sugar-cane, value one anna (rather more than a penny), from a

field in the middle of the night . . . It took me about six times as long to understand what the witnesses said as it would take anyone who knew the language . . . the lingo of the country peasants I find almost completely unintelligible.

Every young man spent a good deal of his first year on cases of this kind and by the autumn he had become familiar with the man who gets up in the night to answer a call of nature and happens to see mysterious goings-on; he greeted with a sigh defence counsel's questions about the state of the moon and the direction towards which the accused was facing when first seen. He knew by now the vernacular terms for a father-in-law's house, a female buffalo and a field of sugar-cane. He had spent a dull month in charge of the Treasury and another in charge of the copying office. He had swallowed his first qualms and certified hundreds of documents which he could not read to be true copies of hundreds he had not seen. He had probably carried out a number of other tasks, such as inspecting a liquor-shop or viewing the bodies of dead wolves, repelling a horde of locusts or welcoming a Viceroy. Now, towards the end of his first year, came the next milestone, his first tour by himself in camp.

'I am going out by myself on a tour of inspection,' wrote Way in November 1891. 'I have to inspect everything, schools, roads, hospitals, dispensaries, ferries, police-stations and most important of all, the records of fields and cultivators kept by the village accountants, commonly called patwaris.'

He was quite right in thinking the patwaris' papers important. They were the mainstay of the whole system, providing not only the basis for the Land Revenue but stability to rural society. An Indian field was usually not much larger than an English allotment, half an acre being a good field, and the problem was to keep a record of every crop and every payment for every plot in an allotment area covering hundreds of miles in every direction. If the entries were to be accurate, there must be constant random checking.

The business of checking did not change much in a hundred years. The young man with a liberal education takes his stand in the middle of the allotment area with a map. It is drawn in Indian ink on cotton cloth and falls over his hand in limp folds like a cheap pocket-handkerchief. There is perhaps a road, a well or a temple to give him a starting-point and this triangular field on the map must surely be the one where he stands. 'This is number 1178,' he says, grateful for the month in the Treasury which has made him so fluent with his numerals. The group of villagers look blank.

'Gracious and Lofty Presence, it is eighty-seven,' says the patwari and the youth resolves that this time he really will remember that in Arabic numerals V as in seven means seven and the other way up means eight. 'This is number 1187,' he repeats firmly and this time everyone seems pleased.

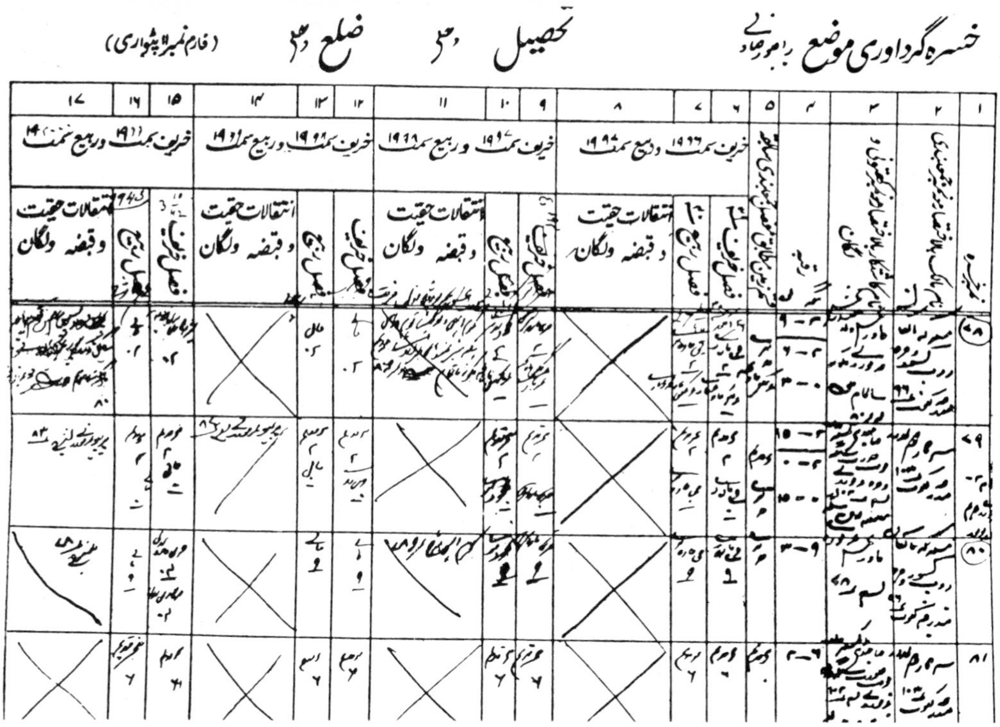

۱۷	۱۶	۱۵	۱۴	۱۳	۱۲	۱۱	۱۰	۹	۸	۷	۶	۵	۴	۳	۲	۱

(Handwritten Urdu khasra record — columns largely illegible)

This is a four-year khasra *or crop record for a village in Delhi district. Reading from right to left the columns show: 1, the number of the field; 2, the proprietor; 3, the cultivator; 4, the area; 5, the soil classification; 6, the crop sown in the Hindu year 1996 (autumn 1939 A.D.); 7, the spring crop in the Hindu year 1996 (1940 A.D.); 8, alterations.*

The other columns repeat 6, 7 and 8 for the following years. See below.

'Whose field is this?' he continues and there is at once a chorus: 'Munnoo's field.' 'Does he plough it himself?' Yes, Munnoo ploughs it. It does not belong to Munnoo. It belongs to the Strawberry-coloured Combine, of whom the senior partner is Gulab Khan. There are seventy-four members of the Strawberry-coloured Combine.

The graduate in philosophy looks at the field book in the patwari's hand. There is something like a newly-hatched tadpole in the column for cultivators and in the Arabic script, written from right to left, that tadpole must stand for Munnoo. He looks at his feet; it is an easy crop to recognize, gram, a small chick-pea, that is just pushing its way up through the rough sharp little clods of sun-baked earth. It does not like a fine tilth. And it is easy to recognize in the book too, for the final *alif* is unmistakable. There is another chick-pea very like gram, but the vernacular word for that ends in a *ye*. This entry is correct.

The next field is a square lying snug against the hypotenuse of 1187; this must be 1193. Yes, everyone agrees to that. It is cultivated by Rahim − for this is a mixed village with Muslim cultivators as well as Hindus − and belongs to the Orange Combine, of which the senior member is a Hindu, Gopal Das, who bought the thirty-three shares out of a hundred and

A few fields on the patwari's *map. The scale on the original is 64 inches to one mile. The long field in the bottom left-hand corner is 10, the top right 175. See previous page.*

eighty-eight which once belonged to Zalim Khan. And this at his feet is barley – no, wheat – no, barley. 'Barley,' he says. 'Wheat,' everyone else says, and they show him how the blade of wheat fits round the stalk as it unfolds and they fetch some barley to show the difference. And it is clearly wheat in the book; the initial *gaf* with its great double stroke like the arm of a steam crane is the most unequivocal letter in the alphabet.

When he feels satisfied that the field book and the map agree, at least for a score or so of fields, the youth will perhaps go into the village. A bed will be dragged out for him to sit on; there are no chairs in the village. It is a wooden frame, with four legs, laced across with hairy string made from hemp. A tall thick glass of greyish tea, generously sugared, generously stirred, is brought him, and there are oranges and perhaps hard-boiled eggs, peeled already and marked with grimy finger-prints. The villagers, in their coarse white cotton, sit on the ground and the young man proceeds to verify the shares of everyone who belongs to the Strawberry-coloured Combine. Gulab Khan's grandfather was one of six brothers who had equal shares and whose names were . . . That was the kind of thing every young man in the service had to do.

In November 1891, Way went to a training-camp at Roorkee, thirty miles from Hardwar, where the Ganges breaks out of the hills. Here with the other men of his year he spent two or three months in study and passed his examinations in languages, law and procedure. Then he was posted to a district and soon became a sub-divisional officer. This was the first real job of every young man. It was his duty to see that the land records were kept up to date and in good order, that all disputes were settled without disturbance of the public peace, that the ferries were run with a minimum of inconvenience and extortion, that the pounds, schools and liquor-shops really were in existence and were properly maintained.

The young man probably took over charge of his sub-division in March or April and for the first six months far too much of his time would be spent in court, deciding formal suits, with witnesses and perhaps counsel. He would also have the opportunity of settling quite a few cases by suggesting a solution and advising the parties to compromise. After all, they alone knew all the facts and if they did compromise, they saved themselves much expense and the terms of the compromise were recorded by the court so that they could not be evaded.

Once the rains were over and the dry cool weather had begun, the S.D.O., if he was ever going to make an officer, was eager to get into camp. His sub-division might be twenty miles long and ten miles across, or it might be as big again. He would choose camping sites not more than ten or twelve miles apart and stay as a rule three nights in each. A cup of tea at dawn and then you would be on a horse and off at a brisk canter. Horse and man would both be keen to keep moving because the cold was still sharp. The fields were grey with dew and villagers were not at all anxious

Camp in 1885. This was not very different fifty years later.

to be stirring so early; their wits seemed numbed with cold these mornings. Perhaps the sanitation of a village six miles away might be the first appointment and then the site of some dispute which had come up in court a month ago, then a school, a ferry or a liquor-shop, perhaps a patwari's papers or a police-station and so back to the tents by ten or eleven in the morning. A bath in a tin tub in the dark little bathroom behind the tent; it smelt of smoke and damp straw but the towels by now would be crisp and warm from hanging over a tent-rope in the sun. A large confused meal, combining breakfast and lunch, and then again the disputes of villagers.

Custom varied at this point. Some men heard formal suits in camp and even permitted counsel; to most it was anathema. It was, they felt, a sad waste of camping-time. Even if no formal cases were heard, petitions would take a long time. 'Petitions!' a court messenger would shout in each corner of the grove, and the patient figures squatting together in a group by the servants' tents would come to life and advance. There would be two or three disputes about fields, about where a field boundary should run, perhaps, or whether Ramu had really said he would let Tulsi plough field number 1239 – the field with the *babul* tree in the corner – if Tulsi would agree to take water from the well every third day instead of every other day. There would perhaps be a woman who had been enticed away from her husband and sometimes the husband would be quite content to let her go if he could have back his savings, the ornaments of silver she was wearing. All these differences could be dealt with perfunctorily and referred to someone else, but with a little trouble, a little goodwill, a little readiness to cut corners, it was often possible to settle them without any more waste of money.

Petitions and reports on things seen on the morning ride would fill the middle part of the day. In the evening, with luck, it might be possible to stroll out with a gun, hoping for a partridge or two, a peacock, a hare, or a few quail, something to keep the pot from going empty. The stroll always produced at least as many peasants as partridges. A man would appear and walk timidly behind for a little, or perhaps ostentatiously beat the bushes for game; it was not quite seemly to introduce the subject at once, but after a little companionship of this kind, out it would come, the field entered in the wrong name, the path for taking the buffaloes to the water blocked by Loharu's malice, the cruel beating administered only yesterday by Rahim Khan's men.

'Look at my *mauqa*!' in pleading accents was the cry heard over and over again in camp. A mauqa is the place where something happened. It may be the scene of a crime or the site of a dispute; to the petitioner it seems crystal clear that once the ruler has seen the mauqa, truth will prevail.

He was a lucky young man who could stay in one sub-division for two or three years. He would learn in the second year what mistakes he had made in the first; he would realize that he never ought to have let the Hindus depart from precedent by holding that apparently innocuous procession at the festival of Ram Lila to which the Muslims had produced such obviously factious objections. He would have learnt the groundwork of his profession and whatever else might happen later he had something firm to build on.

But, sooner or later, the choice would come between the executive line — the department 'of land revenue and general administration' — and the various alternatives, political, judicial, secretariat and a dozen odd branches, opium, customs, salt or excise.

Going to the political was not an easy choice; it involved varied and unknown possibilities. It was one thing to administer Aden or to deal with the desert tribes in the country behind Kuwait or Oman, to be a consul in Persia or the Gulf, to follow John Jacob on the Sind Frontier or Herbert Edwardes further north; it was quite another to spend one's youth in the steamy idleness of a small State, where there was nothing to do between ceremonial visits but wonder when the Raja really would exceed all reasonable limits and force the paramount power to intervene.

As to the judicial, that choice, in the early part of the period, did not arise in the non-regulation provinces, such as Oudh and the Punjab. These had been administered since they were first annexed by the light of a clear conscience and a clear head. In these provinces, the Deputy Commissioner was still all in all. But a change had to be made. No one who went about the country as much as a district officer ought could have time for complicated civil suits. And again, in criminal cases, the district officer could hardly help inclining a little to the side of the police, who had taken such trouble to catch and prosecute the accused. Inevitably, the non-regulation provinces came into line with the others and a judge came to be a judge and nothing else.

The decision was a matter of temperament. There were some to whom a judge's life appealed because it satisfied the intellect. It was possible for a judge to feel when he went to bed that he had done all he could do; he had sat in court and heard the witnesses with attention, he had used the full powers of his mind to reach conclusions. A district officer, conscious of a score of needs for which there had not been time, could never feel that.

If a man did decide on the judicial side, the 'judgey' as the Indian called it, he would deal with both county court and sessions work, turning from civil to criminal work and back and also hearing a great many appeals from magistrates.

The responsibility of a judge in India was heavier than an English judge's, because he did not have a jury. He had, as a rule, but not always, assessors, men of substance, carefully selected, who were asked their opinion – to which the judge need pay no attention whatever. The judge had therefore to decide whether a man was guilty before he sentenced him; he had also a wider discretion than an English judge in respect, for instance, of murder, for which death was not the sole and obligatory punishment. To be a judge, then, was an ambition far from ignoble. All the same, most men preferred to stick to the executive.

The political, the 'judgey', and the Lord Sahib's Office – that is the secretariat – these were the main alternatives to the life of the district. The work of the secretariat was similar to that done by the civil servant in Whitehall, with the difference that there was far more delegation of power, that a junior could do more without referring to his seniors, and that his seniors were people trained in the same way as himself. The result was that in 1939 there were only a hundred officers of the Indian Civil Service in the secretariat of the Government of India, for a population of 350 million. Nonetheless, every district officer despised and hated the secretariat, who would not make up their minds, who hedged and compromised and wrapped up their meaning in provisos. There was of course some truth in it; the secretariat man had more to bear in mind than a district officer and did sometimes tend to think of so many possibilities that he could not decide between them. But he was always liable to go back to a district and there were always to be found in the secretariat one or two who remained obstinately district officers at heart.

The Viceroy and the central secretariat were sometimes engaged in fighting the Government in Whitehall in the interests of India. The cotton import duties provide the classical example of this. The Cabinet in England, devotees of the dogma of Free Trade, would not permit duties on imported cotton goods which would have allowed India to develop factories of her own. India protested; India was rapped over the knuckles; India protested again. India had to give in.

All through this period the Guardians found the heads for the specialized services; as late as 1930, it was still a man from the Indian Civil Service who was head of the departments of Opium and Salt. The Postmaster-General in a province became a specialist in the 1920s, but in 1939 the head of all the postal services for all India still belonged to the service, while the same was true in the long administrative period even of the Inspectors-General of Police and of Forests. There was hardly an important post in the whole range of government to which a man might not be asked to turn his hand.

2 The District Officer

The young man who resisted the temptation to specialize would come through his years in a sub-division and get a chance to officiate for part of the hot weather in a small unpopular district. 'Don't try to do your S.D.O.s' work; see that they do it themselves but give them a chance and don't weigh yourself down with detail,' a wise Commissioner would tell him. In the winter he would revert, probably becoming City Magistrate in a large and troublesome city, under a Senior District Officer. Here his work would be all police, crime and sanitation, with no idyllic camping and no disputes about land. The next hot weather he would officiate for the whole season, and then in a year or two would come the district from which he was not going to revert. Perhaps he would be thirty, but usually less.

G.O. Trevelyan has described a district officer's day in the 1860s.

He rises at daybreak and goes straight from his bed to the saddle. Then he gallops off across fields bright with dew to visit the scene of the late dacoit robbery; or to see with his own eyes whether the crops of the zamindar who is so unpunctual with his assessment have really failed; or to watch with fond parental care the progress of his pet embankment ... [then] the collector returns to his bungalow and settles down to the hard business of the day ... He works through the contents of one dispatch-box after another; signing orders and passing them on; dashing through drafts, to be filled up by his subordinate; writing reports, minutes, digests, letters of explanation, of remonstrance, or warning, of commendation. Noon finds him quite ready for a *déjeuner à la fourchette*, the favourite meal in the districts, when the tea-tray is lost amid a crowd of dishes − fried fish, curried fowl, roast kid and mint-sauce, and mango-fool. Then he sets off in his buggy to the courts, where he spends the afternoon in hearing and deciding questions connected with land and revenue ... If the cases are few ... he may get away in time for three or four games at rackets in the new court ... By ten o'clock he is in bed.

Going home from a party, 1885. They must have changed into evening dress after tennis at their host's home and there should be another man with a suitcase. It was often very like this in the hills – but there was not always a tiger.

'The Collector', wrote Aberigh Mackay, 'lives in a long rambling bungalow furnished with folding chairs and tables and in every way marked by the provisional arrangements of camp life. He seems to have just arrived from out of the firmament of green fields and mango-groves that encircles the little station where he lives ...

'The veranda is full of fat men in clean linen waiting for interviews. They are bankers, shopkeepers and landholders, who have only come to "pay their respects", with ever so little a petition as a corollary ... Brass dishes filled with pistachio nuts and candied sugar are ostentatiously displayed here and there; they are the oblations of the would-be visitors ... They represent in the profuse East the visiting cards of the meagre West.'

Interviewing those 'fat men in clean linen', listening carefully to pick up a hint of truth through the drift of formal compliment and direct flattery, took much longer than Trevelyan seems to have known. But his description was true of most civilians of his day. 'I know of no better company in the world,' he wrote, 'than a rising young civilian. There is an entire absence of the carping pining spirit of discontent ... It is impossible for the civilian to have any misgiving concerning the dignity and importance of his work. His power for good and evil is almost unlimited ... He makes it his aim to turn off his work in good style, trusting for his reward to the sense and public spirit of his chief ... He never speaks of his duties save in a spirit of enthusiasm or of his profession without a tone of profound satisfaction.'

'But, besides the blessings of absorbing work,' Trevelyan continues, 'a civilian enjoys the inestimable comfort of freedom from pecuniary troubles ... Tom's assistant-magistrate keeps four horses and lives well within as many hundred rupees a month. If a man puts off his marriage ... [for a year or two] he may always have a good house and plenty of servants, his champagne and his refrigerator, his carriage and buggy, an Arab for the Mem Sahib and for himself a hundred guinea horse that will face a pig without flinching. He will be able to portion his daughters and send his son to Harrow and Oxford; he may retire ... with a pension of a thousand a year and as much more from the interests of his savings.'

Tom's successors, their pension still a thousand a year, with a pound a quarter of its value and an income-tax that would have made Tom stare, may smile a little wryly at this, but it is pleasant to know that their predecessors had such freedom from anxiety. Trevelyan goes on to wonder: 'Whence comes this high standard of efficiency and public virtue ...? The real education of a civil servant,' he said, 'consists in the responsibility that devolves on him at an early age ... the obligation to do nothing that can reflect dishonour on the service; the varied and attractive character of his duties; and the example and precept of his superiors, who regard him rather as a younger brother than as a subordinate official.' And in an exultant spirit, he proclaims the progress of the English in India, who have not become slothful, luxurious and degenerate. On the contrary, 'each generation ... is more simple, more hardy, more Christian than the last'.

Of course it was foreign rule. This was already a source of pain to educated Indians. But the impact on Indians not educated in Western ways, on villagers and on those 'fat clean men' who came to call on the Collector, was less distasteful than might have been expected. Their own society was static; few born into it were afflicted with the restless ambition of a modern competitive society. And the system did provide peace and a minimum of interference; it generally worked in the interest of the existing order.

Nor were the English Guardians the dignified and forbidding creatures pictured by Plato. They were given to pigsticking, racing and shooting, and, though they could not be bribed, could be induced to smile by news of a tiger or by a subscription to a pet charity. Every man had his *shauq*, his pet enthusiasm, and very often two, of which one was pure recreation and the other philanthropy. There was Brown, whose hobbies were tigers and embankments to store water in the rains; Smith who would go miles for a snipe and planted all the roads with double avenues of trees; and Jones, who was building hospitals when he wasn't pigsticking. And because of their fads, their humour, and their tolerance, many district officers were not merely much less intolerable than might have been expected but were looked on with real affection by the people of their districts.

All the same, the fabric could only be temporary. England herself was progressing steadily towards giving everyone a say in public affairs; India too was some day to move in that direction. But at present the system by which she was governed did not give Indians much say in her affairs. It was too like Plato's state, which was one which Englishmen would never have tolerated for themselves. They had spent a great deal of blood to make it clear that they would not be ruled by anyone, priest, king or baron, who would not account for his authority to his people. Yet just such a rule they did themselves impose on India.

3 Famine

Behind all the satisfaction, there was always in the background the shadow of famine. India is a triangle projecting into the Indian Ocean; more than nine tenths of the rainfall, in most of its vast area, comes in the months of July, August and September, when two sides of the triangle are assailed, one by the South-West and one by the South-East monsoon. In a good year, the two monsoons meet in the middle, everyone has rain, and two crops are taken off the land. In a bad year, the monsoons do not meet, and the centre and the northern part of the triangle seem like a continuation of the Arabian deserts. The devil, the Muslims say, holds an umbrella over Delhi – and not only over Delhi.

In all the central and northern area, the ground for nine months grows harder and harder till it is like dusty concrete. Then come the anxious weeks, when, if God so pleases, the rain will come. If there is no rain, there is no harvest of rice and millet in September and the ground is too hard to sow the wheat and barley that ought to be cut in March. The peasant seldom has grain enough in hand to carry him more than a month or two beyond harvest-time. The grain-dealer of course has stocks, but prices rise and the peasant cannot buy without running into debt. There is scarcity, debt, hunger, and something near starvation. Then perhaps next year there is a poor crop and a partial recovery, then another failure; the dealer's stocks are exhausted and there is no food in the area. This is famine.

Famines there had always been. In the days of Peter Mundy, the bodies were dragged stark naked from the towns to lie by the roadside; women sold their children and men ate each other. The Moguls and their predecessors looked on famine as something beyond the power of human rulers to mitigate. They had some justification.

If there was no grain for men, there was no fodder for cattle and grain could hardly be moved into the starving areas. Bullocks in India are fed mainly on the chopped stalks of millet, a bulky food with not much feeding value; a pair of bullocks moving ten or twelve miles a day would eat in a week all they could carry of this kind of fodder. If they are to deliver a load of three hundredweight and get back alive, their range is barely fifty miles. Elephants and mules are no better. Even as late as 1877, grain lay rotting at the railway stations in Madras, in the very districts where men were starving, because there were no bullocks with strength to drag it away. So long, then, as transport was by means of animals, there was no cure that could be improvised once deaths had begun. The grim course of starvation, flight, and cholera must be faced.

In the first half of the century, there were fewer famines than in the second. This was due simply to the vagaries of the monsoon or, as the peasant would say, to the will of God. Between 1801 and the Orissa famine of 1866 the only major famine in British territory was that which Lord Auckland had found so boring, and that was a long slow famine, a succession of poor years. When that was over, the Government turned to war and diplomacy, the settlement of land revenue and the like, instead of preparing for the next. They thought that famine was something that did not happen very often.

But the Orissa famine of 1866 changed everything. The startling thing

The Secretary to Government. A satirical sketch by Aberigh Mackay, whose Twenty Days in India *is often witty and revealing. His Secretary to Government is just the picture the District Officer usually formed of the Secretary. Note the heads under which he kept his files.*

about the Orissa famine was that it was so sudden, so swift and so complete. In April, 1866, 'the magistrate of Cuttack still reported that there was no ground for apprehension. A few days later, in May, he and his followers were almost starved.' There had been a poor monsoon the previous autumn and stocks were low, but in only five more months the next harvest would be cut, and the grain-dealers must have believed they had enough. Until May, prices did not rise. Then suddenly confidence collapsed. It was like a run on a bank. Everyone strove for what he could get and concealed what he had; prices soared.

At Haileybury, everyone had learnt that political economy was a matter of laws, that money and goods would move by themselves in ways beneficial to mankind. The less any government interfered with natural movements, the better. If there was real scarcity in Orissa, prices would rise, grain-dealers from elsewhere would be attracted and would hurry grain to where it was needed. If the government tried to anticipate this process, they would cause waste and incur loss.

It is a theory that perhaps would work where it is possible to move goods across country the whole year round. But the people of Orissa depended entirely on grain and they were sealed from the outer world for four months. There were no harbours that could be worked in the monsoon. There were no railways. Orissa was like a ship where the stores are suddenly found to have run out. By the time relief came, a quarter of the population was dead.

The rulers of Victorian India were not only reluctant to interfere with the free flow of trade, but also afraid of demoralizing the people. It was hardly to be expected that they should be far ahead of England and in England it was believed that some discouragement ought to go with poor relief. It was desirable that 'the labouring poor' should make every effort to earn their living. And in India although relief must be given when there was famine, it must not continue longer than necessary and as far as possible some work must be done in return.

It is against this background that the famines of the second half of the century must be seen. There was Orissa in 1866 and George Campbell's recommendations; there was Temple's famine in Behar in 1874. There was famine in the North-West in 1868, in 1896 and in 1907. Except for the fifteen years from 1880 to 1895 there were hardly five consecutive years free from famine somewhere.

John Lawrence announced in 1868 that the object must be to save every life; every district officer would be held personally responsible for the loss of a single life that might have been saved. This was repeated by Lord Northbrook in 1873. And by the end of the century, organization had gone so far that direct deaths from starvation were almost unknown.

The first principle of famine doctrine was that work must be provided for every able-bodied man. There must be grain at the relief works which he could buy with the money he earned. As to those too old or ill to work, there was at first no agreed doctrine. Some 'gratuitous relief' there must be but the fear of pauperization was strong with one government, a tender heart stronger with another. One felt there must be no interruption of the normal course of trade, another that famine was like war and everything else must go by the board.

In Temple's famine of 1874 in Behar, George Campbell, now Lieutenant-Governor, wanted to prohibit the normal export of grain from Calcutta. This, he thought, would bring down prices in Calcutta and the grain would automatically flow to the high prices in Behar. He would 'dam up the grain and force it back'. Lord Northbrook, however, was 'as much shocked as a bishop might be with a clergyman who denied all the thirty-nine articles'. The Central Government over-ruled Campbell in the sacred name of Free Trade and imported rice from Burma in quantities which almost equalled the exports. 'The strange spectacle was seen of fleets of ships, taking rice out from the Hooghly and passing other ships bringing rice in.'

There came the famous Commission of 1880, under the chairmanship of Richard Strachey. The views of this Commission were almost the same as George Campbell's but they received more attention and were formulated in the Famine Code. Plans were to be made at once for the works that would be undertaken in a famine. There would be major engineering works in each district and minor village works as well; both were to be as far as possible designed to prevent famine in future, a pond to store water in the rains, a great embankment that would turn the overflow of a river to useful purposes, perhaps a canal, even wells. Wages at the relief works would be fixed according to need and grain would be sold at grainshops at the legal price; there would be an extra allowance for dependants. Those who could not work must be fed by the Government. In normal times, the district must be organized into circles, with an officer already appointed for each circle who would do his best, when famine came, to see that relief went where it was needed.

The plan made in advance was to be the essence of the cure. As to prevention, railways, irrigation and roads were the answer to famine; from now on a sum of fifteen million rupees, rather more than a million pounds, was set aside every year as Famine Insurance. It might be saved up against a bad year, or used on canals and railways that were intended to prevent famine.

But whatever Commission reported, the district officer had as usual to do the work. His main task, once the famine had begun, was to supervise some twenty or more circle officers. What a circle officer actually did in a famine is told well by Herman Kisch, the son of a London surgeon, who arrived in India in 1873 and six months later, in March 1874, was posted to famine duty in Temple's Behar famine. When these letters were written, he was twenty-three years old.

I have under my management . . . he writes on March 17, 1874, an area of 198 square miles . . . I have full liberty to adopt whatever measures I think necessary, subject only to very general instructions . . . When my establishment is complete, I shall have under me at my own office three clerks, 12 sub-superintendents and 24 messengers, while I shall have in the centre of every group of ten villages a store-house, with a storekeeper, a salesman and two messengers, besides watchmen. I am supposed to make myself personally acquainted with the condition of every village . . . and I have never had such hard work. Every day I have been from seven to eight hours a day in the saddle, riding about from village to village and searching out those who are able to work . . . and those who from weakness or disease can now do no work at all. . . . In one of the villages that I visited the condition of the villagers was such that I thought it necessary to have them fed on the spot with cooked food, rather than trust to their reaching alive the nearest store . . . unless I had seen it myself I could not have believed that anyone could live with so thin a covering to the bones. The very colour of the bone was visible through the thin black film that surrounded it . . . In some of the villages, the people are quite comfortably off, while within a couple of thousand yards there is the last stage of distress . . .

I have to organize relief works, arrange for the erection of store-houses, and give directions as to the distribution of gratuitous relief; besides I have to superintend and control the various registers and accounts . . . and give endless minute instructions . . . Today from 6 a.m. till 12.30 p.m., with the exception of breakfast time, I was doing my office work and from 12.30 p.m. till 8 p.m. I was out on my horse . . . Since I came here I have erected 15 Government grain store-houses and opened about 22 Relief works, [he writes by April 8, only a fortnight after he came]. I give employment to about 15,000 men and women per day and am feeding gratuitously about 3,000 more. I have full authority to do what I choose and I do it.

By May 13, Kisch had over forty reservoirs under his own management; some of these were about 'a thousand feet long and nearly as wide; in the rains there will be 20 or 30 feet of water in them and they will have water all the year round'. He had four large grain stores to supply the smaller local stores. 'Each of these four contains from 1,600,000 to 4,800,000 lbs of grain, of which the intrinsic value must be over a million rupees . . . There is, at each store, a man on fifteen rupees a month (about one pound sterling or half-a-crown more) with a staff of messengers and guards on four rupees a month.' He complains of rascality – but was it surprising?

Rain came early in June to raise hopes and by the 15th he could write: 'All day long rice is being poured into my circle . . . Every day two or three military officers come into Bhikwa with thousands of carts, bullocks and horses and mules . . . Each officer brings perhaps 300 or 500 carts with 3 to 5 bullocks each, and they have to move along with mud up to their axles

... I have to run about like mad to see it stored, to the lasting injury of my own and Government horses.' Two temporary light railways had been constructed to bring railhead nearer the famine. To feed Tirhut by bullocks was not the problem it would have been in Mogul days.

Already there were criticisms. It was true that for the first time in Indian history there had been a famine with hardly any direct loss of life from starvation. But had it all been necessary? Had not expenditure been too lavish? Kisch's answer was definite. Even in July he wrote: 'If I stopped the sale of Government grain for two weeks, and the same measure was adopted for only fifty miles around me, in my circle alone the air would be so foul with the dead that it would be impossible to move outside the house.'

By August, anxiety was growing again as the rains had abated, and Kisch was planning to dam all the rivers in his circle. 'I cannot conceive so rapid a system of education as an Indian famine ... When I came up to Tirhut, I knew no more how to dig a good tank or build a grainstore or to store grain so as to avoid injury from damp or heat or to do a hundred other things ... than I have of how to build an English house or play the piano. Now I can do very well the things I have mentioned.'

On September 3, 'we had a tremendous fall of rain during the night and there is now no fear of another famine'.

There might have been twenty or so circles like Kisch's in the district and he says he was the only I.C.S. circle officer. There were a few extra men drafted to the famine area, but the framework of the famine organization was the normal framework of the district. The other circle officers would be Deputy Collectors of the Provincial Service or tahsildars.

Neither the work nor the organization changed much in later famines. The district officer had to make sure that his circle officers were doing what Kisch did – that is, making sure that their subordinates were really distributing food, work, and money where they were needed. That was his main function; his special cares were legion.

The half century from 1858 to 1909 can be looked on as a contest between two evenly matched teams; on one side, the administrators, the doctors, the engineers, who were building roads, railways and irrigation canals, and agriculturalists, with improved seed. But on the other side were the goddess Kali, with her chaplet of men's skulls, and Siva, who is the god not only of destruction but of the phallus. The forces of destruction might seem everywhere to be slowly losing ground but because of his twofold nature Siva cannot be beaten. As the canals made fertile land from desert, his millions rolled in and one generation ate up the gains. For every child saved from smallpox he begat two more, so that three mouths gaped for food where fifty years ago there had been one. The reports of the Famine Commissions follow each other like Banquo's line of kings, each pointing a moral. They suggest improvements, but there is no change in the basic doctrine. And they record a slow but steady improvement in the condition of the peasantry which gives them greater powers of resistance.

It was believed by now that never again need people die from starvation because the rains had failed. Shortage there might be and high prices, but deaths from starvation, no. During the two years of the famine of 1907, the provincial death-rate had, it is true, risen; it rose from a normal figure of 32.59 per thousand to 36.47. This means that additional deaths, above the average, had been in this famine-stricken province rather less than 200,000 out of more than 47 million; most of these extra deaths were from smallpox or cholera. Against this, consider the estimates for the Bengal famine in 1770 and the lamentable famine of 1866 in Orissa. In both of these, district officers thought that about a third to a quarter of the whole population had died; if they were right and if deaths in the United Provinces in 1908 had been on that scale, the additional deaths would have been not 200,000 but 10 million.

The network of railways was by now fairly close for a large continent. In 1909, there were 31,500 miles of railway and throughout the great band of flat country that runs from Calcutta to Peshawar it would have been hard to find a village that was fifty miles from a railway; there were not many that were twenty-five.

It was not a close network compared with England's nor with the United States. But the true comparison is with China, whose civilization is as ancient as India's and whose territory and population are even vaster. Here whole provinces were without railways and the total length open to traffic in 1910 was 3,000 miles, just a tenth of India's.

There had also been steady progress in building up a canal system which by 1909 was the most extensive in the world. The 13,000 miles of primary and secondary canals with 42,000 miles of distributaries irrigated 23 million acres of land. That is half the total acreage of Great Britain. Canals in the North-West or United Provinces brought safety to areas that had previously been uncertain, but men had lived and ploughed there for thousands of years. In the Punjab, irrigation between the rivers meant that a desert suddenly blossomed, that where a few nomad tribes had grazed their camels towns and villages sprang up and good wheat was grown.

The five rivers of the Punjab enclose four areas which once were untilled waste land. The water level was eighty feet below the surface, so that irrigation from wells was out of the question, but for canal irrigation the country was ideal – a desert ready to be peopled. Before the water flowed, a plan was made, a whole countryside was designed – roads, railways, railway-stations, market towns, villages, the mosque, the temple, the village school, the pound, the side-road, the little bridge, the grove of trees for shade, firewood and timber, the meeting-place, the magistrate's court, the police-station. Everyone has seen the model village in an exhibition, with men an inch high, little cows and hens and horses,

There had always been famines in India, but by 1914 most civilians believed that, by canals and railways and timely preparation, famine had been beaten.

shop, church and cinema. But this was real. And it was not a village, but a district with millions of acres of fertile land – made fertile by canal water.

You must picture a landscape divided into squares, each twenty-seven and a half acres, a peasant's holding. Men had to be picked for these holdings who were sturdy and ready to work; they had to be moved. Hard on the heels of the arriving colonists, police-stations and dispensaries had to be built and headquarters for sub-collectorates chosen. Town plans had to be drawn out for grain-markets, general shops, cotton-ginning factories, urban residences and so forth ... Water supplies, drainage, sewage-disposal had to be devised.

Gradually it was done; a time came when the colonies on the Lower Chenab Canal seemed so complete and so successful that they might suitably be combined into the one administrative district of Lyallpur. By 1941 this district, made from the desert, had a population of more than one and a quarter million and a cultivated area over one and a half million acres, its crops being worth six and a half million pounds a year. If the English were to choose one monument by which their years in India were to be remembered, it might well be the canals, the cotton, and the prosperous villages of Lyallpur.

That was one of the Punjab Colonies; there were others. Irrigation,

227

again, was only one part of the contest with famine. Indeed, in the known history of mankind, this antagonist had not before been assailed on so considerable a scale. It may be that different measures should have been taken. There are many controversial points, but even the critics of the regime agreed in believing that, as one of them said, 'no class of men is more anxious to remedy the evils than British administrators who have devoted themselves to the great task of improving the material condition of the people of India'.

It was a devotion that did not escape without loss. At Jubbalpore in the Central Provinces, there is a cross to the memory of the officers of the Central Provinces who laid down their lives during the famine of 1896–1897. There are nine names; five civilians, one engineer, one policeman, two subalterns of the Indian Army. It is one example of the losses of one province in one famine year. There were at that time twenty-two civilians in the Central Provinces Commission; five of them were lost.

Mrs Moss-King's sketch of cutting grass in the compound.

14
THE FRONTIERS

1 Burma and the East

Books by Englishmen about India have tended to emphasize the differences between its many peoples. This has sometimes disregarded the strength of the underlying unity. But the differences were real enough and in the eyes of the English who lived and worked in India they did bulk large. 'What can you expect', asked a character in Kipling – sent from the Punjab to Madras on famine duty – 'of a country where they call a *bhisty* a *tunny-cutch*?'

But the underlying unity was there and in a sense, within India proper, an Englishman's life in a district was not really very different wherever he went. There would be new languages in the South and a strange system of land tenures; more perplexing perhaps would be shades of difference in marriage customs, feasts and the like which looked at first sight familiar. But the bungalow and the court-room were much the same as in the North; the visitor would still have his morning ride and his evening game of racquets. Whether the tea-party was at Trichinopoly or at Lahore, the odes in his honour and the scent of the wet marigolds round his neck would be much the same.

Districts were larger in Madras and a Madras district was divided into divisions, not sub-divisions; the divisional officer lived in his division and was perhaps a little more independent than the northern S.D.O., a little less so than a northern district officer. But his work and responsibilities were not very different; he too settled disputes and supervised the work of village accountants, though he did call them by strange names. Communications were worse in the South and the pace of life a little slower. It was widely held in the South that it was no use casting eyes on Simla or Calcutta; the Government of India was for the Bengal, Punjab and North-Western men and in Madras you must at the most aspire to the Board of Revenue or the provincial secretariat. To the last, the

Government of Madras were inclined to regard the Government of India as a rather vulgar late eighteenth-century innovation.

But if Madras, in spite of differences, was still part of the Indian continent, Burma to an Indian was almost as foreign as England. Burma and Assam are countries of thick steamy forest, of heavy rainfall and rapid rivers; India is dry, baked and dusty. The people are no less different. There are many races and languages, Burmans, Talaings, Arakanese, Shans, Karens, Nagas and others, but all, even the primitives from the hills, seem to resemble each other in gaiety, in a love of bright colours, in a dislike for hard work, in an inconsequent emotional recklessness. And among the civilized people of Burma, the Buddhists, there goes with this an air of being reconciled to the world we live in, a readiness to take life as it comes – and death too for that matter – without making too much fuss.

All this is very unlike India. Whatever critics may say, there are qualities common to all the people of the continent and Indians are serious and introspective people. Their seriousness has led them into religious extremes and they are hedged about with rules and ritual. But in Burma the people are gay and their religion enjoins nothing at which reason jibs. There is none of the hard puritanism of the desert which flowed into Northern India with Islam. Purdah, suttee, caste, child-marriage, all these are unknown. And Indians who have been to Burma shake their heads in horror at people who can lawfully eat anything and who do in fact gladly eat dogs, rats and lizards.

Burma is a poor country but the comforts of life are valued; men and women wear silk when they can, cultivate gardens round their houses, put flowers in their hair. In the villages there is often a *pwe*, which means a play, a feast, or a puppet-show, something to which everyone looks forward and which is conducted with a good deal of artistry. Something of the kind, sport, art, excitement, variety, the Burman seems to find essential. There was more robbery by gangs than anywhere else in the world but even the official Burma *Gazetteer* put it down mainly to the desire for sport and excitement.

A gay and violent people, careless of life, hating monotony and discipline, witty, idle and often beautiful, neat and attractive in their dress – that is the impression left by the Burmese of the valleys and cultivated lands. An untamed, an unspoilt, people, and yet their civilization was far from primitive. Burma for centuries had been Buddhist; there were monasteries everywhere and a monastic brotherhood of some learning. In every monastery, there was a school at which every Burmese boy learned to read and write. Many of the girls could read too and women had rights not yet enjoyed in Victorian England. They owned their own property; they managed their own affairs.

In the hills, among the Karens, the Kachins, and the Nagas, there was another world. Nearly all these tribes took heads and until a man had shown himself a man by bringing home the head of an enemy he did not easily find a wife. War was made on another village with elaborate ritual; the bones of chickens and the gall of pigs were examined for omens; parties were sent to make sure that surprise could be achieved. At a sign of resistance or of preparation for defence the plan would be abandoned, but if the enemy could be surprised they would be mercilessly slaughtered. There were tribes that went entirely naked and tribes among whom money was unknown. It was a primitive half-savage world, remote alike from the monasteries of Buddhist Burma and from India's highly developed Aryan civilization.

Yet Burma, so radically different from India, by the force of circumstance became an appanage of the Indian Empire. For fifty years Burma was an Indian province and a young man who went into the I.C.S. might find himself in Burma. The country became a part of India because of three wars, little wars to Victorian England but important to the Burmans. They were separated from each other in each case by a quarter of a century. The first happened mainly, and the others partly, because of the isolation and ignorance of the King of Burma's court at Ava. The King's House was called the Centre of the Universe and his courtiers really seem to have believed there was nothing in the world but Burma. This made foreign relations difficult.

The Governor-General of India could hardly have been expected to surrender the three richest provinces of Bengal to the King of Burma, as he was ordered to do in 1818. But it is not my purpose to apportion blame for the three wars, nor to recount their circumstances. It is enough to say that the three wars took place and that province by province Burma was added to India.

Three new provinces, Assam, Arakan and Tenasserim, were acquired in 1826 after the First Burmese War. They were administered to begin with chiefly by military officers, for whom life was seldom blessed by that settled comfort which the Victorian English enjoyed at home. Captain John Butler, appointed in 1841 to the civil branch of the service, found himself Assistant to the Political Agent of Upper Assam and in charge of the Hill Tribes. He set out with his wife and child and, after six weeks' journey, reached his headquarters, where 'we were fortunate in meeting with a small bungalow made of bamboos, grass and reed walls; but it was void of the luxury of a door or glass window'. Having plastered the outer walls with mud and laid bamboo mats on the damp earthen floor, he and his family prepared for the rains, 'vainly imagining we were securely sheltered for some time to come'.

But when the 'Burrumpooter' began to rise, it undermined the bank on which this hut was built, 'sweeping away ten paces of the bank three or four times a day'. The family moved to Butler's court-room, but that too followed the hut into the stream and they took to the jungle. A thatched roof was constructed, but the rain was too heavy to build walls and they had to make shift with canvas screens from tents.

That was only the beginning. Butler's tent was one night blown away from over his head and when he took refuge in a police-station the building collapsed about his ears. He and his family were transferred three times in the first two years. One move, taking four days, was made in a boat roofed over with grass to provide two rooms, each three and a half feet wide by nine feet long and three high. The travellers were not once able to set foot on shore and were so bitten by mosquitoes as to be 'literally scarred from head to foot with sores'. However, they were a family, 'not accustomed to make mountains of molehills' and on arrival they 'enjoyed only the more the comfort of a mud-plastered house without doors or windows'. It was during another such journey by boat that 'we were unexpectedly surprised by the birth of our second son James'.

Captain Butler found that the interest of his work made up for all this; Assam was a non-regulation tract and he was Judge, Magistrate and Collector in one. He was 'expected to do everything . . . For six months of the year . . . constantly travelling about the country, inspecting roads, causing them to be repaired, opening new ones, instituting local fiscal inquiries from village to village, enduring great fatigue, exposed to many perils from climate, wild beasts, and demi-savages in the hills.' What compensations Mrs Butler found he does not say.

Arakan was worse than Assam because of the peculiarly deadly form that malaria takes on that coast. Of seventy-nine consecutive Englishmen sent to Akyab, twenty-two died in the station and eighteen were invalided home.

Arakan had also been devastated by forty years of Burmese rule. Many of the Arakanese had fled; they now began cautiously to come back. By 1852, the population and the revenue of Akyab, compared with 1830, had been multiplied two and a half times, the area cultivated nearly four and a half times. This was due to good officers who in spite of fever kept the peace. In the early days, there were so many dacoits that the civil administration of Assam had been almost a form of warfare. It was waged by officers in charge of local levies, a very mixed lot indeed; Fytche, for instance, would not enlist a man unless he was a proved criminal. He thus at one stroke secured the most high-spirited of the population for his own side and reduced the number of his opponents.

There was little in Burma of either the puritanism or the fervour which the English displayed in the Punjab. But some of that spirit was transplanted at the beginning. Arthur Phayre, for instance, went from Shrewsbury to the Bengal Army and as a young man found himself stationed in the North-Western Provinces alongside 'Pickwick' Montgomery and John Thornton, both young civilians learning their work under Thomason. He was so much attracted that, when the chance came of civil employment, he took it eagerly and in the spirit of Thomason and the Lawrences.

Phayre went to Arakan in 1837, and was nine years on that coast. He attained such a mastery of Burmese that Burmans thought he must be a Buddhist. He came back as Commissioner of Arakan and after the war of 1852 was moved to the new province of Pegu – the delta – where he stayed fifteen years altogether, being for the last five Chief Commissioner of British Burma. He left in 1867 and was later four years Governor of Mauritius.

Phayre lived for his work; he never wrote about himself, there are no convenient letters to sisters or mother. He never married and the Burmans 'could only explain the pure life he led by regarding him as a saint . . .' He was plunged into all the business of organizing a new country, just taken over, and his letters to Dalhousie are full of the difficulties that arise in settling boundaries and securing intelligence, full of town-planning, of rents and revenues, teak and drains. A lightship was needed for Rangoon harbour, a chain of police posts for the frontier, dacoits were driving away villagers from the British side of the line. Capitation tax, house tax, the appointment of village headmen, rice and wheat for the troops, elephants in the Taungoo Pass, roads, anchorages, cantonments, committees, the raising of local regiments – all these were his concern and he sticks to them so strictly, stating clear sensible views in such clear sensible language, backed by such a knowledge of detail, that it seems impossible he could have time for anything but official work. Yet he did somehow find time for fossils and archaeology, for Indo-Chinese philology, for the history and customs of the Burmans. And he was not merely industrious. He has the face of a courteous and sensitive man; he was much loved. He went unarmed and would have no sentry on his house at night, no guards with his camp even on a newly formed and very disturbed frontier.

Phayre was not typical and it cannot be denied there were some poor officers. Tenasserim was too far away to be part of Bengal; it was directly under the Government of India and not often visited. Occasionally of course, even in Tenasserim, someone such as John Russell Colvin or Henry Durand would alight on his way to a career, but the general standard at first was nearer that of Impey, grandson of Sir Elijah Impey. Impey sent in no Treasury accounts for nine months and his Treasury was at last found to be short of cash by over twenty thousand rupees. He repaid what he could and then disappeared into Siam, taking with him a local wife with whom he lived happily ever afterwards.

The relations of English officers with Burmese women were quite different from anything that was usual in India. In Hickey's day, almost everyone in Bengal kept 'a female servant' such as Tippee and Gulab, but these were usually low caste women, a means of satisfying a purely animal desire and no more. There were some marriages with Indians, and sometimes men were genuinely fond of Indian mistresses, as Hickey was of Jemdanee, but it was not usual. The custom was dying out in Heber's time, had almost disappeared in Northern India by the age of Thomason and the Lawrences and was never general again among officers – though Burton of the *Arabian Nights* found it general in Sind as late as the 1840s. But in Burma it was different; there was no caste and no purdah; women of all social grades went freely wherever they liked. Women talked and laughed with men, managed their own property and sometimes their husbands' as well; women in Burma had to be treated as personalities.

It was not at all unusual then for an Englishman to marry a Burmese wife. It was common, too, for a man who did not actually go through a ceremony of marriage to live faithfully for many years with a Burmese girl who kept house for him, darned his socks and looked after his money. In Burmese eyes there was nothing discreditable in this and it meant a great deal to many men who would otherwise have been desperately lonely. There was often real affection; it was pleasant to come home to an amiable companion who would talk over what had happened during the day, laugh at a man's troubles, and tease him in a friendly way that would restore his sense of proportion. No doubt he learned more from Ma Phyu than he would from whist or snooker at the club. All the same, most good officers believed that in the end moral standards were lowered and the way paved for corruption.

The more one considers Burma, the more different from India it seems to have been. Kisch, who wrote so clearly of the famine in 1874, was stationed a year later in the Chittagong hill tracts and comments at once on the change. He was pleased with the hospitality the people showed to everyone, with the bright colours of their clothes, with the 'air of independence and freedom which is quite delightful'. 'Their women go before anyone without shame or fear', he writes and adds: 'Nearly all the officers who have been stationed in these Tracts like to go about the District and live in the houses of the natives, eating their food, sleeping in their houses and even adopting their style of dress and habits.'

Upper Burma consists of the country of the Burmans proper and at least as much again of tribal territory. The Burman part of the country was from the beginning administered by reviving a system of village rule which became law in 1887. The law was drafted by Sir Charles Crosthwaite and described by him in a minute which remained part of the Burma Village Manual till the end. It was very simple. For each village there was a headman; the Deputy Commissioner was required to find out who was regarded as a leader and appoint him. The headman had power to try small civil disputes and settle them, to report crime to the nearest Magistrate, to arrest criminals, to resist unlawful attacks, to help the authorities by arranging for transport and supplies when officers were on tour, to collect revenue, make roads, and look after the village sanitation, and act as residuary legatee for any other duties.

It worked, but it could not be applied to the tribes of the hills. Their problems may best be seen against the picturesque career of George Scott, a journalist who turned schoolmaster in Rangoon. Here he acquired a knowledge of Burmese language and customs good enough for him to pass as a Burman and he had ventured in disguise into Upper Burma before it was British. In the course of his many adventures he became aware of the essential difficulty that faced any government – Burmese or British – in dealing with the hill tribes. The hills are occupied by peoples ranging from the Shans, who are Buddhists and culturally can be compared with the Burmese, to the Wa tribes who take heads and go naked. These hill people are on the whole self-contained but from time to time they molest their neighbours. Any power in Mandalay must decide whether to endure occasional raids, which no doubt if unrequited would get steadily worse, or whether to chase the hillman back into his fastnesses and there proceed laboriously and expensively to teach him a lesson. And it must also be decided what lesson should be taught.

To cross the border only to punish and then at once to withdraw – the policy known as butcher-and-bolt – could hardly make the hillmen peaceful citizens. To stay on with military force was not much better and was expensive. To establish friendly relations by peaceful visits required officers of rare courage and devotion. Many were found; some were murdered but some survived and in the end this policy succeeded. Scott was one of the most successful.

Scott joined the Burma Commission in 1886. As in the Punjab after the Sikh wars, civilians from older provinces found themselves on the Burma Commission, side by side with men who had begun in the Indian Army or in some other calling. George Scott was one of those who came from outside Government service. He was soon sent to the Shan States.

The Shan country was divided into small principalities, varying in size from Kengtung, twice the size of Wales, to tiny States of a few villages. The princes of these States, who were known as Sawbwas, had owed allegiance to the King of Burma and had sent him from time to time a tribute of gold and silver flowers, dried squirrels, elephants, musical instruments and ponies. To the English it seemed that the allegiance was now transferred to Queen Victoria, but that someone ought to make sure that each Sawbwa understood what had happened. The French were still spreading their empire in Indo-China and might get there first.

The story of one Sawbwa must do for many; it concerns Kengtung, the largest and most remote. It lay beyond the Salween, more than four hundred miles from the railway, by a track that crossed many mountain ranges. Scott went with an escort of thirty-six sepoys, of whom eighteen were trained and seasoned Sikhs and the other half local men not yet quite dependable. Things went well at first and the Sawbwa sent them gold and silver flowers. Then news came that the Sawbwa's men had opened fire on some of the expedition's mule men and that the Sawbwa himself, apparently to test a new pistol, had emptied it into the back of one of the fallen men. This could not be overlooked – but it would be impossible to bring it home to the Sawbwa. The force at Scott's disposal was negligible; help would take weeks to come; if they were attacked, they would be overwhelmed. Scott reluctantly agreed to accept compensation for the dead muleteer – but when he asked for payment and for formal submission to Queen Victoria, there was an ominous pause. For four days nothing happened. For four days the expedition waited for an attack at any moment – tense – knowing it would be death if the attack came. On the fourth day, the money was paid and the Chief's covenant was formally presented in a *darbar*.

'Some years later,' Scott adds in his own account of this affair, 'when the Chief was handing round cakes to the ladies at a garden-party at Maymyo, he mentioned casually that it was only because of the intercession of his wives that he had not massacred the whole party. On the whole, knowing what he now knew, he thought that the ladies had been right.'

Scott was like a man whom bees do not sting, simply because he assumes they will not. He looks out from photographs with the face of a small boy, humorous and cheeky but determined to get into the eleven. There was a boyishness about him that never vanished. He was still playing football at fifty and noting in his journal and letters that the Gurkha orderlies were getting selfish about passing. He collected stamps and the tops of match-boxes and even had measles four times. He was not the kind of man to consider very deeply where all his activity was leading. He was an ardent believer in the value of the British Empire as a civilizing force; there seemed to him no question that Burma and the tribes were much better off within the Empire than outside; it was enough for him that in the Shan States, where life had been so uncertain, things were peaceful when he left.

The success of Scott and his fellows with the tribes in Upper Burma was proved in the Second World War, when the English were in deep adversity and the hill tribes showed them a loyalty as moving as any in history. But of the rest of Burma, one must conclude that this mature and self-assured people were much less influenced by the English than the people of India.

The connexion was much shorter. Upper Burma was annexed on January 1, 1886, and in the early months of 1942 the Japanese came into the country. That is only fifty-seven years. But even if the connexion had been longer, influence would still have been slight. The English found in Burma a country already unified under one crown and, although the outlying provinces were at first glad to be freed, in metropolitan Burma the people remembered past glory and forgot past misrule. In India, nationalism was a product of British rule; in Burma it was there ready-made. While Burmans on the whole liked individual Englishmen, they seem from the beginning to have felt humiliated by English government in a way which hardly occurred to Indians until late in the century. Nor did they take to Western education as Indians did. Whatever the reason, it may well be that the English period will seem to a Burmese historian three hundred years from now an interlude, longer than the Japanese, but not having contributed much more to the national character and attitude to life. But in the case of India such a conclusion would be out of the question.

2 The North-West Frontier

It would be hard to think of two countries or two peoples in sharper contrast than those of Burma and the North-West Frontier. The mountains of the North-West are rocky and arid, there is little rain and very little vegetation. Goats, sheep, camels and mules are kept, but their existence is precarious, their scanty grazing spreads far over stony and precipitous hills. In the narrow valleys, the summer heat is searing; on the bleak serrated tops, the winter is icy. The sparseness of the grazing, the intensity at either extreme of the climate, drive the people to a life half-nomadic. Bare subsistence is the most the tribesman can hope to extract from the harsh integument of the hills; for a wife or a rifle, he must get money, by trade, service or loot.

It was not a life that encouraged vague goodwill. There was no shade but the shade of a rock and a man looked out on the world with suspicion and hostility. But fidelity within the group and between host and guest, this was a point of honour, while courage and patience were never lacking.

One tale from hundreds may give a picture of these people. Subedar Amir Khan, an officer of the Kohat military police, lived in a valley near the Khyber. He had long ago killed two men from another of the valley forts; what made it worse, he had done it in his own house. They had come to kill him; it was his life or theirs, but his act was regarded by his enemies as a breach of border etiquette. When he went on leave he had to reach his home in darkness. He could never go out by day. At last he retired and settled down, but still he could not leave his home, which on three sides was within rifle-shot of his enemies. On the fourth side, there was open ground, hidden from his enemies by ridges and commanded by the towers at the corners of his own house.

Subedar Amir Khan dug a trench from his home to this dead ground. Here he said his prayers and every evening at sunset went there by the covered way to give thanks to his Maker. His enemies knew his habit but could see no way to make use of it. At last, two of them crept by night to the open ground and stayed there during the whole heat of the following day. They were exposed to fire from the towers if they made the least movement; they had to lie quite still on burning stony ground. In the evening Amir Khan came to say his prayers and they shot him.

The Sikhs had held this country as far as the foot of the hills. Knife, rope, or bullet was all that passed between Sikh and Pathan. The coming of the English instead of the Sikh was a pleasure as positive as the sudden

On the North-West Frontier the harshness of the country did not encourage a vague good-will.

end of toothache. Edwardes in Bannu could work miracles and Nicholson seemed an incarnation of the divine. And Mackeson, whose name they cut short to Kishan, was remembered as Kishan Kaka, Uncle Mackeson, forty years after he was murdered by a fanatic in Peshawar.

The men of that golden age resented any paper work that kept them to their desks. This was all very well when the English first came to the country; to decide on life and death in five minutes under a tree, to settle the Land Revenue of a district in six weeks, was better than anything the people of the country had had before. But something had to be done to ensure that what was an offence in Mackeson's district was not rewarded in Abbott's. And nothing John Lawrence did deserves more admiration than his managing of his brother Henry's team of young men on the Frontier.

Coke he told gently that he could not drop his district and run back to his regiment because it was fighting. Nicholson he checked with a wise amiability for trying to command a brigade at the same time as a district, and Mackeson – but in Mackeson's case he confessed a failure. 'No man appreciated Mackeson's high qualities more than I did, but ... I have written five times officially and three times privately before I could get an answer to an ordinary reference. Everything was in arrears.' There were always men like that, men who did not answer letters, who were always in bad odour with headquarters and worth a dozen careful scribes.

Lawrence laid stress on the settled districts and wanted no adventures in the unadministered tribal areas. The English had inherited from the

Sikhs a line at which the administration stopped short; up to that line there were districts of the Punjab administered by Deputy Commissioners. Beyond that line were wild tribes and the Queen's writ did not run.

John Lawrence insisted that the first duty of his frontier Deputy Commissioners was to show the people of the administered districts the solid advantages of British rule; as to the tribesmen, they must be convinced that we had no intention of going into their country. These were points of emphasis; after he had gone, they were frozen into rigid rules. Soon there were standing orders that no Deputy Commissioner must cross the boundary.

But the tribes were 'our' tribes. They must trade or loot – and there was nowhere but the settled districts where either trade or loot was to be had. And they did loot. Then the Deputy Commissioner was at last allowed to cross the line. When he entered tribal territory for the first time, he went to burn and kill.

When the tribe yielded, they were told to pay a fine of so many rifles and the expedition retired. The tribe were kept busy for some time rebuilding their villages and towers and acquiring means to replace their rifles, but they cannot have felt either affection for those who had chastised them or inclination to reform. It was 'butcher-and-bolt' – and no more likely to succeed here than in Burma.

It was largely due to one man that this was changed. Robert Sandeman shared with Malcolm and Munro a forthright, unprejudiced approach to every problem, a grasp of essentials and a certainty of where justice lay. He found himself Deputy Commissioner of a district a hundred and fifty miles long, within which he was as usual responsible for everything. But Dera Ghazi Khan was a frontier district and he soon became dissatisfied with responsibility for a frontier he could not cross.

Bruce, his assistant, has a tale of how one morning a villager came to see him with something wrapped up in a cloth. It was a human head. The owner of the head had been a tribesman from a mile across the border. He had carried off the villager's wife and the villager had petitioned the Deputy Commissioner for redress. He had been told that as his enemy lived across the border nothing could be done by process of law. He had accordingly dealt with the matter himself. Now he had come to submit to authority.

This state of affairs was clearly intolerable. And there was a further complication. Sandeman's district was in the Punjab and was habitually raided not only by Pathans but by Baluch tribes as well. These were the concern of Sind; here the Chief Commissioner was Merewether, brought up in the school of Frere and Jacob. In Sind, the frontier policy was different, but here too an emphasis had become a rigid rule. It had become a dogma that the Khan of Kalat must always be supported. But now he was engaged in a civil war with the leaders of his clans, over whom he no longer had any control

All this came to a head in a practical way in 1867, when a mixed force of some fifteen hundred armed men, Marris, Bugtis and other Baluch tribesmen, came into Dera Ghazi Khan on a raid. Sandeman and Bruce, with some thirty troopers, raised the country against them and with a force from their own district drove them off, killing their leader and a hundred and twenty of his followers and taking two hundred prisoners.

What was to be done with the prisoners? Merewether from Sind was adamant that they were subjects of the Khan of Kalat – but in fact he was at war with the Marris and Bugtis. Sandeman forgot official channels and did a deal direct with the tribal leaders. They promised not to raid his district and he employed some of them as messengers and as patrols to keep open the caravan routes.

This of course was anathema to Merewether. Sandeman was interfering with his tribes and encouraging them to rebel against the Khan. This controversy lasted a long time but in the end Sandeman got his way by showing that his policy worked. He did it by deliberate disobedience. He ignored standing orders and went for a three weeks' tour across the border. He lived in tribal territory, he moved with a tribal escort, he visited the headquarters of every clan. He risked his life and his career. When he came back he reported what he had done and the tour had been so obviously successful that his disobedience was condoned.

By 1877, Sandeman's policy was accepted by everyone. He was

left, Sir William Merewether, who helped to settle the Sind Frontier under Jacob and Frere. But when he succeeded Jacob, he obstinately turned a general principle into a rigid dogma; right, Sir Robert Sandeman: he became dissatisfied with responsibility for a frontier he could not cross and reformed frontier policy.

16 right, An Englishman's toilet. It is the first half of the century and 'down-country' – towards Calcutta. Things became simpler as time went on and as you moved North-West; 17 below, Young lady's toilet. Servants were cheap and eager for work; 18 below right, At breakfast, 1842. A quiet domestic scene – but the British in India like royalty were never alone.

19 above, *Pigsticking was a dangerous and exciting sport, because the pig had to be followed at full gallop over broken country and was a fierce and courageous animal with sharp tusks. Only the boar was hunted;* 20 below, *Raja Sarup Singh of Udaipur (1842–61) on a boar hunt. This method of hunting the wild boar involved less danger and exertion.*

appointed Agent to the Governor-General in Baluchistan.

In Baluchistan, at least, 'masterly inactivity' had gone down before the new policy of 'conciliatory intervention'. Warfare between the Baluch tribes ceased. Tribal raids on the plains came to an end. Isolated crimes of course there were, but Baluchistan had become a country in which law had effect.

It was not the Baluch tribes only that were pacified. Outside the sphere of the Khan of Kalat, the districts of Pishin and the Zhob became British; further still, the Kurram, in the heart of tribal territory, was taken over and administered. The Kurram was an exceptional case because the people are Shiah Muslims, surrounded by Sunnis, and they wanted protection. Still, all these were Pathan countries and Sandeman himself firmly believed that his system could be extended northwards and that the whole Frontier could be pacified just as Baluchistan had been.

Tribal employment was the cornerstone of his system; the more amenable elements of the tribe must be encouraged and strengthened. This could best be done by letting the tribal leaders present men for service in the tribal levies, thus providing an alternative to loot. Tribal levies could be genuinely useful and should be used constantly. If there was any complaint against the tribe or a member of it, there should be an investigation. Individuals should be judged by a tribal council; if the tribe, or a section of it, had behaved badly, it must be punished by fine.

It was true that Pathans were less obedient to tribal leaders than Baluchis, but it was – Sandeman argued – only a matter of degree. Both understood the idea of tribal responsibility, both had tribal councils or *jirgas*. To an outsider it sounds convincing, though no Frontier officer living will admit that the Mahsuds could ever be brought to obey a Malik unless it suited them. If anyone could have done it, Sandeman was the man. His name was worth all the troops in India. But he died and it was left to Bruce to try the experiment in Waziristan.

Bruce was the younger son of an Irish landowner. He was sent out from Ireland with the promise that he would be appointed an Extra Assistant Commissioner. In most provinces, the district officer had four, five or six assistants, known by different names in different provinces, all doing the same kind of work. Some were in charge of sub-divisions, one would perhaps be City Magistrate, another would have charge of the office. One perhaps would be a junior officer of the Indian Civil Service, and the others would be uncovenanted – that is, appointed direct in India, governed by no covenant with the Secretary of State.

It was these posts that the Act of 1833 had confirmed to Indians, but in Victorian times, many of the uncovenanted were European or of mixed blood. Bruce was 'uncovenanted' but he married his Deputy Commissioner's daughter and was soon promoted to be a member of the Punjab Commission. Before Sandeman's death, he was put in charge of a Punjab

A company of the Royal Artillery crossing a ford of the Kabul River during the Second Afghan War, in 1880.

frontier district, Dera Ismail Khan, the district north of Dera Ghazi Khan. Here he was responsible not only for his own district but for the tribes confronting him, as turbulent and difficult as any on the border. He believed that he could do for Waziristan what Sandeman had done for Baluchistan. He would bring home individual responsibility by means of the tribal council.

In 1893, a European overseer in the Public Works Department, Mr Kelly, with one trooper of a tribal levy, was shot dead in the Zhob. Bruce called the Mahsuds together and demanded from the tribal council the surrender of five men, two who had shot Kelly and the trooper and three others, accused of the murder of an Indian soldier. He was successful; the Maliks brought him the five men. Bruce directed the tribal council to try them and they were tried by all the leading Maliks. They were found guilty by the Maliks and Bruce sentenced them to terms of imprisonment. He dismissed the council to their hills – and within a few weeks three of the leaders were treacherously murdered.

It was a vital moment. If the murder of the three Maliks was judicially punished, there might be some chance of establishing the reign of law in Waziristan. But if these murderers were not brought to book, the Maliks would never establish control. The Punjab Government agreed with Bruce and recommended that a punitive expedition should follow if they were not delivered. But the Government of India believed that an expedition would endanger their negotiations with the Amir of Afghanistan for the demarcation of a frontier; the local problem gave way to wider considerations.

There were two questions – administering the tribes and defending India against Russia. Both questions were argued interminably; this is not the place for a detailed discussion. But two points must be made. The Russian danger was not the bogey of faddists. There were two empires expanding – one westward from the Bay of Bengal, one eastward from the Baltic. And, if Afghanistan was to be maintained as a cushion between the two, some kind of working arrangement about the Border tribes must be made with the Amir. The English could hardly hope to be on good terms with him so long as no one was clear where sovereignty lay among these turbulent and undisciplined people. So the two questions were linked.

Everyone understood where the administrative boundary lay. Beyond that, there was a wide belt of tribal territory in which some tribes were vaguely regarded as British, some were vaguely the Amir's, but neither were wholly subject to the authority of either. There could be no peace till that was settled.

In 1894, Sir Mortimer Durand went to Kabul and the Durand line was drawn between the Amir's territory and that of the tribes. The position of the tribes was at last made clear. They were not British subjects but British Protected Persons, living in a belt of independent but protected republics. There was at last an international boundary. But for this a price was paid; the murderers of Bruce's Maliks were left undisturbed. A year later in 1895, Bruce, with a brigade of troops, went as British Commissioner to demarcate the line on the ground; his camp was attacked at night and heavy losses were inflicted by Waziri tribesmen. His experiment in Waziristan had failed.

Perhaps that would have happened anyhow. Perhaps Sandeman's system could never have worked among so lawless a people as the Mahsuds. But whatever hope there had been now disappeared and in the next half-dozen years, there was established a curious state of intermittent hostility, something not quite a war, and more than a game. It was played – or fought – according to certain rules. It was a rough game and people were killed but both sides found it exhilarating.

It was a strange game. Lord Curzon in 1903 formed a North-West Frontier Province. This gave the English side a better team but did not alter the rules of the game. There were now six frontier districts and six tribal areas, but they were staffed by much the same kind of men as before, recruited partly from the Indian Civil Service and partly from the Indian Army. The regular army was now normally drawn back and trained for war against a foreign enemy, while the task of looking after the tribes was left mainly to irregular tribal forces.

The tribesmen on their side re-armed themselves. Once they had only had muzzle-loading smooth-bore weapons. At first, a breech-loading rifle must be stolen from the British; later, pass-made rifles supplemented this source of supply and then imported rifles landed in the Persian Gulf and brought overland by caravan. This meant that some tribal cash earned from the British government had to be sent in advance to Persian ports. Then British naval action in the Gulf closed down the flow of rifles and the

Afridis could not recover their money. The Afridis petitioned for compensation; they had lost money, they said, because naval action had stopped gun-running. It was as though a burglar should claim unemployment benefits because he had dropped his tools when surprised by the police.

It was all very odd. A few tribesmen in some tribes were irreconcilably hostile, but in most tribes most of the tribesmen credited the Government of India with the infinite mercy that a penitent but recurring sinner counts on from the Almighty. The few were kept at white heat by the *mullahs* or by agents of the Amir. While it suited the English to have a strong and friendly Afghanistan between themselves and Russia, it was no less convenient to the Amir that the tribes between himself and the English should be turbulent and incalculable. And for most of the tribes too the situation was not without its attractions. It suited them to live their old lawless lives in a sort of national park or bird sanctuary, from which they could emerge to commit an outrage and retire in the knowledge that nothing very dreadful would happen.

On the English side, too, most Englishmen liked the Frontier as it was. To the soldier it presented an unrivalled training-ground with real bullets; the Political Officer as a rule felt an affection for the Pathan, for his courage, his sense of humour, and his perverted sense of honour. And if he was a good officer, the Political Agent soon grew to enjoy his own skill at the game. It gave him pleasure to cap one Pushtu proverb with another in the opposite sense; he revelled in esoteric knowledge of the internal divisions of the clans; and to make use of his knowledge gave him the satisfaction that another man would get from potting the red or solving an equation.

There was a tale current in the folklore of Indian clubs and messes which enshrined a truth. A Political Agent was with troops on a punitive expedition; after breakfast with the officers, he took his lunch in a haversack and disappeared; they did not see him again till evening when, sipping a pink gin by the light of a lantern carefully screened from snipers, he asked: 'And how did things go on your side today? Casualties on our side were half-a-dozen.'

Every soldier who went on such an expedition was at first puzzled by this strange compromise between a war and a field-day, and still more by the knowledge that it would be succeeded by a peace no less bogus, a sort of cold peace in which the tribes were forgiven for their misdeeds and paid to be good. No newcomer could understand why, once a tribe had broken its engagements and forced the Government to inflict an expensive punishment, there should be a return to the very conditions which had produced the outbreak.

Finance was the answer. The North-West Frontier Province in 1908 was a deficit Province at a time when all the others contributed to the centre. If for the cold peace there had been substituted all the critic would have liked to see, the roads, the schools and the dispensaries, the bill

Sir Henry Mortimer Durand in 1904. Sir Mortimer Durand settled the international boundary between British India and Afghanistan and ended the long controversy as to whether the best defence against Russia was a Forward Policy or a Close Border.

would have gone up. So the frontier tribes were left alone – except by the mullahs and the Amir's agents. The soldier had his training ground, and the Political Officer was free to tramp the hills after partridge and keep down the murders as much as he could; to share the Pathan's broad stories and enjoy the guest's portion of the roast kid stuffed with raisins and pistachios; to keep his ears open and run the risk every day of the knife or bullet of a fanatic.

15
BACK IN INDIA

1 The Rebels

Flattery was the daily diet of the civilian in India, and constant flattery corrupts; it breeds complacency and an easy optimism, the closed eye and the closed heart. The Guardians would have been super-human if none of them had been inclined to complacency, but they did spend much time considering how their rule appeared to their subjects. Most of them concluded that around three-quarters of the population had for centuries let the legions thunder past and did not mind who ruled them; they were passively loyal; they were better off and preferred British rule to anything they had known before. As for the educated and ambitious – well, clearly we must not *stop* educating them, and for the present, we must put up with their discontent. One day – but clearly not just yet ... The conclusion was unstated.

But there were some who found intolerable this lack of imaginative passion. Take first an Indian, one of the first to enter the service, Romesh Chandar Dutt. He passed the examination in London in 1869, with two other Indians from Bengal, Behari Lal Gupta and Surendranath Banerjea. This in itself was an achievement. It took courage for a Hindu to go to England at all; he had to defy religion and face social ostracism when he came home. And in a foreign country he had to study in a foreign language and be successful in a competitive examination against men answering questions in their mother tongue.

Again, when Dutt came back to Bengal in 1871 and was appointed Assistant Magistrate at Alipur, he had to behave as though he were an Englishman, giving twenty or thirty times a day decisions which were based on a foreign system of thought. He overcame these difficulties and was the first Indian to hold executive charge of a district, becoming Collector of Backergunge in 1883. He was the only Indian in the nineteenth century to be Commissioner of a division, holding first Burdwan in

246

1892 and then Orissa, a charge which was to be a Governor's Province. He was an official member of the Bengal Legislative Council, he was awarded a C.I.E., and he had twenty-seven years' meritorious service when he retired in 1897. He had used his furlough to translate various works from Sanskrit into modern Bengali; he had to his credit translations into English and historical novels in Bengali as well.

Dutt's career was creditable by any standards. He became a lecturer in history at London University and published a number of books, historical and political, the latter mostly critical of the régime in India. He was filled with misery and sympathy when he thought of the famine years which ended the century and he wrote a series of open letters to Lord Curzon proposing reform of the whole revenue system. The noble lord was provoked into the famous resolution of 1902 in which he reviewed Mr Dutt's arguments and proceeded to overwhelm them.

Dutt was a man of more than average ability but he had no experience outside Bengal and he knew nothing about settlement. Lord Curzon had the advice of a dozen settlement officers and a revenue secretary from every province. It was not a fair contest.

Lord Curzon was singularly insensitive to the effect on a man's feelings of being overwhelmed in argument. Sonorous, pompous and usually acid, the sentences flow from his lordship's pen; every paragraph makes a telling point and every other alienates the reader.

Dutt did not dispute the fact that the first cause of famine was a failure of the rains and he put his points with moderation and courtesy. He credited the English with a desire to improve things. He thought however that expenditure was too high and that Land Revenue could be so far reduced that the peasant would be materially better off and better able to resist famine.

'This hypothetical forecast', said Lord Curzon, 'is not rendered more plausible to the Government of India by their complete inability to endorse the accompanying allegations of fact.' He makes a few factual points, as though a battleship should register a few hits with her secondary armament on some despised foe to get the range. Then the big guns loose their salvoes and poor Dutt is blown out of the water. If the Government of India were to accept his suggestions, Land Revenue would everywhere be increased. In Madras it would be roughly doubled. In the Central Provinces, Dutt had wanted to limit the King's share to an average of one-tenth of the total produce. But already the average was less than one-twentieth.

Cruising thoughtfully among the flotsam to pick up survivors, Lord Curzon conceded that the Land Revenue system was not perfect and indicated possible improvements, all in favour of the peasant, to which his Government would try to give effect.

The benefit of Dutt's onslaught was that the Government did carefully re-examine the whole question. Dutt went on to be both Prime Minister of

Baroda and President of the Indian National Congress; he was a man of industry and public spirit on whom it would be pleasant to dwell longer.

On a narrower front, an English critic had already scored some success. S. S. Thorburn knew the Western districts of the Punjab thoroughly; he had confined himself to that area and to one point. Land had never before been *owned*; a man had the right to cultivate but he did not own the soil and could not transfer it. The Sikhs had taken as much of the crop as they could get and he had lived on what they left. Now he found himself the owner, with a capital asset and he was expected to pay a fixed revenue in cash. On average, he was better off than before but in a bad year he would go to the village moneylender. This was always a Hindu, a man who up to now had never dared to raise his voice in the village. In the past, if he behaved extortionately he would be beaten or killed. But now he might get possession of the holding and the law would protect his person. So he would lend a few rupees, and then a few more, and say nothing of getting them back – until the total with interest had mounted to a fair sum and then he would dun the peasant for payment. And then there would be a bond for more still and then a mortgage and in the end the moneylender would get the land.

Some of Thorburn's figures were contested, but every official in the Punjab agreed that something of the kind was happening. Thorburn proposed a series of measures to put an end to it and one by one they were taken up. Indeed, in Bombay most of them were already law. In the Punjab, the Act of 1900 divided the population into agricultural tribes and non-agricultural. The traders were no longer allowed to buy land from peasants and a mortgage lapsed if it was not discharged in twenty years. Credit was restricted, interest limited, precautions against fraudulent mortgages introduced. It was paternal and illiberal and did a great deal of good.

Thorburn was still in service when he began his agitation. He wrote state papers addressed to his government and followed them up by books in which he sharply criticized the Government and individuals. All that happened was that he was ordered to conduct exactly that detailed inquiry in twelve villages which he had himself recommended, and eventually his recommendations were accepted.

The service was still one in which men felt strongly, said what they thought and if their criticism was sound, had a good chance of getting their way.

Another way of dealing with the evils of debt was to provide a better source of credit. Sir William Wedderburn, a baronet by inheritance and a Radical by temperament, had started as early as 1881 to agitate for co-operative village banks. He had worked out a scheme and obtained the agreement locally of moneylenders, peasants, and landowners. His scheme was approved by the Government of Bombay and by the Government of India; after three and a quarter years of discussion with the India Office it was turned down by the Secretary of State. The India Office was a great place for thinking of objections.

Twenty years were lost and it was not till 1904 that Lord Curzon and Sir Denzil Ibbetson passed an Act embodying Wedderburn's proposals. Wedderburn however was not reproved for interesting John Bright, the great Radical M.P., in his ideas nor for addressing meetings while on leave. Nor was this his only agitation. He wanted a more flexible system of revenue collection – though here his suggestion does not sound very sensible. He wanted to revive the old Maratha village committees which would settle disputes by agreement between the parties. This was better. On the platform under the tree in the village, truth is spoken more often than in the law courts. But the memory of the old tribunals had died and undoubtedly there were dangers in reviving them. Sir Richard Temple took the safe line and turned the proposal down. When village panchayats were revived, in the twentieth century, of course things did sometimes go wrong. Patience and perseverance were needed to improve them – but again twenty years had been lost.

Wedderburn was forgiven; he became a Secretary to the Government of Bombay and when he retired the Government of Bombay passed a resolution complimenting him on his good services. Having retired, he devoted himself to the affairs of the Indian National Congress. 'I have been in the service of the people of India,' he said, 'and have eaten their salt; and I hope to devote to their service what still remains to me of active life.' He did. He was President of the Fourth Congress and thereafter for nearly thirty years, during seven of which he was in Parliament, he was the representative of the Congress in London, the counterpart in England of Hume in India.

The Congress had been founded mainly by the exertions of another Indian civilian, Allan Octavian Hume. He had come to India in 1849; he was in charge of a district and had fought bravely in 1857, winning as a leader of irregular forces more than one pitched battle. He stayed ten years at Etawah in the North-West Provinces and was an exceptionally good district officer, showing particular enthusiasm for education and for agricultural improvement. He started juvenile reformatories, and his scheme was taken up by the Government. In 1870, after three years as provincial commissioner of Customs, he became Secretary to the Government of India in the new department of Revenue, Commerce and Agriculture. Hume was chosen as much for his scientific training as for his long and warm-hearted interest in improving the peasant's life, and he was there nine years, an unusually long spell. He retired in 1882, and took up his residence in Simla, where he began to work for the political development of India.

It was Hume's contention that a new spirit of expansive nationalism was arising to which some expression must be given if there was not to be an explosion. He made also the equally strong general point that any proposal for change had to face formidable obstacles, first in the provincial government, then in the government of India, and, last and often fatally, in the India Office. The system was the last in the world to encourage a daring and statesmanlike experiment.

Hume wrote to all the graduates of the Calcutta University asking for fifty volunteers to join in a movement to promote the mental, moral, social, and political regeneration of India:

> There are aliens, like myself, who love India and her children . . . but the real work must be done by the people of the country themselves . . . If fifty men cannot be found with sufficient power of self-sacrifice, sufficient love for and pride in their country, sufficient genuine and unselfish patriotism to take the initiative . . . then there is no hope for India. Her sons must and will remain mere humble and helpless instruments in the hands of foreign rulers.

The result of this letter was the first Indian National Congress of 1885. It had been decided before that date, by Hume on the advice of Lord Dufferin, the Viceroy, to put political reform first and social second; only a government with some popular backing could enforce reforms in such matters as child-marriage. After full discussion, the party was 'absolutely unanimous in insisting on unswerving loyalty to the British Crown as the key-note of the Institution'.

The first session of the Congress was held at Bombay, in an atmosphere of friendly encouragement by both the Governor and the Viceroy. The first Congress asked for a Royal Commission on the working of the administration, prayed for a reduction of military expenditure and deprecated the annexation of Upper Burma. They would abolish the Council of India as an obstacle to reform, and develop provincial Councils on the lines actually made law in 1909. But the longest and most detailed of their resolutions concerned the method of recruitment to the Civil Service.

Hardly anyone, English or Indian, in 1885 envisaged a country ruled by a parliament and by the majority of votes in a wide electorate. What some Indians of the university class did picture was a continuation of the existing system, but with Indian officials gradually replacing English. They wanted, therefore, recruitment to be as late as possible, to give Indians a better chance of competing with Englishmen in English.

Hume was general secretary of the congress until its twenty-third session, held in December 1908. The resolutions of that year begin as usual with loyal homage to the King Emperor, express the deep and general satisfaction of the country at the reforms just announced, and end with a message of cordial greetings and congratulations to Hume, 'the father and founder of the Congress'.

The resolutions that came between are framed in the spirit of Mr Gladstone; they have a flavour of the nonconformist meeting-house, earnest and well-meaning, a trifle doctrinaire, fundamentally warm-hearted. The delegates disapproved of violent outrages and hoped for constitutional progress. They protested against the treatment of Indians in South Africa and against the power still held by the Government under Regulation III of 1818 to confine without trial persons known to be hostile to the Government. The world's history shows few governments who have denied themselves this power, but it is repugnant to the principles of the Great Revolution of 1688. The men of the Congress had been brought up in the mental atmosphere of English Liberalism and they were genuinely shocked. But it was a criticism that would never have occurred to their grandfathers, and the Government of India might well have exchanged the self-congratulatory glances of intelligent parents who perceive that their child has begun to criticize them.

The twenty-third Congress wished also to separate the executive and judicial functions. Here was another idea quite foreign to the soil of India, where, from time immemorial, all functions had centred in the King. The English had introduced the first step away from absolute autocracy, written law instead of personal whim. The second stage, of executive officers with no power to punish, they had treated more cautiously. Even in the older provinces, where there were separate judges, the district officer was the head of the magistracy and could himself sentence an offender to two years' imprisonment. In India, where every religious festival was an occasion when tempers might flare up and lives be lost, there was surely every reason for this slight modification of constitutional principle, but the congress asked for the separation of judicial and executive functions because the principle was liberal. They would have been on firmer ground if they had argued that what was needed was something more Indian, some compromise perhaps between the Maratha system of arbitration by committee and the Mogul system of punishment by executive order. But they were English Liberals.

In those early days, then, some of the resolutions passed in succession at every annual Congress were too English for India. All the same, they were one of the healthiest signs of the times and the mere fact that they were made is something of which we can both be proud.

But something was wrong. Consider the case of Surendranath Banerjea. He, with Dutt and Gupta, went to England in 1868 and next year the three were successful in the I.C.S. examination. There were four Indians that year, these three from Bengal and another from Bombay. All over India, and particularly in Bengal, there were loud rejoicings. But before long, someone discovered that three of the four candidates had given an age for a school examination four years ago which did not agree with the age they had given for the I.C.S. examination. Two of them, including Banerjea, were over age for the I.C.S. if the age they had given before was correct. The Civil Service Commission declared Banerjea and the other man disqualified and their seats vacant. They refused to consider their plea that by their reckoning they were nine months old when they were born.

This was probably mere pedantry. But the India Office took no step to put things right. Banerjea sued the Secretary of State in the court of Queen's Bench and won his case. He and his companion were reinstated. There could hardly have been a worse start to a career.

Worse however was to come. In the course of his first year, Banerjea sent in a false return. On one list he gave a full explanation for delays in dealing with a case – but the same case was included in another list of cases in which no action had been taken because the accused could not be arrested. Carelessness, one would think, but the Bengal Government ordered an inquiry by three senior officers, who came to the conclusion that Banerjea had deliberately intended to deceive his Collector. The sentence was dismissal. Banerjea became a dismissed Government servant, branded for life.

An Englishman would not have been treated in that way. There was a deep-rooted distrust for Indians, a belief that they were not straight-forward, that they could never take the place of English district officers.

Some bitterness of course was due to memories of the Mutiny. That must be the explanation of the Cowan episode. A body of about a hundred Sikhs of a fanatical sect attacked a town; they were defeated by local forces and the deputy commissioner, Cowan – like Bruce an uncovenanted man – blew half the prisoners away from guns without waiting for orders. He was dismissed and the English press thought he had been unjustly treated.

That could hardly have happened in quite that way before the Mutiny but it was for another reason that things grew worse. Henry Beveridge felt that relations between the races were worse in the 1880s than ever before; Sir Henry Cotton thought the same. In the 1860s, nine civilians out of ten had been on the side of the ryot; by the 1880s nine out of ten were against Lord Ripon over the Ilbert Bill.

The real reason is not far to seek. It is easy to forget the immense gulf between the educated Englishman and the Indians whom he met in a district, even in the twentieth century. In a small district, the mental background of the Indian gentlemen who came to visit him was still that of the Hindu epics or of Firdausi's *Book of the Kings*. The civilization to which they belonged had stood still. Between people so different there could be courtesy, kindliness and liking, there could be affection, but no dealing on equal terms. The relationship was paternal, accepted on both sides. It was fixed and settled, like caste; the district officer and his family were one kind of human being, the people of his district another. There was no thought of equality.

In the 1870s and 1880s, and particularly in Calcutta, things began to be different. Here there were Indians of a new kind who could not be regarded as beings of another order. 'Men who speak English better than most Englishmen, who read Mill and Comte, Max Muller and Maine, who occupy with distinction seats on the judicial bench, who administer the affairs of native States with many millions of inhabitants, who manage cotton mills and conduct the boldest operations of commerce, who edit newspapers in English and correspond on equal terms with the scholars of Europe' – such men as these, urged Sir Henry Cotton, cannot be expected to salaam every Englishman they meet in the street, to dismount from a horse or lower an umbrella when they see him coming, to remove their shoes when they enter his house. The educated Indian had stepped right across the gap; he thought and talked like an Englishman and claimed to be judged by English standards.

It was a shock to Englishmen used to the old paternal relationship to find themselves confronted by Indians who claimed equality, and the shock roused a great deal of irrational anger.

To this sense of shock must be added the genuine difficulty that there were still very few Indians with whom it was possible to share a meal or a drink; there was also the treatment of women. It was difficult to be friendly with people whose women were segregated and who practised child-marriage. The Age of Consent Act of 1891, or rather the evil it was intended to cure, was a more important factor in the feelings of this time than is generally recognized. It had its origin in the case of a child wife who died of injuries received on her marriage-bed; Indian Liberals supported the bill – which raised the age for consummation of marriage to twelve – but it aroused bitter opposition among many orthodox Hindus who regarded it as an interference with religion. It was this agitation which started Tilak on his career.

No one can deny, all the same, that there were things at this time of which an Englishman should feel ashamed and at which an Indian has a right to feel bitter. There were cases of rudeness to fellow passengers by train; there were cases – not many, but a sprinkling – of British soldiers when drunk injuring or even killing Indians and escaping with inadequate sentences. There was a feeling in the air summed up in a sentence overheard by Mrs Moss King. At the outbreak of the Second Afghan War, 'a young artillery officer put the present popular feeling in a nutshell. He said: "I know nothing of politics, but I do know that if a nigger cheeks us we must lick him."'

Racial arrogance was more widespread than at any time before or since. A process that had begun in the 1840s was accelerated; fewer and fewer Englishmen were identifying themselves thoroughly with the country. At the same time the English as a nation felt secure, their pre-eminence in wealth and naval power unchallenged, their works manifestly approved by the Almighty.

But in every province there was an ardent minority of the service who hated arrogance and who believed that justice was not always done as between English and Indian. These men were lifelong members of a public service, yet it was still a commonplace for men in the service to write to the papers on political subjects. Continual, unconstructive criticism of course did not help a man's career, but a great deal could be said with impunity. In the darkest days of the Ilbert Bill controversy, Harrison arranged a dinner for British and Indians at which Cotton 'made a speech breathing the spirit of equality'. Both these men stood up for the Bengali against the Government repeatedly; it did not stand in their way to high office and knighthoods.

The racial bitterness was to improve before long. English people became used to the idea of educated Indians, Indian women began to join society, and Indians knew that there were men as generous and warm-hearted as Cotton, Harrison and Hume. 'Do you', Hume appealed to his own countrymen, 'at all realize the dull misery of these countless myriads? From their births to their deaths ... toil, toil, toil; hunger, hunger, hunger; sickness, suffering, sorrow; these alas! alas ! are the key-notes of their short and sad existences.' It was just because there were some Englishmen who sounded that note that on the political side the quarrel that was beginning to develop was so much a family affair.

In Banerjea's long story of struggle he speaks often critically, sometimes bitterly, of abstractions such as the system, the service and bureaucratic rule, but not often in the same spirit of individuals. 'Mr Charles Allen, an officer of great promise ... and a personal friend' – 'Sir Charles Elliott, with whom my personal relations were friendly and even cordial ... but a typical bureaucrat ... who believed the people could not be trusted to manage their own affairs' ... 'Sir Edward Baker, strong, generous and impulsive' – those are the kind of references that fill the pages of Banerjea, who had a right to be bitter if any man had. And consider the dedication of Nirad Chaudhuri's *Diary of an Unknown Indian*, published since independence. 'To the memory', he wrote, 'of the British Empire in India, which conferred subjecthood on us but withheld citizenship, to which yet every one of us threw out the challenge *Civis Britannicus sum*, because all that was good and living within us was made, shaped, and quickened by the same British rule.'

The young Congress movement was in short a quickening of the spirit, a child both of England and India. But while the Congress were talking of Montesquieu and George Washington, Tilak was praising Sivaji for stabbing a Mogul general in the back at the moment he was about to sign a treaty of friendship. While the Congress were welcoming the mild reforms of 1908, Tilak was preaching that if *mlecchas* – non-Hindus, Christians or Muslims – come into your house, you should shut the doors and burn it down with them inside. Ram Mohun Roy had believed that Hinduism must reform itself by a synthesis of the best from Asia and Europe; as that reform began to take effect it bred a new resistance, an angry rejection, a return to the dark side of Saivite Hinduism. That spirit was always in conflict with the element in Hindu nationalism which has so much in common with the English nonconformist radical movement. Fifty years later, it murdered Gandhi.

It was that spirit that alienated the Muslims. Sir Sayyad Ahmad saw that majority rule would mean Hindu rule; he rejected the prospect. The conflict was clearly stated in the first days of the Congress. A beginning had been made to the recession of British power, a healthy and natural development. But no one yet perceived that this meant a struggle that was to split India and to destroy the unity that had been achieved.

2 A Sense of Proportion

F. B. Simson of the Bengal Civil Service, who retired in 1872, was sitting one day in his court when a villager entered carrying the mangled leg of his son. This he laid before the court.

'What sort of a ruler are you?' he cried. 'What are you doing, sitting here arguing with lawyers when a tiger is eating my son?'

It was a view of the Magistrate's duty that agreed with Simson's own. He left his court and shot the tiger. But it was not a view that fitted in very well with the plea of the National Congress for the separation of judicial and executive functions.

Three-quarters of the service at least would have laughed at talk of the separation of powers and would have added that they had more important things to think about. The District Officer had to think, for instance, of the best way of dealing with Brij Mohan, an inspector of Land Records, widely reputed to be corrupt but so far too clever to be caught; of how to raise the money for an extension of the hospital at headquarters; of whether a new primary school at Gopalpur was really essential; of the state of the road to Ramnagar at the thirteenth milestone; of the murder case from Gwalabad and how the defence could be prevented from tampering with the evidence; of what should be done about the pipal trees on the Moharram route at Pitampura.

This last was a problem that occurred again and again. On the tenth day of the month of Moharram, images of the tombs of Hasan and Husain, the grandsons of the Prophet, slain at Karbala, are taken in procession to be buried. They are gaudy towers of tinsel and papier mâché. They jolt, swaying on men's shoulders, through the narrow streets and along the sandy rutted roads between the fields. And then comes a pipal tree, sacred to Hindus. Either the tower or the pipal tree has grown since last year; the image will not pass unless a branch is cut. The Hindus with their six-foot bamboo quarter-staffs wait grimly for the first insult to the sacred tree. The Muslim escort of the tower will not agree to deviation by a yard, still less that the tower should bow its head.

It was a problem that called for a quality for which there is no exact single word in English. But there is a word for it in Hindustani, *hikmat-amali*, a judicious mixture of finesse and tactful management with a hint of force in the background. An Indian inspector of police once persuaded the leaders of the village to call out the landless labourers and dig the roadway deeper. Better still to avoid the confrontation. E. H. H. Edye arranged between festivals for two elephants to graze near an offending pipal tree; elephants are under the special patronage of Ganesh and no one would grudge them a branch or two from a pipal. And next year, to everyone's surprise, the tomb passed easily where before it had stuck.

Skilful management was needed because there was so little force available. There was one British soldier and four Indian soldiers in India to every six thousand of the population. In most districts there were no British soldiers; in very many there were no soldiers at all. There might be seven or eight hundred police in a district to a million or so inhabitants; they would all be Indian except for the Superintendent. A man had to rely on his own wits, his own power of command, his hikmatamali.

Most of the Guardians had been brought up in the tradition of Arnold of Rugby. They had all had to work hard to pass their examination; most of them accepted the ideal of hard work and hard play. And many of them believed that it was the hard play which kept them sane and balanced.

The game of games, easily first in the estimation of all who practised it, was pigsticking. To be good after a pig a man must be a horseman, in any case a great asset to a district officer. And he must also have the power of quick but cool judgment, the controlled but fiery ardour, the determination not to be beaten that are needed in a riot or a battle. Pigsticking was a purgation. The danger and excitement, the ferocity, thus harmlessly given an outlet, sweetened men who might otherwise have been soured by files and hot weather and disappointment, as lime sweetens grass soured by poultry.

The civilian, but hardly anyone else, often hunted pig alone. And to kill a pig with a spear by oneself is an achievement. It is no use pretending that this sport contributed directly to good district management. But in fact the good pigstickers were usually good officers. The district officer who spent all his time with his nose in files did not always have his district in good order; some recreation was needed to keep a lonely man sane. Pigsticking and shooting did take a man among the villagers, to whom the pursuit of animals seemed less irrational than most forms of amusement, and a journey in search of snipe, tiger, or pig seldom failed to produce a petition or the news of some oppression.

Pigsticking and tiger-shooting were the two first sports of the civilian. It was hard to raise a team of civilians for polo tournaments although in the North-West, which became later the United Provinces, teams were always entered for minor tournaments. But there was no chance of practice together and they were usually outclassed. In pigsticking on the other hand the I.C.S. could compete with cavalry and gunners. In 1919, Percy

'Incident in the life of a district officer, 1926.' That was how Percy Marsh described it himself – but it was not usual to spear panthers from a horse. He was one of the best-loved of district officers and a famous pigsticker who won the Kadir Cup.

Marsh scored the double triumph of winning the Kadir Cup and one of the two cross-country races held at the same meeting. In 1898, C. E. Wild and P. V. Allen were both in the final of the Kadir Cup, both having been first in the competitive examination in their respective years.

Victory in competitions is not the point. What has to emerge is the picture of a man who gets through his files quickly because he wants to be out of doors and because he wastes no time on looking up rules; who writes short decisive judgments because he is clear in his own mind and does not seek to justify himself; who expects his subordinates to do their own work and trusts them until he has reason not to; who likes to get about his district and see things for himself.

The men who hunted most among civilians were the men who were remembered in their districts. In the last years, three names in Northern India are particularly remembered in the annals of pigsticking, F. L. Brayne from the Punjab, with over three hundred first spears to his credit, Percy Marsh and Charles Hobart from the United Provinces. Everyone has heard of Brayne's work for village improvement; Percy Marsh was known by every villager in Aligarh and Meerut. Charles Hobart won one of the Hoghunter's Races in 1920 and broke his neck pigsticking – and of Hobart: 'Look,' they would say years later, wherever he served, 'this is where Hobart Sahib sat.' He was often in trouble but received a C.I.E. when at last he retired; the letters he remarked thoughtfully, must stand for: 'Charles's Indiscretions Excused'.

What exactly is meant by sanity and sense of proportion can best be illustrated by its absence. Aubrey Pennell was a man of brilliant intellect whose career at one time seemed most promising. He was a Bengal civilian who volunteered for a spell in Burma; he was picked as Private Secretary to the Chief Commissioner and after some time in Government House went to a district as a settlement officer. He came to the conclusion that the settlement might be run much better on different lines. He said so, with some cutting comments on his seniors; it was arguable that he was right but the upshot was that he ceased to be a settlement officer; the Government of Burma had to choose between Pennell and the rest of the Settlement Department. He became a Deputy Commissioner in Burma but there was a scandal which he wished to expose and everyone else to bury – and Pennell came back to Bengal with a recommendation that he should be employed as a judge.

He began in this new capacity at Mymensingh, where he made some remarks about the conduct of the executive officers in general which the Calcutta High Court ordered to be expunged from his judgment. He then went as judge to Chapra where he almost at once found himself involved in a case which became notorious.

The case came before Pennell in appeal. A man had refused to help the efforts of two young Englishmen to save a dyke; if it broke, the countryside would be flooded. He was influencing others; they beat him and also took legal action. He was sentenced to two months imprisonment, by the District Magistrate, a Muslim.

Pennell took up his case as a matter of principle. A man had been beaten without fair trial; it was oppression. He certainly ought not to go to prison and the case against his assailants must be started afresh. These orders were promulgated in a judgment which included biting criticism of the Bengal Government, of the High Court, of a good many officers, and of various steps that had been taken to keep the matter quiet. The High Court in Calcutta agreed with Pennell's conclusions, though they condemned his language as intemperate, but the judgment reached Whitehall, questions were asked in Parliament and the newspapers enjoyed themselves even more in Calcutta than in London.

Pennell soon achieved even greater notoriety though again he seems to have been right in substance. An Indian Sub-Inspector of Police tried to hush up a murder. The Superintendent, notoriously idle, believed him, but a zealous young district officer heard something on his morning ride, ferreted out the facts and insisted on a trial. Pennell heard the case and after four days' cross-examination charged the Superintendent of Police with perjury, had him arrested and refused him bail. He then spent three weeks writing a judgment in which he analysed the evidence with subtlety and shrewdness, sentenced one of the accused to death and two to transportation for life and acquitted the fourth. Into this searching analysis, however, he wove a scathing, intemperate and witty indictment not only of almost everyone in Bengal, but also of no less sublime a figure than Lord Curzon himself.

Having spent a very enjoyable three weeks writing it, Pennell delivered his judgment in Court, gave one copy to the reporter of a Calcutta newspaper and stepped into a boat in which he spent more than a week on a visit of inspection. During these days no one could get in touch with him; the S.P. was in jail and the district police without a Superintendent, while in Calcutta the *Amrita Bazar Patrika* published Pennell's judgment as a serial. It was three weeks before the High Court could read what Pennell said about them without borrowing a newspaper from their clerks. He was suspended from duty, but it was hard to think what charges should be framed against him; he solved the problem himself by leaving India without permission and was dismissed for that.

3 At Either Extreme

Pennell was perhaps a little mad, but the principles for which he stood were noble principles if temperately pursued. He recalls Snodgrass of Madras, who sixty years before had refused to hand over his district until troops were sent to dislodge him.

There were many others at either end of the scale of normality. Consider first the men of more than usual ability. No one sat for the examination unless he had shown some signs of intelligence; about one in five of those who sat succeeded. Of these, some stagnated mentally but some made steady progress and in every year there were one or two giants. But the empire had now developed to a pitch where one man could not leave his mark on it. If Charles Aitchison, in his ten long years as Foreign Secretary, had not compiled *Aitchison's Treaties*, someone else would have been found to describe the relations of the Crown of England with every State in India – and the result would have been no less ruthlessly discarded in 1947.

Auckland Colvin, a brilliant young civilian of the North-West (later the United Provinces) was in his youth sent to a dull and isolated district as a punishment for articles in Indian newspapers which criticized his seniors; he survived and was deputed to Egypt, where, under Cromer, he put Egypt's finances on a firm footing, and by his articles in the *Pall Mall Gazette* forced Gladstone's Government to accept responsibility in Egypt. He came back to India as Finance Member. He was a man of imposing stature but there were others to take his place.

Look up Antony MacDonnell today in the works of reference and you see him as a list of high offices, Chief Commissioner of the Central Provinces, Member of Council, Lieutenant-Governor of the North-West, Under Secretary of State in Ireland; he sounds like an administrative machine. But the man lived, warm, fierce and dominant. 'If Antony and another man are cast away in an open boat and only one of them can live, it will not be Antony who is eaten,' said a friend. He was remembered in Lucknow fifty years later as a friend of the Hindu, there the underdog. And the words with which he rose to answer Lord Morley in the House of Lords are not those of a bureaucrat. 'I have played', he said, 'upon that stormy harp whose strings are the hearts of men; the noble lord opposite has spent his life writing books about books.' Yet history was hardly changed by MacDonnell.

Consider the imposing figure of Sir Denzil Ibbetson, 'untiring in administration, fearless in doing right, a scholar and a man of affairs'. There is humour and warmth in his face as well as pugnacity and the power of command. Yet, for all his special knowledge of rural indebtedness, someone else could have been found to frame the Co-operative Societies Act of 1904. He is to be remembered for his Census Report on the Punjab and the *Handbook of Punjab Ethnography*; these are brilliant works of scholarship, permanent contributions to ethnology, yet if Ibbetson had never lived someone else would have collected the material. There was no task still left undone comparable with Munro's, which affected everything that the Government did in Madras for the next hundred

Sir Denzil Ibbetson, 'untiring in administration, fearless in doing right, a scholar and a man of affairs'. But by his time, one man could no longer change the system.

years. And though scholars such as H. H. Risley and William Crook will not be forgotten, it is not by them that the English in India will be remembered.

The work of the architects, in short, was almost complete and in the time that remained to the empire it was maintaining the fabric that mattered. This was done by the district officers, men aware of the narrow road the administrator must walk between on the one hand such folly as Pennell's and on the other that other abyss, in which sloth or cynicism or both urge acceptance of things as they are.

Take, for instance, Evan Maconachie; he had a short spell in Simla as Under Secretary but spent the rest of his time either in his Province of Bombay or in States; his recreations were gardening, photographing Indian architecture, and making drawings of insects that are both exact and beautiful. He took any chances that came of shooting and fishing too, but the garden and architecture came first, sandwiched between income-tax appeals, aboriginal tribes, survey and settlement, and reflections that the paternal form of government was not producing enough Indians of the calibre needed for the Prime Ministers of the larger States.

It is in Maconachie's book that written record remains of Frederick Lely. In his early days Lely had been administrator of Porbandar State in Kathiawar, and the people used to repeat a rhyming jingle on his name: 'Lely, Lely, raish na beli — Lely, Lely, protector of the peasant'. And a missionary has a tale of how, preaching one day in the market square of Porbandar, twenty years after Lely had left, he was describing the life of Jesus, as a man with no fixed home, who went about among the people doing what good he could find to do. An old peasant came up, listened for a moment, and then his eye brightened and he began to nod his head. He knew who this must be. 'Lely, Lely,' he said quietly to himself.

It would be pleasant, again, to dwell at length on the country of the Sonthals, a people who were in India before the Hindus, to remember the great days of Yule, who founded the administration of the Sonthals, writing on two sides of a sheet of paper rules which lasted unchanged for thirty years; to think again of George Campbell, who when the Government of India would not let him have what he wanted for the Sonthals replied that in that case he must have soldiers to shoot them — and got his way.

Every district officer in some degree was at war with authority; most men cloaked their warfare in polite words, but some had a genius for making the solemn look ridiculous. Such was Tawney of the Central Provinces, who quite early in his service was rebuked for not appearing punctually when summoned before a superior. He must come at once, whatever he was doing, he was told. It was a rebuke quite foreign to the traditions of the service and Tawney made the most of it. Next time he was summoned he appeared naked, borne shoulder-high in a tin bath-tub by four orderlies.

16
THE END OF AN ERA

It was an India in which personal relations still counted for much, an old-fashioned aristocracy, loosely centralized, in which the provincial Governments consisted of perhaps a Lieutenant-Governor and three Secretaries, and the Government of India was on a hardly larger scale. To this empire, based less on system than on the individual characters of Scots, Irish and English men, came the young man in a hurry, Lord Curzon, trained for the Vice-regal purple by years of self-discipline, study and travel, determined from the day he arrived to carry out his list of twelve major reforms.

To Lord Curzon nothing was ever right unless he had drafted it himself. 'It is no good,' he wrote, 'trusting a human being to do a thing for you. Do everything yourself.' It was a principle that if universally applied would have destroyed the Indian Empire. This was a structure which to an extraordinary extent was based on the delegation of power. The District Officer had to leave his sub-divisional officers, his tahsildars and his patwaris to get on with their own work. He could only check a tiny proportion of it.

This Curzon never understood. And therefore he alienated the services and Indians alike. He often did the right thing, but often in the wrong way. He detached the North-West Frontier Province from the Punjab – but in such a way as to wound the Punjab civilians deeply. For admirable reasons, he divided Bengal and infuriated its inhabitants. He did not see how his words or actions would hurt other people – witness his speech contrasting the Western and Eastern ideas of truth – and the same lack of perceptiveness led him to believe that the Congress and Indian Nationalism in general were about to die.

Lord Curzon arrived in Simla with the laudable intention of reducing the amount of paperwork. Viceroys seldom liked Simla – but then Viceroys had not usually faced the alternative, a hot weather in the plains. They had not usually been away from England long enough to feel

left, Lord Curzon: Viceroy 1889–1905. One of the greatest of Viceroys who had prepared himself for the high office by years of study. But he did not always understand how it felt to be less brilliant than himself; right, Curzon at the Despatch Box in the House of Commons. An unkind cartoon – but that is how he often appeared to other people.

rapturous about the dark little rooms, the smell of ferns and moist earth, the wild roses and the call of the cuckoo. Lord Curzon was no exception. What he rightly perceived – for he was perceptive except about other people's feelings – was the mental isolation of Simla. It was easy to forget in Simla the little squares of earth where the peasant toiled over his rice and millet. And so it was a good step to decide that posts in the secretariat of the Government of India should have a fixed tenure and that between secretariat posts a man should have a spell in his province, and preferably in a district. The rules were not always kept – but they did something to blow away the clouds, to break up the closed circle, to bring in fresh blood.

But as to reducing paperwork – ! Lord Curzon was the last man in the world to do that. He must be told everything. He must be informed at an early stage of every proposal. Nothing must be done without his sanction. And he must not be spoon-fed. No summary would do for him; he must see the original papers. 'Thousands of pages, occupying hundreds of hours of valuable time, are written every year by score upon score of officers, to the obfuscation of their intellects and the detriment of their official work,' he complained. This no doubt was true. All wrote much – but no one wrote so much as Lord Curzon.

Too much paper, too much ink, and still the Viceroy was insufficiently guided and not told enough. In long scarlet gowns trimmed with gold lace, the orderlies at Viceregal Lodge walked every evening in procession to the Viceroy's study, bringing his lordship's evening task. There might be a hundredweight of papers a night; sometimes there would be more. A cubic foot or so of previous references, weighing fifteen or twenty pounds, would come with quite a simple proposal.

But His Excellency was never consulted enough. He was brilliant at the expense of those who discussed a proposal at length before venturing to lay it before him. 'Round and round like the diurnal revolutions of the earth went the file, stately, solemn, sure and slow; and now, in due season, it has completed its orbit and I am invited to register the concluding stage. How can I bring home to those who are responsible the gravity of the blunder . . . ?' But can anyone be sure that, if he had seen the file earlier, Lord Curzon would not have been equally disturbed that so ill-digested a proposal had been submitted to him?

An afternoon outing in Simla, about 1880. It could be very pleasant in Simla and it was easy to forget what went on in the plains.

All the same, Lord Curzon *was* the greatest of the Viceroys, and India has reason to forgive him for much. He did love India, he did perceive the poetry and the glory of his position. He was, in short, as different as anyone could be from Lord Auckland, who was bored. His reign seems to sum up and close the era which began when the Crown took over direct rule. He was the last who could regard the mighty structure with a pride that was hardly mixed with apprehension.

The structure was indeed mighty. A political unity had been imposed that had never before been equalled and had not been approached for two thousand years. Roads, railways, bridges, canals, were far ahead of anything else in Asia; there had been internal peace for half a century, the raids of bandits were no longer a feature of everyday life and robber chiefs had one by one submitted.

It was true that there were conflicts of stress and tension. 'To educated Hindus,' wrote Alfred Lyall, 'the incongruity between sacrifices to the goddess Kali and high University degrees is too manifest.' And Kali may stand for caste and untouchability, purdah and child-marriage. That was a stress within Hinduism, while Muslim India had already begun to display a deep distrust of the undiscriminating liberalism which, they believed, would mean the reign of the moneylender and the Brahman. Finally, Indians were beginning to perceive that, even in his own field of examinations and newspapers and the ballot-box, the Englishman could be met and forced to suffer a reverse, while in arms the Italians had been checked in Abyssinia. They did not yet know that the Russians were to be defeated by Japan in 1904, but the dominance of the European could no longer go unquestioned.

These stresses, which seem so obvious now, were less apparent in 1901; to Lord Curzon it would have seemed that they were no more than the balanced stresses that lock the keystone of an arch in its position. It was his own idea to sum up in the Great Durbar of 1903 the splendours of the era which he did not realize was at an end. There was to be a parade of troops, a state entry, an investiture, a ball, scenes of magnificence never equalled before; not least in the eye of the artist who designed this week of 'becoming pomp and dignity' was a display of Indian painting, jewels and goldsmiths' work, of tapestries, carpets and manuscripts, summoned from every corner of the Empire in the splendour of whose past he delighted. To him the Durbar was the outward and visible sign of an ideal, the heavenly pattern of an Empire to which his life was devoted.

'Is it nothing', he asked, 'that the Sovereign at his coronation should exchange pledges with his assembled lieges, of protection and respect on the one side, of spontaneous allegiance on the other? . . . Is it nothing to lift an entire people for a little space out of the rut of their narrow and parochial lives and to let them catch a glimpse of a higher ideal, an appreciation of the hidden laws that regulate the march of nations and the destinies of men?'

The Great Durbar. 'The crowds, the cavalry, the swaying elephants, the bells, the silver howdah, the cloth of gold – and silence.'

But to the peasant – concerned with canal dues and rust in the wheat, with locusts and rats and his debts to the moneylender – to him it is not easy to talk about the march of nations and the destinies of men.

It is strange to read now that Lord Curzon rejected the hymn 'Onward Christian Soldiers' – he must of course approve every hymn chosen for church services during the Durbar – not because most of the soldiers were not Christian, but because it contained the lines: 'Crowns and Thrones may perish, Kingdoms rise and wane', an unbecoming note of pessimism. But most of the English in India saw the future no more clearly than he.

There is a very simple account of the Durbar written for her children in England by Mrs Macpherson, the wife of a Bengal civilian; it reflects the feelings of many.

There was a special train from Calcutta for those who were going to the Durbar with the Lieutenant-Governor. It halted on Christmas morning, at Dinapore where a hundred and forty years earlier, two hundred English had been massacred by the order of Mir Kasim. 'We walked to the little station church, where Mr Moore, one of the party, held a service . . . Dad and I loved to hear the Christmas hymns and to feel that a few hours later you would be singing them too – "As o'er each continent and island The dawn leads on another day".'

266

Christmas Day wore on, the long, long day of an Indian train journey. 'We rushed through a barren and thirsty land and saw the peasants watering their fields and the blue jays sitting on the telegraph wires and the mud-walled villages and the buffaloes going out to the water with bare brown boys driving them and the bamboo clumps . . . Can you remember the look of it all?' On the day after Christmas they crossed the Jumna, close to the place where the mutineers had crossed it from Meerut fifty years before. At last they were in Delhi, where their tents were 'most luxurious'.

The State Ball was held in the Dewan-i-Am, the Public Audience Hall of the Great Mogul. 'We wandered round the splendid ball-room looking at the many lovely dresses and uniforms and the Native Chiefs simply smothered in jewels.' Supper was in the Dewan-i-Khas, the Private Audience Hall, 'with its marble pillars inlaid with jade and cornelian and much gold tracery – at one end the marble screen through which the ladies of Shah Jehan's Court were allowed to peep at his receptions'. Mrs Macpherson was wearing an emerald given to her husband's great-grandfather by Shah Alam, the last Mogul Emperor, and she wondered whether it felt at home in this revival of forgotten pomp.

But for most people, the crowning event of the Durbar ceremonies was the State Procession from the Red Fort to the Great Mosque.

First, mounted police, then five regiments of cavalry, then artillery, then the heralds, grand in yellow and gold, blowing a fanfare as they reached the mosque. After them, the Imperial Cadets, a corps of young natives, sons of noblemen, all mounted on black chargers with leopard skins, and dressed in white uniforms and pale blue turbans – they were really lovely! And then came the elephants . . . and it was just a dazzling procession, one more splendid than another . . . Six came together first, three and three . . . then a splendid creature covered with silver and gold and carrying a silver howdah in which sat His Excellency Lord Curzon and his lovely lady . . . they came slowly and majestically along, followed by a train of forty or fifty more magnificent animals, all decked and painted and bedizened with cloth of gold and dazzling frontlet pieces and great hanging ornaments over their ears, some wearing silver anklets which clashed and all having bells which sounded boom-boom tinkle-tinkle.

Then came more cavalry and more elephants, a hundred and twenty this time. 'But there was hardly any noise and no cheering to speak of.' And Mrs Macpherson adds: 'the trying thing at all these shows is the great difficulty of finding one's carriage to go home.'

The crowds, the cavalry, the swaying elephants, the bells, the silver howdah and the cloth of gold – and silence.

Three hundred years had passed since Queen Elizabeth's proclamation and now the last stone had been placed on a noble building. To the architects and the masons who had built it, the edifice appeared superb and certainly it had cost a great deal. Two million graves of Scots, Irish and English were scattered through India. There were children's graves, records of a loss that to one pair was a blinding grief, to another a few days of heartache, to a third a sadness long remembered in prayer; there were graves of wives and husbands, soldiers and civilians, boys just landed and men worn out with work. Nor were graves all the cost; much endurance must be counted in as well, much loneliness, hardship, and separation, much toil, much loss of faith, much hardening of the moral arteries.

But had it been worth it? There were three hundred millions who did not raise their heads at the Great Durbar. The Empire which seemed so magnificent to Lord Curzon had not stirred their hearts.

Not that no hearts were affected. Few Englishmen could leave a district without regrets and when the time came to retire there were servants whose eyes filled with tears, there were masters too who turned hastily aside. There were soldiers who would die without flinching for their officers, there were Indians everywhere – landowners, clerks, lawyers, orderlies – who remembered with affection kindly Englishmen who had helped them because they liked them. There were men too to whom the Western ideas of political freedom, justice and tolerance had given a second motherland for which they felt a real love. But they were not stirred by the pomp of Empire.

The Great Durbar was, indeed, a landmark in the history of the people. It was the end of an era. When it was done, the tents were struck, the Princes and English dispersed to their palaces, to their offices and court-rooms and to camps that were less luxurious. 'The trying thing', many must have said, 'at all these shows is the great difficulty of finding one's carriage to go home.'

PART V
The Demission of Power 1909–1947

Tell me, my daughters, —
Since now we will divest us both of rule,
Interest of territory, cares of state, —
Which of you shall we say doth love us most?
                                        King Lear

17
REFORM AND REACTION

1 Two District Officers

A dozen miles from Delhi lie the ruins of Tughlakabad. Mighty ramparts
of ponderous stone, pierced by vast gates, embossed by massive bastions,
enclose a jumble of ruined masonry among which here and there the
fragments of a guard-house or a tower emerge, but in most of which it is
possible only to guess at the builder's intention. The city was abandoned
within a few years of its foundation because water was insufficient; it is
now a lair for hyenas and a nesting-place for owls. The plain around it in
every direction, as far as man can see, is strewn with the tombs of dead
kings and the remnants of forgotten empires.

Metcalfe, a hundred years before, had mused on the insecurity of
empire; to most of the Guardians of 1903 such thoughts would have
seemed fanciful. To most of them the fabric seemed very firm. Yet among
them were men who would see the English Parliament shake from itself all
the cares and business of this Empire, divest itself of rule, interest and
territory. To none of them would it have seemed possible at the time that
the change could be so swift.

This demission of power was not accomplished, like Lear's, by one
regal gesture, but by four, each conceding far more than its predecessors.

First came the Morley-Minto reforms of 1909. Lord Minto succeeded
Curzon rather as his great-grandfather had succeeded Wellesley; in both
cases a masterful Governor-General had become rather too masterful.
The second Minto came with few preconceived ideas except the general
reflection that in training a horse it was as well, now and then, to give him a
rest in his gallops. He had spent his time at Eton and Cambridge with 'a
notable economy of intellectual effort'. He 'saw things clearly and simply
without the irrelevant subtleties with which the practice of law or politics
clogs the most honest minds'.

His partner at the India Office was as different as could be. A Liberal

271

intellectual, who had 'spent his life writing books about books', it was strange that Morley should have formed so real a friendship with Minto. But they agreed in their practical, experimental approach to a change which from their end of the half-century looked much larger than it does from ours. 'The only chance . . .' said Morley, 'is to do our best to make English rulers friends with Indian leaders and at the same time to do our best to train them in habits of political responsibility.'

Their authors, then, did not think of the Morley-Minto reforms as final. Nor were they clear where they were going. As long ago as 1888, Lord Dufferin had proposed that the legislative councils in the provinces should be larger, and some of his proposals had been embodied in the Act of 1892. The Reforms of 1909 grew from this tentative step.

The legislative councils were to be enlarged to a membership of sixty at the centre and of fifty in the larger provinces. They were thus still glorified committees, which were to be partly official and partly non-official. Of the non-officials about one-fifth were nominated by the executive power; the rest were elected, some by voters from small and highly qualified general constituencies, others by special constituencies such as municipal boards, universities, chambers of commerce, landowners – and members of minority religions.

Here of course was a sharp point of controversy and one that was to grow sharper. The Muslims are backward in Western education and must

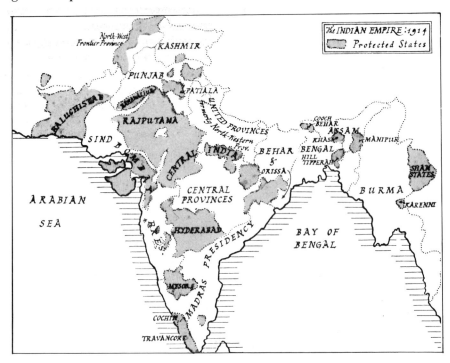

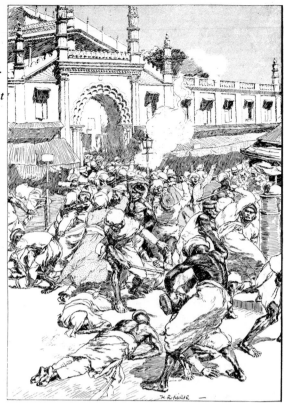

Religious faction fights in Bombay, 1893. An artist's impression, but not a bad one. Riots between Hindus and Muslims were endemic in most big cities.

have special help if they are to hold their own — thus ran the English argument. True, the Hindu conceded, but to give them a separate constituency is to perpetuate the differences between us. No Muslim will be elected unless he oozes communal bitterness. Give them indeed the right to so many Muslim seats, but let the candidates for those seats be elected by a general constituency. Then the Muslim tò be elected will be the moderate. Then we shall have a chance of becoming one people.

That kind of Muslim is no use to us, replied the faithful. You would elect a traitor, one who is no more than a Hindu with a beard. We need a true Muslim, who will protect our rights.

Those were the two arguments. To such a man as Minto, concerned to win this race not the next, the Muslim argument was bound to appeal. Hindus, however, came later to believe that this introduction of separate constituencies was a subtle plot, aimed at dividing the communities and providing an excuse for extending British rule for ever. Nothing could be further from Minto's character and to Morley the idea could only have occurred to be instantly rejected.

The new councils were less democratic than Parliament in England before the Reform Bill of 1832. But they were a step forward for India; members could not merely discuss the budget and bills placed before them, they could also ask questions and move resolutions on any subject of

273

public interest. They did provide a means of testing and creating opinion.

At the same time — and in Minto's eyes it was more important — Indian members were appointed to the Secretary of State's Council and to the Executive Councils of the Viceroy and the Governors.

In the spring of 1909 few responsible Indians asked for more. But appetite grew by what it fed on and soon most educated Indians wanted more — and without delay — and also some idea of the goal. In 1917, the aim of British rule in India was defined as: 'the increasing association of Indians in every branch of the administration, and the gradual development of self-governing institutions, with a view to the progressive realization of responsible government in India as an integral part of the British Empire.'

This declaration led to the reforms of 1919, by which the legislative councils in the provinces were more than doubled in size, about two-thirds of their members being elected. They became small assemblies instead of large committees, while from the elected members were to be chosen Ministers who would advise the Governor on certain 'transferred' subjects. This was the second of the four great steps.

The Governor now became 'the Governor acting with his Ministers', a constitutional figure, in respect of 'the nation-building subjects' — education, agriculture, the control of municipal boards and the like — while in

District officer in a small station. This photograph from 1898 suggests something of the loneliness that often faced a district officer.

respect of the protective subjects – finance, police and general administration – he remained the Governor in Council, the apex of an oligarchy, as he always had been. His right hand was despotic, his left was very nearly responsible to an electorate. This was dyarchy – the technical term for handing over the steering-wheel and retaining control of the accelerator and the brake.

The 1919 reforms were carried a stage further by the 1935 Act, which provided that the provinces should be entirely governed by Indian Ministers responsible to an Assembly. In 1937, the provinces did in fact pass to the control of elected Ministers, each province being under a Premier. The last stage was reached in 1947 when the Central Government 'pared its wit o' both sides and left nothing i' the middle' – but that was only the Fool's comment on Lear's act of demission.

In the course of thirty-eight years political power, which under Parliament had been absolute in the hands of the Viceroy, was entirely made over to elected representatives of the people. Those thirty-eight years were a strange and unexpected test for the caste of Guardians, who up till now had ruled this Platonic empire. They had come to a world in which they had been unquestioned masters, flattered and courted on every hand. Now they breathed a harsher air. They were supposed to be training Indians to be 'fit for self-government', they must give advice instead of orders, and they met constant opposition, slander and abuse. To most of them it was axiomatic that political change should come almost as slowly as biological evolution, just as it had in England. But the people to whom was assigned the role of grateful pupils had behind them a history in which the death of every king was a revolution. They saw no reason why change should be gradual. They were impatient; they did not want to be taught. They wanted to drive the car themselves.

The Guardians had therefore to deal with a changed world, of which each man had his own views. At all levels may be found men who saw in the reforms nothing but doctrinaire folly and men to whom the object seemed profoundly wise. Here is one district officer, who cannot be called typical, but who did possess rather more than most people of some typical qualities.

E.H.H. Edye went from Harrow to Balliol with a classical exhibition, and came to the United Provinces in 1909. He was an able man, but his little vanity was at the mercy of his sense of humour. In his fifth year, he found himself suddenly in temporary charge of a district, one of his first duties being to sign and dispatch the confidential reports which his predecessor had drafted. His own was among them. He did not want to go to the judicial, for which at that time there was a drive, so he added to his own confidential report: 'Judicial capacity beneath contempt.'

He believed that 'if you are abroad three hours before your neighbours, you gain more than three hours' start on them'. But he did not say this aloud; when his friends congratulated him pointedly on having so little work and on always having time for golf or polo, he smiled and reflected: 'It may be easy to win a name for laziness, but to keep it up over a period of years is a laborious process.'

He certainly did all that he could to keep it up, partly as a good-tempered reproof to the pompous or priggish, partly because he was too honest to indulge in eyewash, of which he noted that the kind you buy at the chemist is meant to clarify your own vision, the bureaucratic lotion to obscure other people's. But his idleness was wise, far-sighted, and in reality far from cynical. His mind was at the same time detached and practical; he could see another man's point of view without losing his own powers of 'clear thinking – and, what follows from clear thinking, easy and rapid decision'. 'If you tell your gardener to shoot a cat,' he wrote, 'and then hold his hands while he aims at it, you cannot hold him responsible if he misses.'

He insisted therefore that his officers should do their own work. 'I have said to each of them in effect – "This is your sub-division or your job. These are the lines on which I want it to be run. Now go and run it. If you make a really serious mistake I shall have to over-rule you. Otherwise I shall not interfere. If you want advice, I am here to give it. If you want a definite order, you are free to ask for it. But if you make a habit of wanting either, you will be very little use to me."' This method, he claimed, worked in nineteen cases out of twenty – and it was easy to get rid of the twentieth.

Delegation of power, combined with confidence and trust – these had been the distinguishing marks of this service. Edye did not find many of his superiors who quite came up to his own standards.

It was his argument that 'if you are fit to run a district at all, you will run it best when you are given your head. If you are refused your head, you will have to fight for it.' And he adds that 'fighting for your head is a very pretty art and can be great fun'. He usually found it necessary to 'handle' his Commissioner. The more difficult were 'men of strong character, who for years had run their districts efficiently and well, but on promotion failed to realize that their function had completely changed'. Edye was probably cleverer than most at keeping his superiors in their place, but many district officers felt as he did. The common noun of assemblage for Commissioners was an interference and for their wives an umbrage.

Like all good district officers, too, Edye felt some impatience at the growth of centralized departments. He recognized that it was inevitable, but was sometimes regrettably flippant about their activities. Ordered to fill up a pond where mosquitoes were breeding, he replied that in a perfectly flat country it was impossible to fill up one hole without digging another. The protest was overruled; a year later an official of the department reported that the pond was still there. No, replied Edye, a new pond, formed by filling up the first.

He had a contempt for the Secretariat, where 'you deal, not with men, who may give trouble, nor with things, which may be awkward, but with paper, which cannot answer back'. And he summarizes Secretariat procedure: 'No precedent? Turn it down!' Not always quite true, but often it was very like that. It is quicker and safer to say no, and men are caught in a maze of increasingly complicated routine from which no one has time to consider the means of escape. Indeed, the maze becomes more and more complicated, until no one understands it well enough to plan an escape except the few so used to it that they no longer want to get out — and would have no livelihood if they did.

In Edye's day the spiral of secretarial inflation was getting worse. He points out that in 1909 the provincial government consisted of a Governor, three secretaries and three under-secretaries — seven men. But in 1936 the Governor had to advise him six Ministers, six secretaries, six deputy secretaries, an under-secretary and three assistant secretaries, with four officers attached on special duty — twenty-seven men. Meanwhile, 'no one, I think, would deny that as an engine for the direction and control of the administration it has lost a high percentage of its efficiency'.

He was speaking of the United Provinces, whose population was then roughly that of Great Britain. Whitehall of course would think the Governor's a very moderate staff to administer fifty million people.

It would be pleasant to linger over Edye and his Gambit of the Second Reminder — an infallible device for providing an excuse for disobeying unreasonable instructions — his views on mobs and crowd psychology and his habit of reaching a decision in difficult cases while fishing or pruning roses. It is pleasant to meet in such good-humoured company the moneylender who 'looks as if he had had a morning swim in warm butter', the district officer whose 'value is in inverse ratio to the wear on the seat of his trousers', and the tahsildar whose attitude to his duty is: 'Perish India but the Commissioner's camp must not be short of potatoes.'

But it is his attitude to reform that is important. It is really implicit in his guiding principle that most men can be trusted to exercise responsibility and will rise to the occasion if it is offered them. 'If . . . India has benefited by a hundred years of the control and guidance of the British services, that is no argument . . . that she should acquiesce in, or would benefit by, similar control and guidance for a further period. On the contrary, if in a hundred years the services have not trained India to stand without support . . . they have so far failed in their fundamental task.'

It was not that anyone had set himself to emasculate Indians by refusing them responsibility — but few Englishmen had thought of standing back and making Indians do things themselves. An example was the work of District Boards, of which the district officer was Chairman until the reforms of 1919. 'As a rule he was in fact practically dictator; and the members were quite content . . . Such tasks as seeing that the roads of my district were maintained and improved and flanked with avenues of shade, as getting a drainage scheme for a city financed, designed and executed or building it a market-place, gave me ... the very keenest enjoyment. It certainly never occurred to me at the time that it would perhaps have been wiser to stand aside and insist on a sub-committee of the board making what it could of these undertakings.'

Looking back on the time between 1919 and 1937, the period of dyarchy, when one partner had the wheel and the other the accelerator and the brake, Edye felt that it had been worth while and that a staggering and zig-zag progress had been made. India in thirty years had become a happier country. 'Everything is changed – and everything for the better,' he was told by a friend, a Colonel in the British Army, revisiting India after twenty-five years. 'What he had foremost in his mind was a journey from Bombay on which he had shared a railway-carriage for two days with an educated Indian and had found him a delightful companion. Such a thing would have been hardly thinkable thirty years ago.' Between British and Indian, Edye thought, 'Relations have never been really bad and were never better than now. For this we have to thank, in the Indian his natural courtesy and kindliness, and in the Englishmen, what the Indian recognizes, his fairness and the transparent benevolence tempering the stupidity.'

There was material improvement too. In less than twenty years, the face of the countryside he knew had changed. The old short red-stemmed sugar-cane, not as high as a man, had given place to a ten-foot crop with stems as thick as a child's wrist. The leather bags, in which water had been hauled up from wells, had everywhere disappeared in favour of Persian wheels, which gave a far greater flow of water for less effort. Bicycles appeared in every village, electric torches, and cigarettes; it became the custom to drink tea, a thing unknown among the peasants before 1914. This was material progress.

Edye's conclusion on the political future – in 1936 – was that popular government and the gradual elimination of the English from the services were inevitable. This would mean, at first, 'a perceptible fall in the standard of efficiency, due to lack of administrative experience and tradition. There will also be instances of unfairness and nepotism, due to various social pressures. These drawbacks constitute the price that will have to be paid for a fundamental advance ... The price will fall from year to year but in my view it will not prove too heavy to be paid now.'

'We are passing on a torch', Edye concludes, 'to hands well trained to receive it ... The receiving hands might arguably have been trained more quickly and the torch passed sooner. But what is a matter of ten or twenty years in the history of a continent?'

Everyone did not think as Edye did, but most would have agreed that reforms of some kind there had to be. Sir William Marris told Edwin Montagu as early as 1917, that 'the Indian Civil Servants were very sorry that their day was done; recognized that it was inevitable and were willing to go ahead'.

Even Maconachie, who retired in 1921, wrote 'What race is there should claim superiority to peoples that gave the world a Buddha, an Asoka and an Akbar, religions and philosophies that embrace every religion that has ever existed, an epic literature perhaps unrivalled, and some of the greatest masterpieces in the realm of human art? ... It is absurd to suppose that a handful of foreigners from across the sea can continue to rule indefinitely hundreds of millions of Orientals on the patriarchal lines pursued ... down to the time of the recent reforms.' And he goes on almost in Edye's words: 'The only way to fit men for responsibility is to place responsibility upon them.'

That was written in 1926 and was, as Sir Evan says, by then the view of the majority of the Indian Civil Service. But there were men whose politics were those of Hobbes, who believed that force and the fear of force were ultimately the only factors in any situation. These were a minority; there were more who saw the whole question in essentially practical terms. They could not believe that people such as − and here would follow a few examples − could run the district as well as themselves.

Every revolution throws up not only men with high ideals but scoundrels on the make. India from 1919 to 1947 was going through a revolution in slow motion. In every district, behind the idealists, there were unscrupulous and designing men, careerist lawyers, small landowners in debt and the like. In the nineteenth century these men would have been lickspittles of power − that is, of the district officer. In the twentieth century, they put their money on the nationalist cause and lost no chance of embarrassing and opposing the executive power − that is, the district officer.

To some officers, it was intolerable to think of their district at the mercy of such rascals as these. There were others who could not see the point of spoiling a system which seemed to be working very well and in which the great majority of the people cheerfully acquiesced. Let us consider someone who disapproved of the reforms.

Alexander Loftus Tottenham is a sharp contrast to Edye, though they would certainly have enjoyed each other's company. Loftus Tottenham had been a brilliant classical scholar and might have been expected, as Edye might, to become a Secretariat man. But he remained a district officer in spirit. The contrast with Edye lay in his way of life; no polo ponies, no pigsticking, no shooting, fishing, or gardening beguiled him. Talk and books seem to have been what he most valued, but bathing too came high and he thought he could have lived for ever at Madras with not too much to do and constant bathing.

A confirmed bachelor and never a club man or a player of games, he always, wherever he was, maintained open house and a magnificent table. His house was full of beautiful things, good furniture, much of it designed by himself, blue and white china which he and Charles Cotton had discovered in Madras, and masses of books . . . The first half of the day – hot weather made no difference – was spent out of doors, either in some inspection, often after a long ride, or if there was nothing else to do, in cutting down some unwanted tree. He was not an expert horseman or axeman but made up by energy what he lacked in skill . . . Lunch about the middle of the day was a large and excellent meal, accompanied by a constant flow of wit and, so far as Loftus was concerned, by one or two large bottles of cold beer and a glass of Madeira. He then reclined in a long armchair and piles of files were brought in by a procession of orderlies. With these he wrestled till they were finished, whatever the time. Nothing was left over for the next day and most of the work was done in the long armchair, but every now and then a long note or a draft would send him to his office table and typewriter. A short stroll followed, if there was time, before dinner and then another leisurely meal with excellent food for both mind and body and again there was beer, and two glasses of port, neither more nor less.

This cannot really have been the way he spent every day, for he must have had visitors to listen to and appeals to hear sometimes. But it begins to give an impression of the man. And since it is not easy to take wit on trust, the motto he proposed for the Secretariat – 'First start your hare, then split it' – deserves to be recorded, together with one good-humoured riposte. He entertained the Governor and his wife while they were on tour and, when they had become good friends, Lady Pentland ventured to ask, with a delicate and attractive stammer, whether Mr T-tottenham did not find b-beef and b-beer rather b-brutalizing. To which he replied: 'Well, I don't myself, Your Excellency. But of course if you do, you're quite right to keep off them.'

In spite of his dislike of the Secretariat, he devised a system of reference and office management which was widely adopted, and he became eventually one of the two members of the Central Board of Revenue. He read widely and possessed real knowledge about many things. Botany, Indian art and archaeology, medicine, philosophy, music and religion were among his subjects. He was kindly and genial, one of the most generous and beloved of men, 'with more friends and fewer enemies than anyone I ever knew . . .' though with a strong dislike of sentimentality or pretence, a man to whom 'sin is lack of consideration for others'. 'I hope you aren't going all anti-Semite,' he writes to his sister. 'I take people as I find them, Jew or Gentile, Hindu or Muslim.' Young people sought his company because he was witty and unpretentious. But he thought democracy would only work in a Greek city-state or a Swiss canton, where everyone knew everyone else. 'Now the idea is that every race is fit for "self-government", – really very few are – and certainly not the oriental races.' And again: 'To talk as if the people of India were downtrodden slaves is ridiculous and meaningless. And what does our "yoke" amount to? Little more than keeping the peace internally and protecting them externally.' And again – slipped in with friendly gossip about the victory of his bearer's son in a badminton tournament – 'The vast masses of people are too hopelessly primitive and ignorant to be even *as* able as the masses at home to form a rational opinion about anything.' Or again: 'To contemplate handing over the people of India in the name of democracy to be governed by an oligarchy of people . . . who are more oppressive and more selfish than anything you can conceive . . . is really funny if it weren't tragic.'

He was thinking no doubt of the Brahman monopoly of power, which as a district officer in South India he had spent the best years of his life in trying to mitigate. It was a feeling widely shared. How can we leave these people, who have trusted us, to the mercy of the moneylender and the landlord? The peasant, said Edwin Montagu, must be awakened from his pathetic contentment. There were many like Loftus to ask why. Why destroy a known good, contentment, for some altogether hypothetical ideal?

There were many who shared the view of Loftus; but they were not so many as those on Edye's side and surely it is surprising that there was anyone on Edye's side at all. If India had been ruled by a caste of Guardians who were, let us suppose, Spanish or Roman, French, Portuguese, Turkish or Dutch, can one believe that many would have been found who saw the need to go?

2 A Change of Heart

'I hope', wrote Lord Minto in 1909, 'that public opinion won't take the unreasonable view that the deeds of a few anarchists are proof of the doubtful loyalty of all India.' An attempt to assassinate him with a bomb had just been made and it was the year which saw two murders in London and two in Bengal.

Lord Minto's view was that which until 1919 most people would have taken. The cult of blood and violence, of which Tilak was the chief prophet, was still confined to two centres, Bengal and Maharashtra, the home of the Maratha Brahmans – and to a very small minority in each.

Most educated Indians were mildly nationalist but their dream was of an India governing herself within the Commonwealth. When they thought on political subjects, they still used English terms; they still regarded English ideals with affection, but for that very reason they wanted to govern themselves. The masses were still indifferent to forms of government and, if not exactly enthusiastic about English rule, were inclined to regard it as preferable on the whole to anything else they could imagine.

What had been true till the summer of 1918 seemed to change overnight. In early July of 1918 Mr Gandhi was still speaking of equal partnership within the Empire; he was engaged in a recruiting campaign, urging peasants to attain self-rule by joining the army and winning the war. But a few months later it seemed to him axiomatic that the Government of India must be opposed.

The Acts known as the Rowlatt Acts, which provided a special machinery for dealing with conspiracy, have sometimes been supposed to be one cause of this change of feeling. But it had taken place before they were drafted. Turn to Mr Gandhi's autobiography and you will find that in November, when he read an account of the measures, they did not seem to him to require discussion; he immediately proceeded to the attack. It was not that he condoned assassination; the Acts were opposed with passion because they were a sign of mistrust.

All over the world men thought that when the First World War was over the millennium would come. In India, many had been proud of their country's part in the war and they wanted their partnership in the war to be recognized by some act of royal generosity which would place India at once on a level in the councils of the world with Canada and Australia. Their immediate concern was with status – rank, prestige, fair name in the world's eyes – at least as much as with democracy or responsible institutions. They would have been content if these had come more slowly. But in the discussion which led up to the reforms of 1919, doubt was expressed as to the good faith of Indian leaders as trustees for the people, and particularly for certain minorities. This made bitterness inevitable and co-operation suddenly became impossible between the Government and a large section of Indian Nationalists.

In 1918 the system of the Guardians was still intact to the eye. But the system was to last no longer. It will appear to go on for another quarter-century, but it did really end in 1919. This was because educated Indians were no longer prepared to accept the passive role of being ruled. Nor were they willing to be taught. One partner had expressed a distrust for the motives of the other. Aware that they were distrusted, Indians returned the sentiment and believed they would have to fight for progress.

There was also a change of heart in England. In the past no one had doubted that England would fight to keep India. By 1919, that had ceased to be true. No party in England was prepared to use force on a large scale to keep a partner who wanted to go. Bayonets were now to be worn for ceremonial purposes only. For the next quarter-century the system ran by its previous momentum.

The Kaiser's War had shown that many Indians still preferred English rule to anything else. The proof of this is not that India provided so many troops and so many million shells and rounds of ammunition. This was the result of decisions by Englishmen. The overwhelming proof is that the number of British troops throughout India was reduced to fifteen thousand. Fifteen thousand among three hundred million; that figure alone proves that at the lowest reckoning India acquiesced in her share of the war. But it was more than acquiescence.

There was no conscription. A man went to the colours in India for much the same reasons as Marlborough's or Wellington's recruit. His brother had the land; here was a shilling and a warm coat. There was one other factor present in India, professional pride; here a soldier was proud of his calling, and held in honour as he never was in England. It was a voluntary army — but during the war there was, shall we say, some degree of social and economic pressure to join.

In some villages, more men were ready to go than could be taken; this was always the case in peace. In other areas, competition was stirred up between large landowners to 'give' recruits; there was a badge and a certificate on vellum, signed by the Lieutenant-Governor, for the man who 'gave' a hundred. No sensible district officer would ask questions about a recruit who came forward voluntarily and took the oath without visible compulsion.

The number recruited from start to finish was 1,300,000 to be added to a strength at the outbreak of war, of 280,000. They fought in France, Belgium, Gallipoli, Salonika, Palestine, Egypt, the Sudan, Mesopotamia, Aden, Somaliland, the Cameroons, East Africa, North-West Persia, Kurdistan, South Persia, Trans-Caspia and North China.

This is not the place to discuss the Mesopotamian Campaign and the disastrous decision to advance to Baghdad after achieving with complete success the planned objective, Basra. It is enough to say that it was Whitehall which — against the Viceroy's view — had decided that the army in India should be controlled by the Viceroy's sole adviser in military affairs; it was Whitehall which had confined India's role in any future war to limits which were disregarded within a month of Germany's ultimatum. Brilliant success in Palestine and — in the end — Mesopotamia sponged out the memory of Kut and by the time of the Armistice, India's main sentiment with regard to the war was one of pride and anticipation. There was pride in what the Indian Army had done, in the financial contribution India had made and in the munitions of war she had dispatched. The pride was mingled with a good deal of pleasant curiosity about the form gratitude would take. In this mood, the reforms of 1919 were taken as a slap in the face.

One-sixth of the Indian Civil Service, that is two hundred out of twelve, had been permitted to take commissions in the Indian Army. Recruitment to the service had virtually stopped and there was of course no leave in the ordinary sense of the word. There was much new work; fewer were left for the districts, where work was naturally heavier than usual because of recruiting, rising prices, rumours and general unrest. Men came through the war exhausted. But all this was soon put right. Arrears of leave were quickly wiped off and arrears of intake were met by the addition of young men from the armed forces. There was no reason from the side of the service why the old system should not continue.

But there had been a failure in imagination. Men had been too busy, too wedded to necessity, to organize the willingness of Indians to help. And enthusiasm unharnessed soon sours. To this sourness must be added the worldwide ferment of raised expectations, of men coming back to their villages unsettled by war, of old customs broken and nothing to replace them.

In England it was generally believed that the services in India were opposed in principle to the 1919 reforms. Of course some were; one at least thought of Aristotle and believed the Indian was doomed by his temperament always to be a bondsman. But Lionel Curtis, who spent much time in India discussing reform and was largely responsible for the concept of dyarchy, has recorded at some length the opinion of nine senior I.C.S. men he had consulted. All were in favour of some advance; all expressed some doubts about the detail of dyarchy but five were in favour of the general principle. One was emphatic that there must be one man one vote. The idea that all were opposed to advance was mainly due to two books, *The Lost Dominion*, and Sir Michael O'Dwyer's *India as I Knew It*. The first is written with discursive learning in a style of an attractive peppery brilliance but the second carried more weight because the author put his name to it and because of the part he had played.

Michael O'Dwyer was one of the fourteen children of an Irish land-owner of no great wealth, as much farmer as landlord. He was brought up in a world of hunting and snipe-shooting, of threatening letters and houghed cattle, where you were for the Government or against it, where you passed every day the results of lawlessness in the blackened walls of empty houses.

O'Dwyer passed the I.C.S. examination from Wren's the crammer's and, like most of his year, spent his two years of probation at Balliol. He stayed up a third year to get a degree, read a three-years' course of law in one year and obtained one of the five firsts. He distinguished himself also as a linguist; one gets the impression of a man whose keen hard brain acquired facts quickly but had little time to waste on subtleties.

He went to the Punjab, where it was the first article of faith that the man who is most ready to use force at the beginning will use least in the end. It was the second that juniors must be given a free hand and backed up with unswerving loyalty. In the Punjab, the English were still tense. A hardy, virile and warlike people to control, fierce tribes beyond the Border to be watched; that was the civilian's task in the Punjab.

O'Dwyer went to the Western Punjab, and quite early became a settlement officer. He was in daily touch with the Muslim peasantry. He saw the villagers swarm round himself and his assistants with their disputes; he lived among them in tents for nine months every year, spending most of the day in a good-humoured chaffing battle of wits, they trying to persuade him that all their land was poor, he looking for the best crops with an eye sharpened by the knowledge that the tallest sugar-cane might hold a boar or a partridge. No one who has ever been a settlement officer can forget those months in camp; he comes to think of the peasants as his children.

The burden of debt to the Hindu moneylender was heavy. O'Dwyer heard of it everywhere. And he went next to the Frontier Province, where there is even more hostility to the moneylending Hindu. O'Dwyer, like almost every British officer, had a liking for the Frontier Pathan and for any merry rogue. To cattle-lifting and banditry he was severe, because he wanted an orderly district – but a grim understanding went with the severity; if the boot had been on the other foot, O'Dwyer would have been a cattle-lifter himself. But for the moneylender O'Dwyer felt dislike, contempt and distrust. And he thought little better of Hindu politicians, who had opposed measures meant to free the peasant from debt.

Michael O'Dwyer was the ideal king of Sa'adi and the Persian poets, who keeps order by checking the spring of sedition before it has grown into the river of revolt. He quotes more than once Sa'adi's couplet:

> The spring at its source may be turned with a twig;
> When it has grown to a river it cannot be crossed by an elephant.

He had been in many a Border skirmish and was a fine horseman who had been the death of many a boar. He was proud that while Akbar had reduced the King's share to a third, the British had reduced it to an eighth or a twelfth but he had little mercy for an enemy.

This was the man who ruled the Punjab in November 1918, when Mr Gandhi read an account of the Rowlatt recommendations and determined that they must be resisted. In March 1919 the Rowlatt Acts were passed; on March 30 the first blow in Mr Gandhi's campaign was struck. He had proclaimed a day of mourning and general strike; in Delhi this resulted in rioting and firing.

Somewhere, then, between July and November 1918 the change of heart had taken place and the majority of Indians who had political views had made up their minds against co-operation in the reforms.

Mr Gandhi himself realized very soon that he had made what he called 'a Himalayan blunder' and he said so. He realized now that the people of India were not sufficiently disciplined for peaceful civil resistance. But it was not so easy to turn off the tap as it had been to turn it on.

O'Dwyer always referred to the events of those few weeks as a rebellion. He believed that Hindus of the extremist or Tilak school were trying to incite both the police and the Indian Army to mutiny and at the same time were making advances to Pathan tribes on the Frontier, while the peasants of the Punjab, though not disaffected, were making ready to attack and

A Gandhi Day parade in 1922. After the first wave of enthusiasm for 'non-co-operation' the movement died down in most parts of India. This is a demonstration meant to whip it up again, with a model of a symbolic spinning-wheel, to represent the boycott of foreign cloth.

loot the towns if disorder grew. Intelligence reports of this kind present a problem. Act on them – and they are proved false. Disregard them – and they may come true. Whatever judgment is passed now on the validity of those reports, O'Dwyer believed that they indicated a genuine danger. There were outbreaks of mob violence at a number of places, of which the worst were at Lahore and Amritsar. At Amritsar, the railway station, post offices, banks, the Town Hall, mission schools and mission buildings were attacked, looted and burnt; Europeans were murdered. The mob took control of the city. In the few days that followed, telegraph lines in many parts of the Punjab were cut and trains derailed and attacked. The police for two days had to be withdrawn from Lahore.

O'Dwyer at once asked the Government of India for the introduction of martial law, hoping to retain control himself, but this was not allowed; he was permitted only to advise the military. When it was all over, there was the Hunter Commission and a report from which, apart from Amritsar, nothing very terrible emerged. But Amritsar – and even more what was said about Amritsar – is another matter.

Amritsar city from April 10 to April 12 was in the hands of a mob. On the 11th Brigadier-General Dyer arrived and, the situation being obviously beyond police control, the Deputy Commissioner made over charge to him. Dyer took great care to make public by beat of drum orders forbidding meetings and warning the inhabitants that meetings would be fired on. On the afternoon of the 13th, a meeting was held in defiance of these orders. Brigadier-General Dyer found himself personally in command of a small force – fifty rifles and forty men with *kukris* – all of the Indian Army, confronting a crowd estimated variously at between five thousand and twenty thousand strong. They were in a square, an open place enclosed by houses with few and narrow entrances. In his first military report, and verbally for some days afterwards, Dyer said that he expected the mob to attack and believed that his first duty as a soldier was to preserve the force under his command; he therefore dispersed the mob. He fired one thousand six hundred and fifty rounds, killing over three hundred people and wounding over a thousand more; he stopped when no ammunition was left. That evening the city was completely quiet.

General Dyer's first report implied that he had used so much force as he considered necessary to disperse the mob – and no more. The mob was being addressed by men who later were held by the courts to be dangerous agitators. It was made up mostly of peasants who had come in for a fair, Sikhs armed with the six-foot quarterstaff and many of them with the *kirpan*, the short Sikh sword. Sikhs are a violent people, quick to flare into fury; it was potentially as dangerous as a mob could be. If Dyer had kept to his first report, it would have been difficult for anyone who had not been there to impugn his judgment – though many would have shaken their heads. But he changed his ground and it may well be that his second statement was at least as near the truth as the first. Dyer had been educated in India at Bishop Cotton's School, where most of his companions were the sons of European subordinates or people of mixed blood. It is a soil in which racial intolerance grows very freely.

What perhaps lurked in Dyer's mind was brought to the surface by letters, speeches, and press agitation from the English side. 'I held many meetings and heard on all sides that this incident had saved the situation, and that is my own private opinion.' So wrote an official from a neighbouring district. Much to that effect was said in much less temperate language, and General Dyer came to think himself the saviour of India. He no longer confined himself to what he had said in his first report. He now said that he had determined to influence the whole of the Punjab. This was more than he had any right to do.

That it was near the truth is suggested by other actions, notably his notorious order that any Indian passing that way must crawl along the street where an English woman, a missionary teacher, had been attacked by the mob and left for dead. This order was withdrawn as soon as it came to notice and Michael O'Dwyer took Dyer severely to task for it. It was only enforced for one day but it had a devastating effect on Indian opinion.

Dyer's continuing to fire for so long, his crawling order, most of all perhaps his words later before the Hunter Commission, filled politically minded Indians throughout India with bitterness. They had expected at the end of the war a sudden recognition of their nationhood, an instantaneous partnership. They had been offered instead the position of an articled clerk, which might in the course of a lifetime or so lead to partnership if they were good. Many Indians had been hurt by this offer, and in a mood which to many Englishmen seemed petulant, they had determined to have nothing to do with it. It was a mood which might not have lasted long – but Dyer's words hardened their resolution. They felt, said one after the Punjab rebellion, that the English had come to regard them as a foreign people with whom they were at war.

O'Dwyer himself drew a contrast between this rebellion and the Moplah rebellion a year later. In the Punjab, handled firmly from the start, the total number of lives lost, altogether, from start to finish, was, he claimed, less than five hundred, of whom two-thirds were at Amritsar. The Moplah outbreak – mainly directed at Hindus – broke out in August 1921, at a time when it was important to make the reforms a success; the Government of India tried to conciliate the rebels and were gradually forced into measures more and more rigorous and finally far harsher than anything in the Punjab. In the end, 'more than two thousand Mohammedans were killed by troops and thousands more in other ways . . . while the number of Hindus butchered . . . skinned alive and made to dig their own graves before slaughter, ran into thousands . . .' with other horrors not to be told.

No one of course can be sure that O'Dwyer was right. But after Amritsar, the whole situation was changed. Government had been carried on with the consent of the governed. That consent was now changed to mistrust. And for the rulers a new dilemma was in existence. The officer confronted with the prospect of riot had been brought up to avoid loss of life at all costs. He had been used to having very little force at his disposal and he had known he must therefore use it or display it quickly. He had acted at once with confidence that he would be backed, because the first object of the Government was to keep order.

From now on it was not the first object of the Government to keep order. To the district officer this often seemed in some way dishonest or immoral, but Parliament and the English people were committed to handing over power and to training Indians to govern themselves. From now on they were bound to be responsive to Indian opinion. And Indian opinion, inexperienced in administration, was not yet convinced that firm steps were needed at the first sign of trouble.

18
DISTRICT OFFICER, NEW STYLE

1 Cold Civil War

In the years between 1919 and 1937, India was moving slowly towards self-government but progress was not easy to detect and there was much confusion about what was happening. It was hard to see the long-term aim, easy to take the quickest way of dealing with an immediate crisis. Here is an example, from a letter written home in 1933 by a young man in his fifth year in India:

I have had an exciting and busy week, which I thoroughly enjoyed. I have been left for a fortnight in charge of Lucknow. Everything seemed quiet at first but on Wednesday the Kotwal – the police officer in charge of the city – came to tell me there was trouble between Sunnis and Shiahs – the two main sects of Muslims. One side had published a poster announcing a meeting to which the other bitterly objected and there was likely to be rioting. Most of the city is Muslim and the sects are pretty even in strength; there's a history of fighting between them. I talked to the leaders of both parties for hours and at last I got the party who had published the poster to agree to a statement that they'd had no intention of being provocative, and that if they had hurt anyone's feelings they were sorry. They agreed to this reluctantly and withdrew, but two hours later they were back to say their followers had repudiated them. They hadn't done anything wrong and didn't see why they should apologize. I argued for more hours – but they wouldn't have it. It was an apology and the others had scored off them.

I saw at last it was no use going on, so changed my note. Very well, I said, have it your own way. No public meetings on either side for a fortnight. No assembly of more than twenty people. For the next three days – to cover the time when this chap had been going to speak – we'll have lorries of police dashing about the city and they will break up a meeting as soon as there's any sign of one. And troops will be ready to move in at once if there's any need. I am going straight to the brigadier to see that a battalion of British troops is kept ready for the next three days. And if they do come I shan't hesitate to tell them to shoot.

It worked like a charm. The brigadier grumbled – and it was a strain on the police, but it all passed off peacefully. They obeyed orders and there were no meetings.

A temporary solution had been imposed by a threat of force. It was the kind of thing that was being done all over India. It was dentistry though, stopping holes. On a larger scale, the Secretary of State and the Viceroy could not work quite like that. It was not weak, as some district officers thought, of Lord Irwin to meet Mr Gandhi and try to secure his co-operation. It was both wise and courageous; it was what the English were supposed to be doing.

Indians were no more clear about what was happening than the British. No one – reasoned the peasant – gives up power unless he is forced to. Therefore if the District Board runs a school which the district officer used to run, if the Congress colours fly instead of the Union Jack on a school building, that is a blow in the face to the district officer. And that Indians thought it a blow made it very difficult for the district officer not to think the same.

Dyarchy was meant to be a bridge from authoritarian to popular government; the Guardians were supposed to be instructing their wards in their art, and both were supposed to be going about their business in a spirit of friendly co-operation. But no one wanted to be taught. No one in the average rural district could picture a party system and an opposition which might one day be the Government. In the traditional systems of India, opposition to the ruler is a crime.

Those who wanted political progress thus found themselves in the same camp not only with self-seeking careerists but with criminals in the Western sense, gang robbers for their own gain. In the mind of the peasant and the policeman, criminals and politicians were all alike; they were the party against the Government. The district officer was therefore forced into an intermittent and surreptitious civil war with the very people to whom, according to the will of Parliament, he was going to hand over power.

All this was more or less the case in most of the Hindu part of India. In the Punjab, Sind and Bengal, and intermittently in Assam, there were parties ready to co-operate with the administration.

Most of the time it was cold civil war. The first three years were the worst. Mr Gandhi's influence was stronger then than it was ever to be again, and at that stage he was in alliance with the Muslim movement for the support of the Khalif, the Khilafat. Non-co-operation was his declared policy.

District officers and police did not find things easy; it was difficult to get supplies in camp or to move tents. Forests were burnt, liquor-shops were picketed, every form of government activity was hampered. There was a brief outbreak of political murder in some parts of India.

This extreme phase passed. Round Table Conferences, Commissions, Delegations and Pacts came and seemed important and were forgotten. Sometimes the fight was on and the district officer was encouraged to take firm action. Sometimes the leaders of the Congress would be released and the district officer must make uneasy friends with those he had been fighting. And some on the whole preferred open warfare.

Until far into the 1930s, the district officer in most parts of India could usually count on a good deal of support, quite apart from that he always received from the police. Some of this came from landowners to whom Congress radicalism seemed a threat; more came from men who were old-fashioned and simple, who saw only bad men opposed to the Government and were glad to do something to show their fidelity. Here and there, perhaps, one man took a longer view and calculated that the English did not really mean what they said, that they never did give up anything and never would; it would pay to be on their side. There were Muslims too who did not yet see much sense in the Muslim League and were prepared to do a good deal to avoid rule by the Hindus and moneylenders.

The bluff still held – though by now it was getting very thin. The district officer's power was already less than it had been. There were still titles and gun-licences in his gift but patronage was dwindling. Once he had been able to reward a zealous official or a helpful landowner by making his son a patwari, a clerk or even a tahsildar. But now everything must be done by merit as the result of examinations. Patronage had been part of the whole system of bluff and hikmatamali – judicious management – by which the country had been ruled. But now the district officer must explain to a nice old man who had been faithful all his life that in the competitive examination his son would get no favour at all compared with the son of a lawyer who had spent his life stirring up hatred and contempt for the Government.

Many could be friends with Congress opponents, as Edye could, for instance. Few however could equal Lydall's detachment.

> One of my friends [he wrote] spent much of his time denouncing me . . . as a satanic and cold-blooded murderer . . . In the front row of the audience, carefully taking notes for my edification, would be a police Sub-Inspector, interrupting now and then to ask for a repetition of a difficult passage. Then, the meeting over, the Sub-Inspector would come round to my bungalow with his version of the proceedings. But my perusal of his report would be interrupted by the arrival of the orator himself . . .
>
> 'I'm sure you'll be interested,' he would begin, 'in these rather

beautiful old Assamese paintings. Illustrations to the Mahabharata . . . '
And the small hours would find us still talking hard.

There were also honest men with minds too straightforward to see anything but the tactical situation; to them there were no two ways about it, we were letting down our friends and appeasing our enemies, failing in courage and honour. Such men were happier when Congress leaders were in jail. Others disliked open hostility because they felt it was getting neither side anywhere.

All the time, the English were morally on the defensive – and they had been used to feeling rather self-righteous. They had been incorruptible, their word had been synonymous with truth. Now everything they did was questioned. Anyone who did not like the district officer's views would go to the District Congress Committee, who would send a telegram to the Government complaining of tyranny and high-handedness. The Committee would conduct an inquiry of their own into an affair which the district officer had himself investigated. They would themselves hear evidence – not always taking pains to make sure both sides of the dispute were represented – and produce a report contradicting the district officer's. Politicians, lawyers, the press, and sometimes, it appeared, the judiciary – all seemed to take it for granted that the district officer was not to be trusted.

The cold civil war had, further, to be surreptitious. It was not permissible to say openly what scoundrels some Congress supporters in a district were. Nor was it possible to give official encouragement to those simple-minded people who were ready to support the cause of law and order by taking a six-foot bamboo pole and hitting those wicked folk the rebels.

The Round Table Conference on the Indian Constitution in London, 1931.
'Conferences were held, delegates went to and fro . . . '

While conferences were held, while delegations went to and from London, the district officer had his district to run. And one of the greatest differences in what he had to do was in connexion with District and Municipal Boards. He had been Chairman and virtually dictator. But now there was an elected Chairman and he must be very careful. People would ask him to put right matters that had become the concern of the elected Chairman; it was not easy to be helpful without seeming to be officious. The Chairman might resent even the most carefully worded suggestion – and it was not always easy to convince a petitioner that a recommendation from the district officer might not help him.

The standard of local politics in the early 1920s was often one through which the municipalities of England had passed in the seventeenth or eighteenth centuries. If the factions were evenly balanced, a member might be locked into his bathroom just before leaving home and the crucial vote taken while he was still trying to get out. Or the office clock might be advanced and one party, but not the other, warned to be present ten minutes early. The smaller towns sometimes got themselves into a hopeless tangle, their dues heavily in arrears, their streets dirty and unlighted. Such boards would have to be superseded and handed back to the district officer, who for three years or so would ruthlessly collect arrears of taxation and see that money allotted to services was in fact spent. And then the Board would be re-constituted.

Far more of a civilian's time was now spent in supervision and training of semi-technical workers. Co-operative banks, village forest management, town planning – all these he was expected not merely to understand but to teach. And it was refreshing – if sometimes a little annoying – to note how quickly the devil came to quote scripture. 'No,' said an old and illiterate villager, shaking his head at a proposal made by his S.D.O., *silvicultural principles ke mutabiq nahin.*' It was not in accordance with what he had been taught – he, who ten years before would have happily cut every tree he wanted!

The emergence of local bodies made one change since Trevelyan had described a civilian's day. Another was the increase in the loneliness of being for months together surrounded by people who either could not read at all or who read only the Ramayan or the Koran. In the nineteenth century, a man came in from camp to the headquarters of his district expecting to meet half a dozen men with whom he had shared the last hot weather. There might be a judge, a policeman, a canal man, a doctor; he might be tired of their company before May was out, but he did all the same want for a change to talk to people who were not petitioners.

In the new India of the reforms, the old unguarded companionship among equals was much less likely to occur. In a small district, there were hardly ever to be found so many as four or five officers of the Secretary of State's services. Any member of the Secretary of State's services might be an Indian and in the political circumstances, it was by no means always possible for Englishman and Indian to talk with unbuttoned ease. Perhaps the judge or the doctor would belong to the provincial service; that is to say, he had been promoted, after twenty-five or thirty years of toil, to the kind of post in which a young man of the higher services might officiate after five or six years. Of course, there was plenty to learn from the provincial service, and there was plenty to talk about, tales of crime and village life, of successful scores off the Secretariat, of shooting and the ways of animals. But the provincial service man had seldom been out of India and often there was a fear of causing offence on one side, a determination not to be patronized on the other. This constraint was perhaps more often present between the two grades of service than between Englishman and Indian.

From the end of the 1920s onwards, there were an increasing number of young Englishmen in the I.C.S. who felt strongly that their predecessors had been lacking in sympathy for Indians. 'I belonged to the generation', wrote Hugh Lane, recruited in 1938, 'that thought it was our job in life to live down the land-grabbing nigger-beating sins of our fathers.' After his first eighteen months of settling down, he was sent to Lucknow, where for the first time there was an Indian Deputy Commissioner, Jasbir Singh, a man widely liked and admired; he came of a princely Indian family and ought to have been in the I.C.S., but through some misfortune at the time of the examination had spent far too long in subordinate posts. 'I was soon an ardent worshipper of my D.C.,' writes Lane, 'who trusted me with so much and seemed so wise and experienced himself ... To me he was always a guide, a philosopher and friend and when he died, I felt as though I had lost my own father.' 'An Indian D.C. who treated me as a favourite pupil was, of course, an ideal trainer. I would sit spellbound in Indian Clubs while he gossiped with the strange mixture of types that only India can produce.'

This was not exactly typical; it was a case of a young man happily in love with India. But a change had taken place. Indians of Lane's generation used Christian names to their English contemporaries and they stayed in each other's houses. This had sometimes happened before, but usually there had been a certain reserve. An Indian was bound to feel in his heart that self-government was better than good government. It was easy for him to be over-sensitive and to suppose that he was being snubbed because he was an Indian, when in fact he was being treated with friendly lack of ceremony. Conversely, he did sometimes feel that his English senior was over-careful to be polite to him, where he would have called Smith a young fool and left it at that. But here is the experience of A. D. Gorwala, an Indian who has written of the old service in terms almost too generous to be quoted:

> More important ... was the informal part ... of the training of a young officer ... A good Collector's house was often a second home to the

young administrator. He was encouraged to drop in of an evening. Hardly ever was the Collector so busy or preoccupied that he would not have time for a few words with the young man . . . he might ask the new magistrate to come and have tea with him one evening a week . . . Seated on a comfortable sofa . . . plied with good tea and excellent home-made cake, the touchiness and arrogance so characteristic of the intelligent, inexperienced young prize-winner . . . would fall off like an old garment. Differences of kind or race would sink to insignificance and the young man would, sometimes to his surprise, find himself talking freely, listening with attention . . . pleased at the praise, not hurt at the warning and advice . . .

The young man imbibed standards, sometimes without even being told. Automatically he learned there were certain things one did not do. However awkward the circumstances . . . however grave the consequences to oneself . . . one did not lie. In all emergencies it was one's duty to stand firm. However frightened one might feel, one did not show it. In all one's dealings, the rule must be probity. The throwing of one's own responsibility on one's subordinates degraded one not only in the sight of one's fellows but in one's own eyes . . . While one showed deference to one's elders, one was not frightened of them. If one differed, one expressed one's views frankly . . . It was a great merit of government in this period [that is, up to 1947] that it neither punished frank expression of opinion from its officers nor even resented it.

Another Indian member of the service, a few years younger, Dharam Vir, spoke in almost the same words. 'I often disagreed with my superiors,' he said. 'An Indian was sometimes bound to feel differently. And I usually said frankly what I thought, but I do not think it was ever held against me or taken amiss.' And he went on: 'It was curious. We were all men of the same calibre and background. Sometimes it was chance that one man got into the I.C.S. and a classmate into the provincial service. There was not much in the formal training of the I.C.S. The training lay in being given a job and being told to get on with it. But because we were given that trust and responsibility we soon found ourselves ready to tackle anything in the way they – the provincial service – seldom were.'

With these new preoccupations, the district officer had to consider almost every day one abiding danger. Feeling between Hindus and Muslims was getting steadily worse. Almost anything might serve to touch off angry feeling into riot, loot and murder. As a rule something in the national press heightened feeling and then some local incident, or perhaps only a rumour, started a panic. Crowds would gather, sometimes perhaps in fear and for self-protection. And if two such crowds met and stones began to fly, the gangsters would come out with knives. But an example is best. It happened in Benares in the spring of 1939, but in most of the essentials the same riot took place in half the cities of India between 1919 and 1940. I had the tale from R. V. Vernède who was the District Magistrate; the facts and the pictures are his; I have done no more than put them into writing. He said:

'There is a kind of situation that just gets steadily worse, but there's nothing you can put your hand on. Feeling all through the Province had been getting worse ever since the Congress came to power, mainly because they wouldn't have a Muslim in the Cabinet unless he was a Congress Muslim – and therefore no Muslim at all in Muslim eyes. We asked for more police but they didn't come, and we could do nothing but rehearse and revise our riot schemes in consultation with the military. That year Moharram came at the end of February. We had been keyed up for Moharram of course; the police had been doing extra patrolling all the ten days and the magistrates had all been taking turns at the police stations.

'We had all been keyed up – and I had wondered once or twice whether I had taken stringent enough precautions. Before Moharram began we had arrested some of the main gangsters – just to keep them out of mischief. It's easy to hold them for a few days as known bad characters, under the security sections. I think now that perhaps we should have pulled in a few more.

'Moharram passed off without any serious trouble and I suppose we all relaxed; we had a few days, about a week I think, before we were wound up again for the Holi festival. The Hindus, of course, are the majority in Benares, but not by so many as you might expect in their sacred city. There's a big group of Muslim silk weavers, all illiterate, fanatically religious and very excitable. It's about two Hindus to one Muslim in a population of not much under a quarter of a million. So in a way Holi, when the Hindus were more likely to be excited, was more to be feared than Moharram.

'The riot came just between the two, just when we were relaxed. It came out afterwards that both sides had stored up petrol and kerosene in their houses; but we never did know exactly how it began.

'I got a confused message that rioting had begun about five o'clock on March 3. I had of course talked things over with the Superintendent of Police very thoroughly beforehand; he was Kazim Raza, a Muslim in the Indian Police Service and a good chap; he was first-class, all the way through, though a bit impatient with politicians. We'd decided we could take no risks – our forces were too small. As far as I remember, we had three hundred civil police, armed with batons, and a hundred and eighty armed police with smooth-bore muskets – not much to control a quarter of a million people in a built-up rabbit-warren of a city, all narrow lanes and little closed courts. In reserve was one company of British infantry – the Berkshires, they were. Since we had so little, Kazim Raza and I had agreed to call in the military as soon as trouble began. I rang them up at once and their C.O. kept a platoon at half-an-hour's notice and the rest at two hours' notice; warnings went out to put the riot scheme in operation and I went off to see what was happening. The riot scheme in its first stage was, of course, mostly orders and warnings; orders to the public not to assemble in crowds or carry arms; warnings to the police to requisition lorries and take charge of all arms in the dealers' shops; warnings to the hospitals to be ready for casualties, to magistrates to get to their posts, to the fire service to man the fire-engine. We only had one, a creaking old thing, but it did wonders.

'By about half-past six or seven that evening we had all the warnings out and all the magistrates and police at their posts. It was clear already that we were in for something pretty bad; there were several big outbreaks of fire already and that of course showed that there had been preparations. About half-past seven I got news that the fire-engine with its small escort of armed police was held up by a hostile mob who wouldn't let it get near enough one of these fires to take action. I got in touch with the Berkshires and started off for this fire with one platoon under a newly joined second lieutenant.

'We passed another fire on the way; a group of huts by the roadside. You know the sort of thing there is near every Indian city; thatched sheds, shops selling tea and mineral waters, the houses of vegetable-growers and milk-men. It was all one blaze and not a soul was to be seen. Thatched roofs — and dry as tinder in March. It was too late to do anything. We drove on.

'The fire we were going to was in the silk spinners' quarter. It's odd the way the famous Benares silks are made. The silk is spun by Hindus who sell the spun yarn to the Muslim weavers. That's been so at least since Aurangzebe's day. There was one section of the city where the Hindu spinners lived and worked and all round them were Muslim weavers. And of course it was there the trouble now was. We left the buses in the main street and went down an alley that led us into a small square with houses all round. It was bright moonlight and houses blazing on every side; you could have read a newspaper. But it was like watching a silent film; the flames drowned every other sound. We could see men on the roofs of houses not yet burnt, clear against the flames; we could see them getting stuff out and throwing it to friends below. But all in dumb show. It didn't seem real at all.

'There was no time to spare and it was useless to shout or give warnings. I had settled with the subaltern on the way from cantonments what we would do. If I told him to disperse the mob, he would begin by firing one controlled shot at them. Firing over their heads merely infuriates a crowd and causes more casualties in the end. I gave him the word as soon as we had taken in what was happening. He ordered a corporal to fire one round at the mass of men in front of us who were picking up the stuff as it was thrown out of the houses. It was spun silk on bobbins, done up in parcels. The looters were all Muslim weavers who as a rule had to pay for it.

'By a miracle that one round went right through without hitting anyone.

But it had a miraculous effect – more like a film than ever. In less than sixty seconds we were alone in the close. There were more fires somewhere behind this close and I went with the officer and a section under the same corporal down a side alley. In twenty yards we were in another close with the same scene before our eyes. Flames, moonlight, silence – and dark figures at work against the glow. They hadn't heard the shot; everyone that night was deaf with the roar of flames. I told them another round was needed for this lot and I pointed out to the corporal a man on the cornice of a roof, throwing out bales of stuff. He was clear against the blaze behind him. The corporal was ordered to fire one round and he did; he killed that man.

'There was a stampede. That close was a dead end, though we didn't know it at the time. They could only escape into the houses or out by the alley where we stood. Some went over the roofs, some into the houses. A group rushed straight at us. The corporal didn't wait for orders this time but fired another round at a big man who was brandishing what looked like a thick heavy crankshaft. I was very glad he did fire; in three more strides he would have been on us. The shot brought him down; it took him high in the shoulder and he survived. The rest of the charge jostled past us or melted into the doorways. We realized afterwards they couldn't have seen us; we were in the shadow.

'I went home after that to get my bedding and re-organize myself with Riot Headquarters as my headquarters. We had proclaimed a curfew of course, but had not had time to make the news known. We hadn't a loud-speaker van; there was only one in the province, and – would you believe it? – that belonged not to the police but to the Rural Development Department. That was an anxious night; I suppose I had about an hour's sleep. I went out a good deal to see what was happening, but never very far from headquarters, unless it was to a known strategic point where I could be reached by telephone.

'We were all the time ludicrously short of men and equipment. As to men, I've told you our numbers; with less than five hundred police all told, we had to find guards for every essential service as well as patrolling the city. Corpse collecting, for instance, and the wounded. The people who ought to have gone round as ambulance bearers ran away. We had to find people to do it and protect them as they went round. And with all those small parties dispersed, we had to find men to keep the main streets clear.

'I imposed a twenty-four-hour curfew after the second night; pretty stringent, I know, but I'm sure it was justified. That made it possible to keep the gangsters to small parties in the alleys and closes; after that, large parties hardly ever ventured into the main streets and we had very few pitched battles. We did a good deal of bluffing; when all the lights are out and curfew imposed, an ordinary bus with a civilian driver is pretty impressive at night. Lights blazing and engine roaring, we kept them at it all night long, up and down the main streets; no one could tell there was only one constable inside with a stick.

'The night that stays in my memory is the second. They began shouting war cries. You'd hear the old Muslim war cry go up from the weavers' quarter. *Allah Ho Akbar!* or *Din! Din! Din!* they would shout, all together. And then you would hear *Jai Ram!* or *Har! Har! Mahadeo!* from the Hindus. I suppose we were a bit jumpy by then; it kept everyone on edge. It was next morning I shut down the curfew and said there would be fines on the whole quarter if there were any more war cries. I think as a matter of fact they were defensive; they were meant to show the other side that there was someone awake and ready for them.

'There were eight cases of firing and eight inquiries, not to mention the big inquiry into the whole thing afterwards. They didn't blame me for anything except running about too much; they thought I should have stayed more at headquarters. There may be something in that; it's very difficult to get it just right. I'm sure the District Magistrate should be at the *kotwali* or wherever he makes his Riot Headquarters, not at his house. I'm sure he must go out a bit to see what's happening. So-and-so, you remember, was broke for not going out enough. I had to see how my officers were doing and what the place looked like and above all I had to keep in touch with the soldiers.

'The evening of the third day I managed to collect a peace meeting and form peace committees of the leading citizens. They were a very ill-matched lot; the Hindu leaders tended to be philosophers and the Muslims butchers. It was often a toss-up whether to put a man on a peace committee and trust him to restrain his own side or to arrest him as a fomenter of trouble. Sometimes we began one way and had to end by arrest. The peace committees helped when the back of the thing was broken, but they were always a nuisance in one way. They insisted on having gangs of 'peace volunteers', who often turned into communal rescue parties and made things worse. The Congress party of course claimed to represent both sides, and that didn't help.

'But the Premier* was good. He came to a meeting on the fourth day and did his best to back us up. He accepted, improved and put forward in his own name our suggestion that in any case of stabbing or arson the other community in that section of the city should be collectively fined. We could never collect the fines, of course, but it helped. People at the meeting accused the police of bias and it was then Kazim Raza lost his temper. He was wrong, of course, but he'd had no sleep for four days and he himself couldn't have been fairer. He had all my sympathy.

'That fourth day, when the Premier came, was the second day of the twenty-four-hour curfew and the worst was already over. There had been thirty cases of arson the second day and sixty-nine casualties; by the fourth day it was ten cases of arson and only twelve killed or injured.

*Pandit Govind Ballabh Pant.

We'd arrested four hundred and fifty or so for looting and arson by then. Next day we lifted the curfew two hours morning and evening to let people buy food and after two more days I lifted it altogether in the daytime.

'That's really all. As a matter of technique, I think the three most difficult things are timing and precautionary arrests, which you make beforehand as a preventative; being in the right place at the critical time – and knowing which communal leader to trust and which to arrest. You need general experience and a knowledge of that particular city. Another most important thing of course is good relations with the soldiers. They are always hampered by some doctrine about the concentration of force. We want a line of pickets along a main street to confine gangsters to their own quarters; the soldiers don't like breaking up into small parties. They think it more suitable to be kept in a strength of at least a platoon and marched out against a hostile mob – which is just what we want to avoid. Well, it makes a good deal of difference to the interpretation of their instructions if you know your man.

'It was my only big riot as a District Magistrate. I was in several as City Magistrate, and of course I'd been – I suppose dozens of times – in the sort of situation when one is just on the edge of a riot but by listening to both parties for hours one either persuades them to compromise or imposes a solution. Except for the odd way it began, with no warning and no ostensible cause, it was a classical riot with all the usual features.'

2 Under the Congress

One thing at least the keenest critic could not deny. The English had given India a political unity she had never had before. But the English talked of going; there were really only two possible heirs to political power, the Congress, and the Muslim League; they eyed each other with sharply rising jealousy. There were also the Princes, who did not wish to be subordinate to either heir and each of whom had for several generations been bound to the Crown of England by a treaty which involved obligations for both parties.

It is useless to speculate at length on whether more could have been done to weld the Congress, the Princes and the Muslims into one nation. Perhaps it was a mistake to give the Muslims separate electorates in 1909; it is certain that by 1946 their political leaders had become irrevocably opposed to the kind of state envisaged by the leaders of the Congress. And again, far greater pressure could have been put on the Princes to bring their states into the twentieth century – but the English were scrupulous to observe their rights.

Parliament in 1935 passed a new Government of India Act, a successor to the long line stretching back to 1833 and 1783. The 1935 Act went further than the Act of 1919 and introduced self-government in the provinces. At the centre, there was a more limited advance. This would not become complete until a sufficient number of States joined the Federation, when the Governor-General would become – very nearly – a constitutional monarch with ministers responsible to a carefully balanced Assembly in which there was special representation not only for Muslims, but for Sikhs, land-holders, women, Christians, labour. This never came into being.

The Viceroy dispatched five senior officers of the Political Service to persuade the Princes to come into the Federation. They went to each Prince in turn; they were nowhere successful.

They had been told of the need for haste. But they were sent to each Prince in turn. They had been brought up in an atmosphere of scrupulous regard for the rights of each State. They had been taught to treat with courteous deference the whims of each sovereign princeling. They had learnt to see the good side of an old-fashioned benevolent autocracy. And behind the Viceroy, from whom they received their instructions, was the India Office, attentive to the danger of Parliamentary questions, skilled in legal precedents, concerned for the sanctity of treaties.

Whether it was due to the traditions of the Political Department, to the caution of the India Office, to the procedure adopted or to the British Government's lack of real intention – the mission failed. The five met everywhere objections, bargaining points, conditions for coming in. It was the Princes' own fault; they had been warned, they had had their chance. But it is difficult to resist the feeling that they were warned in a voice so formally deferential, so muffled with historical exactitude and legal complications, that they were virtually invited to bargain and wait and stand out for better terms.

Federation never came into being and thus one chance of preserving unity was missed. The Princes and the British share the blame for that chance missed; for another it is impossible to blame anyone but the Congress Party.

Provinces became self-governing on April 1, 1937, and in the Hindu provinces the Governments which rather hesitatingly took office were Congress Party Governments. The Congress claimed to represent the whole of India, even those who did not agree with them. The Muslim League on one side, the Hindu Mahasabha on the other, were, the Congress believed, communal organizations, narrow-minded and fanatical, out of tune with the new secular world. The Congress would include Muslims in their Cabinets, yes, by all means. But not men determined to represent only their own community. Only Muslims of the Congress Party need apply.

Congress Muslims of course were anathema to the Muslim League who believed that Muslims should represent Muslims and who could not accept the ominously totalitarian doctrine of the Congress. So the split grew.

In the districts, the change of government was viewed by the former Guardians with feelings resigned and wary. On the whole, however, the change proved less startling than might have been expected. For some time, the provincial Government, though not responsible, had been responsive to public opinion, and in composition had been largely Indian.

A scene still vivid in the memory is the installation of an Indian Governor, the Nawab of Chhatari, in 1933. It was in April and already hot; light and air were carefully excluded from the Council Chamber. In the half darkness, the new Governor advanced to take the oath, a tall and imposing figure in white breeches and silk stockings, resplendent with gold lace and sword. He was followed by his Council, three Indians and one Englishman. The Chief Justice awaited him on the dais in scarlet robes and white wig; he too was an Indian. The formal archaic words of the oath were read by the Judge and repeated by the Governor in tones slightly alien to an English ear; more than one of the spectators must have wondered with what feelings a Roman official heard his language used by some such chief as Cogidumnus of Sussex, who was styled *Legatus Augusti in Britannia*.

And the Congress not only replaced a predecessor which had listened to their views, but found that proposals which had seemed easy enough from the other side of the house now presented all kinds of difficulties. The

The Nawab of Chhatari, the first Indian to be Governor of the United Provinces, and a Muslim gentleman of great courtesy and consideration.

change was not much more terrible than a change from Conservative to Labour in Great Britain.

For the Governor and the Chief Secretary it was more difficult than that. Both were met at every turn by suspicion; Congressmen had worked themselves into a state of mind when they believed that to uncover the nakedness of government would be to reveal a tangle of writhing monstrosities. Finding none, they felt sure they were being deceived. The Governor had the burden of discretionary powers which he must use only as a last resort. It was only by persuading the Congress that these powers might never need to be used that he had induced them to take office at all, yet he had responsibilities which might force him to use them. He was a constitutional monarch, but his Cabinet suspected him of having a whip up his sleeve — as in fact he had.

The Governor was a constitutional monarch and the head of the services; he was regarded as their one protector. Yet every adherent of the Congress Party thought it was now within his powers to give orders to the district officer. But the Governor usually found his Cabinet ready enough to support executive authority when disorder began. Indeed, he had as often as not to restrain them. 'Why don't they shoot sooner?' was the question one Governor was constantly asked by his Premier. But he found the same Premier most reluctant to prosecute for speeches which to an Englishman seemed direct incitements to riot.

The Chief Secretary was the channel through whom the orders of the Government were conveyed to their officers. He was the source of postings and transfers. He had now to serve a body whose basic assumptions on almost every point were exactly opposite to those in which he had been brought up. He had been taught that the district officer was in the last resort responsible for his district, must be given a wide discretion and where possible supported. But the new Government began with a feeling of distrust; they suspected that the district officer was more concerned about maintaining his own prestige than about the welfare of his subjects.

The Chief Secretary therefore found himself engaged in continual remonstrance on account of district officers, still more on account of officers of the provincial services. There were some of these who had been regarded by the old Government as particularly trustworthy because they had not been afraid to give sentences to men who were supporters of the Congress. Were they now to be passed over by men whom the late government had regarded as unreliable dabblers in politics? Every Chief Secretary must decide how far he should go in their protection.

It worked, somehow or other. There was enough Congress idealism, there was enough British goodwill. One example will illustrate better than generalizations the odd dilemmas that arose. It is reluctantly I choose an experience of my own, but I have heard no story more to the point.

I was posted to Garhwal as Deputy Commissioner in November 1936. Things had hardly changed since the days of Mr Traill; it was still three days of normal marching into the hills – about forty miles – between any road fit for wheeled traffic and the headquarters of the district; it was more than twenty days' march from Pauri, the headquarters, to the highest village on the Tibet frontier.

But the people now felt it a grievance that they had no road. The district imported grain and to pay for it they had nothing but army pensions. A road would make the grain cheaper to import and would make it possible to export fruit, potatoes, tea. But the road meant more than that; it had become a philosopher's stone, the elixir of life, and when it was built, both women and ewes would bring forth more plenteously, the morning star would sing and the hills skip with joy.

The District Board asked the old Government to build a road. The Government instructed their Public Works Department to prepare an estimate. Their estimate was so high that the Government turned down the project; they could not afford it. The election in the early spring of 1937 was fought by the Congress on a simple platform – a road for wheeled traffic; lower taxes. As the other side had no platform at all, the Congress candidates were elected.

The Congress came into office and found that all over the province awkward promises had come home to roost. They simply could not do all they had said they would do. They took nearly a year to decide about our road and then made a grant to the District Board that could only be called derisory. On the District Board's estimate, which everyone knew was highly optimistic, this would get the road to Pauri in about fifteen years; on the Government's own estimate, by P.W.D. standards, it would take two hundred and forty-nine years.

This was bad enough but financial pedantry made it worse. The first year's grant was allowed to lapse – and then the grant was debited with the cost of the Government's rejected estimate, which ate up the second year's grant. I came back from leave in the summer of 1938 to find that the District Board were threatening to proclaim civil disobedience and non-co-operation against the Congress Government. They were going to incite everyone in the district to stop paying Land Revenue, to cut the telegraph wires, and to disobey the forest laws.

My first reaction was regrettably flippant. I was a civil servant now; I was no longer a Guardian, a ruler of the state. It was not for me to get politicians out of the difficulties in which they had embroiled themselves by hasty promises. Of course, I could not persist in this attitude. I wrote a personal letter to the Premier, Pandit Govind Ballabh Pant, recalling the history of the case and recommending that the Government should make a fresh offer and a very much better one. I suggested that I should summon the District Board and put it to them that their best chance of getting a road was to make peace and ask for reconsideration.

The Premier was a magnanimous man. He forgave me some asperities and he replied, in a personal letter, that he agreed in general terms to most

21 above, *The retreat from Kabul. This followed the most unjust of British wars and was the worst disaster to befall a British army in Asia until Malaya, one hundred years later; 22 below, From Sketches in the Punjab by a Lady, 1854. 'On the Multan Road'. It is a hard dry land, very different from Bengal.*

THE HOUSE (NATIVE) IN WHICH OUR WOMEN WERE SLAUGHTERED BY ORDER OF NANA SAHIB. ON 16TH JULY. 1857. FROM A DRAWING ON THE SPOT BY LIEUT CRUMP. R.A

23 *above, Sepoys were ordered to shoot them; when they refused, the Nana Sahib sent in butchers with knives to do the work;* 24 *below, Durbar at Udaipur, Rajasthan, February 1855. Udaipur stood first in prestige among the Rajas of the Land of Rajas. The ruler of Udaipur was head of the clan descended from the Sun. Sir Henry Lawrence as Resident is sitting on his right hand.*

of what I said. But I was not to summon the District Board; their behaviour had been rebellious and the first move must not appear to come from the Government. I must not summon them, but the news might be allowed to seep round unofficially that if they withdrew their threats and petitioned to be allowed to approach the throne, there was a chance that there might be a bag of sweets in the cupboard.

In Garhwal some members of the District Board took a week or a fortnight on the way to a meeting and went over their knees in snow. It would take a great deal of seeping to reach them. I acknowledged this letter and disobeyed it, writing to the members a personal message. I said I was writing not as the Deputy Commissioner but as a friend. I had been trying to think what we in the district could do to get our road; would they meet me to talk it over? I gave them a date and said I would come to their committee-room to meet them; in India, the man who comes to another man's house is a petitioner. They might easily have refused to come to my court or my house.

They all came. I heard the night before that they were saying among themselves that they would never give in to the Premier. However, when we met next morning, I suggested that we should approach the problem in a practical way. How were we to get our road? Once they launched their civil disobedience, the Premier would never give in till they were crushed. But he must – I could only guess – he must be concerned that they should not start the movement. It would be highly embarrassing; everyone in India would laugh at the Congress. Would they not ask him to receive them and discuss the matter again?

They said they would talk it over by themselves. Two hours later, they agreed that there was a good deal in what I had said. But it was the Government which was in the wrong; it was for the Government to make the first move.

I sent the Premier a telegram in cipher, saying that the Board were anxious to meet him. They had made the first move. Would he name the day – in cipher, please?

He gave me a date and I told the Board that the Premier had invited them to meet him in Lucknow, when he would be ready to discuss the matter in a constructive spirit. He had made the first move – would they go? They went – and the first thing they did after their interview was to send me a telegram in the kind of terms which in England are used after a Cup Final. They had reached a satisfactory solution.

What is typical about this story is the relationship. We, the former Guardians, could not forbear some rejoicing at the difficulties in which the Congress were placed; we laughed at their misfortunes and some of us delighted in pointing out mistakes. But we did what we could to help. The King's Government had to be carried on and Vernède, for instance, conducted his riots at Benares in exactly the same way under a Congress Government as he would have done under a Governor.

19
THE SAME INDIA

1 The Two Schools

While Governments changed, the same India went on. In the twenty years from 1919 to 1939, step by step society became more secular, the state more democratic, the towns more industrial. But in the greater part of India the life of the peasant and of the district officer changed little. Men still heard disputes under a tree, still checked land records in the fields.

There were still tents beneath the dark green leaves of the mango-trees and the camp might still be pitched by the side of such a road as Hawkins had travelled three hundred years before. Perhaps there was a festival and the peasants from near and far must go to bathe; early in the morning, before the first light, the carts would begin to pass and a sleeper would wake to the creaking of wooden wheel on wooden axle, a long-drawn creak, rising and falling as the bullocks lurched in the ruts, dying at last in the distance as others took up the tale. He would hear the peasants singing as they went to the river, men's voices and women's, singing songs they had sung in Akbar's time. Or later, when the sun was low again, he would see them at the ferry, waiting to cross, the women brilliant in their best clothes, apple-green and black, scarlet, deep crimson, yellow ochre and black again, the colours taking a deeper and richer hue in the evening light.

Or perhaps the river had changed its course and a score of villages had been robbed of their fields. The villagers by the river had made a bargain with the Government for five years only; if the river gave them new land, they need not pay on it till the next assessment, but if the river took their old land, they might be excused their taxes altogether. There would be long mornings in the flat sandy ground by the river, when the dew was still pearly and the white blossom still damp among the silver-grey foliage of young peas and wheat; there would be a late breakfast in the shade of a tamarisk bush when the sun was high and the white sand by the river as

Bareilly Settlement: checking land records, 1933. For most of the time, in a great deal of India, things went on just as before, and the basic work of checking the land records and assessing the land for tax continued.

bright as the water; there would be, perhaps, the chance of a snipe or a quail before the ride back to the tents, and certainly there would be long hours checking the patwari's papers, hearing how Ram Kalan had agreed to let Jodhu use the field for two years only on condition . . .

You could still see, in the village where you went to check and to encourage the work of one of the new village committees, a scene unchanged since Akbar's day, the shrine beneath a fig tree, a yoke of bullocks tied in a corner by a manger of mud, a cart with its shaft pointing to the sky. In April, in the level evening light, you would still see the muzzled bullocks treading the straw, a man standing on a platform with hands raised to let the grain fall and the wind winnow away the chaff; grain and straw alike would be palest gold in that warm apricot flood. There might still be one flame-of-the-forest, late in blossom, dusky orange against the sky; along the roadside, the *neem* trees, planted in a double avenue by some forgotten district officer, would spread fresh young leaves, their green as delicate as young beech, against boughs darkly contorted.

You would suppose, from a novel so brilliantly written as *A Passage to India*, that the English in India lived in a state of semi-hysteria, resolutely suppressing a fear that the Mutiny would come again. Perhaps it was so in Bengal; it was not in the North, where a man went all over the district, sleeping in his tent unguarded and unarmed; why should he not? He knew that in every village of his district he would be welcomed with grave courtesy. And in the South, in the intervals of settling the peasants' rent as Thomas Munro had taught them to, civilians placidly continued the

307

'Men still heard disputes under a tree . . .' A drawing by the wife of a U.P. civilian in the 1930s. But they would soon bring a string bed and ask you to sit down.

tradition of Bignold, turning into light verse the instructions which Munro had issued a hundred years before to junior civilians regarding their behaviour to Indians.

> If peptic noises punctuate
>   The flow of conversation,
> Politely pause till they abate;
> No gentleman should deprecate
>   An honest eructation . . .

That exiles still wrote verses does not prove they were free from anxiety.

And of course they were often anxious, about riots, about the future of the world. Indeed, they often seemed rather less anxious than their countrymen in England. There were still *Weeks* in every station of any size. There was Christmas Week in Lahore, not very different from when Kipling had written of it; there were Weeks for the polo or the Races, where everyone met everyone else; everyone, after all, still knew everyone else.

Every year at the Viceroy's House there was a Ball at which something of the splendour beloved by Lord Curzon might still be seen. There was the scarlet and rifle-green of the infantry, making with blue velvet and black a recurrent pattern, sombre and gorgeous, lifted into gaiety by the apricot of Skinner's Horse, by facings of light blue and French grey, by waistcoats of silver lace and aiguillettes of gold, by the more delicate finery of the women, by the brocades and jewels of the Princes. To the eye, there was not much difference between the guests who had attended Lord Curzon's Ball and those who now wandered among the fountains of the Mogul Garden, in the summerhouses of stone tracery and among the staircases and corridors of an architecture massively polite to a variety of traditions. There were more Indians in uniform and in tail coats; there were more saris to soften and vary the colours. The guests no longer had any difficulty in finding their carriages to go home; they drove along spacious uninhabited boulevards, flanked by long avenues of stone lamp-posts, round circles intended to control a traffic that would one day need control, past the cold statues of the Viceroys, and the long empty processional way, to their palaces, bungalows and tents.

There was Christmas Camp, too, with partridges and jungle-fowl and hopes of a tiger in his royal winter coat, with picnics of cold turkey and chestnut stuffing, cold game pies, and cold brandy butter with the pudding. Still mornings there were too in the forest before dawn, every leaf, every blade of grass cold with dew, the air sharp with the fragrance of bruised leaves and of dust wet with dew, the deer hooting in voices shrill with sudden fear, the jungle cocks crowing as darkness grew thin to the East. And there was the mixed soupy smell of elephant and driver, the breathless scramble into the tree above the tiger's kill, the sharpness of dusk when you counted the birds and went into the tents for tea and Christmas cake.

The district notable who was assiduous for honour still felt it wise to contribute a hundred rupees to the Commissioner's fund for midwives and the same to the Collector's for playing-fields, keeping twenty-five for the Joint Magistrate's experiments in village bee-keeping. And in fact many a pet scheme which had been the unofficial love of some patriarch of the past was now an honest woman with her marriage lines and asked to Government House. Brayne's village uplift, once a heresy, was fashionable in the 1930s; all over India, men were trying to persuade villagers to make dunghills outside the villages instead of inside, to clean the streets and open the windows, to conserve humus and use better seed. Co-operative Credit, the mistress of Thorburn and Wedderburn, had become wife to Strickland and to Malcolm Darling.

Soil erosion too was something about which once only a few faddists had been concerned. When the British first came to the Punjab, they found hillsides which had been kept as game preserves by the kings and princes before them. But the new rulers believed in letting men pursue the greatest happiness of the greatest number. They threw the forests open. The peasants cut grass, they grazed cattle and goats, they cut down trees for houses, cattle-sheds and fire-wood. Soon the hillside was bare, the precious living soil washed away, and lost too was the precious moisture that would have been stored, by the spongy leaf-mould of the forest, to emerge in springs and to be used months later for irrigation.

In spite of many efforts by individuals, the government was slow to act; when it did, the first steps were acts of government, to enclose and re-afforest; it was some time before education in self-help began. Now in the 1930s the peasant was urged to protect himself and others; the Co-operative Movement came to help and co-operative societies were formed to establish village reserves of grass and fuel, small forests run by the villagers themselves.

In the 1860s, when Trevelyan had written of the civilian's enthusiasm for his work, there had been two types of men, the protectors of the poor, such as John Lawrence, passionate for improvement, whom some thought inclined to go too fast for India, and thoughtful, philosophical men, Henry Lawrence, Bartle Frere, Alfred Lyall, who saw the value of Indians as individuals and of Indian institutions. They had come to be known as protectors of the noble, because they had often come to believe in some kind of indirect rule through chiefs. Both lines survived.

F.L. Brayne, who tried to teach the peasant to use a plough that went too deep and increased evaporation, was clearly in the line of John Lawrence. No one more clearly belonged to the school of protectors of the noble than Harcourt Butler. His had been a brilliant career even before he rounded it off with ten years as head of a province, of Burma twice and the United Provinces once. He had the knack of talking with easy friendship to anyone and everyone. He liked talking and he liked people; he was interested. He was not concerned about democracy or freedom but that people should be cheerful and enjoy themselves. He liked Indians, and particularly Oudh, with its tradition of courtly politeness. He loved Lucknow and under his rule it assumed in an odd way some shadow of the fantastic air it had borne in the days of the Kings of Oudh. He beautified the city with flowering trees and fountains; he made it once more a city in which people at once thought of pleasure. His principal viziers were Sir Ludovic Porter and the Raja of Mahmudabad; the triumvirate were widely known by a rhyming vernacular jingle – 'Nawab, sharab wa kabab' – that may be loosely translated: 'Food, wine and a lord'. Sir Harcourt was the middle term of the three. When he spoke to the young men of the

I.C.S. who came to Burma in 1927, he said: 'The most important thing is to be accessible to the people . . . to be not an official only but a friend . . . Above all, avoid doing other people's work over again . . . Keep your sense of humour and proportion . . . the business of Government has been described as getting out of one damned hole after another . . .' He has been charged with having been too kind to the Taluqdars of Oudh – but that was the school to which he belonged; he was an *amir-parwa*, a protector of the nobles, and if the type had grown worldly and *bon garçon* since the days of Henry Lawrence, it had also grown genial and human.

It is not so easy to assign to the school of Thomason and John Lawrence the greatest figure of the 1920s and 1930s, Malcolm Hailey. In a sense he combined the best of both schools. He escaped deliberately from Simla and the Government of India in order to get back to the fields and settlement; he became Colonization Officer in the Shahpur District, putting peasants on to the squares of new land reclaimed by irrigation from the desert. He had the plough and the bullocks, the threshing-floor and the corn-bin, before him in all he did. They were always there in the blood of his brain. But the brain was too clear, the grasp of detail and principle too tenacious, to let the figure of the peasant blot out everything else. Realism and common sense made the picture he looked at as clean, as detailed as a Dutch interior. It was no doctrinaire liberalism that made him support Lionel Curtis's proposals in 1917, but a shrewd perception that educated opinion is bound to spread to the public and that public opinion cannot be fought indefinitely, least of all in the name of a democracy. Minute, industrious attention to detail, the sudden revealing glimpse of the whole – to describe his mind is to describe the ideal scholar or lawyer.

It sounds inhuman, but it was not, because with a commanding intellect and a commanding presence went humility and humour and the hallmark of a good Indian Civilian, the power to let another man do his own work. 'You will have a trying day tomorrow,' he said when Chief Commissioner of Delhi to the District Magistrate. 'You will be on the alert all day and will probably have a riot. But I have discussed all your arrangements and I approve of them. One embarrassment at least you shall be spared. I am going fishing.' That could have been said in no other service.

He governed the Punjab for four years and the United Provinces, the highest post in the service, for six. He could govern a province with firmness and restore order, keeping exactly to the narrow way that avoids a pedantic legalism on one side and on the other a cynical connivance at brutality; he could at the same time preside over a Committee with a genial, an almost paternal indulgence. He will be remembered as a Governor; if he had not been a Governor, he would be remembered for the outstanding grasp of constitutional principle which he showed in the discussions before the Act of 1935. And if for none of these things, he would be remembered for the work of scholarship on Africa which he undertook after retirement, nothing less than to make himself an expert on every aspect of the life of a new continent.

But he is not an easy man to write about. You cannot find a fault; there is no dark shading to bring out the high lights. But that cannot be helped. One can hardly expect a man to cultivate vices for the benefit of his biographer.

2 The Same Frontier

There were still men of stature then in the 1930s. Another constant was the Frontier. Here the tribes were still treated like tigers in a national park. They could kill what deer they liked in the park; they risked a bullet if they came outside and took the village cattle. That had been true in 1900 and was still a fair description in 1947.

The backbone of the system was *Khassadari*, a development of Sandeman's principle. The Government paid the khassadars to keep the tribe good. If the tribe misbehaved, the khassadar lost his allowance. On a smaller scale, the principle applied throughout India. You employed a member of a criminal tribe to guard your property. You became a patron of the tribe and the watchman showed intruders the way to someone else's house. It was, all the same, blackmail.

Men still loved the Frontier. No one suffered more continuously than a Frontier officer from that slight mental derangement that afflicted every civil or political officer throughout India more or less. When you first came back from camp, you stared in astonishment at the cold unnatural pallor of your own face in the glass; at the club you could think of nothing to say to these people who never thought of the oppressions of the moneylender and the cost of wheat. As a rule it wore off, but to some Frontier officers, the jirga and the bloodfeud were always the reality, the club and the polo tournament the shadows.

There were no long hours at an office desk, and although there was always the chance of a bullet and often a good deal of discomfort, it was a life that everyone on the Frontier enjoyed. Everyone liked the Pathan, his courage and his sense of humour; far from being aloof, many of these Frontier guardians were half inclined to accept tribal standards. And it was all personal; allegiance was given, if at all, not to a Government but to a man. Nothing illustrates this so well as the tale of a man whom I will call Aslam Khan.

Aslam Khan was a *havildar*, that is a sergeant, in the Guides Infantry. He had been promoted young; he had his Army Certificate of Education; he was a man who stood well with his officers and was sure of a Viceroy's Commission before long. But a moneylender was oppressing his father so he killed him. No one thought the worse of him for that but it was on the wrong side of the administrative line so he reported to the police and went to prison for five years. When he came out, he was appointed orderly to a Political Agent on the tribal side of the administrative frontier. Soon afterwards, the Faqir of Ipi announced that he was going to have the Agent killed, or, failing him, his wife, who was living in administered territory. The Agent picked Aslam Khan, convicted murderer, and sent him to guard his wife and for a year he slept across the door of her bedroom with a loaded rifle to his hand. But that Agent went and another came who did not like Aslam Khan. So he left British service and became the right-hand man of the Faqir of Ipi – fanatical enemy of the British.

The Frontier game was a game of life and death but played with a sense of humour. A patrol once encountered and pursued a raiding party but the lie of the hills soon brought them to a stalemate where neither could move and they began a sniper's battle which would last till dark. But the patrol were firing low and hating to see ammunition wasted one of the gang rose and signalled them the range, as though they were practising at a target. He had after all been in the army himself.

The escort with Charles Duke, Political Agent in North Waziristan, ran into a party who began to fire at them. There was an exchange of shouts and Darim, the *subadar* commanding the escort, came to know that his son was leading the other party. 'But the sahib is in my charge,' Darim shouted, 'I shall shoot you unless you go home.' And shoot him he did, knowing he was his son.

Roos-Keppel was head of the province from 1910 to 1919 and left a lasting name as a good friend and a bad enemy. What was he like? 'Rather like a battleship,' one is told; a large man with a chin like the ram of a fighting ship, cheeks like the sheer of its sides; but he had been loved as well as feared. He had spoken the language like a Pathan and in the 1908 expedition against the Zakka Khel, the Zakka Khel men in the Khyber Rifles fought their own people because of their faith in Roos-Keppel; when the fighting was over, the Zakka Khel leaders crowded round their recent enemy to ask if they had fought well. 'I wouldn't have shaken hands with you unless you had!' was his reply. Roos-Keppel was perhaps the last man among the Guardians who could in practice make or end a war by his own decision.

Bunch Parsons came into the political service too late to reach the highest post, though it had been his aim since boyhood. But he left a name. He never married; the Frontier and his friends on the Frontier were wife, child and home to him. He could keep up with a Pathan youth on his own hills; he seemed impervious to heat or cold, wearing in all climates shorts of khaki drill, the simplest clothes possible, and yet contriving always to look the same trim ascetic figure. Nothing pleased him more than a day spent moving fast over the hills with a few Pathans, young men of the Scouts perhaps or tribesmen. They called him The Touchstone and he had a look that might abash a liar, a look you sometimes see in a naval officer and sometimes in a monk.

There was another school of whom perhaps the best examples were Packman and Iskandar Mirza, one of the first Indians to pass through Sandhurst and into the Political Service. Sikandar, as everyone called him, who later became President of Pakistan, enjoyed getting the better of a man by a cunning trick, intercepting a piece of intelligence that had been bought by the other side, buying it back before it was delivered and substituting something else that would deceive the enemy. It was Sikandar who arranged that a procession which he thought might give trouble should be entertained to tea, quite early in the course of its route, by a party of sympathizers, who had – as it happened – included in the strongly sugared tea one of the most powerful and rapid of vegetable laxatives. The procession dispersed before reaching its objective. This of course was in administered territory; there were no processions among the tribes.

Those are the extremes on either wing; in between came one man who is outstanding in the last twenty years because he was so completely central, so utterly imperturbable, so tolerant and so calm. Sir George Cunningham had been Personal Assistant to Roos-Keppel and Political Agent in North Waziristan; he made his name – it is sometimes said – by never saying a word when he was Private Secretary to Lord Irwin. He was not a reformer or a creator. But he was something else as valuable. He was the holder of the balance, accessible, wise, ready to be friends with Mammon if there was the least chance of Mammon conceding a point, trusted, admired and liked by all, a shrewd judge of men. He was in sharp contrast with Parsons, an edged blade, a man of close friends but not without enemies, intolerant of the second-best, a reformer and a zealot. As Agent to the Governor-General in Baluchistan, Parsons set about purging the country of the anomalies that had grown up since Sandeman's day, things everyone else accepted, indefensible in logic or to an Auditor, but unquestioned because they had been there a long time. Cunningham would have let them bide.

He was Governor of the North-West Frontier Province from 1937 to 1946 and again, at the invitation of the Governor-General of Pakistan, from 1947 to 1948. For the first three years of his time, he had the strange problem of a Muslim Congress Ministry. The people of the North-West Frontier Province had only one idea of politics, which was to embarrass the Government, and as that was what the Congress appeared to be doing in India, their politicians decided to be Congress too. In that improbable partnership they remained until politics suddenly became serious in August 1947.

When this strange party came into office in 1937, they were led by Dr Khan Sahib, a man who had been surgeon to a regiment of the Indian Army and had not the least personal animosity either to British officers or to European ways. Like the other Congress premiers, most of his views were a good deal modified when he came into office and it was seldom that any real controversy seemed likely with the Governor. When difficulty did arise, Sir George Cunningham would ask him round to play bridge and 'lose a few rubbers amicably', after which it was usually possible to come to an agreement.

In 1947, when the new Dominion of Pakistan was set up, Sir George, who had been a year in retirement, was invited to come back as Governor, being the man everyone trusted.* The time that followed he found the most interesting, and also the most peaceful, of his career. It was much better without the Government of India; there was so little paper. Mr Jinnah, the Governor-General, wrote to him, he thought, once only. The nature reserve was maintained, the allowances were paid; everything went on just as before except that the new Government withdrew troops from Waziristan and now lady missionaries found that they could summer peacefully and without protection at Wana, where no woman had been allowed when the place was full of troops.

In the first half of the century, then, there had been no change of principle. There was, however, a change of technique, the introduction of bombing. If it was decided that a tribe should be punished for some atrocity they had committed in the administered area, it was cheaper and quicker to send a few aircraft than a brigade. The Pathan, however, thought it unsporting. 'A great tyranny,' he would say, shaking his head. 'But if you were in our place, wouldn't you drop bombs?' 'Oh, of course we should,' he would answer with a merry peal of laughter. The Government of India recognized the unsporting nature of the technique, and ruled that only small bombs must be used and then only after due warning. Leaflets were dropped to give everyone time to go away – white first and then red. Over a whole area bombs would be dropped occasionally for a long time and tribesmen were supposed to keep out of the way and live in caves. 'They don't like it because they get lice,' one used to be told.

'Proscriptive air action,' of course, was not in the true Frontier tradition; what all parties enjoyed was a brisk fight and then to be friends again afterwards, talking the battle over and congratulating each other on shrewd manoeuvres and well-aimed shots.

Looked at from a different point of view, the local advantage had to be weighed against the moral loss at Geneva, where it was no use explaining that you dropped leaflets first and only used twenty-pound bombs. No one believed it. And to use bombs at all against 'British Protected Persons' did not look well. No one worried about Geneva, but there would have been Frontier support for the view that it was better not to bomb tribesmen at all unless it was really a big affair and part of general military action. And then with the gloves off.

---

* 'Surely he has won the North-West Frontier outright,' said Bernard Fergusson.

20

HITLER'S WAR

———◆———

1 The War in India

In September 1939, the period of Reform came to an end and until 1946 war was the main thing in English minds – but it was not the same for Hindus and Muslims.

The declaration of 1917 had promised 'the increasing association of Indians in every branch of administration'. In the civil part of the administration a good deal had been done to carry this out. For twenty years, recruiting to the I.C.S. had been about half and half English and Indian; as there had been very few Indians taken before 1919, most men with over twenty years' service were English, and there was therefore still a preponderance of English officers – 760 to 540 out of 1,300. But it seemed to Indians that they would never be rid of the English altogether. They were still coming, and it would be thirty years before the last of them retired. Transfer to Indian hands had been carried out much more thoroughly in the Forest Service, in the Public Works Department, and in the services under Provincial Ministries, rather less in the Police. Of the Police and Indian Civil Service it was said that it would not be safe to make them entirely Indian; they were a steel frame, necessary to keep the whole together. That and much more that was said in England undid much of the good of what had been done.

Among the Indians of the I.C.S. were men of the highest calibre. No civil service in the world could hope for abler men than Bajpai, Hydari, Trivedi, H. M. Patel, Gorwala and others. They were a little more like civil servants in England than the old Guardians had been; pigsticking and shooting seldom played much part in their lives. They were more often townsmen in their outlook and in districts they were sometimes a trifle more high-handed. But between Englishman and Indian, over work there was little difference. Trivedi, smoking the foulest of cheroots and saying, 'I tell you, work is its own reward' – no one could have wished for a more loyal or a more able chief. Hydari, too, son of Sir Akbar Hydari of Hyderabad, uniformly cheerful, tolerant, shrewd – no one could be better fitted to be a constitutional Governor. He went on to be Governor of Assam and Trivedi to Orissa, the East Punjab and Andhra.

The second part of the 1917 declaration, the gradual development of self-governing institutions, had not been so successful. For the greater part of the twenty years, there had been no co-operation at all from the largest political party. In the last three years, that party had accepted power, doubtfully and grudgingly, and had learnt a great deal, while many eyes had been opened among their supporters. Lane, recruited in 1938 in the last batch but one, had been a warm well-wisher of the Congress ministry; he wrote that, many months before they resigned, the Indian Deputy Commissioner to whom he had given such admiration and devotion had become disillusioned, 'as he discovered how much the Congress tried to use district officers to further private or political aims. By the time they came to resign there was little that he could find bad enough to say about them.'

Progress had all the same been made. The Congress were better equipped, when they came to take full responsibility, than they had been in 1937 – simply because they had more experience. In the Punjab, where the Muslims were slightly more numerous than Hindus and Sikhs together, a coalition had been formed – the Unionist Party – which included all three communities and whose aim was to maintain the unity of the Punjab and avoid a party division along purely religious lines. In Madras, the ministry had been a marked success. But everywhere progress was threatened by the overhanging crag of dissension between the communities.

As for those who had once been the Guardians, they had become teachers where they had been rulers; some of them had learnt to speak in Assemblies and had become to some extent politicians. Not much enthusiasm had been displayed for that development; it was difficult to feel much interest in an Assembly where votes could be disregarded; it was too much like an undergraduate debating society. Criticism was often ill-informed while, from the Government benches, speeches tended to consist of facts and figures, perfunctorily repeated. But certain conventions were happily established; whatever they might say in their speeches, members met on the way to the division lobbies with good humour and friendly chaff.

In the districts, things had not changed so violently as might have been expected. But there was a change in emphasis. India was a poor country which could not afford luxuries and a district officer had concentrated on essentials – public order, the swift administration of justice, the prompt payment of taxes moderately assessed, the maintenance of accurate land records which would prevent disputes. Those had been the four first things. But by 1939, the emphasis had changed and rural development, co-operative banks and village committees were inclined to come first.

Since 1919, there had been an increase of forty-four officers in the I.C.S., the total rising from twelve hundred and fifty-five to twelve hundred and ninety-nine. This was for the three and a half hundred million of India. The Secretariat had increased by more than forty-four; the districts were weaker in strength than in 1919. Yet the district officer must add to his innumerable duties the maddening and infructuous business of answering parliamentary questions, the host of subjects included under the head of Rural Development, and the labour of persuading where he had been used to command. He did not always find it possible to check land records as he used to do, and cases were taking longer to be settled.

That was why to some at least of the service it seemed that it was time to go. Rule of the old kind was running down; districts were being administered in a new way, which might be better, but was not the British way. A district officer might find, perhaps, when he had time to look, that a peasant had been brought in to headquarters a dozen times before his case reached even the first formal hearing, or that someone had been forced to spend all he had to defend his holding against some fabricated claim, simply because the land records were not up to date. As to Rural Development, most British officers would have agreed that a great deal of what was proposed was admirable if the villagers would do it themselves, but they were sceptical about trying to change habits from above – and much of the effort put into the attempt seemed to them wasteful and incompetent.

In the nineteenth century it had been enough to keep the peace and to see that every man had his own. That could be done by a small number of platonic despots and it had been done admirably. But that was no longer enough. Something more positive was needed and it could only be provided by a government native to the country.

That then was a feeling already held by some in 1939. When war came, every Englishman knew that now the first thing to do was to win it. As in 1914, so when Poland was attacked, there was among educated Indians a wave of sympathy for England and of hostility for Germany. A great deal of that initial goodwill disappeared in the first weeks of the war. As in 1914, there was technically no need for India to declare war; she was automatically at war as soon as His Majesty was. This was not the case with the Dominions; Canada came loyally to His Majesty's aid and India would have liked to do the same.

For a year, Delhi and Simla had been preparing for war. In a year, that technical point could surely have been dealt with. But no one thought of it. It was not malice or arrogance that committed India to the war without consulting any popular leader. It was insensitive, no more than that; no one thought of it – but if anyone had, you may be sure the thought would at once have been killed by legal pedantry.

Whatever the reason, India was automatically in the war and the Congress ministries in the provinces resigned. In the Congress provinces, the Governor ruled as in the old days.

Many senior members of the service believed that this made no difference to the part India played in the war. Not another shell, not another pair of boots, not another recruit would a Congress decision to support the war have produced. And there would have been continual argument about priorities. It is not, all the same, easy to persuade an outsider that to have the people behind you in a war can be anything but a help. The question however is academic; from now on, the energies of the Viceroy and the British members of the services were concentrated on the war and many of them were bitter at the Congress attitude. During those critical years the people of India had, they thought, freedom to say and write what they liked, freedom to associate, freedom to go where they liked – all to a far greater extent than the people of any European country. For the right to vote surely they could wait till it was clear whether there was any likelihood of any freedom at all continuing anywhere in the world.

The Congress did not see it like that. Mr Gandhi began the war with emotion, weeping at the thought of Westminster Abbey reduced to ruins. As the war progressed and the worst had not happened, his attitude changed. The war was a European civil war; Indian dislike for Hitler's racial theories receded; Japan, after all, was an Asiatic nation and there were reasonable grounds for supposing that Japan would win. Mr Gandhi was able to persuade himself that, if only she was dissociated from Britain, India would have nothing to fear from Japan. In 1942 he asked the British to withdraw entirely from India.

The English then disregarded Indian views and got on with the war, while the Congress disregarded both Germans and Japanese and pursued their private aims. The Muslims too had aims of their own. Some years before, the suggestion of a separate Muslim State within India had been put forward as a debating point in a students' society. In 1940 the Muslim League officially adopted it.

Against this background, most of the ex-Guardians continued a routine that was fantastic because so little changed. There was a general rule that no one would be allowed to put on uniform, not even the former soldiers in the Political Service. This was relaxed for very few; Tull, for instance, being very young and a qualified pilot, was released to the R.A.F. and won a D.S.O.; Ian Bowman took casual leave and travelled third-class to Pondicherry to enlist in the French Foreign Legion; after various adventures he was brought back but eventually released to the Army as incorrigible.

But for most people the war meant going without leave, getting very few letters from England and doing much more work. Here is the letter of a young wife, herself a teacher by profession, helping an I.C.S. husband to do his work in the Punjab, in 1941. But not all wives worked so hard as this one.

In Ferozepur we have been on the run all the time without stopping. I have visited four schools and enrolled 110 Guides besides attending a Guide Rally at which about 250 mothers and innumerable children were present. We have given two dinner-parties, one entirely Indian and one European – to lunch once and to tea four times – all Indian – and have spent three mornings judging ten villages, one morning inspecting a Lady Welfare Worker, one afternoon inspecting Health Centres, one evening at a play in a Hindu girls' school and one at an Indian film.

Meanwhile, the Japanese overran Malaya and Singapore and the British suffered their greatest disaster in Asia since the retreat from Kabul just a hundred years before. The Japanese drove them out of Burma, Japanese ships for a week sank what they chose in the Bay of Bengal; their aircraft raided Ceylon. There was not one division in India fit to attack. Hardly any civilian knew quite how bad things were – but anyone could see they were bad. And to the Congress it seemed that an opportunity had come.

Mr Gandhi moved rapidly between April and July of 1942. From an invitation to the British to leave India 'to God, or in modern parlance to anarchy', he proceeded to his statement in July: 'There is no room left . . . for withdrawal or negotiation . . . After all, it is an open rebellion.'

The English, however, are impatient of distractions when engaged in a major war. The Congress leaders were arrested on the eve of their rebellion and, within ten days, the back of the thing was broken. But, for a short time, in the eastern part of the United Provinces and in Behar, things were much as they had been in the Mutiny.

Lines, a young man of twenty-seven or twenty-eight, went to Darbhanga in Behar to take charge of his first district on August 10, 1942, the day after the arrests. 'The Congress High Command', he wrote, 'had planned well and the execution of the plan was good. No time was wasted.' On the 11th, the schools and colleges were empty; on the 12th and 13th, the villagers cut all the roads and railways. The roads were cut at embankments, trees felled across them, masonry bridges demolished, pontoons of the pontoon bridge on the main road sunk; railway lines torn up, 40-foot spans of the bridges removed and dropped into the rivers, the delicate and at that time irreplaceable electrical signalling apparatus at all stations destroyed; telephone and telegraph wires everywhere cut, rolled up and carried off home.

'By the 13th, police-stations and government offices in outlying places were occupied.' A sub-inspector, a head constable and five or six constables – they had not much hope against a mob of thousands. Yet some did escape or defy the mob. 'The man in charge of Laukaha, on the border of Nepal, saved by a couple of hundred Nepalis, armed with spears and battle-axes, driving the Congress attackers from the attack. The Brahman Dube at Jainagar, shooting dead the first man in the mob who tried to enter the police-station, and then with the help of reinforcements holding his own. The stout Rajput at ... ' and so on. A few survived but of the twenty-three police stations in the district, hardly six remained in police hands.

> Our police were staunch enough, once they knew they were expected to be, but a total police force of five hundred men to cover a district with close on four million inhabitants, a district in an uproar, was on the thin side ... I slipped out one night with a handful of armed police and reached Samastipur before dawn – to get the loan of ten British soldiers and one officer! But others were coming and now waverers wavered no more and the police took fresh heart ... The tide had turned and the people generally were by now as certain as we had always been which way it would finally flow.

Lines goes on to speak of the pleasure of getting out into the district again, of the friendliness in so many places and the almost universal relief at the re-establishment of law and order; the cheers for the Collector at Singhia, where not a month before the mob had murdered the Sub-Inspector.

In the Eastern United Provinces, Hugh Lane was now Joint Magistrate at Benares, under 'Bill Finlay, the finest man I have ever had the honour to serve'. They were critical of their orders but obeyed them and on the appointed day 'the well-known and mainly moderate Congressmen in Benares were escorted to jail, leaving those whom we later found were the real plotters of the Rebellion happily plotting away'.

It was later that day that crowds began to pull telegraph poles down and railway lines up; in the latter case, 'they used special spanners, removed the fishplates and lifted the lines bodily, proving how carefully planning had been done'. Culverts, where main roads carried on embankments crossed a ditch or river, were destroyed by digging up the foundations; the mob attacked wayside railway-stations 'taking great care to wreck the valuable control and signal machinery'.

'In a day or two, the back of the Rebellion in Benares City was broken'. As soon as the city was quiet, parties of police were sent out to the villages; they found rural post offices had been looted and – 'a typically short-sighted piece of folly' – Government seed stores. 'The very peasants who had taken part in the looting complained bitterly next year that they could get no seed.' But now reinforcements arrived of armed police and some troops, under the general control of Michael Nethersole, and in Benares the tide turned, and, as Edwardes had said in Peshawar, in May of 1857, 'friends were thick as summer flies now'.

In Ballia, however, a little north and west of Benares, things had been more dramatic. There was no Englishman in the place; Nigam, the District Magistrate, had lived through three years of Congress rule and knew the Congress would rule again. He knew that even if the Japanese did not win the war the English were committed to giving up more and more power. Lane and Finlay both felt the Congress had been mishandled; Nigam must have felt it more strongly. He carried out the arrests as he was told, just as Finlay had. Next day he, too, carefully forbore to disperse meetings or processions and thus give provocation. But on the third day of the trouble, Finlay, perceiving that this was really a rebellion, forbade meetings and dispersed them when they occurred; Nigam forbade them but did nothing when his orders were defied, and then, as things got worse, gave up all hope, released the prisoners from the jail as a gesture of appeasement and ordered the notes in the Treasury – £35,000 worth – to be burnt.

In Ballia town, nearly every Government building was destroyed, the damage including hospitals, dispensaries, seed stores and A.R.P. shelters; in the district two police-stations only remained intact. It should be mentioned that for seventy years Ballia had been a penal district; if a good officer was sent there, he was promised he need not stay long; more often the officer who came to Ballia had some misdemeanour to be forgiven. The district had hardly had a fair chance to form a good impression of British rule.

Lane ends his account of the rebellion with its effect on Europeans:

> Tolerance was rather at a discount; the ghastly fate of two Canadian Air Force officers who were almost literally torn to bits by a mob at a railway station in Behar was described more often than was necessary. Fear always breeds prejudice but we felt also a great measure of honest anger at the wanton damage, especially as it was impeding the war effort, and thus incidentally any hope India had of becoming free ... I freely confess that in those few months my own feeling towards Hindus became very far from charitable and it took me some time to recover.

Few people in the rest of India realized how serious the rebellion had almost been, but most Englishmen knew enough to share Lane's anger. From the more detached point of view of ten years later, one may feel that the Congress were fortunate in not achieving their aims.

2 The War in Burma

For a long time, Burma's chief political wish was to be unyoked from India. That had been achieved by the 1935 Act. But there were many Indians in Burma – and very unpopular they were, because they had come to do work the Burmese preferred to leave undone. And there were many of the Indian Civil Service. In the six months after Pearl Harbor, their daily life was a continuous and feverish improvisation. R. H. Hutchings, an I.C.S. officer from India, was sent to arrange the evacuation to India of those Indians who wanted to go – as most of them did, fearing the

Burmese at least as much as the Japanese. 'It is difficult', he wrote, 'for people who have not worked under war conditions to visualize what they mean in loss of time, lack of precision and demands on nervous energy ... nothing was simple, nothing was normal.' He never knew whether a letter or telegram would reach its destination. 'Every danger, every alarm, every inconvenience, made more refugees' – and made things more difficult for those improvising the exodus.

W. I. J. Wallace at the time of Pearl Harbor was Deputy Commissioner of Amherst district, with headquarters at Moulmein. There was no getting orders, once the invasion had started; a man had to decide what needed doing and do it himself. He had to improvise the means, using any man he could lay hands on. Wallace held charge of three districts in succession and then in three more helped as an additional District Magistrate. It was always possible, he explains, to move about the country with confidence. The people of Burma were even less inclined than Indians to regard the war as any business of theirs, but they 'were still the same people one had worked among for years, sympathetic and helpful, but bewildered and frightened, not treacherous. There was always the risk of air attack and much worse, towards the end of one's time in each district, the fear of being outflanked and killed or captured.'

Wallace had been in Amherst district two years when Pearl Harbor came, with orders, later cancelled, that in the event of invasion the Deputy Commissioner must stay with his people, to look after them under Japanese rule. From Moulmein, the wealthier Indians began to leave for home. 'Burmese, Mons and Karens simply melted into the surrounding countryside,' but special arrangements however had to be made for the Indians – and while Indians had no home in Burma to go to, they were some of them essential to the working of the ports.

The Burmese Ministers had seen no reason to resign as in the provinces of India; they had for some time been engaged in a wrangle with the Government of India about the Indians in Burma and were reluctant either to let them go or to admit that they were essential to the economy of the country. It was the part of Hutchings to play Moses to their Pharaoh, without the special powers of the original Moses. Early in February Wallace successfully passed on most of his Indians from Moulmein to Hutchings in Rangoon; he stayed behind and 'usually took charge in the Civil Defence control room at any hour of the day or night when the air raid siren went ... '

Tavoy, the next town down the coast, was captured in mid-January and with it the Japanese captured the Deputy Commissioner, who was interned till the end of the war. The next week, they were in the Amherst district; from Moulmein the women were evacuated. Only small staffs of essential services remained; the rest had been permitted to go – but 'a faithful few remained on my personal promise not to leave without them'.

Wallace paid visits to the telephone exchange and the telegraph office, the jail and the hospital, all mainly to encourage the staff. He was often at the headquarters of whatever military formation was in the neighbourhood, collected what news he could and passed it on to Rangoon, gave out three months' pay in advance to Government servants allowed to leave, distributed arms to trusted persons who were going to stay behind, spent hours fighting fires after each raid. In the last few hours he destroyed secret papers and codes, burned all the notes in the Treasury and dropped the coin in the river, and finally 'evacuated the faithful – the jail staff and convicts getting away in good order on the last afternoon when mortar shells were already falling in the town'. The Japanese were in Moulmein the next morning, which was January 31.

Wallace was then put in charge of Thaton, the next district. The air raid warning system had broken down here but it was essential to get it going again for the benefit of Rangoon. That was done. Then it was Amherst over again, building walls of sand against the tide.

Pegu, the third invasion district, was the same again, though here the 'heart-breaking problem' was crowds of Indians, setting out on the long journey to India; they were late in starting and 'the war was now close on their heels'.

Everything that was done was an improvised expedient, carried out with an improvised staff. In Mandalay, camps for thirty thousand people had been prepared, hastily and piecemeal; they were transit camps for people on their way north and they were kept filled. Cholera broke out. It became necessary to make fresh camps, move thirty thousand people into them – during the epidemic – and destroy the old camps. Mandalay had been raided and a great part of it burned to the ground. All the time, sick people had to be looked after, those who were fit must be fed, inoculated, and sent on their way, new people received daily. It was done; the camps were moved – all by a voluntary staff of forest officers, doctors, missionaries, school teachers and others.

One scene on the route, one of thousands, is recounted by Hutchings. A young Indian couple are on the road between Kalewa and Tamu. They have two children, a boy of six and a toddler of two. The wife is tired out. The husband takes the boy by the hand and the bundle on his back. He walks on, three or four hundred yards. Then, leaving the boy to rest and guard the bundle, he goes back for his wife. He picks up the child, gives her his arm, and helps her to where he left the boy. He has a hundred and fifty miles to cover to Tamu.

Gledhill, a judge, was in court at Mandalay when the first bombs fell. He sent off his staff to see what had happened to their relations and himself went to the stricken area. He found that the General Hospital had been put out of action and a great part of Mandalay was on fire. Many of the houses were of wood or of grass and bamboo and the fire was never really extinguished till the rains.

That afternoon Gledhill settled into his house, 'in addition to the refugees from Lower Burma I had left there that morning', a number of others, mostly Anglo-Burmans from the stricken area, and then set out on a tour of the town. 'It was decided that the corpses must be removed and with two wagons and some A.R.P. volunteers I set out on this grisly task. I remember the corpse of a pretty Anglo-Burmese girl with terrifying wide staring eyes lying beside the corpse of a grey-haired relative, a good easy Burman decapitated while sitting in a deck-chair under the trees . . . We hurriedly loaded our dreadful cargo and as the light faded directed the driver to the cemetery. The loading was bad but the unloading was too much for my stomach − and for others too.'

In between such duties as collecting corpses and paying out on behalf of the Treasury, Gledhill sat on courts martial and took out the fire brigade. At last he was told to go; he went up the river, loading boats with Indian refugees and distributing rations to them. Eventually he walked out by Tamu.

Gledhill asked the Government of Assam for work and, as they had plenty of judges, he became an Additional District Magistrate. After only six weeks, Gledhill moved on to Silchar, where he was himself Deputy Commissioner. Here his story merges in Assam's. But before going to Assam, mention must be made of Waterfall, Chief Commissioner of the Andaman and Nicobar Islands. The islands contained a convict settlement from India, a few police and jailers, and a company of British Infantry from Rangoon. In preparation for war, the garrison was withdrawn; Waterfall and his Deputy Commissioner, Radice, were left with an islandful of homicides in the face of the approaching Japanese. No help could be sent him; there was nothing to send. A moment came when he ordered Radice to leave, which he did, slipping down to a launch on the west coast of the island and making his way to India. Waterfall remained and was captured; he was in Japanese hands till the end of the war. A year later his execution was described in great detail by an eye-witness to a military intelligence officer, but in fact he survived, paying in full the penalty for his fidelity.

3 The War in Assam

Civilians in Assam and the eastern parts of Bengal were plunged into the war in a way that happened to no one else in India. They had a vital part to play in getting coolies to the airfields; as important were their doings among the tribes, the Nagas, the Lushai, the Kukis and the rest of those people of the hills between Burma and Assam.

The first encounters with these people had not been markedly success-ful. Since the days of Captain Butler, there had been many incidents when small parties had been attacked and murdered. But these had gradually become rarer; in every group of tribes, sooner or later, the Government yielded to the requests of local officers and decided that to keep the peace the hills must be taken over and some elementary administration introduced. One man would be sent up as the first Superintendent or Political Agent, with a platoon or two of riflemen; he would stay ten, fifteen or twenty years and set his mark on the country, as John Shakespear did among the Lushai. Head-hunting was stopped and raids on the plains, but not much else; it was a light and loose administration. The chiefs kept many powers; local customs which did not involve homicide were left undisturbed. Every officer who came to live among these people came to feel a warm affection for them and for their hills.

There was nothing aloof about camping among the tribes who used to be head-hunters. Lydall has described a tour meant to remind them that this practice was forbidden; he would ask conversationally whether they had taken any heads lately and they would deny the fact reproachfully – for they shared his own view that the question was in poor taste – and then he would give a gramophone recital. Another account speaks of waking in a Lushai village to the crowing of jungle-cocks; the writer is sleeping in a hut vacated by the owners for the night. He sees as he wakes the first light between the bamboo of the walls; the bearer comes with a mug of tea, but he is followed by the Chief and two or three Councillors with bottles of *zu* or rice beer. 'No self-respecting Chief will allow his District Officer to get up without a bottle of zu.'

It would be as well to start before the sun is hot. But the Chief has a message from his wife. She has prepared breakfast – rice, vegetables and goat. 'Such an invitation cannot be refused although you had a large dinner at the Chief's house last night.' The meal is a merry one; everyone in the village comes to the door and there are roars of laughter at clumsy attempts to eat rice with the fingers. It is no use trying to stop; hospitality demands that a guest should eat much more than his fill. Then a pipe must be smoked and at last it is time to start.

There is a walk of seven miles to the scene of a boundary dispute, 'down, down, down, a rough path full of loose stones; but the villagers lighten the way, shouting jokes to each other and singing the latest village songs'. There is the meeting with the people of the other village, the dispute itself, which concerns the identification of a stream and means of course another long descent; more zu; more hospitality, and at last the long climb to the village for the evening halt, where 'a great crowd of villagers is waiting you ... There is the inspection of the village records, a little amateur doctoring, of which quinine, aspirin and castor oil are the basis, at last a party, with singing and dancing and of course zu. The district officer too is expected to join in the dancing – but a time comes when he must get to sleep, leaving his people to dance insatiably all night.'

That account was written in 1946 but it was to the same idyllic world that war came in the summer of 1942. And everywhere the primitive tribes displayed a startling, a deeply moving, selflessness and loyalty. In the

Lushai Hills, McCall, who had been Superintendent for nine years, called the Chiefs together and asked them to join in a voluntary bond, signing a promise to join in a Total Defence Scheme for resistance to the Japanese. He explained the scheme at length; it involved guerrilla hostilities, abandoning villages, denying food and water to the invaders, laying booby-traps, destroying bridges, and supplying information to the British only. They were to choose whether or not they would join and he gave them till next day to decide, insisting that they should think it over and sleep on it. The chiefs elected enthusiastically to resist.

The area to be covered was nine thousand square miles. The people of every village arranged a secret hiding-place in thick jungle to which they could withdraw when the enemy came into their area. Secret stores of food were hidden; every village enlisted a band of young braves who prepared ambushes, blockades and stone-chutes. The Japanese made several attempts to enter these hills but met with such difficulties that they seem to have given up the idea.

There was no instance of a Lushai helping the enemy. McCall was transferred at the end of 1943 and his place taken by A. R. H. Macdonald, who almost at once had to put the scheme into force. The Japanese drive towards Kohima and Cachar began and Macdonald went to that part of the country and saw to it that Total Defence was a fact; then, with a force of Lushai braves, crossed into the Chin Hills by night and destroyed the ration dump which supplied the Japanese advanced patrols. Edgar Hyde, too, who had escaped from the Central Provinces, helped in the Lushai country and took over the southern half when it was found too much for one man to manage.

That summer of 1944 was a long-drawn Waterloo; for weeks, the Japanese attacked the British squares. At last a moment came when the attackers were exhausted and now came the moment to counter-attack and to sweep them back. One of those British squares — but they were Indian as much as British — was at Kohima and the other at Imphal. In each, a heavy burden fell on the civil administrator. Pawsey at Kohima, Gimson at Imphal, received from the hill tribes who surrounded them loyal and moving help.

Pawsey had charge of Kohima from the beginning of the retreat from Burma till the end of the Japanese thrust. He had Indian refugees to deal with, labour to find for airfields and roads in the slippery terrain of landslides, floods and earthquakes; mountainous; covered with jungle; swept by the heaviest rainfall in the world and inhabited by tribes who were animists and recently head-hunters. He found time too to go all over his part of the Naga Hills, not once but again and again, going into the villages and talking to the people.

You cannot hurry with such people. However desperate the need for time, you must explain slowly. To them time is not something to be 'saved' or 'wasted'. He had to get away from headquarters, where Brigadiers and

Deputy Assistant Adjutant Generals wanted things, where lawyers, Members of the Legislative Assembly and chairmen of village sanitation committees sat on his doorstep; he must get away from a life where every minute was precious, to eat oranges and drink zu with the Nagas and persuade them to do what he wanted. Intelligence was the first thing; the army found that until they had his direct help their system did not work among the Nagas. Guerrilla patrols, obstacles, raids on food dumps, these came next, and there were rewards for Japanese heads.

Gimson had meant to retire in 1938, but he was asked to come back as Political Agent in Manipur. This was a State, but rather an odd State; the Maharaja had to act in most things that concerned the Manipur Valley on the advice of a Council with a comparatively young I.C.S. officer as President. In the hills, the Nagas and Kukis and the rest, although the Maharaja's subjects, were administered by the President, who at the beginning of the war was T. A. Sharpe. Gimson met Pawsey once a year to compare notes; in 1941, their joint camp broke up on December 8 and that evening Gimson heard on the radio the news of Pearl Harbor.

From that moment 'things fairly hummed'. Refugees were the first problem; camps, tracks, sanitation, food for people coming out of Burma, all had to be improvised. Roads going into Burma were the next; military supplies would have to go in through the Manipur Valley to Tamu and a road must be built that would take military traffic. Labour for roads, labour for airfields; conferences of military officers – 'sometimes three or four going on at the same time, all of which I had to attend, and they lasted until midnight . . . Then in the small hours cipher telegrams which I had to decipher personally.'

Then came the main stream of refugees, a tale often told. At last, everyone thought the exodus was finished and they drew breath. 'But the Japs . . . did not want useless mouths so they sent Indians and Gurkhas across the river to find their way to India. They had no food . . . our nearest camps were three or four days' march away through almost uninhabited and malaria-infested jungle.' It was the monsoon; young children and nursing mothers had to make the journey. When they reached the first camp, most of them had dysentery, malaria or smallpox.

Chinese troops coming out of Burma were the next anxiety, but that paled after Imphal had been bombed; water and electric supplies were cut; the bazar was gutted by fire; 'human and animal corpses lay about for three or four days until we could organize squads to bury them'. Servants and clerks fled:

I am sure that no Political Agent has ever emptied so many commodes as I did in the next few days.

It was seven weeks before the clerks came back. They came in sackcloth and ashes, ashamed and penitent. I cursed them all . . . but was so glad to see them . . . that I could hardly keep a straight face . . . I promised never to taunt them if they behaved well in future and they did not let me down again . . . though the days of the invasion must have been a heavy trial.

Then came the siege, when the Japanese closed in on Imphal and the British and Indian forces kept them out. 'As the defences on the Western side were on the edge of the Residency garden I slept in my clothes for three weeks with a rifle by my side.' Then on June 22, 33 Corps joined up with 4 Corps and the siege was over.

The Nagas and the Kukis and other hill tribes had been heroes. 'They were magnificent,' wrote Gimson. 'Their devoted loyalty stood every strain. Even when the Japs occupied their villages, they co-operated with them as little as possible. Under compulsion, they gave food, shelter and labour, but information was reserved for us . . . A system of ground signals was developed by which Nagas indicated to the R.A.F. where Japs were camping. The people of one village . . . signalled to the R.A.F. to bomb their own village because the Japs were there.'

That might serve as the final verdict on the work for fifty years of Assam district officers.

4 Lambrick and the Hurs

At the other side of India in Sind, H. T. Lambrick was offered in March 1942 a task which might have fallen to Sleeman or Malcolm a hundred years before. He was given special powers in two districts and the task of restoring public confidence in an area almost abandoned by the well-disposed to a fanatical sect known as the Hurs.

Sind is full of hereditary saints, each descended from some famous Muslim of the past whose spiritual authority he inherits. One of these was the Pir Pagaro, an inner circle of whose disciples believed him to be incarnate God on earth. Obedience to him was the sole virtue. They were bound by fearful oaths at initiation and were completely oblivious of any moral standard but their own. These were the Hurs.

The reigning Pir had been tried for murder in 1930 but, though no one can doubt that he had instigated many murders, he was acquitted on a capital charge and sentenced on other charges to eight years' imprisonment. When his sentence expired, provincial autonomy was about to be introduced; everyone knew that in the elections of the spring of 1937 his followers would vote as he told them; candidates he did not approve might easily be murdered by his Hurs. He was therefore courted by political leaders and after the election his price had to be paid by the new Government. It involved the return of the more dangerous Hurs who had been exiled and the relaxation of control over the rest.

Since then things had been getting steadily worse. Violent crimes increased and the Pir began to quote an old prophecy which foretold that he would sit on the throne of Sind. Police were murdered, railways cut and finally the Chief of Police of the neighbouring State of Khairpur was attacked at night when encamped with a large force of armed police; he himself and a number of his men were killed.

There were by now half a dozen large bands of outlaws at work; the police were demoralized, peaceful people had left the area, Hindu villages, if not entirely evacuated, were paying blackmail to the Hurs; postmen, canal officials, keepers of land records, were threatened with death if they went on with their work; cultivation was at a standstill and the Hurs even demanded that taxes should be paid to them instead of to the Government.

The first thing, Lambrick decided, was to restore police morale and end the defeatist attitude of the villagers who were not Hurs; to do this, he must get the police out of their police-stations and lead them to the attack. Night patrols, ambushes, almost anything to attack the Hurs, to keep them on the move and to show that there were still Government forces in being – these were the beginning.

Arms and ammunition not securely held were a danger, inviting attack; these were called in. Next came the rounding up of eight hundred prominent Hurs not yet outlawed or in hiding but known to operate occasionally with the gangs. Detachments from the Frontier Constabulary and the Zhob Militia came to strengthen Lambrick's forces; the Sind Horse, who served Jacob so well, were now regulars and armed with tanks. Three flying columns were organized, each with its own Intelligence staff, with its own guides and trackers. Each was to move swiftly here and there, with no prepared programme, striking wherever they believed there was a chance of meeting the Hurs in the field and beating them.

Before this could happen, one band of Hurs derailed and looted the Lahore Mail, killing many of the passengers who survived the accident. Part of this gang was caught by one of the three flying columns; meanwhile Lambrick was marching, with a small force of Frontier Constabulary mounted on camels, towards a point thirty miles into the Desert where he had heard that two gangs were to rendezvous.

We marched all night and the following day routed one small party, inflicting casualties, but this delayed us and we were compelled to bivouac some miles short of our objective. We had arranged for a supporting force to follow but before it joined us a night attack was made on my party, while a sandstorm was blowing, by a gang which outnumbered us by about three to one. Our police picket was overwhelmed, the majority being killed or wounded ... but the Frontier Constabulary with admirable coolness repulsed the enemy, inflicting heavy loss ... This expedition was certainly a rash one, but in my view justified, for the moral effect of penetrating the Hurs' most difficult country to fight them.

The derailment of the Lahore Mail persuaded the Government of India to train some young troops in the area. First a brigade was sent; later the strength was increased to that of a division; martial law was proclaimed and Lambrick became Civil Adviser to the military Administrator. Twelve months later, the resistance no longer required military action; Lambrick however remained as Special Commissioner for the Eastern half of Sind, with very extensive powers, for three more years.

This Rebellion was directed against the Government, not because it was British – which indeed the Government of Sind could hardly now be called – but because it was opposed to the Pir Pagaro. But its place in this book is to complete a series. Lambrick may fall in beside Sleeman and Jacob; he fought under the same colours and in the same war. And he developed just the same affectionate, fascinated personal regard as they had done for the men he was hunting.

5 The War at the Centre

While Lambrick chased Hurs in Sind and Macdonald blew up an enemy food dump in the Lushai Hills, most men continued their usual work in conditions steadily deteriorating. Many had to learn new tasks, and all added to the normal district work. Air Raid Precautions, Food Rationing, Cloth Rationing – they were all new to India. But the men who did this work enjoyed it. Lines, who was moved some time after the 1942 rebellion to the district which includes Jamshedpur, Tata's great steel city, revelled in the contrast between this modern industrial district and his tours among the Hos. The Hos were cousins of the Sonthals and had been in India before the Hindus. Lines enjoyed 'meeting the friendly carefree aboriginals, visiting their clean attractive villages with their gaily patterned and painted houses, watching the extremely beautiful dances, learning their songs and folklore, tasting their beer – ' and all this derived an additional relish from his ordinary life 'in the great cosmopolitan city

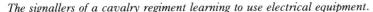

The signallers of a cavalry regiment learning to use electrical equipment.

of Jamshedpur. Tata's steelworks, covering 11 square miles, employing close on 40,000 men, pouring forth more steel in a year than any other steel works outside the U.S.A., with a metallurgical laboratory claimed to be as good as any in the world; tin-plate works employing 6,000 men; A.R.P. as concentrated as anywhere in India; a constant stream of visitors from all parts of the world, generals, industrialists, religious leaders, Governors, Tibetans, members of the British Parliament, Indian political leaders, trade union leaders, all to be met by the Deputy Commissioner.'

Or hear Lane, now with five years' service, as Regional Food Controller in Meerut. 'It was an entirely new kind of job, without precedent and without a book of the rules. It was therefore of absorbing interest and kept me constantly busy.' That is the authentic voice of the service. 'New methods of control, new laws and regulations naturally led to new forms of graft and corruption ... Control was piled on control,' he writes, 'and regulation on regulation; all this led to a mass of paper work which in more organized countries is channelled through many different officials but in India all had to go through the district officer. It was all they could do to keep the wheels from getting clogged and they had no time for keeping in touch with public opinion.'

In Delhi, work covered the same kind of subjects as in Whitehall, but it was dealt with in a different way, because everyone who mattered still knew everyone else and the Secretaries to Government still had direct access to the Viceroy. There was still a distinction between matters of pure administration and those with political implications which must go to Council.

There came a stage when it seemed the war was falling into two halves, when communication with England was possible only by wireless and there was a likelihood that even that might be seriously interrupted. The Eastern Group of territories – India, Australia, Africa and New Zealand – therefore had to become self-supporting in supplies. Delhi was the centre of the Eastern Group and Jenkins in the Supply Department held perhaps as important a post for the war's issue as any man could hold. But

Recruiting for the Indian Army. The Indian Army expanded during the First World War from 200,000 to 2,500,000, the largest army ever raised without conscription. This recruit is getting an advance of pay from an Indian Captain.

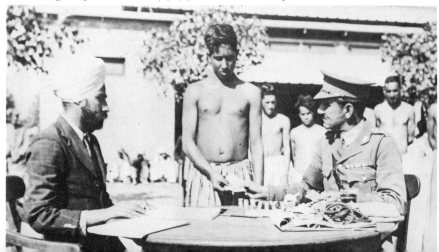

the whole tale of shells, tents, boots, rifles, guns, foodstuffs, will not be told here. It is enough to indicate the scale. The Indian Army expanded from less than 200,000 to 2,500,000, the biggest army ever raised without conscription. In 1943, 113 million garments were made; altogether 50 million pairs of boots were made. And there were delicate things such as surgical equipment and electric apparatus – heavy things such as floating docks, ships and cranes – few of which had been made before in India. It was the last effort of the old administration, now fast running down. It is enough to say that there were a handful of men – Dow, Jenkins, Hydari, Coates, Wood, Hutchings, Trivedi – with the ability to work the system in wartime.

6 The Bengal Famine

Something must be said of the Bengal Famine, which was a failure of the administration in transition. Under the old system famine had been recognized as endemic and there were schemes which could be put into effect as soon as scarcity began. The last famine under the old system had been in the U.P. in 1908; then there had been eleven deaths directly attributable to famine. The death rate was above the ten-year average only in four months out of the twelve.

But in the last months of 1942 and the first half of 1943 Indian newspapers showed photographs of women and children dying of hunger in the streets of Calcutta. The number of deaths in Bengal in 1943 went above the five-yearly average by 689,000. Some of those extra deaths were directly due to hunger and most were indirectly the result of malnutrition. There were 60,000,000 people in Bengal; the extra deaths in that year were more than ten in every thousand.

This was not famine on the scale of the old famines of 1770 and before, when vast stretches of land had gone out of cultivation for lack of people to till it; in 1943 and 1944 – for two years in succession – there was an increase of several hundred thousand acres under the plough. But statistics carry no weight when you have seen children's bones showing through their skin; daily in the towns of Bengal there were heart-rending sights, a shame and a reproach to men of English blood. It was much worse than anything under the pure administrative system since 1866.

There had been no serious failure of the monsoon; the crop in 1942 was only a little less than usual. Supply fell short by three weeks only. But there was no rationing scheme; and in Calcutta about two million out of four were protected and fed by their employers. The whole of the shortage fell on those who were left and for them it was much more than a shortage of three weeks' supply in fifty-two.

Rice from Burma normally made a reserve for Calcutta. In 1943, Burma was cut off. Even so, there would have been enough rice to keep the province in health if it had been properly distributed. A cut of three in fifty is not one that cannot be borne. But distribution was more rigid than usual because boats and wheeled vehicles had been removed from the coastal areas in case of Japanese invasion. And the authorities were late in realizing how bad things were. When they did begin to realize what might be coming, they were faced with a problem that would not have been easy even if the machinery of government had been as taut and as delicate as in 1908.

But it was nothing of the kind. Ministries in Bengal since 1937 had been coalitions, contrived by elaborate personal intrigue. Ministers had to spend much of their energies keeping their places; they had less time than their predecessors for administration.

District officers and the Secretariat were overworked – and while the Provincial Government were busy maintaining themselves, the Government of India were thinking of the war. The Provincial Government were reluctant to admit the seriousness of the situation, to ask for help or to receive advice. The Government of India, even if fully aware of what was happening, could no longer give orders to an autonomous province with an elected ministry. The Viceroy could, in exercise of his special powers, in the last resort override the ministry, and so could the Governor, but only when all else failed. Prices rose steadily. In the ten years before the war, the price of 80 lb. of rice had varied between three and five rupees, usually being nearer three. In January 1943, the price for 80 lb. varied between ten rupees and fourteen; in May it was hard to get any for thirty rupees and soon it changed hands at fifty. There were daily articles on the deaths in the Calcutta streets. But it did not appear to the public that the Viceroy took any action until October 1943 when Lord Wavell went to Calcutta to see things for himself, and ordered the army's great machine to distribute supplies.

left, Lord Wavell and Sir Evan Jenkins at a free kitchen in the Calcutta famine of 1944. Most civilians had believed that careful administration had beaten famine by 1914. But careful administration had become subordinate to politics, responsibility was blurred, and famine reappeared in 1944; right, Mahatma Gandhi leaving Viceregal Lodge in a Viceregal Car, 11 June 1945. The symbol of nationalism is the symbol of pomp and imperialism.

The causes were complex. It was not that the defence forces had bought up all the grain; they did in fact buy very little in Bengal. It was not simply that imports from Burma had stopped; the effect of that was more psychological than economic. It was not simply that transport had been removed from the coastal areas. More than anything else, it was due to panic and to divided control.

At a time when the administration was strained by war and weakened by political experiment, a harvest rather below average started a rise in price. In ordinary times, it would have lasted a few weeks and then rice from somewhere else would have come in. But now there was nowhere else for rice to come from and the air was full of rumours; the Japanese were coming, the English were going, Calcutta was being bombed, all the ships on the sea were being sunk, Burma and its rice were lost, it would soon be every man for himself. To everyone who had money, it seemed that it would be a good thing to buy rice. And a great many people had money. There had been war contracts and compensation had been paid for carts and boats taken up as a precaution against Japanese invasion. Much of that compensation went into rice.

And as prices rose, panic increased and more and more rushed to buy. There was no clear or firm handling from the centre; there were no instructions from the Provincial Government. District officers, jealous for their own charges, forbade the export of grain; neighbouring provinces did the same. In Bengal, there was little grain in the markets and that at a price too high for any but the rich. The rice-growers had enough; the rich had enough. Most of the town middle-classes had seen what was coming in time and bought early. The industrial worker had grain supplied him by his factory. But the casual labourers who bought day by day had nothing; landless labourers from the villages sometimes had nothing and flocked to the towns. It was an urban famine, and that was one thing that made it so shocking; the casualties were concentrated where they could be seen.

The Ministry formed a food department in Calcutta in the autumn of 1942, but it began slowly with no Government drive behind it; by the time it got under way there was no rice to buy. Most of the world's rice is grown in the parts of South-East Asia which the Japanese held. And rice-eaters will not eat wheat.

Everyone was overworked, preoccupied, slow to see what was happening. The Provincial Government pretended they had no real power; the Central Government said the whole business was the Provincial Government's responsibility. Neither can avoid a share of blame. Responsibility was blurred; neither Englishman nor Indian felt it was his failure but the other man's when he saw a pregnant woman lying dead of starvation in the streets. It was high time for responsibility to be clearly fixed. And the English for some time had been moving along a road on which there was no going back; they must go forward; that meant they must leave India.

21
THE END

―――――――――

'Most sensitive Indians', writes Lane, 'looked on victory not as the end of anything but as the beginning of a vast forward movement.'

It was true, and it bred a certain resentment in the English. 'If we had not concentrated on winning the war, you would not be making your plans for freedom,' was the feeling in some English minds. And a reciprocal irritation was present on the Indian side, because the English were not eager to share in plans for a new India. Plans – if they are to be realistic – must be made by the people who are going to carry them out. Almost everyone in the Service now pictured an independent India and few believed that it could rightly hold a place for themselves. They must think of where to live in England and how to educate the children. Yet, distracted by such thoughts as these, tired by the war years, they must still hold on to their districts in a world in which the old bluff hardly held good any longer. If after all it was true that the English really were going, the District Magistrate had nothing to offer, either as reward or punishment, and the quicker he made way for someone with real power the better.

Everyone then, English or Indian – and by now the Service was almost half Indian – was thinking of what was to come next. Hardly anyone in 1946 was giving his heart and soul to the task of the moment. No one, however, thought the end would come quite so soon as in fact it did. The change of Viceroys was announced in February 1947; in August 1947 came the end of British rule.

It is perhaps illogical to be so resolute in war as the English have shown themselves for some six or seven centuries and yet so concerned about human life in times of peace. Whether because they have become accustomed over the centuries to being a small people in a small island, or whether because they are at heart more Christian than they suppose, the English do still think an individual life is important.

But there was another view. 'We are a nation of ninety million Muslims,' a Muslim, later President of Pakistan, said to me in 1946, 'what does it

25 above, 'Loyal Sepoys at Target Practice'. It was often forgotten how many sepoys remained faithful to their Colours; 26 below, 'Troops of the Native Armies'. G. F. Atkinson, the author of Curry and Rice, published in 1859 this unflattering impression of some of the troops sent by native states to help their British allies.

27 left, *Delhi Durbar: 1901. The Retainers' Procession: Lord Curzon designed every detail of the procession and lost no opportunity of including the picturesque; 28 below, The Maharajah of Patiala in the Delhi Durbar. Patiala was one of the Sikh States and the young Maharajah was one of the Imperial Cadets.*

matter if we lose ten million to gain our freedom? There will be eighty million of us left.' That is a way of seeing life that may seem natural to those sprung from the teeming loins of Asia or Germany; it was not the way the Indian Civil Service had been trained to look at things. When in 1931 four hundred lives were lost in the Cawnpore riots, the District Magistrate's career was finished; it was a disaster. As near as could be, in a country with some four hundred million inhabitants, the English had tried to ensure that no one should fall to the ground by violence without an inquiry and a report to Government. It had been the first maxim of the English that there should be no interference with religion, but that was overridden where homicide was involved; they had interfered even with customs sanctioned by religion – to save widows from the pyre, travellers from the noose, and infant daughters from suffocation.

To the Viceroy and to his official advisers it had been a cardinal principle to avoid loss of life. There were other considerations too. No political party in England was prepared to use force on a large scale to enforce a settlement on any considerable section of the people. It was out of the question to fight for the subjugation of India and just as unthinkable to force Muslims to submit to Hindus. That was a pivot on which all thought had to turn. On the other hand, we had given India political unity and we wished to preserve our handiwork. Nor could we lightly abandon interests which had on the whole supported British rule – the Princes, the depressed classes, the aboriginals, the planters – all the minorities who anxiously claimed some special protection. And we wanted to hand over power to someone who could keep the country stable.

This made a complex position from which to bargain. And until Mountbatten, no Viceroy had a free hand – while the Congress and the Muslim League were unhampered.

To simplify is always to falsify. But it is only by simplification that action is achieved. For years the problem of handing over power had been clogged by detail and the scrupulous assumptions that everyone must be protected, unity must be preserved and life must not be lost. It required great courage to disregard the scruples and simply let go. It was dangerous and courageous; it was the right thing to do.

This was a shock to many who had once been Guardians. They saw the price paid and not all saw that without the price the disengagement was impossible. Nor did all of them perceive that the price grew with delay. It is only necessary to count the dead, month by month, from the day of Germany's defeat to see how true this was. It had to be done quickly. In England it was believed that the Congress was in danger of disintegration, that India was in danger of falling into the hands of the Communists. This was not so. But bitterness was growing day by day.

Need the price have been so high? Unity, the minorities, the preservation of life – on all three counts the bill was a large one. But Pakistanis today are adamant that any hope of unity was lost as far back as 1919, when

337

Mr Gandhi decided not to co-operate in the reforms and instead to win his movement backing by appealing to the religious emotions of the Hindu peasantry.

Unity was part of the price and the Princes also were sacrificed. No doubt it was deplorable that there was no democratic constitution in Hyderabad State, but His Exalted Highness the Nizam had for nearly two centuries proudly styled himself Faithful Ally of the British Government and until the spring of 1947 his affairs had been partly controlled by his faithful allies. The same applied in some degree to every Prince; now all were told, surely with either cynicism or pedantic blindness, that they were free to make such terms as they chose with whom they liked. 'Paramountcy is not transferable', – that was the cry raised. But paramountcy was a concept invented to describe the relationship between the English Crown and the Princes; it had been invented to fit circumstances and it could, surely, be modified to fit new circumstances. The phrase was meaningless jargon. Paramountcy in fact *was* transferred. No State except Kashmir had any choice; the rest had to make terms with a more powerful neighbour. It would surely have been more realistic, more just and more honest to direct that transfer of paramountcy.

Nor is it surprising that there should have been sadness and shock among men who had worked in the Punjab. In that province, there was just – but only just – a Muslim majority over Sikhs and Hindus together. It had therefore been the ideal of the Unionist party to maintain a united Punjab under a Government in which a Muslim should lead, but Sikhs and Hindus should be represented by ministers. It was inevitable that British officials should sympathize with such aims and try to avoid a situation in which all the Muslims should be in one party and everyone else in the other. This was avoided until early in March of 1947, when events forced zealotry on one moderate Muslim after another and the last remnant of the Unionist Muslims resigned from office. The Muslim League could not quite command a majority in the Assembly and did not wish to take office; the Governor, Sir Evan Jenkins, had to assume personal charge. He was faced with that division of the Punjab on clean-cut communal lines – Muslim against Hindu and Sikh – that had always been regarded as the most dangerous possible contingency.

No one knew how many had been killed in the rioting of August 1946 in Calcutta; an estimate had been four thousand but there were perhaps many more. There had followed the killings of Hindus in East Bengal and of Muslims in Behar; in the United Provinces again there had broken out a pointless, senseless slaughter. There was fear of the unknown on both sides; it would suddenly flare up. In ordinary communal trouble there were usually points to guard, some point of focus, a mosque or a temple or a pipal tree. In a city, main thoroughfares could be patrolled. But this new horror was unaccountable; no one could foretell where it would come next. In a village where Hindus and Muslims had lived peacefully side by side for centuries, sudden fear would blaze up and the weaker would be slaughtered with every kind of barbarity, babies being killed before their mother's eyes, women and children burnt in their huts. No district officer could prevent it by force unless he could station a platoon in every village.

The tale of deaths had been mounting steadily. In March 1947, it spread to the Punjab and here it was worse; here the numbers were evenly matched and here there was real ground for fighting. If it was possible to wipe out the Sikhs and Hindus in Lahore, then the Muslims would be unquestioned masters of the city.

The first outbreaks in March were brought under control; there followed a lull and then a communal war of succession which lasted until the British had gone. In June it was announced that the date on which power would be handed over was August 15, 1947, that there would be two successor states and that the Punjab would be divided. It was a province of thirty million virile and warlike people; the long discussion had whipped them into a state of religious frenzy. They had been told that the authority which had held the ring for a century was going almost immediately, that their province would be divided into two parts by a boundary driven through an area homogeneous in everything but religion, a boundary which would probably convert its two principal cities into frontier towns. It was not surprising that there should be disorder.

By early August, it was reckoned that five thousand people in the Punjab had been killed and three thousand seriously injured since the beginning of March; the number of people homeless as a result of arson no one tried to estimate. These figures were shocking but there was evidence that many people in the Punjab were preparing for August 15 as a day of reckoning that would far surpass anything that had so far occurred. That was in fact the case. On that day of anger, slaughter began. It went on and on. No one knows how many were killed; one estimate is half a million dead and twelve million homeless.

It was a time when, to villagers of the Punjab, and to those soldiers and policemen who never ceased to be villagers, it must have seemed that heaven and earth were moving. Every party of refugees had to face the risk at every moment of attack by armed men who, when they did attack, slew without mercy. The men of the Indian Army did not know what was happening in their own villages. They had seen blackened ruins around them, desolate mud walls standing in the ashes of their own thatch with the corpses heaped in the yard. They could only guess what things were like at home. In that hour, when all they knew was failing, one thing stood firm – though only just – the discipline of the Indian Army.

That slaughter was one reason why some men left with a feeling that their life's work had been wasted. It is not easy to look at things with cool detachment when you have spent your life trying to prevent bloodshed and leave the scene of your work with corpses piled indiscriminately shoulder-high at your garden gate. The Congress suggested, before the day of anger, that British officers in the Punjab were stirring up trouble themselves in their own districts – a thing which in his own interest anyone but a lunatic would avoid – and that they were doing this in the interest of the Muslims. The Muslims were not behindhand with the reverse allegation. Since both sides brought the same charges, one may suppose that impartiality was maintained.

A charge was brought too that in those last months British officers were indifferent to what became of their districts. This requires two comments. First, it had long been the practice to post British officers to the storm-centres where riot was likely, because it was much easier for a British officer than for an Indian to maintain a middle course between Sikh and Muslim. When riots came, they came where they were expected, that is to say, where there were British officers. Secondly, to deal with a riot takes the courage which comes of confidence. And in those last two or three months, confidence was impaired.

Officers had been used to carrying out the partition of a peasant's holding between his sons. The quality of the soil in every field, the flavour of the fruit on every tree, would be discussed and weighed and, at last after many hearings, a balance struck in which all these things, as well as area, were meticulously taken into account. Now they saw a mighty empire divided with little attention to the interests of the parties. All their experience seemed to be ignored. In such circumstances, a man might well hesitate before taking that robust action which might avert calamity but might also be pilloried as brutality.

Wherever blame lies, trains rolled into Delhi and into Lahore loaded with the dead. No wonder that there were heavy hearts. Men left the Punjab with pistols cocked, ready if need be to fight during their last train journey in India, and probably not for themselves but for some carriage-load of defenceless folk who might otherwise be slaughtered on the way.

It was not so in most of India and for most men feelings were far from simple. One young man wrote:

> I will not dilate upon the personal distress of this uprooting, since it was only a distress of my own mind and I suppose selfish, not to be compared with the trials of our colleagues in the Punjab and Bengal, still less with the ghastly experiences of the minorities in those Provinces. Enough that though I felt it my duty to leave India, I shall never cease to yearn for another glimpse of a land that gave me so much happiness.

There were older men who found their thoughts turning to the past, to the blood that had been shed so liberally to win what was now given away. In such a mood, the mind might dwell on the bullet-pitted walls of the Residency, on the moment of decision at Assaye, on the countless days and nights of toil and danger, the sweat and anxiety that had gone to bridge a river, to break a dacoit, to bring home the mean murder of some

Sir Maharaj Singh (Harrow, Balliol and Indian Civil Service), Governor of Bombay, at the march past of the Somerset Light Infantry, the last British troops in India.

defenceless woman, or to the more prosaic task of simply ensuring that each man's field was properly entered in the papers.

There was a mood of lonely wakefulness in which the two million English graves that marked that immense effort seemed wasted. But in the daytime, it would be clear that the effort was neither ended nor wasted, that what had been done was its own reward. And there were Indians in the services who, in their own way, not as mere imitators, would continue what had been begun.

A few stayed, a very few, both in India and Pakistan, but most felt that to stay could only blur responsibility. Once that decision was taken, there were practical things to think of, passports and visas, packing and passages, where to live and how to earn enough to educate the children. Beneath were regrets for chances missed and things not done, friendships not pursued and letters left unanswered – all the sadness of leaving, and the sadness double when opportunity has been so great and the little done so little. The faces that came to the window of the railway carriage and that came back in dreams to most were the faces of simple people, servants and orderlies, people who had worked cheerfully and not always very efficiently for very little, who had perhaps brought a cup of tea every morning, had stood gravely by the bedside in sickness, had perhaps told of a child's death with choked utterance. For others the memory was of bewildered voices asking for help that could not be given.

That was sentimentality to be firmly repressed. And if – as he bent once more to the luggage labels with eyes a little blurred – his thoughts could not be controlled and he must look back, hardly one man would have chosen his life differently. As to whether the job had been well done, that was a question time alone could settle. It was something that the two dominions did not want to leave that odd association of peoples that had once been called the British Empire.

341

It had been a long journey since Hawkins had landed and the subjects of the Great Mogul had made him welcome 'after their barbarous fashion'. Varied and often inconsequent it had seemed but it ended in a mood of astonished warmth on one side, of wry relief on the other, both expressed with dignity.

Let the formal events be formally recorded. On February 28, 1948, the farewell parade to the last British troops in India was commanded by Lieutenant-Colonel Prithi Pal Singh of The Sikh Regiment. The 1st Battalion of The Somerset Light Infantry, the last British troops in India, bear on their cap badges the word *Jellalabad*, in memory of the illustrious garrison of which they had been a part in the least just of British wars, a hundred years before. On this last parade, they were presented with a silver model of the Gateway of India, with an inscription 'to commemorate the comradeship of the soldiers of the British and Indian Armies', and the dates – 1754–1947. The date looked back to the arrival of the battalion that was later the 1st Battalion of the Dorsetshire Regiment, – *Primus in Indis*. Indian Guards of Honour from the Indian Grenadiers, The Maratha Light Infantry, The 2nd Royal Battalion, The Sikh Regiment and The 5th Royal Gurkha Rifles, presented arms in a Royal Salute; the bands played *God Save the King*; The Somerset Light Infantry presented arms in a Royal Salute and the bands played *Bande Mataram*, which six years before had been the rallying song of insurrection; the King's Colour and the Regimental Colour were trooped through the Gateway of India, the bands playing *Auld Lang Syne*.

It was over. The long years of partnership and strife were ended and divorce pronounced.

March past of the 1st Battalion: The Somerset Light Infantry, to the strains of Auld Lang Syne. Men of the regiment bore on their cap badge the word Jellalabad, in memory of the illustrious garrison of which they had been a part in the least just of British wars, a hundred years before.

EPILOGUE

The curtain has fallen but it is a civilized custom to drink a glass of wine with a friend and discuss the play before going home. Was it tragedy or triumph, bitter and meaningless or insipid and flat? Would other actors have played it better?

Look back to Akbar's three aims, a united people, a stable treasury and a stable peasantry. All three seemed at one time in sight, but now unity has gone, the second and the third are precarious. Look to another aim, glimpsed by Munro and Elphinstone, by Macaulay and the Act of 1833, explicitly proclaimed in 1917 – and it is clear that the change from government *for* Indians to government *by* Indians has been carried through successfully. As to the ultimate value of the whole incursion, not perhaps for two centuries will it be possible to judge whether English ideas have bred with Indian as Roman did with Gaulish.

On the surface, much remains. In Delhi, Karachi and Lahore, bugles call you from sleep as they did in Kitchener's time. In the Shalimar Gardens or the Red Fort, you will see the Pipe-Major swagger before his men in Campbell tartan or Royal Stuart and toss his baton with the old assured arrogance; you will see pipe banners gay with the arms of officers long dead, *pagris* as stiffly starched and spats as immaculately pipe-clayed as before. The precise movements of ceremonial drill, the wording of a legal document, a judge's assumption that his word will bind a government to whom it is unwelcome, a parliamentarian's deference to the Speaker – all these are still there and may last. They may even survive a formal abandonment of all links with the Commonwealth, as things English and Spanish have survived in the Americas.

Goodwill and kindly feelings are another matter, a volatile and perishable commodity. Soon after the Kaiser's War, a brigand made himself famous throughout the United Provinces and far into Behar and the Punjab. He left few women unviolated and no man alive to give evidence against him in the villages he raided. He was feared and hated; in the end,

343

he was hunted down and caught by a policeman whom everyone knew as Freddy Young. There was a play called *Sultana Daku*, a favourite at fairs all through Northern India, in which at first Freddy Young was the avenging hero and the crowd cheered when the villainous Sultana was brought to book. But as the play was repeated year by year the parts were reversed, until Sultana was the hero, a gallant Robin Hood who befriended the poor and robbed the English, while Freddy Young became the comic villain, fat and cowardly, continually calling for whisky.

For Tod and Sleeman, for Malcolm and Munro, in the 1820s — when the memory of anarchy was fresh — Indians of all classes felt respect and even affection. Even at the end of the nineteenth century, Nirad C. Chaudhuri has described, in his *Autobiography of an Unknown Indian*, his impression, while he was growing up, that there was a protecting Government who would always look after the people. 'Overhead there appeared to be, coinciding with the sky, an immutable sphere of justice and order, brooding sleeplessly over what was happening below.' But that feeling 'vanished at one stroke with the coming of the nationalist agitation in 1905', Chaudhuri wrote. It was not however Freddy Young the policeman who had changed. India had changed; India had outgrown the system.

The times had changed and in the twentieth century something more was needed than a rule that was just, impartial, benevolent and considerate. India was passing through three revolutions at the same time, social, industrial and political. And in revolutions there is no room for impartial leaders. India now needed a leader of her own people, a partisan with strong, indeed violent, views on such questions as child-marriage, industrial slums and manhood suffrage.

Let us accept then without more ado that the system of rule by foreign Guardians was a temporary expedient. It was a Trust, held until India was ready for the English to go, as Munro and Elphinstone had recognized. At its best, some three hundred million people were ruled by a body of never more than twelve hundred picked men, with some fifty thousand British troops behind them. It was a bluff, which worked because the administration was light. It was much more just than any the people had known before, and it brought a tranquillity and prosperity they had not known for centuries. The system was sometimes referred to in the 1920s and 1930s as a steel frame. But it was really more like a weaverbird's nest than a steel frame. All kinds of odd fragments were woven into the fabric, things found on the spot and made use of because they worked.

The men sent from Britain to rule India had often been brilliantly successful with such people as the Hos, the Nagas and the Lushai. They had liked simple people; they had done well with peasants, soldiers and servants. They had not been so successful with the new kind of Indian educated in Western ways. But from the time of Elphinstone and Macaulay they had recognized the need for Western education and later they had accepted the fact that the service was to be Indianized.

It was said that they were aloof. Perhaps they were. They did not marry in India, they retired to England. And India – like the African possessions of the Crown – was governed as a separate entity, not as part of metropolitan England. The French and Portuguese possessions beyond the seas were, on the other hand, parts of metropolitan France and Portugal. It was surely one consequence of this separate organization that the last British troops left India with a dignity in sharp contrast with the French departure from Indo-China. And the aloofness of the Guardians too was an asset when the time came to go. How much more difficult it would have been if, as Lord Roberts and Kipling had wished, Kashmir had been made into an Asian Rhodesia, peopled with retired British soldiers!

The East India Company had served a useful purpose as a device for insulating the administration of India from the more sordid squabbles of Whig and Tory. What is more, it had bequeathed to the Crown an incomparable instrument for government, a civil service 'minutely just, inflexibly upright', well enough paid to be above corruption, independent and confident because assured of a career that could only be interrupted by gross misconduct. This instrument was forged by the East India Company long before Whitehall possessed anything of the kind.

The administration in India had the immense advantage over those in the later African territories that it was possible to set up the framework of government before the invention of the electric telegraph and close control

Fourteen years after independence, tribesmen in Peshawar bring sheep as tribute to the Queen.

from England. Use was made of Akbar's machinery and whatever local institutions could be adapted. The whole was controlled by a cadre of district officers, rigorously picked, but trained almost wholly by doing what in fact they were learning to do. Because they were so few they had to let their subordinates do their own work. Confidence that they would be backed up from above was the hall-mark of their profession and they acquired a confidence in themselves and a confidence that they would be obeyed, which meant that they *were* obeyed. Few administrations can have ruled so many with so slight a use of force. Everything was done through Indians and by Indians to whom power was delegated.

No greater Englishman than Warren Hastings ever ruled in India; it had been his ideal to influence without direct rule. But though indirect rule may be well suited to a primitive people, who, once they have passed beneath the yoke, are ready to accept the ways of their conquerors, it is surely hardly enough to awaken to new life a people possessing an ancient and complex civilization which has ceased to develop, who are highly contemptuous of foreigners and foreign ways. Gaul and Britain could be Romanized by indirect rule but not Judea, Hellas or Egypt. Indirect rule may suit Africa but it would have been likely to leave Bengal stagnant.

It is by the new spirit which it awakens that a foreign conquest is justified. Voltaire atones for the wrongs of Vercingetorix and it is by the new vigour of India and Pakistan that the old system must be judged.

In the last stage, Indian nationalism throve on a repression which it would hardly have received from an indirect system. That it throve in unexpected ways is surely a sign of health. The English were not permitted to play the part for which they had cast themselves. Instead of becoming the kindly and paternal guides of a people meekly content to imitate, they were directed in the last stage to perform the more stimulating and creative – if less pleasant – function of a counter-irritant, a moral mustard-plaster, which restored the circulation and began a brisk reaction.

It was a Platonic empire. The best thinkers among the English in India, the most far-sighted politicians in Whitehall, had always looked forward to a day when the work would be complete, when the English would go. They had consciously professed to provide rulers who would be Platonic Guardians, sheep-dogs not wolves.

When all has been said, one simple point remains. It was put clearly by Lord Wavell in an informal speech made after he left India. The English would be remembered, he believed, not by this institution or that, but by the ideal they left behind of what a district officer should be. At the other end of the long line, Warren Hastings had expressed a similar thought. 'It is on the virtue,' he had said, 'not the ability, of their servants that the Company must rely.' And if today the Indian peasant looks to the new district officer of his own race with the expectation of receiving justice and sympathy, that is the memorial of the English.

NOTES ON THE AUTHORITIES

The list that follows is meant only to indicate the books I used most for the first edition and to acknowledge the original manuscripts and notes lent to me:

PART I

The First Letter Book of the East India Company, 1600–1619: Letters Received, 1602–1613: Early Travels in India, 1583–1619, ed. W. Foster, Humphrey Milford: *The Embassy of Sir Thomas Roe*, Hakluyt Society: *Travels in Mogul India*, Bernier, Humphrey Milford: *Rise and Fulfilment of British Power in India*, Thompson and Garratt: *A History of England from the defeat of the Armada to the death of Elizabeth*, Edward P. Cheyney: *India at the death of Akbar, From Akbar to Aurangzebe* and *Agrarian Systems of Moslem India*, W. H. Moreland: *The Economic History of England*, Lipson: *Travels of Peter Mundy*, Hakluyt Society: *Akbar*, Vincent Smith: *Akbar*, Laurence Binyon: *Albuquerque*, Rulers of India series: *Early Records of British India*, Talboys Wheeler: *Keigwin's Rebellion*, Ray and Oliver Strachey: *The History of India as told by its own Historians*, Elliott & Dowson: travels of de Mandelslo, Fryer & Hedges: unpublished papers of the 1680 volume of the English Factories series: *New Account of the East Indies*, Hamilton: Diary and Papers of Streynsham Master: *The Life of Lord Clive*, Sir George Forrest, also lives by Sir J. Malcolm and G. B. Malleson: *Military Transactions*, Orme: D'Urfey's *Pills to Purge Melancholy* for songs about the two East India companies: *The Indian Civil Service*, L. S. S. O'Malley: *History of Hindostan*, Orme.

PART II

The Siyar-al-Muntakherin, tr. Raymond: *Echoes of Old Calcutta*, Busteed: *Memoirs of the Revolution in Bengal*, Printed for A. Millar in the Strand, 1760: Letters of the Court of Directors: Scrafton's letters: Letters of the Select Committee: Verelst's *Government of Bengal*: The Cambridge *History of India*: *William Bolts, A Dutch Adventurer under John Company*, W. L. Hallward, Cambridge University Press, 1920: *Hastings' Letters*, ed. Sydney C. Grier:

347

Warren Hastings and the Making of British India, Penderel Moon: *Warren Hastings*, G. R. Gleig: *Life of Lord Teignmouth* by his son, Lord Teignmouth: *Studies in the Land Revenue History of Bengal*, R. B. Ramsbotham: *Memoirs of William Hickey*: *Journal* of Bishop Heber: Roberdeau's sketch is in *Bengal, Past and Present* No. XXIX, Jan.–June 1925: *The Indian Police*, J. C. Curry: Dodwell and Miles's Civil List, 1780–1836: *Wellesley*, P. E. Roberts.

For the inscription on Clevland's monument I am indebted to Mr R. M. Lines, I.C.S. Kipling altered, and improved, the inscription on Clevland's monument and advanced its date. He transplanted Clevland to the C.P. and grafted him on to a family tree very like that of the Outrams.

For social history, *The Nabobs*, T. S. P. Spear: *British Social Life in India*, Denis Kincaid: *The Nabobs of Madras*, H. H. Dodwell.

There is a wealth of light material on social history, such as d'Oyly's *Tom Raw the Griffin*, and for a later generation, *The Chronicles of Budgepore*.

The chances of retiring on a pension were poor in the eighteenth and early nineteenth centuries. In 1784, the figures given in Parliament were 508 appointed during the 22 years since 1762, of whom 150 were dead, 320 were alive and serving in India and 37 had returned. Taking 250 names at random from Dodwell and Miles's Civil List of 1838 – it begins with appointments in 1780 so covers nearly 50 years – I find 112 are serving, 85 died in India and 48 retired or died in England.

PART III

Life of Sir Thomas Munro, Gleig: The Cambridge History, J. T. Gwynn on the *Ryotwari Settlement: The Fifth Report* of the Select Committee: *Life of Malcolm*, Kaye: *Life of Elphinstone*, Colebrooke: *Elphinstone*, J. S. Cotton, in the Rulers of India series: *Annals of Rajasthan*, Tod: *Rambles and Recollections, Journey through the Kingdom of Oudh* and Reports on *Thuggee*, Sleeman: *Oriental Memoirs*, Forbes: *Journal of a Residence in India*, Maria Graham: *Suttee*, Edward Thompson: *India's Cries to British Humanity*, Pegg: *Confessions of a Thug*, Meadows Taylor: *Memoirs of Old Haileybury*, Sir Monier Monier-Williams and others: *Malthus and his Work*, James Bonar: *Notes on Indian Affairs*, F. J. Shore: *James Thomason* in the Rulers of India series by Sir Richard Temple: *The Journal of a Pilgrim*, Fanny Parks: *Curry and Rice*, Atkinson: *John Lawrence*, Bosworth Smith and the smaller life in the Rulers of India series: *Henry Lawrence*, Edwardes: *Honoria Lawrence*, Maud Diver: *A Year on the Punjab Frontier*, Edwardes: *Lives of Indian Officers*, Kaye: *Sepoy War*, Kaye: the Reports on the Punjab for 1852 and 1853.

The quotations in Chapter 7 which are mentioned as typical are from *Henry Crawford, H.E.I.C.S.* with notes by R. G. B. and from *A Memorial of Three Generations of the Urmiston Family* – but there are many parallels. The words about the Devonshire home are from *The Tomb of His Ancestors*.

CHAP. 8. There is no biography of Jonathan Duncan; the D.N.B. refers to Higginbotham's *Men whom India has known*, but the account of him there is even shorter than in the D.N.B. He is referred to in the Cornwallis Correspondence, in Wellesley's dispatches, in the lives of Elphinstone and Malcolm, in Heber and indeed in almost any book that mentions Bombay in the first ten years of the century. His struggles with infanticide are described in Kaye's *Administration of the East India Company; A History of Indian Progress*.

On Mr Traill I have included some hearsay remembered a century and a quarter later; Shahi, where Mr Boulderson waited for Bishop Heber, was a favourite camping-ground in my first subdivision, and part of Mr Traill's kingdom was the district of which I held charge.

The travel books of Lord Valentia and Moorcroft though interesting and readable do not help much for my present purpose. Nor do Forster and Buchanan.

Narrative by Major-General John Campbell of operations for suppressing Human Sacrifices and Female Infanticide, mainly about the Meriah sacrifices, is a straightforward account of the kind of thing many people did. Campbell's predecessor, Macpherson published a pamphlet. The proceedings of the three Governments, Madras, Bengal and India, were published by authority in 1854.

There is a good deal about human sacrifice in India under the head 'Human Sacrifice' in the Encyclopaedia of Religion and Ethics published in Edinburgh in 1920.

CHAP. 9. Kaye's *Life of Metcalfe* is a good solid Victorian biography with plenty of letters and minutes quoted in full. Edward Thompson's is more likely to appeal to the general reader, but there is a tolerable deal of Thompson to every pennyworth of Metcalfe.

I have quoted from Miss Eden's *Up the Country*; Captain Trotter's *Lord Auckland*, in the Rulers of India series, professes to be a biography but is a scathing indictment of Lord Auckland's foreign policy. The Cambridge History discusses the first Afghan War at length and where a point can be made for Auckland makes it. But I do not see how he can be absolved.

CHAP. 9. The memoirs of John Beames were not published in 1953 and I was indebted for them to his grandson C. H. Cooke. They have since been published as *Memoirs of a Bengal Civilian*, Chatto, 1961. And see also passim *Mr Verdant Green, Tom Brown's Schooldays*, and Trevelyan's *Lord Macaulay*.

CHAP. 10. The story of Napier's telegram – *Peccavi*, I've Sind – seems to be apocryphal. Sir Hugh Dow, last Governor of Sind but one, traced its origin to *Punch* in 1846; it was capped ten years later, on the annexation of Oudh, by the couplet:

> '*Peccavi*, I've Sind,' said Lord Ellen so proud;
> Dalhousie, more humble, said '*Vovi*, I've Oudh.'

CHAP. 11. The Mutiny: There is nothing so good on the causes of the Mutiny as Kaye's *Sepoy War*. G. O. Trevelyan's *Cawnpore* and *The Competition-Wallah*, for the defence of the little house at Arrah, provide excellent background: so does Cooper's *The Crisis in the Punjab*, and Lord Roberts's, *Forty-one Years in India*. There are the official reports of Deputy Commissioners in the Punjab and a record of the services of Haileybury men in the Mutiny is included in Monier-Williams's book. Edward Thompson's *The Other Side of the Medal* should be read; it does not profess to be impartial but it is definitely untrue to say that the greased cartridges were forced on the mutineers at Meerut. The only case I have found of Indian soldiers using the greased cartridges was in Sind; the men were mutineers who had looted the cartridges from an Ordnance Depot.

I do not think the Sepoy's loss of prestige at Oudh has been given enough weight as a cause of the Mutiny. Having been secretary of one district soldiers' board, president of another, and secretary of the Indian Soldiers' Board, I may be inclined to lay too much stress on this but I do not think so. Nor has the religious attitude of British Officers been sufficiently stressed, while I am inclined to think that too much weight has been laid on the reduction in the number of British Troops. The total reduction in the seven years before the Mutiny was three thousand. Twenty thousand more might have prevented the Mutiny, but I find it hard to believe that three less caused it.

For the Cooper story, Cooper's official dispatch is published as well as his book; both are nauseating. They need to be checked with the account given in Bosworth Smith's *Life of Lawrence*. Thompson must have read this but differs from it without saying why.

For the period from 1784 to 1834 I was indebted for much help to Mr B. B. Misra of the Patna University whose scholarly work on the administration of the East India Company was not published at the time.

PART IV

Sir Bartle Frere, John Martineau: for Frere, see also *The Exploitation of East Africa* and *Isandhlwana*, both by R. Coupland: *The Memoirs of John Beames*, lent me by C. H. Cooke: Bignold's poems are collected with the title *Leviora: Life of Lyall*, Mortimer Durand: *Twenty-one Days in India*, Aberigh-Mackay: Plato's *Republic* (in translation): *Competition for the Civil Service*, Sir Percy Waterfield, which appeared in *Oxford*: Mr R. A. H. Way's letters to his mother were sent to me by himself and have not been published: The unpublished memoirs of A. R. Bulman: *A Civilian's Wife in India*, Mrs Moss King: 'Binks of Hezabad' comes from *Departmental Ditties: India: Its Administration and Progress*, Sir John Strachey: for famine, see Sir Verney Lovett in the Cambridge History and Sir John Strachey's *India*, also Sir George Campbell's *Memoirs* and the reports of the 1880 and 1908 Commissions: for grain rotting at the stations in Madras in 1877, my authority is *Work and Sport in the Old I.C.S.*, W. O. Horne: the letters of Herman Kisch (later published as *A Young Victorian in India*) were kindly lent me by his daughter, Mrs Waley-Cohen: *History of Upper Assam*, Shakespear: *Travels and Adventures in the Province of Assam*, Captain John Butler: *Forty Years in Burma*, Dr Marks: *Scott of the Shan Hills*, Mitton: G. E. Harvey's chapters on Burma in the Cambridge History: Professor Hall's *Introduction to the History of Burma* and the *Dalhousie-Phayre Correspondence*, also G. E. Harvey's *History of Burma* and his short *British Rule in Burma*. *The Soul of a People* by H. Fielding is useful background on Buddhism and the Burmese but to be taken with handfuls of salt: Phayre's obituary by Yule in the Proceedings of the Royal Geographical Society: *Burma Past and Present*, Fytche: *Burmah*, F. Mason: *The North-West Frontier, 1890–1908*, Collin Davies: *Life of Sir R. Sandeman*, Thornton: *Eighteen Years in the Khyber*, Warburton: *The Forward Policy and its Results*, Bruce: *The Indian Borderland*, Holdich: *Allan Octavian Hume*, William Wedderburn: *William Wedderburn*, S. K. Ratcliffe: *Romesh Chandra Dutt*, S. N. Gupta: *A Nation in the Making*, Surendranath Banerjea: *New India*, Sir Henry Cotton: *Musulmans and Moneylenders in the Punjab*, Thorburn: *The*

Punjab Peasant in Prosperity and Debt, Malcolm Darling: *The Land of the Five Rivers*, Trevaskis: and *Ancient Law*, Maine. Romesh Chandra Dutt's *Famines in India* is answered by Lord Curzon's Resolution of January 16, 1902: *India Called Them*, Beveridge: Sir Auckland Colvin's correspondence with Hume, entitled *Audi Alteram Partem: Speeches on various Occasions*, Rash Behari Ghose. Annie Besant's *How India Wrought for Freedom* contains the resolutions of all the early Congress meetings; there is also a good deal about how the rosy fingers of the Dawn Maidens touched the Indian sky and the Sun of Freedom rose to irradiate the Motherland: *The Little World of an Indian District Officer*, R. Carstairs: *Life in the Indian Civil Service*, Sir Evan Maconachie: *Twelve Indian Statesmen*, George Smith: *Life of Lord Curzon*, Ronaldshay. The Census Reports of the Punjab, 1881, and of India, 1901; Ibbetson's Settlement Report of the Karnal District.

CHAP. 13. There is a detailed account in L. S. S. O'Malley's book *The Indian Civil Service* of the many changes in the age limits for the examination. Changes were made in 1855, 1860, 1865, 1866, 1879, 1892, 1906 and 1921. No two Royal Commissions held exactly similar views but I do not feel the detail is of much interest except to students of education and to other Royal Commissions. Roughly speaking, up to 1892, boys were taken at the school-leaving age and given two or three years in England on probation; after 1892 the examination was meant for university graduates who had a shorter period of probation. Educated Indians such as Surendranath Banerjea felt the earlier age a great handicap to Indian candidates and pressed strongly for the later age.

I have long thought that the artistry with which he presents his arguments conceals for many people the horror of Plato's conclusions. He is, I believe, the father of Hegel and Nietzsche and of the Prussian and the Fascist state and I do not see how he can be absolved of some responsibility for Marxism, and indeed for all theories of the state that equate us with ants and bees. I am grateful to Lord Samuel for lending me K. S. Popper: *The Open Society and its Enemies*, in which these views are worked out in detail.

I have had full notes on canal colonies in the Punjab from Sir Geoffrey de Montmorency, who was Governor of the province from 1928 to 1933, and from Sir James Penny, Mr C. V. Salusbury, and Mr H. S. Williamson. I have, as so often, far more detailed information on this subject than I can use without upsetting the balance of the book and feel grateful to these officers for the trouble they have taken and apologetic that I have not been able to give it more space.

CHAP. 14. On Burma, I am indebted to writers so different as Maurice Collis, J. K. Stanford, and G. E. Harvey, all originally Indian Civilians, and to Professor D. G. E. Hall, not only for their various writings but for what they have told me in conversation.

The literature on the Frontier is immense; Mr Davies prints a bibliography described as 'Select' which covers twelve pages. I am indebted to a note by Sir James Penny on Dera Ghazi Khan and to conversations with many Frontier officers, both civil and military, and particularly with Sir Francis Wylie, Sir Arthur Parsons, Sir George Cunningham and Charles Duke. Needless to say, they have not seen what I have written and would not necessarily agree with it.

CHAP. 15. There is a full account of the Cowan episode in Sir Douglas Forsyth's *Autobiography and Reminiscences*: see also Khushwant Singh: *The Sikhs*.

On pigsticking I have used notes sent me by Sir Percy Marsh, General Wardrop and others, for which I am most grateful. I have referred to an unpublished book by E. H. H. Edye and another by S. T. Hollins of the Indian Police, and used a good deal of personal hearsay. For Pennell, I have to thank Messrs Ife and Reid for information.

CHAP. 16. I am very grateful for Mrs Macpherson's Journal of the Durbar, a simple and to me moving account of something that will not happen again, and also to R. A. H. Way for notes on Whish and other subjects and to Sir R. H. Macnair, Sir Benjamin Robertson and several others for notes on Tawney.

PART V

See the Cambridge History: *Indian Unrest*, Valentine Chirol: *My Experiments with Truth*, M. K. Gandhi: *Mahatma Gandhi*, Louis Fischer (but this is not reliable for facts): *Life of Minto*, Buchan: *Dyarchy*, Lionel Curtis: *An Indian Diary*, Montagu: *India as I knew it*, O'Dwyer: *The Lost Dominion*, Al Carthill: *A Nation in the Making*, Surendranath Banerjea: *India Insistent*, Harcourt Butler: *The Simon Report*: The Government of India Act, 1935: *Mission with Mountbatten*, Alan Campbell-Johnson: *The British Impact on India*, Griffiths: *Constitutional History of India*, Keith: *Kingdoms of Yesterday*, Sir Arthur Lothian: *The India We Served*, Sir Walter Lawrence: *Pomp of Yesterday*, Sir Kenneth Fitze (unpublished) and other memoirs by political officers: *Madras Occasional Verses: Autobiography of an Unknown Indian*, Nirad C. Chaudhuri.

CHAP. 17. Conversation with Lionel Curtis and Lord Hailey has been a great help and I have quoted from the report on the 1919 disturbances which Lord Hailey wrote for the Punjab Government. E. H. H. Edye's unpublished papers were lent me by Mrs Edye; for the letters of Loftus Tottenham and a note on his life and character I am indebted to Sir Richard Tottenham, his distant cousin.

CHAP. 18. The letter about Lucknow is my own, edited. I could find nothing else that illustrated my point so directly. I have quoted from *Enough of Action*, Edward Lydall, only part of which is about India, and from *The Role of the Administrator*, A. D. Gorwala (The Gokhale Institute of Politics and Economics). I have also used a note by Hugh Lane, *The Young Man in the last Ten Years* and notes by H. Macdonald-Tyler of Madras on the non-co-operation movement. Much of this chapter is based on personal experience and conversation. My debt to R. V. Vernède is acknowledged in the text and I have also used a note by D. S. Barron.

CHAP. 19. I have used some privately printed poems of J. A. Thorne; a note on *Soil Erosion in the Punjab* by Sir James Penny; Sir Harcourt Butler's speech was lent me by J. K. Stanford; other speeches of his were lent me by L. M. Jopling.

For the Frontier, see *Mizh, A Monograph on the Mahsuds* by Evelyn Howell. Everything else about the Frontier comes from conversation. As before, I owe much to Sir Francis Wylie, Sir George Cunningham, Sir Arthur Parsons and others.

CHAP. 20. I am very grateful for material received from R. N. Lines, Hugh Lane, Sir Robin Hutchings, Messrs Wallace, Gledhill, Gimson, Bowman, McCall, Lambrick, Bell and Sir Henry Knight.

CHAP. 21. Most of the information contained in the last chapter comes from conversation. It has been one of my difficulties that many of those most intimately concerned in the last days do not wish to be quoted or do not feel themselves at liberty to allow their papers to be made use of. I am very grateful for the loan by the Somerset Light Infantry of a copy of their Regimental Journal. I am grateful to Brigadier Humphrey Bullock for information as to the number of British graves in India and to Lt-Gen. Peter Rees for the history of 4 Indian Division, which is admirable on the last days. I have also used a note by Philip Nash.

EPILOGUE. *Briton, Boer, and Bantu*, Macmillan: *The Cape Coloured People*, J. S. Marais: *The Spanish Empire in America*, C. H. Haring: *The Rise of the Spanish Empire in America, The Fall of the Spanish Empire in America*, Madariaga: *The Cambridge Ancient History*, vols. X, XI, XII: *Roman Colonial Administration*, Stevenson: *A History of the Later Roman Empire*, Bury: *China, a short cultural history*, C. P. Fitzgerald: *Society in China*, R. K. Douglas: *The Ottoman Empire under Suleiman the Magnificent*, Libyer.

I thank F. N. Crofts for the index to the new edition as well as the old.

Picture Credits

The author and the publishers would like to thank the following sources for permission to reproduce black and white illustrations: the B.B.C. Hulton Picture Library for pictures on pp. 99, 214, 238, 242 and 266; John Christie for the picture on p. 211; the Mary Evans Picture Library for the endpapers (showing a temple in the Deccan) and for the pictures on pp. xvi, 32, 33, 65, 76, 97, 104, 148, 163, 194, 209, 218, 227, 264 and 273; Fox Photos for pictures on 334 right, and 346; the India Office Library for pictures on pp. 17, 25, 34, 35, 36, 49, 79, 91, 93, 103, 114, 123, 126, 132, 201, 240 right, 260, 292, 302 and 307; the Keystone Press for pictures on pp. 331, 332, 334 left, 341 and 342; the Mansell Collection for pictures on pp. 8, 15, 118, 146, 161, 274 and 286; Sir Percy Marsh for the picture on p. 257; Eric Midgley for the picture on p. 212; I. W. Lewys-Lloyd for that on p. 307; F. N. Crofts and the family of Sir Carleton Moss-King for the pictures taken from his mother's sketchbooks on pp. 28, 134, 179, 206 and 228; the National Portrait Gallery, London for pictures on pp. 7, 26, 46, 51, 78, 84, 145, 149, 185, 186, 191, 203, 240 left, 245 and 263; Norah Vivian for the picture on p. 308.

For the colour plates thanks are due to the following: Ardea, London, for nos 16, 17 and 18; the Chester Beatty Library and the Gallery of Oriental Art, Dublin for no. 3; the Bridgeman Art Library/British Library for nos 22, 23 and 26; the Bridgeman Art Library/Guildhall Library for nos 12 and 13; the Bridgeman Art Library/India Office for nos 8 and 24; the Bridgeman Art Library/National Army Museum for no. 21; the Bridgeman Art Library/National Maritime Museum, London for no. 4; the Bridgeman Art Library/Victoria and Albert Museum for nos 1, 2, 7 and 20; the Mary Evans Picture Library for nos 6, 25, 27 and 28; the India Office Library for nos 10, 11, 14 and 15; the Mansell Collection for no. 19; the National Maritime Museum, London for no. 5 and the Victoria and Albert Museum for no. 9.

INDEX